I0868066

A Poetic Genealogy of North African Literature

FLASHPOINTS

FlashPoints publishes books that consider literature beyond strictly national and disciplinary boundaries and that are distinguished by their historical grounding, their openness to multiple genres and media, and their theoretical rigor and conceptual reach. In a Benjaminian mode, the series focuses on instances of literature that wrest tradition from conformism, contributing to the formation of new cultural constellations. Titles in this series engage theory without losing touch with history. They approach topical aesthetic and social concerns that operate critically in the present. They are grounded in comparative analysis—often based on archival research—yet eschew uncritical positivism. FlashPoints aspires to reach an interdisciplinary audience within literary studies, broadly defined, concerned with moments of cultural emergence and transformation and the poetics of cultural forms. Each book is published in print and made available in Open Access through the California Digital Library, reflecting the series' commitment to simultaneous publication in both forms since the beginning.

A complete list of titles begins on page 307.

A Poetic Genealogy of North African Literature

Thomas C. Connolly

NORTHWESTERN UNIVERSITY PRESS | EVANSTON, ILLINOIS

Northwestern University Press
www.nupress.northwestern.edu

Printed in the United States of America

10 9 8 7 6 5 4 3 2 1

Library of Congress Cataloging-in-Publication Data

Names: Connolly, Thomas C. (College teacher), author.
Title: A poetic genealogy of North African literature / Thomas C. Connolly.
Other titles: FlashPoints (Evanston, Ill.)
Description: Evanston : Northwestern University Press, 2024. | Series: FlashPoints | Includes index.
Identifiers: LCCN 2024039659 | ISBN 9780810147768 (paperback) | ISBN 9780810147775 (cloth) | ISBN 9780810147782 (ebook)
Subjects: LCSH: North African poetry (French)—History and criticism. | French poetry—Africa, North—History and criticism.
Classification: LCC PQ3982 .C66 2024 | DDC 841.009/961—dc23/eng/20240828
LC record available at https://lccn.loc.gov/2024039659

For Josephine and Anthony

In memory of Coleman, Bridget, Kenneth, Honoria

Le plus beau serait de penser dans une forme qu'on aurait inventée.

—Paul Valéry, quoted in Abdelkébir Khatibi,
Figures de l'étranger dans la littérature française

Contents

Acknowledgments

I am grateful to all those at Northwestern University Press for supporting this project and for including this book in the FlashPoints series. I thank especially Faith Wilson Stein, senior editor for scholarly titles, Professor Susan Gillman, and the two anonymous readers for their generous feedback and expert analysis. I hope I have responded appropriately to their valuable comments and suggestions. Many thanks also to Mary Klein, Anne Gendler, Maddie Schultz, Maia Rigas, Charlotte Keathley, and Courtney Smotherman, as well as to Matthew John Phillips for brilliantly crafting the index, and to Lily Sadowsky for her rigorous copyediting. All remaining errors, omissions, and infelicities are my own.

Early versions of some chapters, or parts of chapters, have been published elsewhere. A version of chapter 2, "Orpheus, *pied-noir*: Sartre, Sénac, and the Poetics of Algerian Becoming," appeared in *Sartre, Jews, and the Other: Rethinking Antisemitism, Race, and Gender* (De Gruyter Oldenbourg, 2020). I thank the editors Manuela Consonni and Vivian Liska for their permission to republish the article here. A version of chapter 3 appeared as "Mohammed Khaïr-Eddine's Secret Music" in *Sounds Senses* (Liverpool University Press, 2021). I am grateful to the editor of this volume, Yasser Elhariry, and Chloé Johnson at Liverpool University Press, for permission to reproduce this article. A version of chapter 4 was first published as "Berber Spider: Tahar Djaout, Arachne, and the Afterlife of Oral Poetics" in *MLN* 133, no. 4 (September 2018): 1099–1122 (Copyright © 2018 Johns Hopkins University Press). I am grateful to Suzanne Roos and the editorial board of

MLN for granting this permission. An early version of chapter 6, "Corporeal Fantasies, False Bodies: Ways of Seeing in Abdelwahab Meddeb's *Phantasia*," appeared in *Expressions maghrébines* 19, no. 2, a special issue entitled "Abdelwahab Meddeb ou des itinéraires d'un 'passeur de cultures'." My thanks to the editor of that volume, Réda Bensmaïa, and to Edwige Tamalet Talbayev for their very helpful editorial comments. A version of chapter 7 appeared in French as "Rimbaud islamique? Le vertige artificiel de 'Fleurs'" in *Parade sauvage: Revue internationale d'études rimbaldiennes* 29 (2018). My thanks to Félix Lemieux at Classiques Garnier and to Robert St. Clair and Denis Saint-Amand, editors of *Parade sauvage*, for their permission to reproduce the version here. I also thank all the anonymous reviewers of these articles for their constructive and encouraging feedback.

Some of this work was first presented at conferences and universities in the United States and Europe, which afforded me the invaluable opportunity to discuss the material with many people much more knowledgeable and capable than myself, and I am grateful to them all for their intelligent insights and recommendations. I presented "Islamic Rimbaud: Submitting *Illuminations* to Islam's Aniconism" at the Society for French Studies Annual Conference in Glasgow in June 2016; "'Plus d'éclipses': Mohammed Khaïr-Eddine, Modern Moroccan Painting, and the Edges of the Figurative" at the International Colloquium of 20th and 21st Century French and Francophone Studies in Bloomington, Indiana, in April 2017; "'Corps négatif': The Afterlives of Mohammed Khaïr-Eddine in Modern Moroccan Painting" at the Society for French Studies Annual Conference in Durham, England, in July 2017; "North African Poetry in French: The Example of Mohammed Khaïr-Eddine" at the Council on Middle East Studies Colloquium at Yale University's MacMillan Center in November 2021; and "Trans-Mediterranean Baudelaire: On Some Motifs in Abdelwahab Meddeb" at the Nineteenth-Century French Studies Conference in New York, New York, in November 2022. I especially thank Nicolas Valazza and his colleagues in the Department of French and Italian at Indiana University, Bloomington, for the opportunity to present "Virgin of Nowhere: Abdelkébir Khatibi's Secular Mysticism" in February 2023. Most recently, I am very grateful to Adrien Cavallaro and Delphine Rumeau for the invitation to present "Le polygone étoilé: Rimbaud au Maghreb" at a conference entitled "Le rimbaldisme 'aux confins du monde': Approches de la réception mondiale de Rimbaud" at the Université Grenoble Alpes in May 2023.

I was able to undertake research for this book in Morocco, Algeria, Tunisia, Italy, Spain, and France thanks to generous financial assistance from the MacMillan Faculty Research Grant, the Baron Research Grant from the

Yale Program for the Study of Antisemitism, and, on two occasions, the A. Whitney Griswold Faculty Research Grant—all through Yale University. The additional costs of publication, including the rights to reproduce several images and poems, have been covered by grants from the Schofield Fund in the Department of Comparative Literature at Harvard University and the Frederick W. Hilles Publication Fund at Yale University. I am extremely grateful for this support.

The work undertaken here would never have been possible without the great resources of the various Yale libraries. I thank especially librarians Elizabeth Johnson, Samuel Jungeblut, and Michael Printy for all their help locating material from across the globe. For their generous assistance, I am also grateful to the staff at Le Centre d'études diocésain, Les Glycines, in Algiers; the Bibliothèque de l'Alcazar in Marseille; and the Bibliothèque Nationale du Royaume du Maroc in Rabat.

I am indebted to Rajae Benchemsi and the Fondation Farid Belkahia for generously allowing me to reproduce Farid Belkahia's *Afrique* (1985) on the front cover of this book. For permission to reproduce the anonymous Attic drawing that features on the opening page of Nabile Farès's *L'état perdu, précédé du Discours pratique de l'immigré* (Actes Sud, 1982), I thank Michèle Farès. I thank the estate of Francis Bacon for permission to reproduce the triptych of paintings by Francis Bacon titled *Three Studies of the Human Head* (1953), as well as *Fragment of a Crucifixion* (1950). I am grateful to Josie Shenoy and Louis Jacquet at DACS for their assistance here. Thanks to Verónica Montes at the Museo Nacional del Prado in Madrid for her kind help in obtaining permission to reproduce Diego de Silva Velázquez's *Las hilanderas o la fábula de Aracne* (1655–60). My sincere thanks to Denis Martinez for his permission to reproduce his image *Arachné*, which first appeared in Tahar Djaout's *Solstice barbelé* (Naaman, 1975). For permission to reproduce "Le corps subverti: Tatouage" from Abdelkébir Khatibi's *La blessure du nom propre* (Denoël, 1974), I am grateful to Lalla Mina El Alaoui Khatibi. I thank Ana Isabel Gamero González, Margarita López, Francisco José Ortíz Bernal, and the Chapter of the Cathedral of Seville for authorizing the reproduction of *The Immaculate Conception with Miguel Cid* (1619) by Francisco Pacheco. For permission to reproduce the anonymous illustration *Muḥammad Receiving His First Revelation from the Angel Gabriel* from Rashīd al-Dīn Ṭabīb's *Jāmiʿ al-tawārīkh* [Compendium of Chronicles] (1314), I thank Danielle Howarth, Daisy Stafford, and the University of Edinburgh. I thank Laura Seitter and the Walters Art Museum, Baltimore, for the rights to reproduce the illuminated chapter heading for "Sūrat Ṭā Hā" from an eighteenth-century Qur'ān inscribed in the

Maghreb. My thanks to Ramdane Achab, Ali Chibani, Jonas Elbousty, and Khalid Lyamlahy for their help in securing these permissions. Thanks also to Kuani White-Lascelles at Northwestern University Press and to Faton Limani in the Department of Comparative Literature at Harvard University for their help in coordinating a number of these requests.

Since much of the work undertaken in *A Poetic Genealogy of North African Literature* is predicated on the analysis of poetic texts, several poems, or parts of poems, appear in the original language. I am extremely grateful to Jacques Miel for his permission to reproduce passages from Jean Sénac's poetic oeuvre and to Natalie Miel and Rémy Aron for their kind collaboration. I thank Alexandre Khaïr-Eddine for his generous permission to reproduce a passage from Mohammed Khaïr-Eddine's *Moi l'aigre* and Marie Lemelle at Éditions du Seuil for her help in securing this permission. I am thankful to Amina Meddeb for authorizing the reproduction of an excerpt from Abdelwahab Meddeb's novel *Phantasia*. Thanks to Nathalie Beul Vandenberghe at Gallimard for permission to reproduce passages from Mohammed Khaïr-Eddine's *Soleil arachnide*. I thank Hilary Plum, editor at the Cleveland State University Poetry Center, and translator Conor Bracken, for permission to reproduce an excerpt from his superb version of Khaïr-Eddine's *Scorpionic Sun*. My thanks also to Julija Šukys, Hervé Sanson, and Kai Krienke for their kind collegiality and support.

As I began to write this book, I edited a special double issue of *Yale French Studies* on "North African Poetry in French" (2020), which enabled me to learn from a number of brilliant specialists in the field of North African studies, as well as several formidable poets, artists, and translators. I am grateful to Rita Alaoui, Dia Al-Azzawi, Tahar Bekri, Fouad Bellamine, Mustapha Benfodil, Réda Bensmaïa, Mahi Binebine, Beïda Chikhi, Dominique Combe, Patrick Crowley, Jalel El Gharbi, Yasser Elhariry, Olivia C. Harrison, Jane Hiddleston, Jill Jarvis, Pierre Joris, Tibari Kantour, Rachid Koraïchi, Abdellatif Laâbi, Sonia Lee, Nawel Louerrad, Denis Martinez, the late Mohamed Melehi, Mohammed Mourabiti, Donald Nicholson-Smith, Peter Skafish, Habib Tengour, Hamid Tibouchi, Soraya Tlatli, Lara Vergnaud, Teresa Villa-Ignacio, and Alyson Waters.

I have been fortunate to be able to teach parts of this material to both undergraduate and graduate students at Yale over the past few years, welcoming Réda Bensmaïa, Yasser Elhariry, Teresa Villa-Ignacio, and Pierre Joris to some of the early sessions. I thank them and all my students and auditors, especially Kate Aitkenhead, Griffin Berlin, Mohamed Walid Bouchakour, Onyx Brunner, Bailey Decker, Alaman Diadhiou, Finley Doyle, Claire Elliman, Vyann Eteme, Elita Farahdel, Abigail Fields, Pierre Folliet, Tsivia

Frank-Wygoda, Sophia Helverson, Raoul Herskovits, Ismail Jamai Ait Hmitti, René Kooiker, Ethan Levinbook, Logan Lewis, Vicky Liu, Ester Luna, Kexin Meng, Isaac Mijares, Helena Mileo, Awuor Onguru, Marielena Soledad Rodas, Anna Salzman, Luca Scoppetta-Stern, Hana Stankova, and Dani Zanuttini-Frank.

I am extremely grateful to all my colleagues in the Yale French Department, where this project has been supported and encouraged at every step. I thank Ramla Bedoui, R. Howard Bloch, Agnes Bolton, Dominique Brancher, Morgane Cadieu, Marlene Daut, Edwin Duval, Nichole Gleisner, Bethany Hayes, Jill Jarvis, Alice Kaplan, Ruth Koizim, Soumia Koundi, Christopher L. Miller, Matuku Ngame, Lauren Pinzka, Maryam Sanjabi, Françoise Schneider, Christophe Schuwey, Constance Sherak, Candace Skorupa, Léo Tertrain, Alyson Waters, and especially Pierre Saint-Amand and Maurice Samuels for their careful advice and guidance. My thanks also to Shawkat Toorawa in the Yale Department of Near Eastern Languages and Civilizations for his kind assistance.

Finally, my thanks to all my friends and family, to Miriam and Valery, to everyone at Old Bridzor and beyond, and above all to Helena, Yaël, and Gabriel. This book is dedicated to my parents and to the memory of my grandparents.

Note on Language

As this book is intended to be accessible to any reader of English, all quotations from foreign languages have been translated. Where poetic texts are quoted, the source language has also been provided. Unless otherwise stated, all translations are my own.

Text from non-Latin scripts, including Arabic, Greek, and Hebrew, has been transliterated according to the American Library Association–Library of Congress (ALA-LC) Romanization tables.

A Poetic Genealogy of North African Literature

INTRODUCTION

The Interruptive Discourse of Poetry

RUPTURE

One of the most striking works of modern Maghrebi literature written in French can be ascribed to the novelist and poet Nabile Farès (Collo, 1940–Paris, 2016). Published in 1982, *L'état perdu, précédé du Discours pratique de l'immigré* [The Lost State, Preceded by the Immigrant's Practical Discourse] begins with the following lines:

> O. Ce livre n'est ni un poème, ni un roman, ni un récit. Simple parole qui, sous la voûte des polices et des arrestations, creuse ce privilège d'être au-delà de l'insignifiance. Paroles lancées à l'intérieur du livre, comme éclaboussures de vies mordues, il plaide, malgré l'ostracisme auquel il est soumis, pour un devenir d'autres paroles, éloignées des mises en garde ségrégatives.

> O. This book is neither a poem, nor a novel, nor a story. Simple discourse that, under the arch of police and arrests, pursues this privilege of being beyond insignificance. Words launched within this book, like splashes of bitten lives, which pleads, despite the ostracism to which it is submitted, for a becoming of other words, removed from segregationist cautions.[1]

This opening stems in part from the introduction to a similarly revolutionary collection of poetry in prose, namely René Char's wartime notebooks, *Feuillets d'Hypnos* [Leaves of Hypnos]: "Ces notes n'empruntent rien à l'amour de soi, à la nouvelle, à la maxime ou au roman" [These notes do not draw from self-love, the short story, the maxim, or the novel].[2] In both instances, the initial lines mark a rupture, a break from some preexisting myth—the myth of having to accept National Socialism and the occupation on the one hand, and colonialism and its postcolonial afterlives on the other. For Char, legendary poet and resistance fighter, the interruption of one myth momentarily enables the creation of another, as he claims that "a dry grass fire"[3] might as well have edited his notes, setting in motion a myth of poetic genius and spontaneous composition. Farès, though, soberly retains the original myth in his sights, providing it with an unmistakable figure, almost a target to aim for, a bull's-eye: "O."

The "O" that opens Farès's text is a trace we might usually overlook, literally "ob-literate," or just forget—*oublier.* "O" is a consonantless utterance, both with and without structure, a simple and infinite mark. It is as much the sound of presence as the inscription of absence, a perfect summons, perhaps even a "pure, revealing word."[4] Jean-Luc Nancy might say that the "O," this "great anonymous voice,"[5] is "the opening of a mouth immediately adequate to the closure of a universe."[6] As an "*ō mega*" or "great O," it intends a beginning as much as an end, a great myth encompassing both earth and sky, binding *lógos* to *kósmos*, or what Friedrich Hölderlin called the "poetic view of history" to the "architectonics of heaven."[7] It is a trace that does not require interpretation. It does not even allow for interpretation. It is what Friedrich von Schelling once termed a "self-explicating mythology."[8]

Farès writes in the wake of, and against, the "O." His "practical discourse," a text woven between the book ("livre") and the word ("parole"), is a restless pursuit of the becoming-of-other-words ("le devenir d'autres paroles") that necessarily leads to "ostracism," to exile from the "O," to exclusion from its founding myths. Such "ostracism" could be understood in its historical sense, from ancient Greece, as the temporary expulsion of a citizen whose power or influence is considered dangerous to the city-state. It is this temporary dislocation into statelessness that enables a practice of writing that Farès sometimes calls allegory, sometimes literature, and perhaps even sometimes poetry—although none of these terms is entirely apt, hence his negative definition of what we are reading: "neither a poem, nor a novel, nor a story." Nancy says that no name fits here: "The place or time of the interruption is incommensurable."[9]

If this groundbreaking but little-read text pursues what Farès calls the "privilege" of being "beyond insignificance," beyond myth and its tautology, beyond the reach of the state and its police, it is because it is never entirely bound by a simple logic of signification, never entirely closed or open, never tied up by a single mythology. Instead, it opens itself to the plurality of discourses, scripts, and images that inhabit and animate the Maghreb and that will be a focus of this book. Farès's reader is encouraged, wherever possible, to dismantle the "O" of origins, to perceive its potential for undecidability, drawing to begin with on the calligraphic imaginary of languages outside French. In the Arabic script, for example, "O" or "ه" signifies the number five, or "خمسة" [khamsah]. In the tifinagh script used to write Tamazight, or Berber languages, "O" approximates the letter "yar," or "r." Or, as we read later in Farès's text:

SIGNES.

Cinq en arabe: en berbère ( ) insolite
ou suspendu

SIGNS.

Five in Arabic: in Berber ( ) unusual
or suspended[10]

Farès's attention to the multiple codes, languages, and scripts that operate across the Maghreb ensures that our reading is often "unusual / or suspended." What Nancy calls the dividing line—that is, the line of reading—is never allowed to rest in this text, to conclude where one narrative passes to another, or where one poem passes to another, or where one thought passes to other thoughts: "It is in the degree to which it is unfinished and unfinishing that it is literature."[11]

In his defining study of francophone Maghrebi literature, *Experimental Nations*, Réda Bensmaïa adopts and reformulates Farès's interruption of the "O" by asking what kind of "machine of expression" could account for all the functions—"affective, psychological, ethical, poetic"—of the multiplicity of linguistic practices at work in the Maghreb "without crushing them or reducing them to a single, abstract whole."[12] What form of literature would be capable of simultaneously embracing "such diverse *terrains* and heterogeneous *temporalities*"?[13] Bensmaïa acknowledges the role of the theater in forming national popular cultures across Morocco, Tunisia, and Algeria—

the three countries of the Maghreb—especially as practiced in the latter by Abdelkader Alloula, Slimane Benaïssa, and Kateb Yacine.[14] Theater's orality means that it "can muster everything it needs to play in a variety of keys: word, gesture, mime, music."[15] The "sociocultural conditions of dislocation" brought about by prolonged periods of colonization across the Maghreb should have meant that the novel was "incapable of carrying out this work."[16] And yet it is in the novel that writers such as Kateb Yacine, Mouloud Feraoun, Mouloud Mammeri, Mohammed Dib, and Assia Djebar first elaborate what Nancy calls "a complete, original word, at times revealing and at times founding the intimate being of a community,"[17] a novel myth through which "the world makes itself known" in a complete and decisive way.[18] Or as Bensmaïa puts it, "Writing was contemporary and synonymous with the *laying of the foundation of the nation to come.*"[19]

Bensmaïa identifies Nabile Farès as the writer who first warns of the dangers of too closely identifying the space of literature with the crystallizing political forms of national consciousness. More recently, Edwige Tamalet Talbayev has shown how the interruption brought about by Farès's work is a reaction both to the affect of realist expression in such works as Albert Camus's *L'envers et l'endroit* [Betwixt and Between] and *Noces* [Nuptials] and to the increasing authoritarianism of the Front de libération nationale [National Liberation Front] (FLN), the political movement that brought about independence from colonial rule in Algeria and was established on "the twin pillars of reified state-mandated nationalism and ossified Islamic identity."[20] More than most, Farès is alive to the risks of a "mythological realism"[21] to any emergent nation: "Algeria's pitfall was its beauty, and now its pitfall continues to be a realist vision."[22] As Nancy insists in relation to the National Socialism that preoccupies Char in *Feuillets d'Hypnos*, "In this sense, we can have nothing more to do with myth."[23]

A Poetic Genealogy of North African Literature seeks to establish itself in the space created by Farès's vigilant gesture of resistance—not so much in what Georges Bataille calls "l'*absence de mythe*" [the *absence of myth*][24] but in what Nancy terms "*l'interruption* du mythe" [*the interruption* of the myth].[25] If, in *Experimental Nations*, Bensmaïa addresses the "increasingly radically refractory and exploratory practices of the Francophone writers from the Maghreb,"[26] then this book seeks to extend his approach specifically to instances of poetry. Poetic writing, such as that deployed by Farès in *L'état perdu*, often presents obscure modes of expression that require alternative critical approaches to the narratological methods developed throughout the twentieth century to read works of prose. Instead of turning away from the poetic at the point where it becomes indecipherable, this book engages the poetic on its own terms, allowing its idiom to dictate the search for significance and amplifying what the poems themselves have to say.[27]

The Moroccan author Abdelkébir Khatibi, whose writings and thought enable much of the work undertaken in this study, speaks of poetic writing as being a form of dissymmetry, which requires readers not to seek reflections of what is already known but to be open to the unexpected and to the possibility that they themselves will be transformed over the course of their encounter with the text. Reading these poetic texts will, accordingly, inaugurate discussions on topics as varied as poetics, aesthetics, religion, visuality, painting, ekphrasis, orality, and inscription. In the words of critic and translator Pierre Joris, poetic works such as those studied here "stretch the imagination of what the lyrical can be."[28] Few works remind us to be on the lookout for what poetry might become more than Farès's radically subversive text.

LYRIC, POETRY

Although Joris hails the "lyrical," the noun "lyric" does not often appear in this book. It is common, particularly in the world of anglophone literary criticism, to speak of genealogies of lyric, often tracing long arcs back to antiquity, sometimes at the expense of more recent contributions to our understanding of what poetry is or can do. Toward the end of the 1970s, Gérard Genette claimed that major mid-twentieth-century theorists of the lyric genre—including Northrop Frye, Philippe Lejeune, and Tzvetan Todorov, among others—"blindly project onto Aristotle, or Plato, their own contributions and thus 'bury' their own difference, their own modernity,"[29] despite the fact that "for more than a century, we have considered as 'more eminently and peculiarly poetry' . . . precisely the type of poetry that Aristotle excluded from his *Poetics*."[30] This repeated what a sixteen-year-old Arthur Rimbaud had written a hundred years earlier: "In Greece, as I've said, verse and lyres *give rhythm to Action* [vers et lyres *rythment l'Action*]. The study of this past charms the curious: many are delighted to renew these antiquities."[31] More recently, Virginia Jackson and Yopie Prins have shown that "the concept of lyric as the oldest form of poetic expression is actually a relatively recent notion; specifically, it is a post-Enlightenment idea, developed steadily over the course of the nineteenth and twentieth centuries."[32]

And yet, in contemporary scholarship, lyric retains a theoretical and philosophical weightiness that is rarely accorded to poetry and the poetic. Its "utopian horizon"[33] can be as vast as the world itself, as when Ayesha

Ramachandran argues for a view of Renaissance lyric, commonly understood as encoding the precise standpoint of the human individual, as "an alternate means of exploring and expressing the global."[34] When Yasser Elhariry artfully draws on the fourth-person singular mode of Jean-Michel Maulpoix to define "Mediterranean lyric,"[35] he proposes a tripetalous Franco-Arabic flowering in the works of Serge Pey (b. Toulouse, 1950), Emmanuel Hocquard (Cannes, 1940–Mérilheu, 2019), and Habib Tengour (b. Mostaganem, 1947), but he does so only after privileging a genealogy that passes through German and French Romanticism and is resolutely Western in its origins.[36]

Here, the terms "poetry," "the poetic," and "poetic writing" are generally—although not exclusively—preferred over "lyric." Not only do these terms allow for a greater variety of inscribed forms, many of which are ambiguous, minor, or marginal; they also privilege partial, fragmented, or otherwise obscured trajectories, facilitating the displacement of established epistemological paradigms. The francophone poet and Lebanese diplomat Salah Stétié (Beirut, 1929–Paris, 2020) conceives of his own poetry as an infinite practice in language, undertaken simultaneously at the center and at the periphery of life, that gives temporary form to the incommensurable: "In the face of all the intellectual superstructures created by man to explain or justify his presence in the world and his probable disappearance from the world, as well as his possible projection into other worlds, in particular into a world that would exist after death, but also in the face of ideologies, philosophies of all kinds that claim to shed light on this or that aspect or this or that process of man's action in the universe . . . , poetry [la poésie], more humble but also more ambitious, strives, on the basis of lived experience, on the basis of our enigmatic condition, to provide its own lesson on how things are."[37]

In place of an "intellectual superstructure," this book proposes the more modest practice of reading poetry open to difference, to linguistic plurality, to the incidental and accidental, to the unfinished and unfinishing, to "points of rupture, knots of dissidence and of resistance,"[38] to the unpromising, unpopular, unknown, and often obscure. It allows for fragmented and temporary approximations of poetic traditions, for unanticipated divergences, for unfamiliar constellations of modernity. It attempts to be attentive to the unique and uniterable logic of each poetic text, to the operations of each "machine of expression"[39] and each "poem machine [machine du poème],"[40] abandoning itself to the moment of reading and enabling the unfolding of each text's revolutionary potential in what Khatibi calls "an infinite translation."[41] Above all, it allows for what Stéphane Mallarmé describes as the "elocutionary disappearance" [disparition élocutoire] of the subject "who yields the initiative to words, through the clash of their ordered inequalities; they light each other up through reciprocal reflections like a virtual swooping of fire across precious stones, replacing the primacy of the perceptible rhythm of respiration or the classic lyric breath, or the personal feeling driving the sentences [remplaçant la respiration perceptible en l'ancien souffle lyrique ou la direction personnelle enthousiaste de la phrase]."[42] Mallarmé perceives the poetic text taking the place of the ancient "lyric breath," just as much as it does the second of Johann Wolfgang von Goethe's "natural forms of literature," "the enthusiastically excited one" [die enthusiastisch aufgeregte], namely "Lyrik" [lyric].[43] Jean-Marie Gleize describes this same shift in more mundane terms as a "despectacularization," that is, "the growing autonomization of a discourse that shows, tells, or exposes less and less, and is more and more intransitive and literal."[44]

By ceding the initiative from the subject to language, poetry might be understood as what Khatibi calls a linguistic "expansion," a liberation of language that also provides the poet, "at the moment of his or her ecstasy, with the illusion of limitless freedom."[45] The history of modern poetry in the nineteenth and twentieth centuries is one of experimentation and innovation, of freedoms and illusions of freedom that require constantly renewed readerly attention and reflection. Such inventiveness is often treated with suspicion by those on the outside. It is the fear of what poetry might do that the author and journalist Tahar Djaout parodies in an early prose poem titled "Lecture interdite" [Forbidden Reading], in which the protagonist sneaks into the public library to check out "un livre poussiéreux qu'il avait longtemps convoité" [a dust-covered volume that he had coveted for a long time] before running out, the book tucked under his shirt, for fear of losing his job as a civil servant and his reputation as a serious and honest man. There, poetry is crudely defined as "production taxée depuis longtemps d'ésotérie et de nocivité" [production long taxed with esoterism and noxiousness].[46] Where society would restrict poetry as a product that is acceptable only to the degree to which it can be monitored and made profitable, the poet releases language, letting it go the moment it becomes uncontrollable.

It is this that Khatibi evokes when he compares the poet to the musician who plucks at the three strings of the Japanese shamisen: "The poet sometimes feels the line of words breaking and, as if dazzled, sets them free. Where can they run and fly? Into oblivion, into contemplation, into pre-sleep . . . Now they return with muffled steps (each step is a fleeting moment of unity between the thought and the form of the poem), visiting the site of the poet, his motionless body, inspecting his breath, his breathing, the back and forth of his dreams."[47] The darkness in which the musician sits and plays is, like the space of poetry, a smooth space, "occupied by events or haecceities more than by formed and perceived things," "a space of affects more than of properties,"[48] a space that constantly slips striation and regulation.

DISCOURSE, FIGURE

Farès's text is replete with reminders of language's power to signify visually—including figurative processes such as metaphor, the visual appearance of the poetic text itself, and the engagement of the text with concrete visual images, sometimes through the trope of ekphrasis—as well as of the significatory power of nonlinguistic semiotic systems. Immediately after the title page of *L'état perdu, précédé du Discours pratique de l'immigré*, the reader is confronted with an anonymous, undated Greek illustration in black ink (fig. 1). A paratextual note on the facing page reads:

> NOTE / Le dessin de présentation est un emprunt attique où se mêlent les différents éléments de la symbolique berbère et méditerranéenne encore utilisée aujourd'hui. Les chiffres d'immatriculation qui parcourent ce livre (chiffres au sens de *codes* ou *déchiffrements*) sont autant chiffres de chapitres que chiffres imposés par une immatriculation, ou l'inscription d'un nom et d'une langue qui, toujours selon la même histoire, furent *empruntés*. Voyages au cœur des signes—donc—où le serpent figuré  manifeste le sens d'une *réalité*.[49]
>
> NOTE / The introductory illustration is Greek and borrows a mix of different elements from Berber and Mediterranean symbolism still in use today. The registration numbers that run through this book (numbers in the sense of *codes* or *decryptions*) are as much chapter numbers as numbers imposed by a matriculation, or the inscription of a name and a language that, always according to the same story, were *borrowed*. Journeys to the heart of signs—therefore—where the figured snake  manifests the meaning of a *reality*.

If, as intimated in the final phrase, the image is fundamental to poetry, it is because the image bears traces of the encounter between the real and lan-

FIG. 1. The anonymous Attic drawing that appears on the dedicatory page of Nabile Farès's *L'état perdu, précédé du Discours pratique de l'immigré* (Le Paradou: Actes Sud, 1982), 7. Reproduced by kind permission of Michèle Farès.

guage, dramatized here as a journey "to the heart of signs" where a figured snake "manifests the meaning of a *reality*."

In *Discours, figure* [Discourse, Figure], Jean-François Lyotard notes that when we focus on the presence of the figure in language, we realize that, by itself, language does not refer to very much of reality as we experience it.[50] It may gesture toward the real, but it ultimately refuses or is refused by it. There appears to be, within language, a desire to have and to be what it is not. In the journey "to the heart of signs," where the divergent functions of seeing and saying overlap, Lyotard takes the side of the eye and its ability to perceive figures that cannot be reduced to representation, "the half-light that, after Plato, the word threw like a gray pall over the sensory, that it consistently thematized as a lesser being."[51] To take the side of poetry, this verbal discourse of images, would be, as Lyotard maintains, to dismantle the self-sufficiency of linguistic discourse and to argue for what has often been dismissed as "falsity, skepticism, the rhetorician, the painter, the *condottiere*, the libertine, the materialist."[52] When Lyotard distinguishes between "defining speech, which tries to force the designated into invariant structure relations and to assimilate completely the designated into signified," on the one side, and "expressive speech striving to open itself up to the space of vision and desire and to produce figurality with the signified"[53] on the other, he speaks of the divide between what language is and what it is not but wants to be. The discrepancy between what is desired and what is lacking in language makes for what Lyotard calls the "épaisseur" or "thickness" of discourse. It is in this thickness that the figure takes shape. Although the figure is present in discourse, it represents an order that would dismantle language, that would abolish both the spoken and the written word. The image in language is parasitical, feeding off its lettered host, draining it of its force, but rarely to the point that language would cease to be its vehicle. Or as one critic wrote when Lyotard's book first appeared, "The figure is above all *deconstruction* of writing, rupture of the imposed order of discourse."[54]

The paradoxical nature of the relationship between language and figure is perhaps nowhere more in evidence than in the repetition, in Farès's note, of the word "chiffre" or "figure." Etymologically, "chiffre" comes from the Arabic "صفر" [ṣifr] meaning "zero," "nothing," "void." As "zero," "ṣifr" is not symbolized by the inscription of a circle, such as the "O" with which Farès opens his text, but by a dot as imprinted by the nib of the "قلم" [qalam] used for calligraphy: "·." Although the French "chiffre" insists on numerability, this same numerability is denied by its ancient Arabic source. And although the Arabic "ṣifr" signifies nothingness, it is represented by a trace that is all presence and contains no absence. A similar paradox inheres in the repetition of "immatriculation," or "registration," throughout *L'état perdu*. "Immatriculation" stems from the Greek "μήτηρ" [mētēr], or "mother," which in turn gives rise to two homophonous words in Latin with divergent meanings, both of which figure prominently in Farès's text. On the one hand, "mātricula" is a "public register," a diminutive form of "mātrix," which is a "list" or "roll." On the other, "mātrix" is a "womb." A central method of colonial control takes on the aspect of a curiously ambivalent figure, now split between bureaucracy and parturiency. Farès's persistent recourse to images of the "ventre," or "stomach," especially in states of exposure, radically undermines the dry logic of immatriculation and emphasizes the subversive abilities of the poetic figure.[55]

The snake that inaugurates Farès's book—illustrated in the quotation above but repeated subsequently in the text as a series of juxtaposed "X's"[56]—is meant to reassert the legitimacy of visual modes of signifying, particularly those modes that fracture the conventional, prosaic use of the French language. These are modes that deny the exclusive logics of the alphabet, or of the aleph-bet, or of the abjadiyyah, that rupture social and religious interdictions, that reject the imposition of registers and laws that restrict bodies, stomachs, and tongues, and that refuse clear distinctions between verbal and figural modes of signifying. Throughout *A Poetic Genealogy of North African Literature*, images interrupt, complicate, and enhance the discussion of poetic texts. On some occasions, but not all, these are images that the poetic text appeals to. These include colonial era maps and topographical diagrams, several European paintings from the fifteenth through the twentieth century, contemporary Maghrebi art, ancient practices of tattooing, Qurʾānic illuminations, and medieval Islamic illustrations, all of which allow for the disruptive liveliness of the figure.

RUDIMENTS

Farès's snake also reasserts the legitimacy of pre-French, pre-Islamic, and even pre-Roman modes of signifying—in other words, of the pagan. It is this concept that the narrator of his novel *Un passager de l'Occident* [A Passenger from the West] explicitly espouses when he identifies the pagan as the source of "a very old belief that is against everything" but that has been "occulted in the country where I was born," despite the fact that "Algeria was a supreme place of paganism before becoming the rangeland [la terre de parcours] of Christianity's and Islam's edifying discourses."[57] In later writings, such as *Instructions païennes* [Pagan Investigations] and *Rudiments païens* [Pagan Rudiments], Lyotard also points to the pagan as that which affirms the singularity of events.[58] Unlike religion and mythology—great "O's" that negate events in favor of a larger, transcendental meaning—the pagan refuses to serve a higher purpose. In a similar way, Farès's poem affirms itself and refuses to be folded into utility, let alone the bureaucracy or technocracy of the state, even as it purports to be a "practical discourse." In modern poetry, we see this pagan affirmation in the degree to which the referential function of language is minimized. We also see it in the degree to which the text constitutes a reality that is met in the moment of reading. In a poem such as Farès's, language does not primarily refer to an external, greater truth, in which its meaning is grounded, a historical narrative, or a political or social reality. It is itself the event. As Martin Heidegger declared in a speech in 1950, "Die Sprache spricht," that is, "Language speaks."[59] This is what the modern poem invites us to read and experience.

The poem, as discourse and figure, presents the possibility of being interruptive at any moment it is read or uttered, and in any sphere, maybe even far from the geographical, political, and social realities of its inscription. While the focus of this book is on Maghrebi poetry, these are texts that might impinge upon any domain. My aim here is to trace and amplify the disruptive effects of poems whose power has mostly been experienced and then forgotten, or whose import was perhaps never fully grasped. There is much that has remained hidden in this body of work, latent energies and emotional intensities that have not yet been emancipated, events that have been working away in invisible ways in the background. This aim might be formulated differently by turning to one of Lyotard's later concepts. The "differend" can be understood as a call not to judge according to preestablished conceptual structures—what Immanuel Kant, in the first introduction to his *Critique of the Power of Judgment* calls "bestimmende," or "determining," judgments—but to invent the criteria necessary for judging a conflict or event in a way that ensures no injustice is done to any party, that is, through "reflektierende," or "reflecting," judgments.[60] The differend relies for its institution on a feeling, a sense, an aesthetic sensibility that "demands a certain impoverishment of the mind, a disarming of the intellect's mastery."[61] The poems studied here may not always lend themselves to preexisting critical and conceptual structures, hence their partial sidelining and silencing. But if we abandon ourselves to their unique modes of creating sense—their minor worlds—then we may learn how to judge more reflectively, in a way that is more attuned to thinking's inherent indeterminacy. Farès's version of the pagan, expressed here in the figure of the snake, is meant to point to modes of free expression that break open the "O" of myth, away from the restraints of French literature as much as those of French colonization, not to mention earlier religious, linguistic, literary, political, and social forms of restriction and reduction.

Farès's text is not easy to read and has so far elicited only flashes of critical response, not least in the unfailingly illuminating writings of Réda Bensmaïa.[62] Many of the texts examined in this book are similarly difficult to read, although only rarely is this obscurity gratuitous. As Édouard Glissant wrote on seeing Kateb Yacine's theater in the late 1950s, "The language of this oeuvre is poetic, which is to say that it does not hesitate to express obscurely what is obscure in man but can also burst into precise contours, for there are some truths that must be said without deviation. Such a language, alternately burning bright and somber like a summer night, quick and effective like a good tool in the hand—such a language is well suited to the undertaking: it does not sacrifice grandeur for expansion, or vice versa."[63] Underlying *A Poetic Genealogy of North African Literature* is a conviction shared by many of these poets that poetry does indeed operate on the social, on the political, on the environmental, on the sexual, on the historical, and so on, but in ways we might not initially recognize or expect. Alongside movements in critical thought, modern poetry can also be a site for what Bensmaïa calls a "profound rethinking of the relations of inequality, hierarchy, subjection and domination,"[64] although elsewhere he notes that it is not sweeping declarations of ideological principle or significant political rupture that allows change to take place. Instead, change occurs only through "contamination, cutting, grafting, an asymmetrical assemblage of heterogeneous signs"[65]—irrational rather than rational breaks: "To write? Yes. But writing as wandering, strolling, migrating. To write like a nomad and produce books that will be like war machines against the ideological apparatuses of the totalitarian state and their registration cards."[66] Habib Tengour puts it starkly when he states, "Political narrative is a discourse that conceals the real; poetic narrative is itself the real."[67]

Understanding the poem as pagan, as a differend, or as constantly in a state of migration is crucial to understanding, and being better positioned to critique, the historical privileging of the francophone Maghrebi novel over the poem. This preference continues to prevail in North American universities—which, at the turn of the millennium, poet Charles Bernstein dubbed not just "nonpoetic" but "antipoetic"[68]—as much as in contemporary French and francophone scholarship. Here, the novel promises to lend itself to cultural and postcolonial modes of critique, in ways that the "turbulent" poem—open to "the irregular, the nonquantifiable, the nonstandard or nonstandardizable, the erratic, the inchoate"[69]—cannot, or at least not with the same degree of ease. The preference for the novel applies more broadly to the nonacademic reading public, too, as noted by the poet Abdellatif Laâbi (b. Fès, 1942) in an article on the unjustly neglected poetry of the trailblazing Algerian novelist Mohammed Dib (Tlemcen, 1920–La Celle-Saint-Cloud, 2003).[70] The Moroccan poet explains the gradual sidelining of poetry over the course of the second half of the twentieth century, "in the wake of an apodictic declaration of the novel's superiority as the major literary genre" based on the "questionable grounds that fiction was favored by the largest readership," as a choice that "hewed fast to a market logic that judges what it calls 'cultural products' by the yardstick of profit."[71]

The minor status of poetry is not something that the poets studied in this book appear to be troubled by. Many of them admit that poetry will never have broad appeal. Speaking of Goethe, for instance, Khatibi recognizes both the unusual effort required to read his poetry and poetry's self-sufficiency, the fact that poetry does not necessarily require readers to be significant in the way that the novel does: "The authenticity of a poet is always conditional; language is sufficient unto itself: it does not dictate any rule of truth; its aim is to elaborate the experience of whoever has the ability to invest in it, to lose themselves in it, and perhaps to invent it, by a happy coincidence."[72] In the notes that precede his anthology of contemporary Algerian poetry from the early 1980s, Djaout stresses that there is no easy way to approach this type of literature: "As poetry makes no concessions to anything (not even to teaching), it was never a question for us of choosing texts according to their 'accessibility' but of offering the student 'entire' poems, even if it means requiring effort from them—the effort without which no discovery is possible."[73] Those who opt to devote this effort to reading, to give themselves up to the disorienting logic of the poem, might be transported and transformed. Khatibi says of Goethe that he "never ceases to dazzle us, to challenge our body's intelligent sensibility—we who are lovers of risky poetry."[74] *A Poetic Genealogy of North African Literature* is designed to contribute to the creation of a community of lovers of risky, precarious, turbulent poetry.

A POETIC GENEALOGY

This book is the first English-language study devoted to the poetic works of modern North African authors writing in French. Besides Farès, it examines six major Maghrebi authors active in the twentieth and early twenty-first centuries, all of whom engage in poetic writing and some of whom will already be familiar to the English-language reader for their works in prose. The authors examined include Jean Amrouche, often considered the pioneer of poetic writing in French in the Maghreb, who was active during the final three decades of colonization in Algeria and who died weeks before its independence; the pied-noir Jean Sénac, whose writings coincide with the end of French rule and the first decade of independent Algeria; Mohammed Khaïr-Eddine, who published widely in Morocco and France between the 1960s and 1990s; the journalist and novelist Tahar Djaout whose life began with the Algerian War and ended with his murder at the start of the civil war; and Abdelkébir Khatibi and Abdelwahab Meddeb, leading intellectuals in late twentieth- and early twenty-first-century Morocco and Tunisia, respectively. The study concludes with a chapter on Arthur Rimbaud's poetic engagement with Islam and the Qur'ān, an irreplaceable intertext to which reference is made repeatedly throughout this study.

If this work puts forward a "poetic genealogy" of modern North African literature in French, it does so in the sense proposed by Khatibi, who speaks of an "imaginary genealogy"[75] made up of the elective affinities between texts. He likens these affinities, with quiet reference to Mallarmé's composite essay "Crisis of Verse," to virtual trails of fire across precious stones, whose "genealogical wake liberates a poetic memory."[76] Khatibi also silently draws on Michel Foucault's provisional definition of genealogy as "the union of erudite knowledge and local memories," which allows for the impulsive, unpredictable, speculative dimensions of literature, rather than any "claims of a unitary body of theory which would filter, hierarchise and order them in the name of some true knowledge and some arbitrary idea"[77] of what constitutes modern francophone literature in the Maghreb. The "lines of force"[78] that connect this constellation of poets and poetic works by no means preclude other connections, perhaps obscured here but also full of generative potential. This book is written in the hope that alternative, dissenting, contradictory poetic genealogies will be proposed in the time to come. Accordingly, and following the call of Friedrich Nietzsche in his preface to *Morgenröte: Gedanken über die moralischen Vorurteile* [Daybreak—Thoughts on Moral Prejudices] for the slow, philological attention of a goldsmith rather than the rush to comprehension of the philosopher, the reader of this book may decide to abandon a linear mode of reading for something more divagatory.[79] Each chapter could be read in isolation as well as in sequence, and might therefore be understood as a diversion, a delay, a distraction, perhaps a "demeure," a place we inhabit for a time and that may dislocate how we think about North Africa and how we read its literature.

Most literary histories identify Jean Amrouche (Ighil Ali, 1906–Paris, 1962) as the founder of modern francophone poetry in the Maghreb, despite the fact that his poetic production was not only slight, limited to two collections published in Tunis in the 1930s, but also of limited resonance and perhaps ultimately of questionable quality.[80] Although widely lauded at his death in April 1962, just weeks before the declaration of independence, few French-language poets in Algeria or the broader Maghreb appear to identify Amrouche as a guide in any practical sense. He himself would focus increasingly on political journalism and activism in favor of Algerian self-determination from the early 1940s onward, ultimately serving as an unofficial intermediary between Charles de Gaulle and the FLN during the Algerian War. If Amrouche ever obtained fame, it was as creator of the literary radio interview, in which he assumed the role of "Midas's barber"[81] to prominent personalities such as André Gide, Paul Claudel, Jean Giono, and André Malraux,[82] as well as academics including Louis Massignon.[83]

Instead of searching for the origins of Maghrebi poetry in French in the poet's early works or even in his seminal presentation and translation of Kabyle songs as recalled by his mother, Fadhma Aït Mansour Amrouche,[84] in chapter 1, I examine an uncollected poem written in 1959 that appears as a preface to a book of poems by Henri Kréa.[85] It is here that Amrouche's reading of younger Algerian authors, including Kateb Yacine, appears to have a late, transformative effect on his own more conservative poetics. Drawing on Aimé Césaire's analysis of this poem, we see how the fluvial network that irrigates Kateb's *Nedjma* is replaced with the past and present rivers of Amrouche's native Kabylia, thereby enabling an alternative poetics of Algerian independence.

In Jean-Paul Sartre's seminal essay "Orphée noir" [Black Orpheus], which first appeared as a preface to the Senegalese poet Léopold Sédar Senghor's *Anthologie de la nouvelle poésie nègre et malgache de langue française* [Anthology of New Black and Malagasy Poetry in French], the mythical Greek singer is presented as a model for Black poets writing in French in the postwar period.[86] According to Sartre, it is the Orphic nature of the Black francophone poet's relation to negritude—his heroic descent toward it and his fatally imperfect retrieval of it—that makes his the only great contemporary revolutionary poetry. Chapter 2 explores the effect of this preface on poets who write poetry in French outside of France during the period of decolonization and who are neither French nor Black by considering the case of Jean Sénac (Béni Saf, 1926–Algiers, 1973), an Algerian whose astonishing poetic talent was supported by the likes of René Char and Albert Camus. From his early writings, Sénac is motivated by a desire to bring about the liberation of Algeria from French colonial rule and envisions an emancipated nation that accepts and celebrates the diversity of its people, not only its Arab and Amazigh populations but also the members of its European community who relinquish other nationalities. Although this appears somewhat feasible under the presidency of Ahmed Ben Bella, the arrival of Houari Boumédiène in the coup d'état of June 19, 1965, ushers in a narrower vision of Algeria, from which Sénac, a fervent Roman Catholic, unable to speak either Tamazight or dialectal Arabic, is increasingly excluded. In *Avant-corps* (1968), Sénac fixes on the poem as a privileged locus for social and sexual, if not political and national, revolution, developing concepts such as the "corpoème" [corpoem] and the "Corps Total" [Total Body] and for the first time openly celebrating his love of other men.[87] Central to this new poetics is the elaboration of a counter figure to Orpheus, namely the biblical Jacob, who represents Sénac's search for a new foundation for poetic subjectivity to parallel that sought by Frantz Fanon, "away from the Manichean foundations of colonial life."[88]

The poetic oeuvre of Mohammed Khaïr-Eddine (Tafraoute, 1941–Rabat, 1995) is most often interpreted with reference to his 1970 novel, *Moi l'aigre* [Me, the Bitter One], where the protagonist, a writer, commits himself "once and for all to the cause of linguistic guerrilla warfare!"[89] This electric phrase has become the leitmotif of Khaïr-Eddine's work, enabling an equation between its extreme opacity and violent political resistance. Any impression of violence would appear to be confirmed by audio recordings of the poet reading his poems, such as that broadcast on *France Culture* in 1975, where he shouts his poems aloud.[90] And yet, as chapter 3 begins by showing, there is a curious discrepancy between the violence of the reciting voice and the rhythm of its delivery, a rhythm that Khaïr-Eddine ascribes to his ancestors and that he claims was transmitted to him genetically. As he says, "I call it my secret music."[91]

Here, I identify and amplify elements of Khaïr-Eddine's secret music, enabling more nuanced ways of understanding this difficult, sometimes repellent oeuvre. Following Gilles Deleuze and Félix Guattari, who stress that rhythm only comes about through the encounter of different milieus, I juxtapose Khaïr-Eddine's poems with paintings by Francis Bacon.[92] Much as in Khaïr-Eddine's poetics and in the performance of his poems, the shout or scream is a central figure in Bacon's iconography, from his crucifixion paintings in the mid-1930s to his multiple "copies" of *Portrait of Innocent X* (1650) by Diego Velázquez. Deleuze's reading of Bacon's painting in *Francis Bacon: Logique de la sensation* [Francis Bacon: The Logic of Sensation] provides a guide to the complex interplay of body, voice, violence, rhythm, and art that also allows us to draw out some of the hidden dynamics of Khaïr-Eddine's secret music.[93] An untitled poem in *Soleil arachnide* [Arachnid Sun],[94] never previously subject to analysis, is read here alongside a triptych by Bacon to identify rhythmic territorializations; the effects of attendant, diastolic, and systolic rhythms; and the presence of flutes, drawing on both Ovid's account of the contest between Marsyas and Apollo and Plato's debate on the relative benefits of the flute and the lyre. In Khaïr-Eddine's poems we encounter, among other things, a relationship to sensation not far removed from Marsyas's pipes and Bacon's paint. Khaïr-Eddine is shown chiefly to be a poet not of extremes, nor of violence or of iconoclasm, despite his shout, but rather of uneven rhythms.

Tahar Djaout (Aït Chafâa, 1954–Algiers, 1993), one of the first of many intellectuals to be murdered in the "décennie noire," or black decade, of the Algerian civil war, is nowadays celebrated as a journalist and novelist. He was also an important poet, whose often opaque poems are unique sites of experimentation in what modern poetry in French can do. In chapter 4, I juxtapose some of Djaout's earliest poems, released in Canada in 1975, alongside one of his last novels, published in 1991, allowing aspects of their unique logic to motivate the other text in unexpected ways.[95] *Les vigiles* [The Vigilantes] tells of the reinvention and modernization of a traditional loom by a mathematics teacher, the unnecessary administrative obstacles placed in his way by the local authorities in collaboration with the vigilantes of the title, and the unforeseen success of his invention at an international fair. Instead of pursuing the sociological, political, historical, and narratological perspectives adopted by previous critics, I read the novel for what it tells us about the continuing significance of poetry in modern Algeria. Specifically, the novel is set against the backdrop of the struggle for official recognition of Amazigh language and culture in the wake of the publication, in 1980, of an anthology of Kabyle poetry edited and translated by the author Mouloud Mammeri.[96] "Arachné," a cycle of five poems that appears in *Solstice barbelé* [Barbed Sunstead], Djaout's first collection, is read with reference to the myth of Arachne as recorded in Ovid's *Metamorphoses* and in the scholia to Nicander of Colophon's *Thēriaka* [Θηριακά]. This reading of Djaout's poems allows Arachne's obscured presence in *Les vigiles* to come to the fore, suggesting that, despite his shift from poetry to the novel, Djaout remains determined to ensure the continuance of Berber orality, and its particular beauty and power, within modern francophone literature.

The poetic works of Abdelkébir Khatibi (El Jadida, 1938–Rabat, 2009) are less read and critiqued than his novels, philosophy, semiology, sociology, or art criticism, but the principles required to read his poetry are not different from those he teaches us to deploy in reading phenomena of popular Maghrebi culture. For Khatibi, reading is "an erotic awakening, on the beach of being,"[97] and whether the text be a tattoo, a carpet, a piece of jewelry, or a poem, the reader is expected to take risks, to reach between different systems of signification, participating in the "erotic transport"[98] of the intersemiotic gesture. The reader of Khatibi's poetic texts, including *Dédicace à l'année qui vient* [Consecration to the Year That Comes],[99] "Notes de mémoire pour les femmes" [Memory Notes for Women] and "Notes de mémoire pour les hommes" [Memory Notes for Men] in *Par-dessus l'épaule* [Over the Shoulder],[100] as well as *Aimance* [Lovence],[101] among other works, might find that there is much here that is sensed more than it is grasped. Words dazzle momentarily, with the brief promise of communion, before meaning seems to slip away.

Symptomatic of the mystery of these texts is the enigmatic appeal, throughout Khatibi's poetic writings, to the figure of the female virgin. Chapter 5 therefore includes an examination of his ekphrasis of *The Immaculate Conception* (1619) by Diego Velázquez, philological attention to Islamic accounts of the Virgin Mary's conception and motherhood, and a comparison between the folds that partially conceal Khatibi's virgins and the tattoos investigated in texts such as *La blessure du nom propre* [The Wound of the Proper Name].[102] Where the tattoo is part of a semiotic system that has no syntax, the fold, which signifies through a dialectic of what it conceals and reveals, is inherently syntactic. Thus, the virgin partly covered in folds is shown to be a figure not only for Khatibi's poetic writing but for his lifelong attempt to wrest the French language away from its deep historical investment in Christian theological concepts, in place of which Khatibi presents a new secular and erotic poetics.

The book's penultimate chapter consciously pushes the boundaries of the poetic by examining *Phantasia* [Phantasia], a poetic novel by an author, philosopher, and poet whom Christian Jambet dubs "a marvelous geographer of this topography of the invisible,"[103] namely Abdelwahab Meddeb (Tunis, 1946–Paris, 2014).[104] Much like Khatibi, Meddeb is concerned with the innovative ways that poetic language creates meaning, focusing in this novel, as the orthography and meaning of its title suggests, on a complex interplay of images and letters. Although recent criticism has focused on the author's relation to Islam, particularly its Sufi forms, no attention has yet been paid to his extensive engagement with Christian, notably Roman Catholic, culture, theology, and aesthetics. Specifically, Meddeb turns at several crucial points both in *Phantasia* and elsewhere to the Christian doctrine of the Incarnation, that is, the belief that God took on the form of man in the person of Christ. In an article published in 1995, Meddeb opines that the Incarnation remains "the one thing that Islam has not yet formulated,"[105] and in a discussion about the uncreated Qur'ān, draws a parallel between a fourteenth-century Persian miniature showing Gabriel instructing Muḥammad to read and the scene of the Annunciation, when Gabriel announces that Mary will give birth through the Holy Spirit.[106] Meddeb thereby suggests that the Holy Book of Islam is itself a form of incarnation, although he acknowledges that contemporary Muslims would not accept this image. Throughout *Phantasia*, Meddeb permits the Incarnation to infiltrate projections of the modern Muslim imaginary, exposing the reader to numerous ekphrases of Christian works of art, of which one, Jacopo da Pontormo's *Deposition* (1528), is examined here. Whereas Khatibi seeks to repeatedly defer the Incarnation to poetic expression, and to thereby deconstruct the presence of Christianity within the French language, Meddeb, more concerned with fashioning a tolerant form of contemporary Islam, demonstrates the astonishing imbrication of Christian representations of the Incarnation and decorative Islamic calligraphy.

A Poetic Genealogy of North African Literature concludes by considering the prose poetry of Arthur Rimbaud (Charleville, 1854–Marseille, 1891) from the perspective of his engagement with Islam and the Qur'ān. In "Le surréalisme maghrébin" [Maghrebi Surrealism] a parody of André Breton's manifesto, Habib Tengour recalls how a left-bank editor once complained to him that authors from the Maghreb all take themselves for Rimbaud and notes, with reference to the decade that the Carolopolitan poet spent in what was then Abyssinia, "I'm sure that Rimbaud never gave a toss about being a North African in Harar and that the publisher in question is a pedant, despite his undeniable qualities."[107] And yet the poets discussed in this book—and many others who write in, from, or to the Maghreb—also appeal to Rimbaud with more insistence and urgency than to any other precursor, be it Ibn Khaldūn, or Si Mohand, or Baudelaire, or Augustine. For instance, in "Poubelles précieuses" [Precious Trash], Sénac aligns Rimbaud with the Persian and Shāfi'ite poet Shams-i Tabrīzī (Tabriz, 1185–Khoy, 1247/1248), as well as with a host of so-called poet-thugs of the twentieth century, including "Yesenin, Voznesensky, Yevtushenko, Allen Ginsberg, Genet, Artaud, Anna Gréki, Patrick Mac Avoy, Yahia S. Ben Hadji."[108]

In a letter dated August 18, 1992, addressed to Patrick Hutchinson, founding editor of the literary journal *Détours d'écritures*, Khatibi also describes his fascination with the Ardennes poet, pondering in particular his sudden abandonment of poetry. How could a spirit as otherworldly as Rimbaud "sacrifice this prodigious liberty to a radical silence"? "How do you burn up all the cards of life in a single poem?"[109] Khatibi's desire to understand Rimbaud's shift into silence at one point led him to consider writing a novel entitled *Arthur R.* Although the book never saw the light of day, Khatibi visited Charleville, the poet's hometown, where he found himself asking how he could ever "imagine a novel in the shadow of Arthur R. without going to the Orient?"[110] In 1981, at the invitation of the president of South Yemen, Abdelfattah Ismaïl, and in the company of the Syrian poet Adonis, he visited the city of Aden: "I was able to go to the place where Arthur R. had vegetated, facing the promontory of the Indian Ocean."[111] This is where Khatibi's own research and project came to an end.

The narrator of Djaout's novel *L'invention du désert* [The Invention of the Desert] does something similar when he goes to Aden partly to retrace the steps of Ibn Tūmart (Igiliz, 1080–Tin Mal, ca. 1130), the Berber leader and founder of the Almohads, partly to retrace those of Rimbaud: "I had to determine who really inhabited me: Ibn Tūmart or Rimbaud? When the sun beats down too hard, they become tangled up like twin shadows. I know Rimbaud's face better, whereas Ibn Tūmart's journeys are more familiar to me. Both wanted to change the world and came to these lands, where prophecy had once thundered under the absolute sun, a sun that grinds the rocks and makes one's spirit aerial. Did they find anything here? Sadly, this is a country where nothing weighs heavily enough to leave a trace on a ground fashioned by the wind. The only effective strategy for this implacable planet would be one of attrition that deliberately excludes the passage of time."[112]

There is no evidence to suggest that Rimbaud ever set foot in the Maghreb itself, despite his extensive peregrinations, but it is a place to which he was tied from the start. His father, Frédéric Rimbaud (Dole, 1814–Dijon, 1878), who served in the French colonial army in Algeria, read and spoke Arabic, leaving behind a cache of Arabic books and papers when he abandoned his young family. Personages such as Jugurtha (Cirta, ca. 160 B.C.E.–Rome, 104 B.C.E.), king of Numidia, and ʿAbd al-Qādir (Guetna, 1808–Damascus, 1883), leader of the resistance to the French invasion of Algeria in the 1830s, figure in Rimbaud's first poems, and the imaginary of Islam and the Qur'ān frequently punctuates his poetic writings. Chapter 7 proposes a reading of the prose poem "Fleurs" [Flowers][113]—alongside nineteenth-century orientalist Albin Kazimirski de Biberstein's rendering of the Qur'ān into French;[114] George Sale's[115] and Claude-Étienne Savary's[116] eighteenth-century versions in English and French, respectively; and Ludovico Marracci's late seventeenth-century rendition in Latin[117]—as an instance not of visuality, as poems in *Illuminations* [Illuminations] are often interpreted, but of aniconism.[118] With reference to Khatibi's concept of "artificial vertigo," developed in *Maghreb pluriel* [Plural Maghreb],[119] I ask if an Islamic critical perspective might provide a more accurate understanding of the ways in which the visual is manifested and dissimulated in Rimbaud's prose poetry.

Although concerned primarily with North African poetry written in French, *A Poetic Genealogy of North African Literature* is constantly alert to productive investments of this poetry in other languages, not only "الدارجة" [al-dārijah], the colloquial form of Arabic used across the Maghreb and spoken by some but not all of the poets included in this study, but also Tamazight, or Berber, including notably Kabyle; the classical Arabic of the Qur'ān; the classical Greek or Latin that records the myths of Orpheus and Eurydice, Marsyas and Apollo, and Arachne and Pallas Athena; the Hebrew from the account of Jacob and the angel in "Genesis"; and even, in one case, modern Swedish—all languages of the Maghreb, if not of the Mediterranean. It is, in short, a book that entertains the drama of what Julia Kristeva calls the "intercultural vocation" of literatures in French.

CHAPTER 1

Kabyle Rhapsody

Jean Amrouche and the Makings of Modern Maghrebi Poetry

Cerco un paese innocente.

PRECURSE

The beginnings of Maghrebi poetry in French are often traced to the small poetic oeuvre of Jean El Mouhoub Amrouche. He has been dubbed the "founder" and "pioneer of French-language Algerian literature"[1] and "the first French-language Algerian poet worthy of the name."[2] Other Maghrebi poets published in French before Amrouche, including Salem El Koubi (Tlemcen, 1875–Paris, 1921), author of *Contes et poèmes de l'Islam* [Tales and Poems of Islam][3] and *Rosées d'Orient* [Orient Dews],[4] but their works have not yet caught the attention of literary critics and historians.[5] For Jean Déjeux, one of the first to write extensively on Maghrebi poetry in French, poets such as El Koubi were satisfied to emulate their metropolitan counterparts, showing that they could write "without errors of syntax, in an academic style, with a regimented vocabulary,"[6] whereas Amrouche was the first "to take cognizance, in literary and aesthetic terms, of the gravity of the situation."[7] This opinion is echoed by Tahar Djaout, for whom Amrouche alone represents the first generation of Algerian poetry in French, which, after a period of hibernation, resurges in the 1950s—"this time abundantly and definitively."[8] Jacqueline Arnaud calls Amrouche "the precursor,"[9] although he always yearned to be more than this. As Jules Roy (Bougara, 1907–Vézelay, 2000) puts it, "He desperately sought consecration, a sign. He would have liked to be a prophet in his country."[10]

Amrouche is no prophet, at best a problematic precursor, and even the most enthusiastic evaluations of his work are troubled by the question of what the poet actually achieves. Guy Dugas opines that Amrouche's early poems "seem awkward, superficial, perhaps even without great genius."[11] Déjeux admits that his literary oeuvre is "largely the work of his youth,"[12] that he never matured as a poet, and that he was instead limited to "ceaselessly announcing the great work that he did not know how to bring to completion."[13] In his postwar anthology of francophone Maghrebi authors, Albert Memmi (Tunis, 1920–Paris, 2020) summed up Amrouche's career in poetry as "an enigma, a short but dense work, that does not manage to avoid the fragmentary nature of many North African oeuvres" and about which "it is difficult to draw useful conclusions."[14] In the opening chapter of this poetic genealogy of North African literature, I seek to understand Amrouche's inability to develop as a poet and to reflect on how this may have inflected the fortunes of francophone Maghrebi poetry. I also show how—much later than is commonly accepted, just before his death, and largely unnoticed—Amrouche appears to achieve a mature poetic, if not prophetic, voice.

Jean Amrouche was born in Ighil Ali in the Soummam Valley in February 1906 to Antoine-Belkacem Amrouche and Marguerite-Fadhma Aït Mansour, both Kabyle converts to Roman Catholicism. As Jean later explains, "A twist of fate meant that I was raised in the Catholic faith and spoke French as a mother tongue."[15] The Amrouche family migrated to Tunis in 1910, where they obtained French nationality and where Jean studied at the École normale d'instituteurs before he moved to the École normale supérieure in Saint-Cloud, on the outskirts of Paris, in 1925. It was during his years as a student in the French capital that Amrouche became convinced that he was predestined to be a great poet, giving rise to poems such as "Certitude" [Certainty]:

> Pourtant ma jeunesse
> Éclatera sur le monde
> En fusées d'astres inconnus,
> Et mon chant vêtira la terre et le ciel
> Du lourd manteau de ma voix.
>
> And yet my youth
> Will burst upon the world
> Like bolts of light from unknown stars,
> And my song will cloak the earth and the sky
> With the heavy mantle of my voice.[16]

Amrouche was twenty-eight when *Cendres* [Ashes], his first collection of poems, in which these lines appear, was published in Tunis. Composed over a six-year period, which includes the years between 1930 and 1934 that he spent teaching at a lycée in Sousse, Tunisia, these poems betray numerous, initially cryptic, autobiographical references. As the poet's biographer, Réjane Le Baut, points out, all but two of the poems in the collection are dated, enabling us to align their gestation with events in Amrouche's life.[17] These include his rapid marriage to and divorce from Lucienne Darribère in 1932. In October of that year, Amrouche was found guilty by the "tribunal correctionnel" in Sousse of an act of violence against his wife, for which he was punished with a day's labor and one franc in damages. A daughter, Marie Claire, was born in January 1933. When Jean's conviction was discovered by his employers, he was forced to leave Tunisia for Bône, now Annaba, in Algeria. He returned to Tunis in 1937 to take up a job at what was then the Lycée Carnot, where one of his pupils was Memmi. In his debut novel, *La statue de sel* [The Pillar of Salt], Memmi closely models Marrou on Amrouche and attends especially to what was then known of his teacher's biography: "It was said in hushed tones that he was a violent man, brutal even. He is said to have divorced; his wife, who was French, apparently couldn't put up with his bad temper any longer. People insinuated that he had even hit her; and then they pretended to blame her for it: Who on earth would ever marry a foreigner? What else would you expect from a mixed marriage?"[18]

Poems in *Cendres* such as "Ombre" [Shadow], written between February and March 1933, transitively reflect this period of Amrouche's life:

> Autour de moi, au fond de moi,
> L'angoisse est un lac de ténèbres:
> Noir sur noir, j'y suis étouffé,
> Et mes bras ne peuvent briser
> Les flots glacés du désespoir.
>
> Around me, inside me,
> Anguish, a lake of shadows:
> Black on black, I'm drowning in it,
> And my arms cannot break
> These frozen waves of despair.[19]

This negative aesthetic is characteristic of the entire collection, as Le Baut and others have demonstrated. *Cendres* is marked by silence ("Le mur épais du silence . . . Les larmes du silence, seules, / Baignent mes yeux brûlés" [The thick wall of silence . . . The tears of silence, solitary, / Bathe my burnt eyes]);[20] darkness ("le nocturne orage" [the nocturnal storm]);[21] pathos ("J'ai trop longtemps pleuré dans les bras de la femme" [I cried for too long in the arms of the woman]; "Des sanglots lourds montaient à sa gorge séchée . . . Une étoile sanglote au fond de ma mémoire" [Heavy sobs rose to her dried throat . . . A star sobs deep in my memory]);[22] anguish ("Cri perdu dans la nuit des secrètes angoisses" [Cry lost in the night of secret anguish]);[23] the urge to commit violence ("J'ai voulu briser la porte à coups de tête, / Fuir / Éclater ce front de feu" [I wanted to smash the door with my head, / Flee / Blow up this brow of fire]);[24] the threat of madness ("Les nerfs désaccordés s'étirent sous le feu crépitant / Du soleil" [A clash of nerves stretch out under the crackling fire / Of the sun]);[25] and thoughts of death ("J'aurais aimé mourir sur la route" [I wish I had died on the road])[26]—expressions of despair that are redeemed in part by multiple dedications to the living, mostly male friends and colleagues.

A telling measure of Amrouche's inability to achieve the level of poetic expression sought in *Cendres* can be seen in the private diaries of the Malagasy poet Jean-Joseph Rabéarivelo (Antananarivo, 1901–Antananarivo, 1937), with whom Amrouche exchanged poems and letters in the mid-1930s, although they never met in person.[27] Rabéarivelo, then the foremost poet of French expression in Madagascar, was largely self-taught and the author of a handful of volumes, including *La coupe de cendres* [The Cup of Ashes].[28] After the Second World War, Léon-Gontran Damas would include Rabéarivelo in his landmark anthology of francophone poetry, casting him as one of the founders of literature written in French by those living under French colonization and citing "the strong personality of the poet, the penetrating power of his accent, a new rhythm, a composite originality, a very particular sensitivity, a melancholy both rich in metaphor and serene."[29]

When Rabéarivelo first encountered the name of Jean Amrouche, in correspondence with Armand Guibert,[30] he was excited at the prospect of reading his work, as he makes clear in a diary entry dated May 1, 1934:

> And *Mirages*, a review "published in the realm of Barbary," what a marvelous thing, dead in the purest realization of its momentum! There, I discovered another young poet, Jean Amrouche, whom Guibert talks about in his letter. He is, he says, a Berber of the purest stock. His remarks on Poetry touched me all the more deeply, as they coincide—through time, space and . . . silence—with my own conception of the 'honey of life' ['miel de la vie'].[31]

By May 28, and now in possession of *Cendres*, Rabéarivelo is noticeably less enthused about his discovery:

> But perhaps I am even more melancholy at the idea of having to revive the *Cendres* of Amrouche here in the humidity of Iarive: the atmosphere here will hardly help me, and I will be forced to postpone the day of wonder to an indefinite and, who knows, distant date! The problem is that, from what I've been able to read so far, the book that the young Kabyle has just sent me is quite cryptic [est bien secret] . . .[32]

Only on July 20 will Rabéarivelo exclaim, ". . . Amrouche, the African that I finally managed to read entirely and in one go."[33] And on July 31,

> He is a Kabyle who writes in the language of Ronsard.
>
> I have read and reread a substantial collection by him: *Cendres.* I took great pleasure in it. But, and I "shout" it in my letter to Guibert, Amrouche must, for his own sake, remain Kabyle—*if only for when he is dead.* In other words . . . but I think with dread of the dedication he made of his triptych to DEATH.
>
> I shout to him that it is already enough that we are going toward the Conqueror with the "disease" of our *Intelligence,* that, when we will be returned to Earth, we should still offer our NOTHINGNESS to the West . . .
>
> Will he listen to me?
>
> It is true that he is, it appears, a Christian, a fervent Christian . . . And so, for him, the mortal body does not matter and can go and annihilate itself any old place. That only the Soul counts.
>
> No! Oh, unknown friend but so close to my heart! No! Let's give nothing more than our SONGS [nos CHANTS] to the Foreigner—our BLOOD too if necessary—but not the rest that we owe to our RACE, to the EARTH, to our DEAD . . .[34]

Rabéarivelo's testimony is curiously revealing, as he identifies the need for Amrouche to liberate himself from France and to write as a Kabyle, although this is a realization that Amrouche himself will only make over time.[35] In Athens in the summer of 1937, at the end of a vacation in Greece and Italy with Amrouche, the musician Marcelle Schveitzer, and her husband Marcel, Guibert received a letter from Rabéarivelo that began, "By the time you read this, I will have been returned to the earth, to the grasses of my country . . ."[36] The letter was just one part of an elaborate project by the Malagasy poet to document his own voluntary death, which saw him not only send word to his friends apprising them of his by then completed suicide but also write until the poison he had taken prevented him from writing any more.[37]

On the day of his death, Rabéarivelo had written, "It's no joke: to be a Latin born among the Celts and with the appearance of a Celt [un latin né parmi les Welches, et avec les traits d'un Welche]—I say this without any mockery whatsoever . . . No, it can't go on like this."[38] Déjeux suggests that it was this same impossible combination of French and non-French, of Latin and Celt, of colonizer and colonized, that would torment Amrouche and that gave the greatest Malagasy poet of his day no choice but to end his own life—"having not been able to achieve the synthesis and to find the balance between the culture of his ancestors and the culture of the French."[39] Two decades later, Amrouche looked back over Rabéarivelo's career in such a way as to invite comparisons with his own dubious poetic legacy:

> Jean-Joseph is less exemplary for his successes, fragmentary and questionable as they are, than for his errors. He was not cut out for victory but for defeat. His liveliness, his spasmodic and disorderly enthusiasm, are signs of his profound weakness, that of a confused conscience and a confused soul. More than anyone, in order to live he needed a star to guide him, to hold him firm in believing in the existence both outside of himself and in his innermost self of a *place* and of a *formula* [d'un *lieu* et d'une *formule*], a belief that would have maintained the integrity of his being and the cohesion of his indestructible identity against all temptation and in the fiercest of storms.[40]

The "star" Amrouche evokes here in the 1950s is his own religious faith, but in the 1930s, this "star" had tried to take on the shape of literature. Three years after the publication of *Cendres*, and after some cajoling from Guibert, Amrouche's second collection, *Étoile secrète* [Secret Star], appeared.[41]

LUMINOUS NORTH

Before the end of the 1930s, two more poet deaths would test Amrouche's belief in his guiding star. In March 1939, the Lithuanian French-language poet Oscar Vladislas de Lubicz Milosz died at Fontainebleau aged sixty-one.[42] His mystical, religious poetry was a major source of inspiration for Amrouche, as is made clear by the dedication of *Étoile secrète* to him.[43] In October, it was reported that the French poet Patrice de La Tour du Pin, then in his early twenties, was missing in combat and presumed dead.[44] He was later revealed to have been wounded, captured, and imprisoned in camps in Hesse and Silesia—but not before Amrouche and Guibert had completed his obituary and prepared it for press.[45] As Gabriel Audisio put it, Milosz and du Pin were Amrouche's prophets,[46] to whose ranks we might also add Giuseppe Ungaretti, whom Amrouche called "the poet of inner auscultation."[47]

Among these poetic "prophets," the one to have the most impact on the development of Amrouche's poetics throughout the 1930s, and especially on the composition of *Étoile secrète*, was undoubtedly du Pin. Born in Paris in 1911, he was, much like Amrouche, not only an aspiring poet but also a committed Catholic, whose first collection, *La Quête de joie* [The Quest for Joy], was published privately in 1933.[48] Du Pin's poetics was noticeable for the originality of its voice and for the almost complete absence of surrealist aesthetics. When Henry de Montherlant discovered du Pin in 1934, he commended his distinctive style in a letter dated April 17 of that year: "Your poetry is full of mystery. Each poem presents not an intellectual problem, like those by Valéry, but instead an enigma for sensibility and the imagination."[49] Guibert was so impressed by *La Quête de joie* that he sent it immediately to Amrouche, then newly divorced and living in Bône. Amrouche responded with an extended analysis of the collection, which appeared shortly afterward in a small compilation of essays as "La pensée de Patrice de La Tour du Pin" [The Thought of Patrice de La Tour du Pin].

For Amrouche, the discovery of du Pin is nothing short of transformational:

> One only ever rarely encounters, embraces a thought as vast, as dynamic, and as dominating as this. Few poems transform you to this degree, make of you a different being. The thought of Patrice de La Tour du Pin imposes itself like a powerful magnetic field. It overwhelms you with its brute elementary force; with the prestige of its fascinating images; and finally, with the sweetness of a legendary setting and characters who have the appeal of flowers, and of snow, and of distant childhood memories. It moves with prodigious ease in a concrete universe that the poet engages in his carnal life with an indubitable self-evidence, and, at the same time, it is detached from the earth

> and hovers in a universe where all those who do not have the sense of mysticism will find it hard to breathe.[50]

Amrouche's expression of enthusiasm echoed that of many others at the time, including the right-wing polemicist Robert Brasillach, who noted, "It is rare to see a poet in the act of being born."[51] In du Pin, Amrouche discerns "a spiritual guide" as well as "a guide to death," in other words, a poet able to restore to poetry "its dignity as artistic priesthood" [sa dignité de sacerdoce artistique].[52] The mystical quest for spiritual joy pursued in *La Quête de joie* later led du Pin to formulate a broader concept of "théopoésie," or "theopoetry," in which the poet is encouraged to embrace tenderness, to seek out solitude, and to speak of faith with the heart, away from the dictates of theology.[53] It is what Toby Garfitt defines as "the organic union of the life of faith and the craft of poetry."[54] There are three major aspects of du Pin's nascent theopoetry that Amrouche identifies and incorporates into his own work at this time. These include the elaboration of a poetic landscape, the implication of the carnal into the spiritual, and fragments of du Pin's verse itself.[55]

First, du Pin's poetic province, or "unknown country" as Amrouche later calls it, is one of woods, marshes, and open fields—much like the landscape around his family's ancestral home at Le-Bignon-Mirabeau, seventy miles southeast of Paris, or like Milosz's portrayal, through poetry, of his native Lithuania.[56] The marsh or bog, "cet obscur marais"[57] [this dark swamp], is especially invested with mystical qualities:

> A l'aube on voit monter la torpeur
> Du marais, des bancs de brouillard immenses . . .
>
> At dawn you see torpor rise
> From the marsh, immense banks of fog . . .[58]

For du Pin, the marsh is an unrivaled locus for the generation of myths: "Car les marais sont tout embués de légende" [For the marshes are all fogged up with legend].[59] In his introduction to a translation of du Pin's prose from the late 1940s, the English poet Stephen Spender approximates du Pin's verse with the early work of William Butler Yeats, contrasting his "misty, shrouded, wooded landscape," where readers lose themselves, with Walt Whitman's "open prairie, with occasional swamps, ponds and bosks," where "the reader always knows where he is and can see what he is coming to."[60] With du Pin, the poet loses himself so as to find himself anew:

Moi que la lente fièvre des marais démange,
Qui voudrais m'enfoncer plus avant dans l'oubli,
Dans le lâche brouillard des poèmes étranges . . .

And I, irritated by the slow marsh fever
Would like to sink ever deeper into forgetfulness,
Into the loose fog of strange poems . . .[61]

In "Anges sauvages" [Wild Angels], initially intended as the title poem of the collection, the "quest" for spiritual "joy" leads north:

Et nous avons marché tous les deux vers le Nord,
Vers le Nord lumineux et vif des hauts gâgnages,
Où vibrent follement les abois et les cors,
Quand surgissent les grands voiliers d'anges sauvages
Qui ne retrouvent pas la porte des cieux morts!

And both of us walked in a northerly direction,
Toward the luminous and lively North of the high pastures,
Where barks and horns resonate wildly,
When the tall ships of wild angels ride forth,
Unable to find the gates of a defunct heaven![62]

As if to remind himself and his readers of the limits of poetry, du Pin's seekers of joy are often disappointed:

Mais, rien, rien . . . maintenant le ciel est vide et sale:
Le vent du Sud? il va pleuvoir un jour entier:
Pourquoi m'avoir promis une aurore royale?
Et ces meutes qui ne cessent pas d'aboyer,
Que voient-elles, le cou tendu dans la rafale?

But, no, nothing . . . now the sky is empty and dirty:
The southerly wind? it will rain the entire day:
Why then promise me a royal dawn?
And these packs that won't stop barking,
What do they see, necks stretched into the gale?[63]

The wild angels, invisible but sensed by the hounds, represent a "yearning for love and fulfillment."[64] However, throughout *La Quête de joie*, angels are hunted like migratory birds—a leitmotif that most impresses Montherlant—and are often encountered dead or dying, hosted on the ground by a murder of crows, or hanging lifeless in the branches of trees.

Amrouche's *Étoile secrète* includes a cycle of six poems entitled "Le livre de l'ange" [The Angel Book] that imitates du Pin's elaboration of a northern poetic landscape populated by angelic beings, as is clear in the opening poem, "Présence de l'ange" [Presence of the Angel]:

> Sur fond nocturne et champ de mort
> Les pierres jouent avec leurs ombres,
> Le ciel est noir, le lac est noir;
> Au fond de la doline l'eau est morte,
> Le vent fou par torrents afflue de l'orient,
> Et les corbeaux muets surgis du Val de Mort
> Cernent le pic d'Agha de lourds anneaux funèbres.
>
> Against a nocturnal background and a field of death
> The stones play with their shadows,
> The sky is black, the lake is black;
> At the bottom of the sinkhole the water is dead,
> The mad wind rushes in torrents from the east,
> And the mute crows surging from the Vale of Death
> Circle Agha's peak in heavy funereal rings.[65]

Albert Memmi will complain that these poems "have nothing North African in them,"[66] but throughout both his collections of poetry, Amrouche makes a concession to the mountainous spaces of his native Kabylia in his repeated reference to schist, or what in Kabyle is called "ijdi." In *Cendres*, "le schiste sec" [the dry shale] conceals the "os oubliés" [forgotten bones] and "membres séchés" [dried limbs] of the souls of the dead—"os rendus au schiste sec" [bones returned to the dry schist].[67] In *Étoile secrète*, the reader is told, "Tu seras dans ton lit de schiste" [You will lie in your bed of shale].[68] Elsewhere, "schiste" will feature in the poetry of Mohammed Khaïr-Eddine, whose work is considered later in this book, when he describes the Anti-Atlas Mountains of southern Morocco—where he was born and raised—as "des schistes où dorment les psaumes calleux" [schist rocks where callused psalms sleep].[69]

In general, though, Amrouche prefers to take inspiration from du Pin and Milosz's boreal climes, aiming to preserve the territorial anonymity of his poems—the better to lend them what he calls "la parfaite nudité de l'espace intérieur" [the perfect nudity of the inner space].[70] Or, as du Pin puts it:

> Nous n'avons plus besoin de carte ou de boussole;
> Ces pays sont marqués comme lieux inconnus.
>
> We no longer need map nor compass;
> These lands are marked as unknown territories.[71]

The second aspect of du Pin's poetics that ostensibly impacts Amrouche's conception of poetry at the time is its audacious entertainment of carnal pleasures. Jean-François Lyotard says of Paul Claudel that "his entire oeuvre arises from this drama, for a Christian, of being able to achieve a semblance of serenity through the agreement of a pine and a maple, to experience a fervent faith—both desire and pleasure—in the sensory."[72] Throughout *La Quête de joie*, a similar paradox inheres in the evocation of "chair," or "flesh," which describes the bodies of female lovers as much as it does Christ's deteriorating corpse. Images of tortured corporeality in lines such as

> Le Christ maigre et désossé et tordu dans sa chair
> Par la lâcheté d'âme des autres
>
> The Christ emaciated and deboned and twisted in his flesh
> For the cowardice of others' souls[73]

send distorting echoes through otherwise unrelated lines, such as

> Et que j'étreins ta si douce chair de femme,
> Lumineuse et caressée tout le printemps . . .
>
> And that I embrace your female flesh, so soft,
> Luminous and caressed all spring-long . . .[74]

On occasion, the devotional veers implacably toward the erotic, as in the following depiction of Christ crucified, where the so-called "Quêteur[s] de Joie,"[75] or "Seeker[s] of Joy," clasp their mouths to the man-god's wounds, catching the blood within the poem before it can drip down to the chalices and cloths of conventional Christian iconography:

Ils ont jeté leurs oriflammes rouge et blanc,
Et les calices qu'ils remplacent par leurs bouches,
Tellement ils ont peur de perdre un peu de sang.[76]

They have cast aside their red and white banners,
And the chalices, which they replace with their mouths,
So afraid are they of losing even a little blood.

Amrouche goes so far as to establish these sacred and profane instances of incarnation as the basis of all poetry: "There are no poetic ideas. All poetry is incarnation. The idea therefore presents itself here not in its icy purity but as the soul of a form that quivers with all the tremors of the flesh. *La Quête de joie* is a poem where sensuality, an unbridled sensuality, has a magnificent role to play."[77] Du Pin repeatedly acknowledges that although carnal pleasure can never lead to divine pleasure, it does not preclude our eventual passage toward this ideal state of ecstasy.

Du Pin's attention to divine and human flesh enables us to comprehend why both Amrouche and du Pin privilege forms of the semanteme "déchirer" [to rip, tear] throughout their writings. For both, it describes a tearing between the urges of original sin and the desire for divine redemption. In three of the four gospels, the death of Christ is marked by the tearing, or "déchirement," of the catapetasma in the Temple in Jerusalem—"a trembling of the veil in the temple, with significant folds, and, a little, its rending [et un peu sa déchirure]," as Mallarmé puts it at the end of the nineteenth century.[78] For Amrouche, "déchirer" also captures his lifelong struggle between two identities: one French, the other Kabyle. Few biographers or critics writing in French on Jean Amrouche fail to evoke the term in one form or another.[79] Later in life, when Amrouche largely abandons poetry to devote himself to the cause of Algerian self-determination, he will assert, "I am not a professional politician but an intellectual, perverted, fanciful, irresponsible, and torn" [Je ne suis pas un politique professionnel, mais un intellectuel, perverti, fantaisiste, irresponsable et déchiré].[80]

Both poets are likely aware that "déchirer" stems from various historical forms of the German verb "scheren" [to shear, cut], which can in turn be traced to the Greek "κείρειν" [keirein] [to shear, ravage, destroy, consume, devour] and to the Latin "caro" [flesh, or in French, "chair"].[81] In "La plaie" [The Wound], du Pin deliberately draws the reader's attention to this nexus of sense by inviting us to think beyond the acoustic cluster of "chair" and "déchirer":

Le ciel qu'il leur faut pour tressaillir
Hors les déchirures de la chair . . .

The sky they need to shudder
Outside the tearings of flesh . . .[82]

Amrouche echoes this in the poem "Unité" [Unity]:

". . . N'est-ce le dur scalpel qui déchirait nos chairs,
Et du repos, jamais ne nous permit l'espoir?"

". . . Is it not the hard scalpel that tore our flesh,
And rest, never allowed us hope?"[83]

This brings me to the third aspect of Amrouche's engagement with du Pin's theopoetics, one more substantial than the previous aspects, as it involves the appropriation and modification of passages of the latter's poetry. Throughout *Étoile secrète* especially, Amrouche incorporates fragments of *La Quête de joie*. Consider the poem "Laurence printanière" [Vernal Laurence],[84] in which du Pin celebrates what he calls "l'orgie dionysiaque de la chair" [the Dionysiac orgy of the flesh].[85] Amrouche is not inclined to be as explicit as du Pin in sexual matters but nevertheless recasts du Pin's erotic images within his own poems. Where Du Pin writes,

Ces seins qui sont gonflés de soleil et de sève

These breasts swollen with sun and sap[86]

Amrouche responds, in the poem "Paroles de l'ange" [Words of the Angel], with the following lines:

Comme la sève ivre des plantes au cœur des aubiers laiteux
Et la montée du sang à la cime des seins.

Like heady plant sap in the heart of milky sapwood
And the way blood flows to the tips of the breasts.[87]

The twelve syllables of du Pin's alexandrine are structured on the repetition of "s," which occurs five times, as well as on the acoustic transition from "ces" to "seins," "sont," "soleil," and "sève." There is here not only a progression of nasal vowels in "sein," "sont," and "gonflé" but also movement from the voiceless labiodental fricative "f" in "gonflés" to the voiced labiodental fricative "v" in "sève," as if approximating in the pronouncing mouth—with the shift from unvoiced to voiced consonant—the way blood flows to the tip of the aroused breast. Amrouche reaches for the image of the breasts and attempts a similar alliteration on "s" in "du sang à la cime des seins." But what makes du Pin's line so pertinent is the position of the "v" in "sève" at the extreme end of the single verse, which seems to protrude into space, even as it conveys a sense of excess vitality in the notion of "sap." Amrouche deploys "sève" as the third word in a line of eleven, not only enveloping the "v" but repeating it in the following verbal unit "ivre," which deprives "v" of its special—visually and acoustically protrusive—significance. The translation of du Pin's dodecasyllable to two verses, only one of which has the tidy, predictable rhythm of the alexandrine, and the inclusion of a loose simile in "cœurs des aubiers laiteux" [heart of milky sapwood] fail to reproduce du Pin's tight sense of excitement.

Déjeux says that Amrouche "experienced a sort of jubilation when he appropriated Patrice de La Tour du Pin's language to express his own aesthetic pleasures, as well as the sense of moving toward liberation by going back in time to the sources of innocence,"[88] but even as du Pin's voice is appropriated, there is a consistent desire to weaken its force. Christ is omnipresent in du Pin's poetry, even when he is absent. As one poem puts it, "Et nous ne voyions pas que tout gravitait autour du Christ" [And we didn't notice at the time that everything revolved around Christ].[89] Just as Amrouche retains and dampens the sensual qualities of du Pin, deflecting some of the most insistent imagery, he is less likely to appeal to Christ by name, despite establishing the poetics of *Étoile secrète* squarely within the bounds of Christian thought. A striking instance of this occurs when du Pin describes angels as

> Comme des Christ phosphorescents en plein essor
>
> Like phosphorescent Christs soaring high.[90]

When Amrouche appropriates this line he transforms it, not only by putting the soaring angel to sleep but also by removing the explicit reference to Christ, allowing only the phosphorescence of his supernatural presence to remain:

> Dormeur phosphorescent parmi les faunes vierges . . .
>
> Phosphorescent sleeper among virgin fauns . . .[91]

Amrouche's adoption of du Pin's aesthetics and theopoetics might usefully be contrasted with his critical perception, in November 1936, of poems written by his friend Gabriel Audisio: "While drinking tea, I had a look at some of Audisio's poems. None achieves that tone of cante jondo, that tone of solemnity, of religious celebration of the entire world that is the tone of poetry."[92] Besides the absence of the required gravity, Amrouche opines that Audisio's poetic images "do not possess this arousing power of a universe in the sky of the soul." He continues, "They evoke the real but not the surreal that is the true domain of Poetry."[93] And he concludes that Audisio lacks the desire and the will to operate in dark matters: "He is probably too much of a man of Mediterranean light. He lacks this sense of the night, on which I will no doubt continue to meditate, as well as on this Rilkean notion of 'open life.'"[94] In the eighth elegy of *Duineser Elegien* [Duino Elegies], Rainer Maria Rilke attributes an openness of vision to animals denied to human beings: "Was draußen *ist*, wir wissens aus des Tiers Antlitz allein" [What's outside we only know from the animal's countenance].[95] It is this impression of "open life," as well as a sense of the poetic potential in obscurity missing in Audisio, that du Pin's eloquent example provides.

It is common to assume that Amrouche turned away from poetry after *Étoile secrète*, although Dugas asks whether we should not say that poetry turned away from him.[96] Le Baut writes that Amrouche comes to the realization that "he is not a source, not the great poet who will rise up over Africa, in the wake of the greats he admires, a Milosz or a Patrice de La Tour du Pin, even less a Claudel or a Saint John of the Cross."[97] Jane Hiddleston has argued that Amrouche's poetry should be understood as "an anguished search for a means of communication that would overcome the poet's isolation, and, in establishing complicity with a reader, would reintroduce him into a human community."[98] She concludes that "more often language fails the poet, and the images of darkness, obscurity and separation foreshadow his eventual abandonment of the genre."[99] A sense of Amrouche's debt to du Pin—as well as to poets such as Milosz and Ungaretti—is crucial if we are to more fully understand what he sought to achieve with this modest poetic oeuvre. As Amrouche himself insisted in 1942, "An asceticism and mysticism specific to poetry must be defined and lived."[100] In spite of their perceived limitations, these poems will remain an important touchstone for francophone poets writing in, from, and to the Maghreb, their potential perhaps even metamorphosing over the course of time. In a review to mark the republication of *Étoile secrète* in 1983, Tahar Djaout maintains that Amrouche's mysticism is one that transcends religion: "Drawing away from religious asceticism, Jean Amrouche's poetic language here bursts into opulent poems, gorged with skies, saps, storms, fruits, and women."[101]

"CHANT," "ASEFRU"

> . . . le chant, jailli dans un déchirement . . .[102]

> L'ombre est devenue
> capricieuse. Le chant
> appelle une phrase
> claire.[103]

In 1938 Amrouche moved back to his parents' home in Maxula-Radès, a suburb of Tunis. Concerned by the poor health of his mother, Fadhma Aït Mansour, he asked her to recall the Kabyle songs that he had heard growing up. *Chants berbères de Kabylie* [Berber Songs of Kabylia], a collection of eighty-seven songs translated from Kabyle into French, was published in Tunis the following year.[104] Amrouche traced the motivation behind this project to his 1937 summer holiday in Greece with Guibert and the Schveitzer couple, "an indissoluble team of travelers,"[105] during which he had heard traditional Greek folk songs that reminded him of similar oral traditions in Kabylia.[106] As Amrouche told Véra Florence in an interview for Radio-Genève in 1961, "I discovered the folklore of my country, the monodies of my country, quite late on."[107] He may also have been encouraged by the example of Rabéarivelo, who, before his premature death in 1937, had published collections of what were purported to be translations of songs from his mother tongue, the Merina dialect of Malagasy, into French.[108]

The poems in *Chants berbères* are quite unlike Amrouche's own poems from the 1930s. Although certain traces of Amrouche's poetics remain—such as the primacy of "enfance," or "innocence," as presented in his writings on Milosz—gone is the mystical search inspired by du Pin. Instead, these are poems to do with everyday activities, absence, exile, love, celebrations. Where Amrouche's own verse is resolutely Christian, here the context is Islamic, and "Christian" serves as shorthand for the French occupier.[109] And yet, in his introduction to the anthology, composed in October and November 1938, Amrouche's understanding of poetry appears to undergo a shift. This shift can be traced to the tension that inheres between two appellations, which, I suggest, intend slightly different conceptions of poetry, namely the French term "chant" and the Kabyle term "asefru."[110]

As the title of the collection makes clear, the songs are initially translated as "chants" [songs], from the Latin "carmen," or the plural "carmina," which can be spells or incantations, the magic formulas required to open what is cryptic or closed. Amrouche writes of Milosz that his poetry "does not sing outside of us [ne chante pas hors de nous] but rises from the depths of ourselves, awakening a song [un chant] composed in an unknown world, which immediately makes itself recognized as the song [le chant] we could have composed had we been delivered from our chains [nos chaînes]."[111] For both Milosz and Amrouche, "chant" is closely related to magic, childhood, and religious liturgy. Similarly, for du Pin, "chant" is the definitive unit of poetry, "the simplest of the functions of the spirit."[112] The word "chant" obtains such significance in Amrouche's presentation that the very form of the word becomes a structuring principle of the text, its organizing acoustic unit, as the opening lines make clear:

> As far back as I can trace the course of my life, the slightest event that surfaces in my memory is accompanied by the rocking of the songs [chants] of my country. There is not a rustling of the heart, not an image on the interior sky, to which the inflection of a melody, a rhythmic time, a shudder of their verbal flesh [chair verbale] does not respond by sustaining them. These songs [chants] are in tune, by virtue of a kind of connaturality, with the ebb and flow of my interior life. This is the essence of any deep song [de tout chant profond]. If I try, in this presentation, to describe their charm [leur charme], I well know that I will not reach the source of their radiance, the source where the tears they make shed are born.[113]

The repetition of "chants" achieves additional dislocated resonance through the alliteration of the phoneme /ʃ/ in "chair" and "charme," which consolidates the acoustic armature—the musical key, so to speak—of the preface. This phoneme also features prominently in the paratext that precedes the preface. In addition to its auditory presence in Amrouche's name, /ʃ/ echoes in the dedication "*Aux poètes clairchantants . . .*" [*To the 'clairchanting' poets . . .*],[114] where "clairchantant" translates the Kabyle "iferrahen," which literally intends those who rejoice, who bring joy.[115] "Clairchantant" is then repeated in the final phrase of the preface, as if in musical resolution.[116] Within the preface, we are told that "these clairvoyants and 'clairchantants' are neither magi nor prophets. They go to the fields [champs] like all the others or sell their cheap wares in the town. They don't make a profession out of singing [chanter]."[117] The woman who cradles her child, thinking of those who work far away, sings [chante], as does the woman who works the millstone or spins or weaves wool: "In the cafés, in the fields [aux champs] . . . the pilgrims on the roads [sur les chemins] . . . the events of rural and pastoral life [la vie champêtre et pastorale] are celebrated with songs [chansons] and dances."[118] Conscious above all of his metropolitan audience, Amrouche identifies "le plain-chant" and the "songs," or "Lieder," of Schubert as comparable instances of "chants" in Europe.[119]

The prominence of the phoneme /ʃ/, in the written forms "ch" or "sch," not only means that its presence becomes inherent to the text, a feature of its textual body; it might also be interpreted as a visible and audible trace of an otherwise hidden Christian structure to Amrouche's presentation, one comparable to the Greek letter "χ," or "chi," used to covertly represent "Χριστός" [Christos], or Christ, in previous eras. This would not be out of step with Amrouche's thinking at the time. In "Pour une poésie africaine" [Toward an African Poetry]—an essay written in late 1940 and early 1941 and dedicated to the memory of Rabéarivelo, "hero and victim of the Spirit of Poetry"[120]—Amrouche will speak of the need for African poets to feel Africa living in the depths of themselves, "bearing it like a mother bears her infant" [la porter comme une mère porte son enfant], developing the gestational concept introduced in the introduction to *Chants berbères*.[121] He will also exhort them to "put on Africa" as Saint Paul told the early Christians to "put on Christ" [Il faut que le poète africain se revête de l'Afrique, dans le sens où Saint Paul dit à ses disciples: 'Revêtez-vous du Christ'].[122] The notion that this presentation of *Chants berbères* might be underwritten by an obscured symbolic Christian framework is only strengthened when, in the second section of the introduction—entitled "Les poëtes" [The Poets]—Amrouche asserts that these songs express the "great pain" of mankind's fallen state, a Christian concept notably not shared by Islam, and likely not shared by the anonymous singers themselves.[123] This occurs in a passage that is also, perhaps not coincidentally, structured on the phoneme /ʃ/.

Even as Amrouche covertly insists on the transcendental task of poetry, of the "chant" as "carmen" or "charme"—in keeping with his own intimate, spiritual Christian poetics—there are signs that he is aware that these songs propose a more critical concept of poetry. This occurs when he acknowledges the importance of another related but specifically Kabyle term, namely "asefru":

> The poet is one who has the gift of ASEFRU [Le poète est celui qui a le don d'ASEFROU], that is to say, the ability to make clear and intelligible what is neither. The poet sees deep into obscure souls,

elucidates what anguishes them, and restores this to them in the perfect form of the poem [dans la forme parfaite du poème].[124]

The Kabyle term "asefru," capitalized by Amrouche, could be translated into English as "poem" or "poetry," or into German as "Dichtung." It can describe a fixed poetic form as practiced most famously by the great nineteenth-century Kabyle singer Si Mohand ou-Mhand (Tizi Rached, ca. 1848–Aïn El Hammam [Michelet], 1905).[125] For Si Mohand, the "asefru" is almost always a "neuvain," or nonet, consisting of three stanzas ("taseddart"), each containing three verses ("tafirt"), with seven syllables in the first and third verses and five syllables in the second, each tercet following an *aab* rhyme pattern. This form is sometimes called the "asefru-neuvain"[126] or the "Kabyle sonnet," although Mouloud Feraoun likens it less to the Western sonnet than to the villanelle in three stanzas or the virelay in two rhymes.[127] Youssef Nacib compares the five and seven syllables of Si Mohand's "asefru" to Verlaine's "impair,"[128] as celebrated in his 1874 poem "Art poétique" [Art of Poetry].[129] He even asserts that we can speak of Verlaine's "isefra" (plural of "asefru"), an intriguing idea that deserves further examination, given that Amrouche compares his transcribed Kabyle songs to Verlaine's *Romances sans paroles* [Songs without Words] (1874).[130]

In his early writings on Kabyle poetry, Mouloud Mammeri remarks how much human reality is compressed in the modest prosodic space of the "asefru": "In nine verses, Si Mohand said everything. Breathless poetry of an irritated world in a hurry to come to a close, and that no longer proceeds in ample and serene developments as it did previously, but instead in short cries, through a process of antithesis, because everything in life can now be summed up as the collision of two opposing forces: two generations, two modes of living, two languages. The time it takes for a tear to form, sometimes the space of a brief smile, and it is already past."[131] It is on account of this marriage of formal perfection and liberal content that Si Mohand's skill is often attributed to angelic intervention. Mouloud Feraoun is one of many to retell this legend of origin: "One day, it is said that an angel came to him and made this proposition: '*Rhyme and I will speak, or else speak and I will rhyme.*' Si Mohand chose to speak. This is why his divine rhymes lend themselves to such profane utterances, for the whimsical poet, privileged with this rare gift, was less concerned with glorifying the angels than with conveying his own torments."[132]

Most of the songs recorded in *Chants berbères* are not instances of the "asefru" in this precise formal sense. It appears that by "asefru" Amrouche intends something broader, a poetic embodiment of simplicity lacking the ornate artifice of established poetic forms in the French tradition, such as sonnets by the likes of the Parnassian José-Maria de Heredia: "These are not glasshouse flowers," Amrouche assures us. "They are not forced."[133] These poems do, however, have in common with forms such as the sonnet "the benefit of enclosing great wealth in severe forms." Amrouche elaborates, "Speech is compressed, even suppressed; verses often attain the density of the final period, which, summing up everything in a prestigious image, reveals immense perspectives."[134] As Mammeri and Nacib remind us, "asefru" can also mean "clarification" or "resolution."[135] It derives from the verb "ssefru" [to make explicit or, when applied in a practical setting, to thresh wheat].[136] "Ssefru targit" is "to explicate a dream,"[137] and "fru taluft" is "to find a solution to a difficulty."[138] These various applications come from the verb "efru," meaning "to sort" or "to separate," as chaff is sifted from corn or as light is separated from the dark. The Kabyle "efru" therefore resonates semantically with the ancient Greek "κρίνω" [krinō] [separate, distinguish, decide], which in turn provides such terms as "critic," "criticism," and "crisis." "Asefru" similarly designates a self-conscious, critical use of language, and it is in this sense that Amrouche identifies it as the single quality that most defines Kabyle poetic discourse.[139]

There are hints that Amrouche is not yet comfortable with this progression from "chant" to "asefru," from "song" to "consciousness of song," from the poem as spell to the poem as criticism. He deliberately plays down the intellectual force of Kabyle orality ("Kabyle is not a language intended for intellectuals"[140]) and insists that its favorite themes "exclude the entertainment of verbal acrobatics."[141] Nevertheless, between the end of the 1930s and the early 1940s, Amrouche's concept of poetry undergoes a radical, irreversible transformation. In 1941, Amrouche will describe the poems of Pierre Emmanuel as follows: "Development of the poem: the internal force of the poem, each word stuck to the other words to form a single body with them, free and cemented to them by an invisible mortar made of silence and a sort of electric current (rudimentary simplicity of syntax)."[142] Here, he clearly draws, consciously or otherwise, on his understanding not so much of "chant" as of "asefru," such that this description of Emmanuel's poetry might be applied to any number of the Kabyle songs he translates into French. In 1942 in an essay on du Pin's *Psaumes* [Psalms], Amrouche formulates the shift from "chant" to "asefru" in even clearer terms, when he insists, "The poet can no longer be satisfied with song; he also needs the consciousness of song" [Le poète ne peut plus se satisfaire du chant, il lui faut aussi la conscience du chant].[143]

RHAPSODIC RIVERS

> l'écume grasse clapote au pied des pierres
> rouillées évoquant les trocs d'olives de froment
> et la fantaisie des rhapsodes
> qui se transmettaient secrètement le mythe d'
> Aphrodite[144]

To better appreciate the effect of this development in Amrouche's conception of poetry, we have to consider his later, mostly neglected poems. "Rhapsodie sur le seuil" [Rhapsody on the Threshold] may be unfamiliar to most readers, as it does not appear in either of Amrouche's early collections, nor in the recently published anthology of his uncollected poetic texts.[145] The prose poem was written as a preface for *La révolution et la poésie sont une seule et même chose* [Revolution and Poetry Are One and the Same Thing], a collection by the Algerian poet Henri Kréa (né Cachin; Algiers, 1933–Paris, 2000) published in 1960.[146] The second person address with which this poem begins therefore refers—at least in part—to the younger poet, as does the call, in the fourth paragraph, to recognize "the voice of a Son articulating the word, true and hard, against the current of your songs."[147] It is a poem that seeks to establish the relations between "chant" [song], "chanson" [song], "contre-chant" [counter-song], and "poème" [poem], as is evident in the opening fragment:

> Lecteur, frère, ami, ne cherche pas ici le déploiement des jours des nuits de l'été en sa force, les beaux accords des nostalgies conjurées, ni le chassé-croisé des connivences cachées: Tu n'entendras pas d'emblée le chant.
> Poème avant le chant, poème au-delà du chant, poème à chant suspendu pour le dire du jour premier qu'érige le mascaret d'un printemps de colère.[148]

> Reader, brother, friend, do not look here for the unfolding of days of nights of summer in its strength, the lovely chords of conspired nostalgia, nor the criss-crossings of obscured connivance: You will not immediately hear the song.
> Poem before song, poem beyond song, poem of suspended song for the telling of the first day established by the tidal bore of a spring of anger.

Although based in part on an earlier, unfinished poem, Amrouche dates this text "Paris, Novembre 28, 1959."[149] He therefore situates it in the wake of his unanticipated dismissal, on November 6, by the French prime minister Michel Debré from Radiodiffusion-Télévision Française (RTF), where he had presented the radio program "Des idées et des hommes" [Of Ideas and Men] since October 1948. His removal followed the accusation made by deputy Jean Legendre that Amrouche's publications in the press in favor of Algerian independence were undermining the French military effort in Algeria.[150] This text was also completed in the aftermath of Charles de Gaulle's acceptance—made on television on September 16—that "the women and men who live in Algeria will be able to decide their own fate once and for all, freely, with full knowledge of the facts."[151] De Gaulle identifies three possible outcomes of this inevitable exercise in "autodetermination." The first is "secession," which he warns will lead to "horrendous poverty, terrible political chaos, widespread slaughter, and then the bellicose dictatorship of Communists." The second is the complete integration of Algeria within France, extending equal rights to all its citizens "from Dunkirk to Tamanrasset." The third is Algerian self-government in close union with France. As is clear from this poem, and from those of Henri Kréa that it precedes and celebrates, as well as from his journalism, Amrouche would be satisfied only with the advent of Algerian sovereignty:

> Fin d'un hiver centenaire; soudain au cœur de l'automne une entrée de cymbales canonne et déchire le temps.
> Et le sommeil sans fin, et la résignation muette qu'on croyait éternelle, et la prosternation, volent dans la gloire du peuple debout à la proue de l'Histoire.
>
> Non la rivière ramageuse mais l'oued sauvage, mâle tragique, roule ses galets vers la mer, avec les endormis dans le limon, les immolés, le sang, la lymphe et le pus parmi les lauriers-roses;—avec les songes des maîtres ruminant au berceau de leurs couches balancées, avec le saint frusquin des chaînes, des lois, et des tranquilles consciences gonflées de vents.
>
> . . .
>
> Un temps nouveau s'éveille au cœur d'un automne de débâcle et de restitution, proclame et sacre un printemps de gésine et de

fondation, remonte le temps des morts en flots de paroles verticales; et voici la grâce du baptême sur le dol à son origine, innocent et sauvage, ignorant son nom souillé de larmes et de sang dans la subversion de l'honneur.
Le temps nouveau lavé d'orage et couronné de foudre accole le temps antique, et de l'inceste sublime Abel seul sans Caïn surgit dominant les grèves du futur!

Poème purifié du chant, poème au mépris du chant?
L'espoir humide verdit pourtant, germe vif sous le reg incendié au lit fossile d'un Igharghar de mémoire parmi le déhalement des rocs.
Brisée la mélodie d'enfance (qui ruisselait des lèvres saintes) sous la masse à coups redoublés de la colère, il en reste des mesures mutilées dans le tohu-bohu des cris noués aux cris.
Assez pour l'orphelin à l'écoute, assez pour la nostalgie navrée jusqu'au sang, assez pour que dans la gerbe des mots tout brûlants de la forge étincelante ressuscitent ensemble indivises la Mère en larmes et la Patrie.

Ah! tendresse, tendresse refusée, tendresse perdue et retrouvée, enfin acquise à jamais sur la pente d'un jour, sourire du cœur rompu, par toute enfance abandonnée aux génies du désert, de la montagne, et de celle-ci qui seule mérite le nom de Mer, sois reconnue, saluée, et communiée!
Igharghar légendaire au long de tes peintures, frise des monts sur le ciel de jade et de safran, Soummam et Sebaou aortes du sang libre, et vous contes du soir, dictons, silences et soupirs des flûtes de roseau,
horizons d'antimoine et de henné, et vous encore odeurs premières menthe, figuier, olive solaire, vigne de la chèvre sèche et de Noé, myrthe, benjoin,
et toi, Sel,—
sous l'oeil sombre frangé d'hyacinthe, fixe et sans larme, plus haut plus bas que toute peine humaine, vous n'êtes plus qu'*attente* dure et *patience* gelée.

Ce sont mots souverains au double fil du temps en ce présent terrible: l'attente vers l'aval guette le fils, Espoir enfoui au gouffre du futur; et la patience vigie vers l'amont interroge les Mânes qui n'ont jamais fini de vivre et d'ordonner.

Tel, le poème avance au front d'une armée d'images, de blocs de pensées catapultés, et se refuse en vain au chant.

Car la colère délivrée dans l'écume est fille première-née de la tendresse orpheline.

Lecteur, frère, ami, écoute la plainte à contre-chant jaillie d'un cœur aimant, c'est ta plainte haute dans la vengeance et le juste défi.

End of a centenary winter; suddenly in the heart of autumn a clash of cymbals cannonades and tears up time.
And endless sleep, and mute resignation that we thought was eternal, and servility, fly away in the glory of a people standing at the prow of History.

Not the bubbling river but the wild wadi, tragic male, rolls its stones toward the sea, in its silt the sleeping, the sacrificed, the blood, the fluid and the pus among the oleanders,—with the dreams of the masters ruminating in the cradle of their swaying beds, with the holy trinity of chains, laws, and consciences at peace, all swollen by wind.

. . .

A new time awakens in the heart of an autumn of meltdown and of restitution, proclaims and anoints a spring of labor and of foundation, runs back against the time of the dead in floods of vertical words; and here is baptismal grace at the very origins of the fraud, innocent and wild, ignoring its name stained with tears and blood in the subversion of honor.
The new time washed by storm and crowned by lightning abuts ancient time, and from sublime incest and without Cain, Abel alone emerges dominating the shores of the future!

Poem freed from song, poem in spite of song?
And yet damp hope turns green, living seed under the burned-out *reg* in the fossil bed of a legendary Igharghar among the warping of the rocks.
Broken the melody of childhood (which streamed from holy lips) under the mass of anger, with repeated blows, there remain measures mutilated in the tohu-bohu of cries knotted to cries.
Enough for the orphan who listens, enough for nostalgia saddened to the point of blood, enough that in the sparking forge the spray of burning words together resurrect as one the Mother in tears and the Fatherland.

Ah! Tenderness, tenderness refused, tenderness lost and refound, obtained at last forever on the slope of a day, smile of the broken heart, by every childhood abandoned to the spirits of the desert, of the mountain, and of this one that alone deserves the name of Sea, be recognized, saluted, and in communion!
Igharghar legendary throughout all your paintings, frieze of mountains on the sky of jade and of saffron, Soummam and Sebaou aortas of free blood,
and you evening tales, sayings, silences, and sighs of reed flutes, horizons of antimony and henna, and still, you, first scents, mint, fig, solar olive, dry goat's vine and Noah's vine, myrtle, benjamin,
and you, Salt,—
under the dark eye fringed with hyacinth, steady and tearless, higher lower than any human suffering, you are nothing but hard *waiting* and frozen *patience*.

These are sovereign words double threaded by time in this terrible present: downstream expectation lies in wait for the son, Hope buried in the abyss of the future; and patience the look-out upstream interrogates the Souls of the Dead who never finished living and setting things straight.

This is how the poem progresses at the head of an army of images, of chunks of catapulted thoughts, vainly refusing song.

> For anger delivered in the foam is the firstborn daughter of orphaned tenderness.
>
> Reader, brother, friend, listen to the counter-song of complaint sprung from a loving heart, it is your lofty complaint in vengeance and true defiance.[152]

When Aimé Césaire sought to mark Amrouche's passing in April 1962, his eulogy included a brief but incisive reading of "Rhapsodie sur le seuil."[153] In his analysis, Césaire focuses above all on the poem's fluvial logic, noting "the frequency with which two geographical notions return to Jean Amrouche." But these, he says, "should not be understood geographically: the notion of upstream [la nation (*sic*) *d'amont*] and the notion of downstream [la notion *d'aval*]."[154] Besides this poem, Césaire likely has in mind Amrouche's essays on Rabéarivelo[155] and Ungaretti,[156] both from 1958, in which these notions are reprised. Césaire initially compares this coupling of terms to the ancient Chinese dualist concept of yin and yang and to the "thesis" and "antithesis" of European dialectic thinking: "In Amrouche there is the dialectically united couple of *upstream* and *downstream*," two stakes in time [literally "deux postes du temps"] that are essential to Amrouche's poetic "mission." Césaire identifies downstream as the present, as action, as "innovation, metamorphosis, and ultimately revolution." He continues, "*Downstream* is the modern world; it is French culture, it is Guillaume Apollinaire, it is Gide, it is Claudel, it is the—universal—human and man's daily struggle, like that of the fatherland, for freedom and dignity."[157] Upstream is the past: "'The upstream of fabulous ancestors,' as Amrouche puts it. It is also the night of Mothers, from where the poetic word emerges."[158] This is Algeria, Kabylia, Ighil Ali—the village of his birth, the Berber songs of his childhood, or as Amrouche himself writes, "evening tales, sayings, silences, and sighs of reed flutes, horizons of antimony and henna, and still, you, first scents, mint, fig, solar olive . . ." "Which poet," asks Césaire, drawing from the closing line of Rimbaud's prose poem "Vagabonds"[159]—and echoing Amrouche's comments on Rabéarivelo quoted above—"has not been haunted by this obsession" to "find *the place and the formula* [trouver *le lieu et la formule*]?"[160] For Amrouche, the place is generated by the formula that sees upstream and downstream coexisting in the same moment and movement.

Césaire seeks to draw a lesson from the resolution of these two contradictory dynamics: "If we are obliged to reagglutinate all these remarks around moral notions, we will find the *two Amrouchian virtues*: upstream, *fidelity*; downstream, *hope* [les *deux vertus amrouchiennes*: vers l'amont, la *fidélité*;

vers l'aval, *l'espérance*]."[161] Or, as Amrouche himself puts it, "These are sovereign words double threaded by time, in this terrible present: downstream *expectation* lies in wait for the son, *Hope* buried in the abyss of the future; and *patience*, the look-out upstream, interrogates the Souls of the Dead who never finished living and setting things straight."[162] For Césaire, Amrouche's singular greatness inheres in this constant negotiation of poetry and history: "The pathetic grandeur of Amrouche [Grandeur pathétique d'Amrouche]: to have maintained, at the cost of what suffering, with what self-denial too, the double tension; to have sacrificed neither upstream nor downstream, neither his country nor universal man, neither the Manes nor Prometheus, and, we might add, neither Christ nor Jugurtha. Jean Amrouche is great for having refused to rest and to have refused any surgery. And this is how he fulfilled himself."[163] In this brief but astute analysis of Amrouche's poetics, Césaire reveals affection and esteem for his fellow poet. To a life that might be considered "rhapsodic," in the sense that it is made of many ill-fitting parts sown together, Césaire momentarily brings a sense of totality.[164]

Although Césaire maintains that we should not take "l'amont" and "l'aval" in their strict geographical sense, the naming of rivers—the Soummam, the Sebaou, and, on two occasions, the Igharghar—suggests that this poem wants us to do just that. Abdellatif Laâbi speaks of Kateb's *Le polygone étoilé* [The Starred Polygon] (1966) as inscribing itself "in the itinerary of what we could call 'Maghrebi cosmogony,'"[165] and Amrouche appears to aim for something similar here. The Soummam, whose name stems from the Kabyle word for "acidic," begins at the confluence of the Oued Sahel and the Oued Bou Sellam in the mountains at Akbou and runs into the Mediterranean Sea at Béjaïa. The contemporary Kabyle author El-Mahdi Acherchour (b. Sidi Aïch, 1973) describes it as follows:

> rivière des cycles respectés
> vallée des sous-âmes
> suprême billet de secrets voyages
>
> river of retained cycles
> valley of the sub-souls
> supreme ticket of secret journeys[166]

The Sebaou also flows from around Akbou but in the opposite direction to the Soummam, past the city of Tizi Ouzou and into the sea close to Dellys. Amrouche's poem is an attempt to situate the "aortas of free blood" of the new Algeria—or what Rimbaud once called "route[s] hydraulique[s] motrice[s]" [hydraulic motor roads][167]—in the heart of Kabylia, close to his home village of Ighil Ali. By evoking such rivers in this poem, Amrouche aims to stitch together a new geography for Algeria, establishing a "seuil" [threshold] that is not only historical, national, or geopolitical but also geological and poetic.[168]

I suggest that Amrouche's fluvial rhapsody bears traces of an encounter that takes place in the second half of the 1950s, namely with the writer Kateb Yacine (Constantine, 1929–Grenoble, 1989). At first, it might seem unlikely that these two authors should have very much in common. Where Amrouche is a Kabyle Catholic with broadly right-wing political opinions, who once said that "the truly great poets are Christian, be it obvious or obscured,"[169] Kateb is a secular Muslim, brought up speaking colloquial Arabic and taught to write in French at school, who makes no secret of his adherence to Communism. It appears that Kateb thought as much before meeting Amrouche shortly after the Second World War, at a time when the latter was editor of *L'Arche*:[170] "This first contact was glacial. Amrouche represented for me the worst image of French Algeria: that of a Christianized Kabyle. With my extreme left, nationalist convictions, I believed him to be irreparably corrupt."[171]

It was only later, specifically on June 23, 1956, when the two authors met to record a radio interview for RTF to mark Kateb's recently published novel *Nedjma*, that Kateb began to understand Amrouche's deep and active commitment to the cause of Algerian independence. The two men would diverge on how best to secure this outcome. When Charles de Gaulle returned to power later in the decade, Amrouche would be convinced that the general was uniquely positioned to bring peace and freedom to Algeria, whereas Kateb continued to hold de Gaulle responsible for the massacres at Sétif, Guelma, and Kherrata on May 8, 1945, which the writer had witnessed in person, and in the wake of which he had been imprisoned for three months. Later, Kateb would acknowledge Amrouche's efforts toward securing independence, being one of those who assumed "the thankless role of the first emissaries, of those who were correct too far in advance."[172] Elsewhere, Kateb would say, "As a man, Amrouche had the sacred fire. He was very lucid. He too wanted Algeria to be independent. And he was a poet [Et c'était un poète]."[173]

Meeting Kateb in 1956 had a powerful effect on Amrouche. During their discussion, he points to Kateb's uniquely "extravagant lyricism" and "epic realism," which, in his words, "makes you the only writer among North African writers on whom, personally, I base great hopes."[174] This sentiment is reaffirmed in a letter sent to Jules Roy in October of that year: "The man [Kateb] is equal, if not superior, to his book. On the future of Algeria, on the relations of Arabic and French, he has vast and profound views."[175] In advance of their meeting and recorded discussion, Amrouche had prepared seventeen pages of notes, mainly from his reading of *Nedjma*, in which he celebrated Kateb's language for its "invention, not imitation of foreign models."[176]

"Rhapsodie sur le seuil" appears to show that *Nedjma* also had a transformative impact on Amrouche's conception of his own poetic praxis, as Algerian rivers play a pivotal role in the novel too.[177] First and foremost, the river Rhummel appears as emblematic of the author's youth: "I recalled my adventurous childhood; true; I was free, I was happy in the bed of the Rhummel; the childhood of a lizard along a vanished river."[178] The Rhummel—which runs from the mountains at Ferdjioua onto the plains around Constantine, where Kateb was born in 1929, and from there into the Oued El Kebir, from where it flows into the sea at Sidi Abdelaziz—depends on seasonal rains to flow: "The rare flow of the Rhummel, its power always in suspense, collecting nothing more than brief, hopeless showers, like an infusion of blood to an old man whose bones already lie withered . . ."[179] Although other rivers also feature prominently in the novel—such as the Seybouse, which runs into the sea just south of Annaba[180]—the Rhummel is the privileged current of comparison, enabling analogies and providing moments of clarity within the text's obscurity. The mysteries of Rachid's genesis are compared to those of the Rhummel as it runs underground at Constantine: "The Rhummel, which does not flow for more than a few weeks a year, dissipated in the rock, with neither lake nor estuary, a pseudo-torrent vanquished by the enigmas of the terrain, just like Rachid, an only son born out of time to a father murdered before his birth."[181] It even becomes a figure of historical dispossession, treachery, and loss:

> Just as the Rhummel, betrayed in its torrential violence, delivered according to a course other than its own, just as the betrayed Rhummel flows into the sea through the Oued El Kebir, memory of the river lost in Spain, pseudo-Rhummel escaped from its destiny and from its parched bed, in the same way [de même] Rachid's father, murdered in the nuptial grotto, was torn from the warm body of his mistress, by the rival and close relative Si Mokhtar, who married her in secret, and it was then that [et c'est alors que] Nedjma was conceived, a star of blood sprung from murder . . .[182]

Kateb here traces the Oued El Kebir, literally "the great wadi," into which the Rhummel flows, back to the expulsion of Muslims and Muslim converts to Christianity, or Moriscos, from the Iberian Peninsula between 1492 and the early seventeenth century—the Guadalquivir being the river "that the Moors driven out of Andalusia could not transport with them, Guadalquivir, Oued El Kebir . . ."[183]

It is the Rhummel, though, that provides a figure to which Kateb will return to describe his own process of creation.[184] When, in 1963, Kateb looked back at his composition of *Nedjma*, he continued to draw from his novel's riverine logic: "I was like a wadi in an unexpected storm."[185] In turn, the oued, or wadi, has become a figure of choice for critics seeking to capture the secret of Kateb's obscure method. When, around 1970, Kateb abandoned writing in French to compose dramatic works in dialectal Arabic, Jacqueline Arnaud said it had always been a matter of time before he returned to writing in French: "Against Rimbaud's silence, we can set the Katebian themes of endlessly renewed waves of Numidian horsemen, or of the dry wadi, reduced to a subterranean current until the flood, or the resurgence."[186]

The "oued" that Kateb and his critics evoke comes from the Arabic "وادي" [wādī], meaning "valley," "riverbed," or "river." It defines an irregular hydrological regime that only flows with water when it rains heavily. The Arabic word describing a flood of water or a torrential stream is "سيل" [sayl], from the verb "سال" [sāla], meaning "to flow" or "to be or become liquid." This, in turn, gives rise to the term "سيالة" [sayyālah], a "rivulet," which, as Abdelkébir Khatibi later points out, metonymically describes a tattoo inscribed as a vertical line between the lower lip and the chin before spreading across the neck and chest in the manner of a carpet design.[187] In his discussion of Sufism, Abdelwahab Meddeb mentions the use of the Arabic "شطّ" [shaṭṭ], the seasonal flooding of a river, to denote the expression of divine sentences by inspired mystics that surpass normal human capabilities,[188] which Louis Massignon, with more circumspection, entitles "theopathetic locutions."[189] Meddeb proposes "débord" [overflowing] as a rough equivalent for "shaṭṭ" in French, before noting that the term can also be used to characterize the sparks that fly from the friction between two millstones and, as such, might also be equated with the French "fusée" [burst of liquid or flame, flare, rocket], which term Baudelaire used to describe his late aphoristic reflections.[190]

Amrouche, though, has recourse to a somewhat different term than those used by Kateb, Khatibi, and Meddeb to describe sudden flows of water. In place of Arabic or Kabyle definitions, and their French approximations, he proposes a French word that has a long history in Algeria, not least on account of its use in colonial hydrology: "the tidal bore of a spring of anger [mascaret d'un printemps de colère]." "Mascaret" describes the infrequent and unpredictable tidal movement of waves in an estuary, such as the Pororoca that runs up the Amazon and that features in a poem Guillaume Apollinaire wrote in September 1915: "Vagues du Prororoca [*sic*], l'immense mascaret" [Waves of the Pororoca, the immense tidal bore].[191] It comes from the Occitan "mascar," which is to be "splattered in black" and was mostly used to describe the coloring of the head of an animal.

It is therefore intriguing to note, in passing, that in *La Quête de joie*, du Pin's speaker claims to be able to predict such natural phenomena as the tidal bore on account of his animal instinct:

> Car j'ai le nez d'un chien de chasse, pour prévoir
> Les tempêtes qui font déborder ma rivière
> . . .
> Nous passerons avant la vague qui détruit
>
> For I have the nose of a hunting dog, to sense
> The storms that make my river overflow
> . . .
> We will pass before the wave that destroys[192]

When André Gide writes to du Pin on December 1, 1933, to congratulate him on his new publication, he advises the young poet to let himself go and refers to this line specifically: "Do not fear 'the storms that make my river overflow.'"[193]

By the late 1950s, Amrouche had long learned to forgo du Pin's caution and abandons himself here to the uncontrollable flow of such rivers and their inevitable rhapsodies. Like the river evoked by Khaïr-Eddine, Amrouche's bears things in excess:

> . . . le fleuve crie pour avoir trop porté
> comme un serpent
> noir il broie roches et cèdres
> jusqu'à la mer qui le comprend . . .
>
> . . . the river cries out for having carried too much
> like a black
> snake it crushes rocks and cedars
> as far as the sea by which it is comprehended . . .[194]

The irrepressible movement of these rivers of change also confirms what Amrouche had dimly sensed when still in thrall to du Pin and the Catholic mystics in the 1930s: "The poems will be born when the salt on the motionless lakes of the desert adopts life's palpitation, when the Angel smiles on the dark edges of my silence."[195]

To emphasize the institution of a new fluvial regime through his poem, Amrouche twice calls on the river Igharghar. It is a river that is often marked on maps—such as those from the 1880s by the geologist Georges Rolland—with a vertical inscription (fig. 2), to which Amrouche appears to refer when he speaks of this new moment that "runs back against the time of the dead in floods of vertical words" [remonte le temps des morts en flots de paroles verticales]. This vertical inscription can also be found on Rolland's transversal maps of Algerian topography, such as those depicting elevation along a North-South or East-West axis (fig. 3). The Igharghar differs from the Soummam and the Sebaou both by its location—it runs from

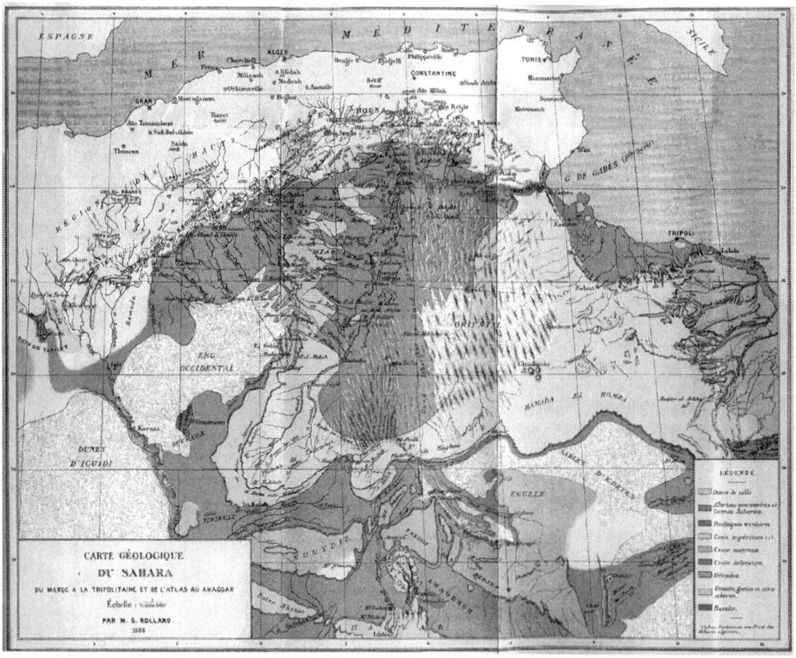

FIG. 2. Georges Rolland, "Carte géologique du Sahara du Maroc à la Tripolitaine et de l'Atlas au Ahaggar, 1886 / Geological Map of the Sahara from Morocco to Tripolitania and from the Atlas to the Hoggar Mountains, 1886." Reproduced in Georges Rolland, *Chemin de fer transsaharien: Géologie et hydrologie du Sahara Algérien; Planches accompagnant les deux volumes de texte* (Paris: Imprimerie nationale, 1890), plate 4.

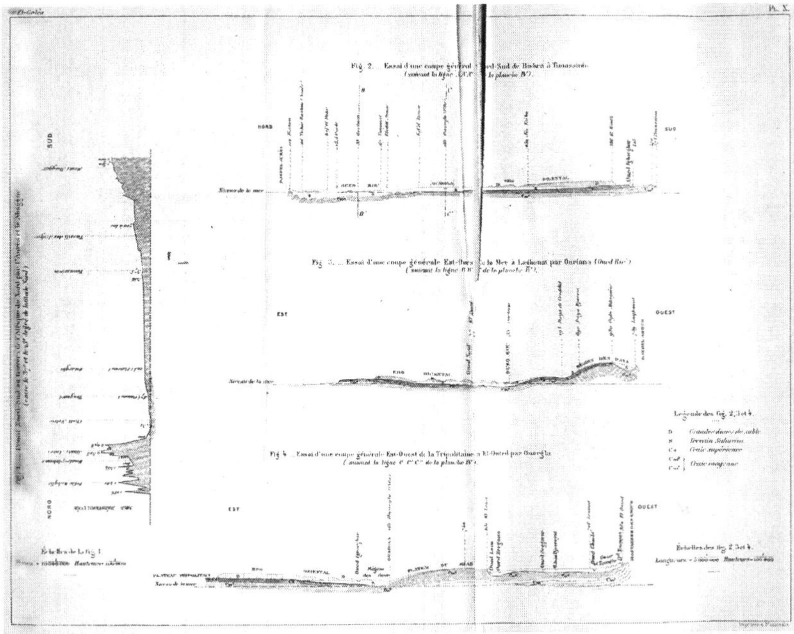

FIG. 3. Georges Rolland, Four transversal topographical sketches to scale depicting elevation: 1) Along a North-South axis between the Mediterranean Sea and the Hoggar Mountains via the Aures Mountains; 2) Along a North-South axis between Biskra and Timassinin; 3) Along an East-West axis between the Mediterranean Sea and Laghouat via Ourlana (Oued Righ); 4) Along an East-West axis between Tripolitania and El Outed (Ksour Range) via Ouargla. "Mission d'El-Goléa / El Goléa [El Menia] Mission." Reproduced in Georges Rolland, *Chemin de fer transsaharien: Géologie et hydrologie du Sahara Algérien; Planches accompagnant les deux volumes de texte* (Paris: Imprimerie nationale, 1890), plate 10.

the Hoggar mountains in the south of the country, northward through the Algerian Sahara ("the burned-out *reg*") to the "Seuil de Gabès" [Gabèsian threshold]—and because it is now a mostly dry riverbed. As the *normalien* and geographer Émile-Félix Gautier wrote around 1920, rivers such as the Igharghar are a fragment of their former selves: "Today's [Saharan] rivers are dwarfs lost in valleys that no longer fit them, because the valleys were carved out by gigantic ancestors. . . . We find there, deeply engraved in the earth, valleys of great Quaternary wadis, practically dead today, but whose networks are still easily recognizable."[196] In the early 1930s, the prehistorian Henri Begouën described the Igharghar specifically as "an admirable *fossil* river [fleuve *fossile*]," adding that "we are in the presence of a skeleton that lends itself admirably to a general study."[197] Gautier also notes that in contrast to the sudden, regular, and potent floods of the Saoura in the north, "which are concentrated in a single channel and sweep it like a tidal bore [à la façon d'un mascaret], from end to end, up to five hundred kilometers from the source,"[198] no such thing could ever come to pass with the Igharghar: "There is certainly no question that a flood starting from the Hoggar, however powerful it might be, could ever travel as far as the great chotts at the foot of the Atlas, along a channel whose continuity is immensely broken. It is not just unreal; it is unimaginable."[199]

Amrouche adopts Begouën's description of this ancient river when he evokes "the fossil bed of the legendary Igharghar," gesturing less to the cultural and ethnic past of Algeria, as he did in his *Chants berbères* and in various essays and speeches, than to the country's obscured ecological past, in which the Sahara would have been temperate, verdant, and fertile. However, he counters Gautier's notion that the Igharghar can no longer serve as a conduit, asserting via his poem that here, at the end of the decade, on the verge of independence from colonial rule, the "flood" will come not only from the Rhummel, the Oued El Kebir, the Sebaou, and the Soummam but also from the Igharghar in the south, that is, from the entirety of the country and its history.

Kateb's poetic influence is central to Amrouche's late poetic development, but this does not stop the older poet from both displacing and broadening what he perceives to be the younger poet's narrow geographical focus, or what Arnaud calls the "quadrilateral polygon of Sétif-Guelma-Constantine-Bône."[200] Although the Igharghar runs north, it does not reach that "which alone deserves the name of Sea."[201] Instead, as Gautier notes, "It is separated today from the nearby Mediterranean by the threshold of Gabès [le seuil de Gabès], and on this threshold, despite all their efforts, geologists have not yet found the slightest trace of an ancient river junction between the basin and the sea."[202] Edwige Tamalet Talbayev demonstrates how *Nedjma* and its related texts enact "the reallegorization of national myth in a Mediterranean mode, inserting the Algerian nation that Kateb's writing helped form into a transnational, more historically capacious map."[203] Here, the Igharghar enables Amrouche to propose a vision of a nation that is not exclusively maritime but also fluvial, arterial, geological, continental. On the threshold of an independence that he will not live to see, Amrouche imagines Algeria as rhapsody, as simultaneously African and Saharan, as much as Mediterranean. Now far from the placelessness of du Pin, Amrouche casts himself as the poetic cartographer of a newly recognized nation.

"Rhapsodie" comes from the Greek verb "ῥάπτω" [rhaptō] [to stitch, sew, weave], itself from a Proto-Indo-European root conveying the sense of turning or bending, and "ᾠδή" [ōidē] [song, legend]. It is generally understood to be an oral form used to recount epics. In his dialogue *Ion,* Plato dismisses the rhapsodic mode because, although it serves as a channel for divine speech, it is delivered in a state of emotion or excitement and therefore lacks "τέχνη" [technē] [skill, mastery, poetic art].[204] In the case of Amrouche's poem, "rhapsody" describes a series of eighteen phrases in prose that are divided between eleven fragments of irregular length—a medley of disparate parts, woven together as in a patchwork. When in *L'entretien infini* [The Infinite Conversation], published a decade after this poem was written, Maurice Blanchot provides a definition of the rhapsodic form, he characterizes it as a "perpetual repetition from episode to episode" and the "interminable amplification of the same."[205] This is why Baudelaire, in a letter to Sainte-Beuve, dubs the narrator of his prose poems, later published as *Le spleen de Paris* [Paris Spleen], "a new Joseph Delorme hanging his rhapsodic thought on every incident encountered on his stroll and drawing from each object an unpleasant moral."[206] The rhapsode, or "song-stitcher,"[207] works to both create and repair discrepancies, to pick and fill holes, thereby stretching the work "until it evaporates."[208] In other words, rhapsody is a model of thinking based on but not limited by repetition, or—as Blanchot puts it—a type of poetry in which criticism is already embedded.

When in the early 1940s, Amrouche had stated the need for "an asceticism and mysticism specific to poetry," he concluded, "The poet can no longer be satisfied with song; he also needs the consciousness of song."[209] Rhapsody is an instance of song that is conscious of itself as song, of song that has become critical, that consciously resists the "prestressed rhythms" and the melodies of childhood, as well as the mythical projections of innocence, timelessness, and utopia. This poem actively distinguishes itself from the "chant" of Amrouche's earlier poetic endeavors and meditations, as well as the "asefru" of Si Mohand and the many other anonymous singers whose songs were reproduced in *Chants berbères.* As we read at the close of the opening fragment of "Rhapsodie sur le seuil,"

> . . . Tu n'entendras pas d'emblée le chant.
> Poème avant le chant, poème au-delà du chant, poème à chant suspendu . . .

> . . . You will not immediately hear the song.
> Poem before song, poem beyond song, poem of suspended song . . .

Blanchot reminds us that the rhapsode is not simply "a faithful imitator, an immobile practitioner."[210] He or she does not just repeat what has come before. Instead, the rhapsode carries repetition forth, a "repetition disturbed by incidents,"[211] a tradition distracted by "new peripeteia."[212] Roland Barthes tells his audience at the Collège de France in the late 1970s that the rhapsodic "distances the Object,"[213] thereby removing what Khatibi identifies as the "theological poison" of "أصالة" [aṣālah], or "originarity."[214] This means that the rhapsode does not need to have been the hero whose feats he or she recounts in their song, slightly distorting the previous telling with each repetition. The heroism celebrated in epic rhapsody is in fact the artificial sustaining of an event that vanishes as quickly as it appears. The hero is lost to the event of heroism as soon as it has occurred.

It is therefore of little consequence, within the logic of rhapsody, whether it was Amrouche who achieved the glory of precursor of which he once dreamed or whether it was Kateb or some other poet. As Blanchot insists, "The epic has neither beginning nor end. And so it must be with the hero: appearing, disappearing, simple and gracious material support for a marvelous act that is inscribed in legend but not in history, because his action is for nothing and is not meant to be effective; it is a beautiful flash in the sky, not the crude furrow dug into the earth."[215] In place of the hero, as Barthes tells us, it is "*Writing*" or "l'*Écrire*" that is magnified.[216] It is perhaps only in "Rhapsodie sur le seuil" that Amrouche enters into writing—that he achieves something that touches on the prophetic, that he is able to inaugurate a poetic modernity for the Maghreb—not alone but alongside Kateb Yacine, Henri Kréa, and others. As Édouard Glissant assures us, "It is no longer a question of discovering unknown lands, explorations no longer set out to reveal the secrets of rivers, mountains, and deserts. Instead, it is the marvelous and infinite and rare multiplicity of peoples' imaginaries, of their contacts and also of their reciprocal reactions that remain to be discovered and meditated."[217]

The vision of Algeria proposed in Amrouche's late poem is one that is conscious of poetry as much as of history, of myth as much as of liberation. Unseen by most, in "Rhapsodie sur le seuil" Amrouche moves away from the incompatible binaries that structured much of his early poetry and thought toward what Khatibi will term a "pensée-autre" [thinking-other],[218] that is, a decentering of established epistemological paradigms, here through poetry. Amrouche takes almost a lifetime to realize that the future of Maghrebi poetics lies not so much in the impossible marriage of France and Algeria, or of Kabylia and Catholicism. The dual and its perpetual "déchirements" must be abandoned in favor of a less predictable, rhapsodic model. Algeria is irrigated by numerous currents that each follow their own laws, some of which flow into the present, others into the past, some continuously, others in seasonal bursts, and still others not at all. Such rivers are rhapsodic not only within their own fluvial logic but also in their relation to each other, some of which they will touch and others of which they will never encounter. These currents are not undisputed authorities but competing, marginal, fragmentary voices, figures of Algeria's plurality or perhaps of what Khatibi will later call a "wandering topology, split, androgynous dream, loss of identity—on the threshold of madness" [Topologie errante, schize, rêve androgyne, perte de l'identité—au seuil de la folie].[219]

CHAPTER 2

Orpheus, pied-noir

Jean Sénac and a Poetics of Algerian Becoming

SARTRE'S ORPHEUS

In "Orphée noir" [Black Orpheus], the preface to *Anthologie de la nouvelle poésie nègre et malgache de langue française* [Anthology of New Black and Malagasy Poetry in French], edited by Léopold Sédar Senghor, Jean-Paul Sartre adopts the mythical poet as a vehicle for his presentation of contemporary Black francophone poetry.[1] Sartre is an unlikely champion of Black poetry, in part because in *Qu'est-ce que la littérature?* [What Is Literature?], first published the previous year in *Les temps modernes*, he had promoted prose at the expense of poetry as the genre best equipped for political and social engagement;[2] in part because Sartre—white, Protestant, and metropolitan—had limited familiarity with Black poetry in French or any other language. Yet, as Richard H. Watts writes, "For better or for worse, the one writer or critic to do more than any other to put francophone literature on the cultural map is Sartre."[3] Here, I begin by reconsidering the figure of Orpheus as presented by Sartre—to judge its purpose, success, and limitations, and to ask to what degree the figure responds or fails to respond to the predicament of poets writing in French outside of France during the period of decolonization who are not Black. Specifically, I examine the poetic writings of Jean Sénac (Béni Saf, 1926–Algiers, 1973), art critic, radio presenter, pied-noir supporter of Algerian independence, and perhaps one of the most talented poets to have written in French in the postwar period.[4] The author Rachid Boudjedra (b. Aïn Beïda, 1941) calls him "the greatest poet in the Maghreb."[5] I argue that Sénac responds belatedly but decisively to Sartre's Orpheus by proposing a counter figure to better grasp the plight of the pied-noir poet writing in colonial and, eventually, postcolonial Algeria.

Orpheus may be the archetype of the Western poet, but he is not an obvious choice to represent the postwar writer. Reflecting on "poésie maudite" [cursed poetry] toward the end of the Second World War, Aimé Césaire points to Prometheus the thief, Oedipus the assassin, and even the obsessive-compulsive Christopher Columbus as more pertinent models.[6] In *Metamorphoses*, Ovid recounts how Orpheus's marriage to Eurydice is cut short when she is bitten on the ankle by a serpent and dies.[7] By virtue of his song—which is such that all manner of flora and fauna draw toward him to hear him sing—Orpheus is able to enter the gate of Taenarus. He persuades the shades to release his bride on the condition that he not look back until they have both reentered the world of the living. Orpheus does look back and so loses Eurydice for a second and final time. Sartre reads Orpheus's turn as the error built into all poetic language: "This sense of failure regarding language considered as a direct means of expression is at the origin of all poetic experience."[8] Modern poetry begins where language breaks down and fails its speaker, where it is no longer possible to sustain the illusion of harmony between word and being. Poetry does nothing more than suggest being in and through the "vibratory disappearance of the word."[9] As Stéphane Mallarmé put it in the critical poem "Magie" [Magic], "évoquer, dans une ombre exprès, l'objet tu[,] par des mots allusifs, jamais directs, se réduisant à du silence égal" [to evoke, with intentional vagueness, the mute object, using allusive words, never direct, reducing everything to an equivalent of silence . . .].[10]

Sartre develops the notion of a modern Black Orpheus by asking his readers to consider not only the fatal, last-second turn but also the initial descent into the underworld. The Black poet pursues negritude—his Eurydice—in an untiring descent into his self: "It is a quest, a systematic reduction, and an ascesis, accompanied by a continual effort to go deeper."[11] Drawing on inaccurate cultural stereotypes,[12] Sartre claims to see evidence of this descent into the "greatest lyricism" in a series of extreme behaviors—rolling around on the floor; singing of angers, regrets, and hatreds; exposing one's wounds—that are normally associated with trance and demonic possession: "It is when [the Black poet] seems suffocated by the serpents of our culture that he appears the most revolutionary."[13] The Black poet is driven by the belief that he is meant to become one with negritude. But the moment he turns to look at it head on, it disappears in smoke and the walls of white culture rise up: "*their* knowledge, *their* language, *their* morals."[14] It is the Orphic nature of the Black francophone poet's relation to negritude—his heroic descent toward it and his fatally imperfect retrieval of it—that, Sartre asserts, makes Black francophone poetry the only great contemporary revolutionary poetry.[15]

SÉNAC'S JACOB

In 1968, some twenty years after Sartre's projection of Black Orpheus, Jean Sénac published what many consider to be his best book, containing three collections of poems: *Avant-corps* [Fore-Body], *Poèmes iliaques* [Ilium Poems], and *Diwân du noûn* [The Nūn Dīwān].[16] As his close friend, the poet Rabah Belamri (Bougaa, 1946–Paris, 1995) later affirmed, "Sénac never felt so attuned to his poetic word and to the universe as when he was writing *Avant-corps*."[17] For those who had followed Sénac's publications in avant-garde literary journals in France and North Africa—as well as collections since the breakthrough *Poèmes* [Poems], included in Albert Camus's prestigious Espoir series at Gallimard—*Avant-corps* appeared to reassert the purpose and potential of poetry in a still newly independent Algeria.[18] From as early as 1950 and the creation of poems later published in *Matinale de mon peuple* [Awakening of My People],[19] Sénac is motivated by the desire to bring about the liberation of the Algerian people from French colonial occupation. Much of his work projects the vision of a liberated country that accepts and celebrates the diversity of its inhabitants—not only Arabs and Imazighen (although Sénac acknowledges that they will make up nine-tenths of any independent Algeria) but also members of the European, or pied-noir, community who relinquish their claims to other nationalities.[20] He writes, however, from within an unusual constellation of factors that alienate him from the social, cultural, and religious norms of Algerians living under colonial rule—as an actively gay, ardent Catholic, unable to speak either Tamazight or "اللغة الدارجة" [al-lughah al-dārijah], the dialect of Arabic spoken across the Maghreb.[21]

It is a quandary captured in a poem written in November 1966, which Sénac dedicated to the poet Jamel Eddine Bencheikh (Casablanca, 1930–Tours, 2005):

3

Cette terre est la mienne avec son amère liturgie,
Ses éclats orduriers, ses routes torves,
L'âme saccagée, le peuple las.

Mienne avec son soleil cassant comme un verglas,
Les dédales affamés où nos muscles se perdent,
Et tant de vanité qui pousse comme une herbe
Là où rêvaient des hommes-rois.

Avec son insolent lignage, ses cadavres climatisés,
Ses tanks et la puanteur du poème
A la merci d'un cran d'arrêt.

A l'heure de dérision je l'appelle à tue-tête.
Une aile où se poser! Un sourire habitable!
Une jambe affermie où commence un chemin!

Je ne la quitterai pas. Escaladant le mythe.
Je connais ses chardons, ses genêts, sa torpeur,
Mais toujours dans le roc insinuant l'espace
Un escargot secret—et tel ongle rageur!

Cette terre est la mienne entre deux fuites fastes,
Deux charniers, deux désirs, deux songes de béton,
Et le chant d'une flûte en mes veines surprend
Le mal de Boabdil sous les murs de Grenade.

Mienne hors de la raison, mienne hors de vos saisons.
Vous pouvez mordre et mordre,
Sur une science si tendre, une joie si têtue,
Le chaos n'aura pas de prise.

3

This land is mine with her bitter liturgy,
Her vulgar radiances, her sinister routes,
A plundered soul, a weary people.

Mine with its sun brittle like black ice,
The famished labyrinths where our muscles waste away,
And such vanity that grows like a weed
There where men, kings dreamed.

With her insolent lineage, her air-conditioned corpses,
Her tanks and the stench of the poem
At the mercy of a flick knife.

At the hour of derision I shout to her out loud.
A wing to land on! A habitable smile!
A sturdy leg that provides a pathway!

I will not abandon her. Ascending the myth.
I know her thistles, her bushes of broom, her weariness,
But always in the rock insinuating space
A secret snail—and such a painful nail!

This land is mine between two auspicious escapes,
Two mass graves, two desires, two dreams of concrete,
And the tune of a flute in my veins takes
Boabdil's misfortune under the walls of Granada by surprise.

Mine out of reason, mine out of your seasons.
You can bite away,
On a science as tender as this, on a joy this stubborn,
Chaos will have no purchase.[22]

Avant-corps, in which this poem appears, marks a watershed in the life and career of Sénac. It is the work where he most unambiguously asserts his erotic fascination with men, at a time and in a place where public manifestation of such desire was not widely accepted. It is also the collection in which his agitation in favor of the self-determination of the Algerian people acquires a new emphasis. In the first years of independence, it appeared that the ideals promoted at the Soummam Valley Congress in 1956 might yet be realized. At that time, the political objective of the FLN for independent Algeria was to create something resembling a secular, democratic, and multiracial social republic. These principles were largely formulated by the FLN leader Abane Ramdane (Larbaâ Nath Irathen, 1920–Tétouan,

1957), who drew on the ideological objectives of the defunct Mouvement pour le triomphe des libertés démocratiques [Movement for the Triumph of Democratic Liberties] (MTLD), a pre-independence Algerian nationalist political party. Frantz Fanon would promote a similar vision in *L'an V de la révolution algérienne* [Year V of the Algerian Revolution].[23] But by the time Houari Boumédiène became chairman of the Revolutionary Council of Algeria in the bloodless coup d'état of June 1965, there was less interest in the notions of diversity, tolerance, and multiculturalism promoted throughout Sénac's writings. When Sénac was stabbed to death in his basement apartment in Algiers in August 1973, Assia Djebar said that it showed that "a little more than ten years after independence, the country was already rejecting its tradition of openness and plurality."[24] *Avant-corps* does not abandon its vision of a liberal Algeria, but there is a sense of resignation to the new political and social status quo and a renewed focus on the poem as the privileged locus for social, sexual, political, and national revolution.[25] This is what Sénac refers to variously as the "Corps Total" [Total Body] or, more commonly, the "corpoème" [corpoem]—a textual event, in which the poem, the (usually male) body, and the broader community enter into a mutually motivating network of desire. As he writes in the preface to *Avant-corps*, "Cette aventure iliaque, cet avant-corps ne sont que des prolégomènes vers un verbe réconcilié, une chair heureuse, le Corps Total" [This iliac adventure, this fore-body are only prolegomena toward a reconciled word, a happy flesh, the Total Body].[26]

Integral to Sénac's project to pursue the Total Body and the corpoem is the elaboration of a figure who asks to be compared to Sartre's Black Orpheus, namely Jacob. While Sartre, like Memmi, "labors under the dichotomies of colonial domination,"[27] Jacob enables Sénac to propose a figure of struggle that—though presented in a poetic rather than prefacial mode—critically condenses and articulates the challenges facing the francophone, and especially the pied-noir, poet in independent Algeria in the late 1960s. We know that the episode recounted in Genesis, in which Jacob wrestles with the angel, held special significance for Sénac because it appears in full—in Louis Segond's translation[28]—in *Ébauche du père* [Sketching the Father], the only completed volume of his project to write a multivolume autobiographical novel.[29]

As a boy growing up in Oran in the 1930s, the narrator recounts how he used to read the Bible to his mother from one side of a curtain, while she sat on the other side, defecating and reading the local newspaper. When alone at night, the narrator would pick up the Bible, enthralled by its images of "light and blood," and often turned to the account of Jacob's encounter at Jabbok. It is an account that Charles Baudelaire—who also quotes it in full, as translated in the seventeenth century by Lemaistre de Sacy, in his discussion of Eugène Delacroix's mural on the topic (fig. 4)—describes as a "bizarre legend":[30]

> Jacob remained alone. Then a man fought with him until the dawn. Seeing that he could not defeat him, this man hit him in the socket of his thigh [cet homme le frappa à l'emboîture de la hanche]; and the socket of Jacob's thigh was dislocated while he fought with him. He said: Let me go, because the dawn is rising. And Jacob replied: I will not let you go, until you have blessed me. He said to him: What is your name? And he replied: Jacob.

FIG. 4. Eugène Delacroix, *Jacob Wrestling with the Angel*, oil and wax on plaster, 1849, 1860–1861, 751 × 485 cm. Église Saint Sulpice, Paris. Bridgeman Images.

> He said again: Your name shall no longer be Jacob, but you shall be called Israel; because you have fought with God and with men, and you have been the victor. Jacob questioned him, saying: Let me, I pray you, know your name. He replied: Why do you ask my name? And he blessed him there. Jacob called this place Peniel; because, he said, I saw God, face to face, and my soul was saved. The sun was rising, when he passed Peniel. Jacob limped from his thigh.[31]

The account in Genesis of a physical contest between human and angelic beings may have informed that of Muḥammad's conflict with Gabriel on Mount Ḥirāʾ, when the Prophet's refusal to respond to the angel's imperative to read or recite the first verse of the Qurʾān leads to three such meetings, only after the last of which Muḥammad accedes. As Khatibi explains with reference to the account recorded by the early Muslim historian Ibn Isḥāq (Medina, 704–Baghdad, 767), "It was necessary for the prophetic body to suffer a terrifying ordeal, for it to be detached from merely human 'reason' so that the message—illegible to the addressee—might exist."[32] In the context of Sénac's novel, the passage informs the description of other struggles. One, more mundane, is the encounter with a Spanish sunbather, with whom the narrator daydreams he is making love. The other is the confrontation that brought about Sénac's conception, when his mother, Jeanne Comma (1887–1965), was raped by a neighbor in a hat boutique in Mostaganem. Sénac never knew his father and took his family name from Edmond Sénac, whom his mother divorced in 1933 when Jean was seven years old. Attention should be paid to the comma in Sénac's work, as it is his original, maternal—we might even say Spanish—signature.[33] Notably, the only variation Sénac makes in his transcription of Segond's translation from the Hebrew is the addition of a comma in the penultimate phrase.[34]

This episode in Genesis is also a vital intertext for *Avant-corps*. It helps to explain certain features of the preface, including the importance of naming in Sénac's notion of the poem: "Nous vivons parce que nous sommes nommés. Toute vie se fait en nous par le nom qu'elle exalte" [We live because we are named. All life is made in us by the name that it exalts].[35] The rhetorical mechanisms of giving and receiving the name provide narrative structure in the account of Jacob's combat with the angel. The angel asks Jacob his name and then changes it to Israel. When Jacob—now Israel—asks the angel's name, the angel not only does not give the name but also asks why Jacob would want to know. The angel's name is a question, a refusal, and a blessing. Derrida might call it a ruse.[36] Jacob then renames the place where the encounter with the anonymous angel takes place, such that it is no longer Jabbok but Peniel. It is in provoking debate around the possibility and conditions of giving the name that Jacob becomes a figure, for Sénac, of modern poetry. Sénac thereby directly counters a definition of poetry proposed by Sartre: "Neither do poets . . . think of naming the world anymore and, in fact, they name nothing at all, because naming implies a perpetual sacrifice of the name to the object named, or, to speak like Hegel, the name is revealed to be inessential compared to the thing that is essential."[37]

Implicitly drawing on Jacob's experience at Jabbok, Sénac insists on the power of naming, even as he acknowledges the difficulties that naming involves:

> Mais transcrire, c'est aussi déchiffrer, ordonner le message et lui restituer son feu. C'est arracher le corps à ses ténèbres et lui donner dans le vocabulaire un espace de transmission. C'est inventer. Qu'un mot s'accorde à un autre mot et le mythe met en place l'image à souffle continu: l'univers respire, l'homme existe.
>
> But to transcribe is also to decipher, to organize the message, and to restitute its fire to it. It's to tear the body from its shadows and give it, in words, a space of transmission. It's to invent. If one word is in tune with the next, then myth installs the image within a single breath: the universe breathes, man exists.[38]

The labor of transcription, of deciphering, and of organizing syllables in Sénac's conception of the poem suggests that he is writing with intimate knowledge of the ways in which the Hebrew text itself gives further significance, resonance, and texture to Jacob's resistance. Any reader of the original text will be struck by the close coincidence of certain verbal units. Jacob is properly "יעקב" [Ya'aḳov] from "עקב" ['aḳev], meaning "heel," a reference to the heel of his twin brother, Esau, which Jacob was holding when he was born. As Sénac writes:

> Et n'oubliez pas (dit Antar) que dans le ventre de sa mère il tenait déjà le talon de son jumeau.
>
> And don't forget (said Antar) that in his mother's womb he already had his twin's heel in his grasp.[39]

Jacob's name also closely resembles the name of the river he is to cross, the Yabboḳ ["יבק"]. Furthermore, when Jacob, or Ya'aḳov, "wrestles" with the stranger, the verb used in Hebrew is "ויאבק" [ṿaye'aveḳ], in which all the sounds—if not strictly speaking all the letters—of both Ya'aḳov and Yabboḳ are contained.

The partial confluence of these three Hebrew words—their inability to fully distinguish themselves from each other—dramatizes, on the level of the word, the struggle between Jacob and the angel, neither of whom is able to vanquish the other, even when the angel "touches" the "hollow" of Jacob's "thigh."[40] Jacob agrees to release the angel only once he has been blessed, but the angel only blesses Jacob when he is no longer Jacob. When Israel does cross the river, it is no longer Jabbok but Peniel. Curiously, even this dislocation is not allowed to stand. In the verse immediately following the naming of Peniel, there is a further, unexpected dislocation: "And as he passed over Penuel the sun rose upon him, and he halted upon his thigh."[41] The final fragment of this verse appears to suggest that Jacob limps as a result of the fight. But the parallel dislocation of Peniel into Penuel suggests that the dislocation is a function of naming and renaming. This double dislocation—of the name and of the thigh—coincides with the crossing of the river and the rising of the sun.

Exegetes often see the divinity's departure in the sun's arrival, but for Sénac the appearance of the sun is an invitation to inscribe his poem within the consonantal fault lines of the biblical narrative. The sun is Sénac's own figural signature, as it appears in the form of a circle and five dashes at the end of many of his poems and letters. In this, he is perhaps inspired by the Persian poet, Islamic scholar, and Sufi mystic Rūmī (Balkh or Wakhsh, 1207–Konya, 1273), who often signed his poems with the word "شمس" [shams], meaning "sun," in reference to his master and friend, the mystic Shams-i Tabrīzī, who some traditions say was murdered by Rūmī's followers, jealous of their master's attention.[42] The sun persists as a figure for Sénac in the work of subsequent Algerian poets, not least Tahar Djaout, whose first collection of poems, written shortly after Sénac's murder, includes the line "Sénac tonsure anachronique de prêtre solaire" [Sénac sun priest's anachronistic tonsure].[43]

Sénac is alert to the poetic potential of the linguistic and corporeal dislocations that take place in the ancient account of Jacob's encounter with the angel.[44] In section 11 of the conversation poem "Étreinte" [Embrace],[45] a character called the "genius of the [Arabic letter] nūn" brings donuts [beignets] to a group of male friends gathered on the beach at Pointe Pescade (now Raïs Hamidou): "C'est seulement pour ceux qui se baignent!" [They are only for those who swim!], he cries. That is, the "beignets" [/bɛ.ɲɛ/] are only for those who agree to "se baigner" [/sə bɛ.ɲe/]:

Beignets, baigner, Peniel (pensait le Maître du Noûn, et il rêvait à l'alchimie des mots. Car l'alchimie, qui est une science capitale (en exil) à laquelle il faudra bien revenir un jour, est aussi une transmutation par le Mot. On peut nous brûler vif, l'Homme finira bien par se découvrir!).

Donuts, swimming, Peniel (thought the Master of the Nūn, and he pondered the alchemy of words. For alchemy, a capital science (in exile) to which we must return one day, is also a transmutation by the Word. They can burn us alive, Man will end up discovering himself!).[46]

The "beignet," or donut, features persistently in Algerian poetry both in and outside of French. The Kabyle singer Si Mohand ou-Mhand was at one point a donut seller in what was then Bône (now Annaba), as he sings, in Mammeri's translation:

Par indigence de tout bien
Je me suis fait marchand de beignets
Oublieux de toute écriture

On account of utter poverty
I became a purveyor of donuts
Oblivious to all writing[47]

On one occasion, Si Mohand is said to have dropped the pipe he used to smoke drugs into the donut mixture, causing several of his clients to fall ill and forcing him to flee the city.[48] For Sénac, though, the donut is more than anecdotal, as can also be seen in his poem "Schéma de la misère" [Diagram of Poverty]:

Le soleil a quitté les mots.
Le poème est un beignet froid.

The sun has abandoned language.
The poem is a cold donut.[49]

In this solar thinking, Sénac echoes his colleague-in-poetry Anna Gréki (Batna, 1931–Algiers, 1966), who died in labor at age thirty-four and in whose poem "Le pain le lait" [Bread, Milk] the donut is in lunar orbit around childhood:

A ras du sol dehors des beignets
Lunes plates que mordent à dents
De lait des enfants qui savent rire

On the ground floor outside donuts
Flat moonlets bitten into by children
With milk teeth who know how to laugh[50]

More recently, in Kaouther Adimi's novel *Nos richesses* [Our Riches], the anecdotal, acoustic, and astrophysical investment of the donut explored by Si Mohand, Sénac, and Gréki gives way to disillusionment, when Abdallah's bookstore is sold by the state to be transformed into a donut shop, with "beignets" replacing books: "There will be every possible type of donut: sugar, apple, chocolate."[51]

The acoustic progression from the ridiculous ("beignets") to the banal ("baigner") to the divine ("Peniel") in Sénac's poem demonstrates the unique potential of poetry to bring about radical change through small verbal dislocations. When Sénac says that the role of the poet is to transcribe, to decipher, to organize the message, to restitute its fire, to tear the body from the shadows, and to give it, in words, a space of transmission, he describes the series of dislocations dramatized in the biblical account of Jacob's struggle and crossing. Jacob is the supreme figure of the modern poet:

> Toute sa vie (dit Yahia) il fut étreinte et ruse. Tant de mesquinerie, de marchandage, avait besoin de la Maison de Dieu et d'échelles et d'anges. Il n'est de grande poésie qui ne sente son purin.
>
> His entire life (said Yahia), he was embrace and trickery. So much meanness, and bartering, needed the House of God and ladders and angels. There is no great poetry that does not bear his stench.[52]

DISLOCATING ORPHEUS

Implicated in Sénac's promotion of Jacob as the perennial emblem of great poetry, there is both a rebuttal to Sartre's claim that the only great contemporary revolutionary poetry is Black francophone poetry and a rejection of Orpheus—Black or otherwise—as the figure of this poetry. Sénac's elaboration—through poetry—of a mythical figure for what great francophone poetry must be invites us to better identify the limitations of Sartre's election and presentation of Orpheus, both within the context of Sartre's preface and beyond.

First, anyone familiar with the myth of Orpheus, as presented by either Ovid or Virgil, might be taken aback to see Sartre propose Orpheus as a figure for the struggle against colonialism. As Sartre writes, the Black person has "more than all others, suffered from capitalist exploitation; he has acquired, more than all others, the sense of revolt and the love of liberty."[53] Césaire describes negritude in similar terms: "It is a jolt, a jolt of dignity. It is refusal, I mean refusal of oppression. It is combat, that's to say combat against inequality. It is also revolt."[54] But Orpheus is not a common figure for the oppressed, nor for resistance. He is one whose unique talents in song allow him access to and egress from even the realm of the dead. He is an unimpeachable interloper into the Other, an agent of absolute opposites. His talent is so complete that projectiles hurled at him stall in midair and fall at his feet.[55]

In short, Orpheus is the total poet. In turn, this may recall Pierre Bourdieu's description of Sartre as the total intellectual.[56] By this, Bourdieu intends one who is uniquely able to transgress the invisible frontier between philosophy and literature, between the weight of the concept and the elegance of writing, between reflexivity and naivete.[57] It is as a total intellectual that Sartre is able to suspend the regular order of things, unnaturally completing and bringing to fruition the work of those who have gone before him, much as he attempts to do in his preface on Black francophone poetry. Sartre is aware of the incongruous application of Orpheus to the struggle of the Black francophone poet for self-determination and seeks to repair this. When projecting Orpheus onto Césaire, for instance, Sartre invests the figure with a new, Ophelian narrative, in which the poet drowns in his words: "His back turned, his eyes closed, so as to be able, finally, to touch the black water of dreams and of desire with his feet, and to let himself drown there."[58] In another instance, the Black poet "stands upright and freezes like a bird charmer, and things come and perch on the branches of the fake tree." Sartre continues, "This is a way of catching the world but magically, through silence and stillness."[59] Sartre's Orpheus now drowns, now stands silently rooted to the spot—novel variations to the myth that come naturally to the total and totalizing philosopher-poet.

Second, the mythical Orpheus entertains a detached relation to the heterosexuality espoused for the most part in the poems selected by Senghor for his anthology. In *Metamorphoses*, Orpheus is prevented from consummating his marriage to Eurydice by her premature death, continues to pursue union with her even though she has died, and when he fails to bring her back from the dead, shuns the love of other women.[60] Sartre's controversial negotiation of the interrelations of Black poetry, negritude, and sexuality is mostly founded on Orpheus's alienation from sex. When the Black poet makes love to a Black woman, the sexual act seems to Sartre to be a celebration of the "Mystery of being."[61] Being emerges from Nothingness "like a member becoming erect" [comme une verge qui se dresse].[62] And yet in analogue images in Césaire's *Cahier d'un retour au pays natal* [Notebook of a Return to My Native Land], to which Sartre presumably refers, the phallus takes form not in being but in earth:

> terre grand sexe levé vers le soleil
> terre grand délire de la mentule de Dieu . . .
>
> earth great sex raised to the sky
> earth great delirium of God's penis . . .[63]

Césaire thus firmly situates sex in the world of matter not metaphysics. Similarly, Sartre draws on Orpheus's stilted relation to sex to restrict Black sexuality to predictable ceremony: "His labor, it is the repetition, from year to year, of sacred coitus."[64] There is no acknowledgment here of the thrill of the casual encounter, of the spontaneous burst of instinct, of what Sénac, writing in his journal calls "l'amour généreux, multiple, risqué, démesuré, insolite" and ultimately "l'amour fou" [Generous, multiple, risky, immoderate, weird love. Mad love].[65] This is despite the fact that the examples of sex provided by Sartre in poems by Senghor, Jean-Joseph Rabéarivelo, and particularly Léon Laleau—"spasmes lourds d'homme en rut" [heavy spasms of man on heat][66]—do not describe holy ritual so much as common human passion. Sartre's characterization of Césaire's poetry as "a perpetual coupling of women and men metamorphosed into animals, vegetation, stone, with stones, plants, and beasts metamorphosed into men"[67]—or what he calls the "profound unity"[68] of vegetal and sexual symbols that constitutes the greatest originality of Black poetry—can also be traced to Ovid's *Metamorphoses*, where Orpheus himself narrates the transmutation of the likes of Hyacinthus into a flower and of Myrrha into a myrrh tree.

Orpheus cannot be said to adequately represent either the anti-colonial struggle or the celebration of heterosexuality at stake in the poems presented in Senghor's anthology. If Sartre persists with Orpheus, it is primarily because Orpheus is an agent of extremes, the singer whose song is implacably powerful, the man able to enter and exit the province of Hades. He is therefore well suited to the unambiguous terms of Sartre's dialectic model. Sartre claims that the modern French poem has surrendered all authority to words and no longer has any relation to the body: "The poem is a dark chamber, in which words bang insanely into each other. Colliding in the air, they set each other on fire and fall in flames."[69] Here, Sartre paraphrases a passage from Mallarmé's late critical poem "Crise de vers" and is guilty of hyperbole. Mallarmé speaks merely of "la disparition élocutoire du poëte" [the elocutionary disappearance of the poet],[70] which cedes the initiative to words "par le heurt de leur inégalité mobilisés" [mobilized by the jolt of their inequality]:[71] "ils s'allument de reflets réciproques comme une virtuelle traînée de feu sur des pierreries . . ." [they light each other up with reciprocal reflections, like a virtual trail of fire on precious stones . . .].[72] But Sartre's message is clear. What were mere "reciprocal reflections" in Mallarmé have become "fires" [incendies], and the words themselves "burst into flames" [tombent en flammes], in a complete conflagration of verbal units and systems of signifying. When Sartre goes on to suggest that negritude poetry will die with French before it can resurrect with French, we are invited to see these fires as the progression of French poetry to its destructive extremes, coinciding with political and social reality as the colony comes to its inevitable and violent end: "It is only when [the words] have disgorged their whiteness, making this ruined language a solemn and sacred superlanguage, that [the Black poet] adopts them."[73] According to Sartre, negritude—and with it, Black poetry—is little more than a step, a stage, the antithesis in a vast dialectic progression, in which the theoretical and practical affirmation of white culture is the thesis: "Negritude is destined to destroy itself, it is transitional not terminal, a means and not an end."[74]

There has been considerable opposition to Sartre's implication of negritude in the dialectic that results in the proletariat. When Césaire explains his reasons for leaving the French Communist Party, he cites the party's prioritization of class over race as a major factor.[75] It is likely that he would apply a similar critique to Sartre's abolition of negritude here. In his 1952 *Peau noire, masques blancs* [Black Skin, White Masks] Frantz Fanon wrote, "When I read this page, I felt that my last chance had been stolen from me" because "conscience needs to lose itself in the night of the absolute, the only way to obtain self-consciousness."[76] The evident shortcomings of Sartre's Orpheus remind us that we would be wrong to take Sartre entirely at his word when he proposes to dissolve negritude and Black poetry into a greater class struggle. Orpheus is something of a fraud, able to persuade those who cannot be persuaded, almost able to bring the dead back to life, a prototype for Christ's duplicity. Sartre, too, is playing a trick on his readers. We should perhaps have realized this when he projected Black francophone poetry—with which he has limited familiarity—as the only great revolutionary poetry. The same might be said of Sartre's projection of excessive, if not melodramatic, humility, from the depths of which he states that no white man can read—let alone comment on—Black poetry, before doing just that. There is, in other words, little in the figure of Orpheus to hold on to, no body to struggle against or to struggle with. We think he is one thing, but when we go to touch him, he becomes something else. Sartre's Orpheus is constantly on the point of becoming Eurydice.

ORPHEUS, PIED-NOIR

In contrast to Sartre's Black Orpheus, Sénac's Jacob is a figure that demands, and achieves, an encounter with the Other, and thus there is a parallel to be drawn with the way Fanon develops Sartre's thinking on colonization and decolonization.[77] Hegel says that it is in opposition with the Other that the subject experiences desire and thereby sets out on the route leading to dignity of the spirit: "It is only by risking one's life that one conserves one's freedom."[78] Fanon continues, "Human reality in-itself-for-itself can only be achieved through conflict and through the risk that conflict implies."[79] Sénac similarly understands the importance and risk of struggle in the pursuit of human dignity. This is especially evident in the third and final collection included in *Avant-corps*, entitled *Diwân du noûn* [The Nūn Dīwān]. In "Interrogations" [Interrogations], another conversation poem, we are told that the injury suffered by Jacob is the inscription of a letter, the Arabic letter "ن" [nūn]:

3

Cuisses. Si donc Jacob s'arc-boute et prend assise
Sur le cri des pleureuses ou la surprise
D'un berger entre deux roseaux,
L'Ange tamponne sa peau
D'une consonne bleue où le combat s'éclaire:
Pour qui sait lire il y a là toute l'injustice du Père,
Ses tricheries, la corde, la glu dans le pommier;
L'Ange ne fait que rappeler

La première impudence et sur la hanche exalte
Ce chant de dérision en un chiffre de basalte.
Nous l'appellerons Noûn.

3

Thighs. So if Jacob braces himself and builds
On the cry of the mourners or the surprise
Of a shepherd between two reeds,
The Angel stamps his skin
With a blue consonant in which the combat becomes clear:
For whoever knows how to read, here is all the injustice of the
Father,
His duplicities, the rope, the birdlime in the apple tree;
The Angel merely recalls
The initial impudence and on the hip elevates
This song of derision to a figure in basalt.
We will call it the Nūn.[80]

The inscription of "ن" [nūn] is meant to mark the victory of God over man, but Jacob refuses to be labeled in this way:

Mais se rebiffe Jacob et la ruse de l'Homme
Ne touche pas sa chair au-delà des caniveaux
Où les siècles croupissent . . .

But Jacob digs his heels in and the Man's ruse
Does not touch his flesh beyond the gutters
Where centuries stagnate . . .[81]

Jacob escapes because he operates in a language other than the one he has been branded with, a dislocated language, a language free from the stasis of the sacred, a language that exploits ambiguities and always renames before it proceeds. Just as Genesis plays on the similarity and difference of "Ya'aḳov," "Yabboḳ," and "ṿaye'aveḳ"—and "Étreinte" on the verbal and acoustic proximity of "beignets," "baigner," and "Peniel"—so too does "Interrogations" invite us to speculate on the excess of meaning generated by the proximities and extremities of the letter "nūn," or "noûn" in the French transcription. Acoustically, "noûn" evokes both the first-person plural pronoun "nous," which in the diegesis of the poem identifies a group of friends sunbathing by the sea at Pointe Pescade, north of Algiers, as well as the various manifestations of "nu" [naked], particularly in the male nudity that repeatedly distracts the conversation poem.[82] This is what René Char—Sénac's lifelong mentor—called "l'énergie disloquante de la poésie" [the dislocating energy of poetry].[83]

8

Et c'est là que Jacob est vainqueur. La cohorte
Des Anges peut lacérer ses côtes; comme sur une porte
L'Homme (l'Ange privilégié, le chef)
Tambouriner de la nuit à l'aube, plaquer des tampons, bref,
Hurler tout un alphabet d'Eden et sa cabale
Dans le sang même de Jacob prostré, que dalle!
Dieu—à cette réponse qu'il implore—n'a pas accès
Et se consume dans sa création comme en un abcès.

8

And it is there that Jacob is victor. The cohort
Of Angels might lacerate his ribs; as if on a door,
the Man (the privileged Angel, the chief)
Can pound, from night to dawn, tackling him hard, in short,
Screaming the entire alphabet of Eden and its cabal
In the very blood of prostrate Jacob, sod all!
God—to this response that he implores—does not have access
And is consumed in his creation as in an abscess.[84]

In part, Sénac is affirming the continuing importance of French as a mode of expression, contradicting his earlier statements on the role of French poetry in an independent Algeria, which he described as transitional and as preparing the way for the "Great Arabic Oeuvre" [Grande Œuvre arabe] to be written by the "Arab poets of tomorrow."[85] In an article published a week before his murder in August 1973, he writes, "Literature in the national language (Arabic), literature written in French, each will have its share" [Littérature de langue nationale (arabe), littérature de graphie française, chacune aura sa part].[86] But beyond this, he is promoting a practice of poetry in which struggle and suffering have their natural place. Jacob—like the poet unwelcome in both the colony and the postcolony—is able to withstand the forces that would eliminate him, the angelic lacerations, the drummings and beatings, the shoutings and bleedings. The final line of "Le poème au gué de Jabbok [The Poem at Jabbok's Ford]," the opening poem of the cycle, reads,

> Quel Ange
> Frappe une fois de plus à la hanche celui
> Qui osa arracher à ses ailes une plume
> Pour achever la Création?
>
> Which Angel
> Strikes once more the hip of him
> Who dared pluck a feather from his wings
> So as to complete Creation?[87]

The ability to struggle and to resist, to hold one's own in combat with the divine, but also with Arabic expression, is how the poem comes into being. It is this imbrication of poetry in combat, of combat in poetry, and of interlingual conflict that is missing in Sartre's presentation of Orpheus.

ENDS

Sartre's reduction of Black francophone poetry to a movement in the dialectic provoked the anger of Fanon, who exclaimed, "The generation of young poets has just received a sucker punch. . . . Sartre's mistake was not only to want to go to the source of the source, but to cut this source off."[88] Later, in *Les damnés de la terre* [The Wretched of the Earth] (1961), Fanon insisted that violence was necessary to displace the colony: "Violence detoxifies. It rids the colonized of his inferiority complex, of his contemplative attitude, of his despair. It makes him intrepid, rehabilitates him in his own eyes."[89] Simone de Beauvoir recounts how Sartre came to realize "that it is only in violence that the oppressed can attain their human status."[90] It is in this context that Sartre agreed to provide a preface for *Les damnés de la terre*, in which he asserts, "Yes. Violence, like Achilles's spear, can heal the wounds it has inflicted."[91] Sénac had been asserting the legitimacy of violence in the anti-colonial struggle since the early 1950s:

> Et dans cette nuit sociale
> tu nous as dit ton nom

Algérie
et tes lettres sont douces à nos lèvres
tes luttes douces dans nos veines

And in this social night
you told us your name
Algeria
and your letters are sweet to our lips
your fights sweet in our veins[92]

Sénac's Jacob provides a figure of effective engagement through poetry for the francophone poet in the new Algeria, even though—or perhaps because—he is not a conventional figure for the poet. He represents Sénac's search for a new foundation for poetic subjectivity, to parallel that sought by Fanon, "away from the Manichean foundations of colonial life."[93] He thereby disrupts the standard binary categories of divine and human, of the man (Jacob) and the nation (Israel), of the heterosexual and the homosexual, of the family-man and the loner, of the firstborn and the secondborn, of the proprietor and the usurper, of the colony and the postcolony. Jacob is a pied-noir Orpheus, combining the violence necessary for revolution with the love required to build a new nation:

> Ce que j'aime en Jacob c'est l'homme dans sa laideur, toujours haussée d'un point jusqu'au sublime, jusqu'au geste. Lavée. Passée à fresque. Ce que j'aime dans cet homme face à l'Homme (dit Yahia) c'est son humanité, la nôtre.
>
> What I like in Jacob is the man in his ugliness, always raised by a point to the sublime, to the gesture. Washed. Frescoed. What I like in this man faced with Man (says Yahia) is his humanity, which is ours.[94]

Unlike Orpheus and Sartre—both of whom are aberrations, geniuses, supremely and uniquely talented individuals—Sénac's Jacob is a man in whose desires, fears, ambiguities, and limitations we may find evidence of our own humanity.

CHAPTER 3

Rhythm-Chaos

Mohammed Khaïr-Eddine's Secret Music

ma flûte s'implique et termine

RHYTHM-CHAOS

It is rare to come across readings of the Moroccan poet Mohammed Khaïr-Eddine that do not refer to a passage in his 1970 novel, *Moi l'aigre* [Me, the Bitter One], where the protagonist, a writer, suddenly hits a rich vein of form and finds he can write with ease:

> When I left work, I went home. I stood in front of an old typewriter that I called *Ouragan* [Hurricane], and I typed. I wrote my texts without thinking; I had understood that the plans, notes, and other criteria essential to the elaboration of a novel were of no use to me. I was writing practically blind. But I ought to note that books are first made in my brain before being thrown down on paper. I wrote with such speed that my own hand, when I picked up a pen, was unable to follow me. More often than not, I would churn out an epic poem, and that was it. One day, though, I must have touched upon a good vein. At that point, I had arrived at the most total state of sterility. My writings were of no interest to anyone. I dealt with nothing, let alone myself. Perhaps this is where true creation begins. I had left whining sentimentality and random reminiscences behind me. Mallarmé must have experienced something similar. That said, he droned on for long enough! But the "Coup de dés" [Toss of the Dice] saved him. At that time, I had already rejected all form, shattered normal meter, including that of blank verse. I listened only to the twitchy

> rhythm of things. A creaking door could inspire me as much as a man coming out of a particularly hazardous adventure. But I was only really in love with the sound of *Ouragan*. It seemed to me that each of her keystrokes dismantled the word being typed as if under the effect of high fusion. I had absolutely nothing more to say, I just listened. But one day came when I spat out a true vein of gold: I ejaculated a text unlike anything I had written to that point in time: a crackle of bullets and a surge of muffled screams. It was through this text that I understood that I had to commit myself once and for all to the path of linguistic guerrilla warfare [C'est par ce texte que je compris que je devais m'engager une fois pour toute dans la voie de la guérilla linguistique]![1]

"La voie de la guérilla linguistique" has become the leitmotif of critical writings on Khaïr-Eddine.[2] It is usually understood to mean that literature can and should be equated with violent, even paramilitary, struggle. And yet there is much in Khaïr-Eddine's poetic corpus that does not appear to be implicated in the militant pursuit of political and social justice and that has, as a result of this critical focus, been wholly overlooked. I argue that this brilliant, electric, infectious phrase occludes alternative approaches to Khaïr-Eddine's work, that it silences other things that Khaïr-Eddine has to say. To continue to get to grips with some of the many dimensions of this poet's often obscure writings, we may have to momentarily set this poetic manifesto aside, allowing others of his texts to speak. This will enable us to dislocate and reformulate some of our assumptions about Khaïr-Eddine, his work, and his place in modern francophone Maghrebi poetry.

In an edition of the weekly radio program "Poésie ininterrompue" [Uninterrupted Poetry], broadcast on *France Culture* on October 19, 1975, Khaïr-Eddine, then at the height of his fame, was invited by his interviewer, Lucette Finas, to begin by reading from two of his works.[3] The first fragment—from *Agadir*, his best-known work then as now—is a monologue by a seer who claims to know

> comment s'écrit l'avenir et comment
> naît une rose
> dans les somptueux jardins des rois sicaires
> une rose de sang
>
> how the future is written and how
> a rose is born

in the sumptuous gardens of the Sicarii kings
a blood rose[4]

The second is an untitled prose passage from a collection that had just appeared, *Ce Maroc!* [This Morocco!].[5] The opening poem of this collection—which contains the verse "ma voix fut roide comme le tonnerre" [my voice was stiff like thunder][6]—goes some way to capturing the aural dynamics of the one-hundred-and-sixty-second segment because the poet does not read, or recite, so much as shout out his texts. Once Khaïr-Eddine has completed this mini recital, his voice returns to normal. Unperturbed, Finas remarks, "When you read, the listener is struck by the fact that your diction is a continuous shout [un hurlement continu] or, more accurately, continuously shouting [continuellement un hurlement]."[7]

Few who knew Mohammed Khaïr-Eddine fail to mention the quality and sound of his voice. Jean-Roger Bourrec recalls "a wide and deep voice, persuasive and full mouthed, that said everything bluntly with a gravelly roughness."[8] The poet, novelist, winner of the 1987 Prix Goncourt, and fellow Moroccan, Tahar Ben Jelloun (b. Fès, 1944), speaks of his friend's "often thunderous presence" [sa présence tonitruante].[9] He explains this as a manifestation of the poet's irrepressible desire for immoderation in all things: "He had passion only for the excesses of life, would drink too much and smoke too much, although intoxication never prevented his poetic source from flowing."[10] Abdelmajid Benjelloun (b. Fès, 1944) says that Khaïr-Eddine was never a "cursed poet" [poète maudit], as the French poet Paul Verlaine described himself, his former lover Rimbaud, and a handful of others in 1884. No, instead Khaïr-Eddine was a "cursing poet" [poète maudissant].[11] The poet Jean-Paul Michel, who edited and republished much of Khaïr-Eddine's work following his death in 1995, specifically remembers the poet singing passages from Mallarmé out loud, as if intoning an Islamic text, creating "an incredible comic effect, his long ululation mimicking the call to prayer."[12]

If much of the testimony around Khaïr-Eddine's life evokes his acoustic presence—his wide, deep, often violent voice—much of the criticism around his proteiform literary oeuvre focuses on his readiness to say "everything bluntly." In critical readings of Khaïr-Eddine's work, there has been an implied equation between the violence of his poetic delivery, and the syntactic, grammatical, semantic, and thematic violence of his texts. It is as if one form of violence justifies or explains—or even necessitates—all the others. For some, this violence is directed at conventional literary forms. Marc Gontard, for instance, in a landmark critical study from the 1980s on the violence motivating Maghrebi literature, describes Khaïr-Eddine's language as "wild," a ceaseless process of fragmentation that creates "a truly plural discourse."[13] It is true that this poet has limited interest in the rules of versification or genre norms, or in the accessibility associated with mainstream literary expression.[14] For others, Khaïr-Eddine's violence is one of refusal. He is the "écrivain du refus," whose "cry of revolt" targets instances of social and political injustice, particularly those perpetrated under Hassan II during the "années de plomb" [years of lead], known in Arabic as "سنوات الرصاص" [sanawāt al-ruṣāṣ].[15] For still others, his violence is more ontological—more Rimbaldian—a violence aimed at all established orders and conventions, "language, society, religion, and morality."[16] Habib Tengour accords Khaïr-Eddine a privileged place on his parodic roster of Maghrebi surrealists—"Kheireddine [*sic*] is surrealist in alcoholic delirium"[17]—and hints at the presence of madness: "From time to time, language is illuminated by the jerky current of fire and mud. Nedjma is proof of this, and certain spurts of Kheireddine [*sic*] also bear traces."[18] In Tahar Djaout's experimental novel *L'exproprié* [The Dispossessed], Khaïr-Eddine is a model of spasmic revolution and convulsive debauchery: "Among shards of glass bottles and tubs of urine, the Royal Police spoke to me at length afterward about another Berber named Khaïr-Eddine, deflowerer of nuns and plunderer of mausoleums where hashish blooms."[19] But however we choose to interpret the object of Khaïr-Eddine's violence, be it literary, psychotic, social, or ontological, he is generally regarded as one of the Maghreb's most unsparing iconoclasts. It shouldn't be too much of a shock to hear him shouting on the radio.

In this chapter I analyze and explore the gap between the perceived violence of Khaïr-Eddine's verbal delivery and that of his poetry by reading a poem that has never before been subjected to critical scrutiny.[20] I note in passing that to "explore," from the Latin verb "explōrāre" [to inspect, inquire], originally meant "to scout the hunting area for game by means of shouting."[21] I situate the impetus for this investigation in an acoustic crack in Khaïr-Eddine's reading on *France Culture*, a clear dislocation between the rhythm of the shouting voice and that of the written text. In the first of his two readings, for example, the poet inserts an explosive stress—represented below by a short vertical line—every second, third, fourth, or fifth syllable:

> Je ˈlis sur mon ˈos, je ne lis ˈpas je ˈvois plutôt
> sur mon ˈos

> I ˈread from my ˈbone, I do ˈnot read I ˈsee rather
> from my ˈbone[22]

At other moments, the acoustic structure of individual verbal units is inverted, such that a word like "l'instiga'teur" becomes "l'in'stigateur," and "impecc'able" becomes "im'peccable." Most strikingly, in "peuple" [/'pœpl/], which appears six times in quick succession, the poet stresses the first syllable with such force that the terminal "-le" is inverted, giving /'pœpɛl/. There are suggestions here of what Mladen Dolar has called an "antinomy of meaning and the voice."[23] Or, as Finas puts it, "This screaming doesn't necessarily follow the lines of meaning of the text itself. On the contrary, your shouting raises each fragment of the text and transforms it into a sort of verbal fetish, or if you prefer a 'fétiche-cri'—a fetish-shout."[24]

Some fifteen years later, in an interview with Abderrahmane Ajbour, Khaïr-Eddine will explain these rhythmic discrepancies by pointing to his Berber—specifically Shilha (in French "chleuh")—ancestry and to the place of his birth and childhood, Azro Wado, next to Tafraout in the Anti-Atlas Mountains. This is the site of "la montagne sèche, rougeâtre, impossible à franchir, le vieux Sud" [the dry, reddish mountain, impossible to cross, the old South][25] and of "la montagne violette . . . avec des diffractions jaunes et mauves quand le soleil l'embrase par-derrière du côté du levant" [the violet-colored mountain . . . with yellow and mauve diffractions when the sun sets it ablaze from behind on the eastern side].[26] As he explains to Ajbour, "I am only bringing to light what is already in me, this rhythm, which is that of my ancestors and which was transmitted to me genetically. I call it my secret music" [cette rythmique qui est celle de mes ancêtres et qui m'a été transmise de façon génétique. J'appelle cela ma musique secrète].[27]

The association Khaïr-Eddine makes here between his shout's dislocated rhythm and the secret music of a poetics might be compared to the marriage of steps and song in the refrain as presented by Gilles Deleuze and Félix Guattari. For them, the refrain is "territorial, a territorial assemblage" that "always carries earth with it."[28] Khaïr-Eddine's shout relates to his native countryside in similar ways: "When you cross . . . these lunar landscapes," he explains to Finas, "you scream [on hurle], you want to scream [on a envie de hurler], because suddenly you find yourself alone; you have a good shout [on gueule un bon coup], and it reverberates throughout the entire mountain."[29] Once uttered, the scream does not just disappear but fashions the landscape: "What can you see?" he asks, "You only see stones and a voice that multiplies to infinity. This incrustation of the landscape and the echo, which breaks down and dies. But no sooner is it dead than you want to bring it back to life again."[30] Mallarmé speaks of a similar, albeit silent, dynamic on the "lunar" landscape of the white page: "et, quand s'aligna, dans une brisure, la moindre, disseminée, le hasard vaincu mot par mot, indéfectiblement le blanc revient, tout à l'heure gratuit, certain maintenant, pour conclure que rien au-delà et authentiquer le silence" [and, when aligned, in a break, the least, disseminated, chance conquered word by word, unfailingly the white returns, just now gratuitous, certain now, to conclude nothing beyond and authenticate the silence].[31] Whereas for Mallarmé silence returns "authenticated," for Khaïr-Eddine the voice adds another imperceptible layer to the surface of the earth, sealing—in its dying echo—the rhythms, the music, and the part of chaos that the cry contains.

Following Deleuze and Guattari, who stress that rhythm only comes about through the encounter of different milieus, I propose to unearth something of the structures of Khaïr-Eddine's secret music by juxtaposing his poetry with the work of the Irish-born English painter Francis Bacon. I do this despite the assertion of at least one expert that Bacon's work is not "companionable."[32] The open, screaming mouth becomes central to Bacon's iconography with his first crucifixion paintings in the mid-1930s and continues to grow in importance in the dozens of his "copies" of the *Retrato de Inocencio X* (Galleria Doria Pamphilj, Rome, 1650) by Diego Velázquez. These include the iconic *Study after Velázquez's Portrait of Pope Innocent X* (Des Moines Art Center, 1953), in which a spectral figure, seated on his papal throne, streaked with black bars, and enclosed in a makeshift yellow fence, screams—"thunderstruck," as Claude Imbert puts it, "by the invisible evidence of an unspeakable disaster."[33] By the early 1950s, Michael Peppiatt writes, the scream becomes "obsessive, dominating all other concerns."[34] Bacon's scream is commonly linked to prominent antecedents, such as the still of the nurse shot in the eye on the great steps of Odessa in Sergei Eisenstein's *Battleship Potemkin* (1925), and to Nicolas Poussin's *Massacre of the Innocents* (Musée Condé, Chantilly, 1628), where the scream emanating from the mother's half-open mouth is echoed and amplified by the ellipse of limbs and weapons. Louis Marin insists it "could without hesitation be taken, well in advance of Munch's celebrated work, as *one of the most extraordinary pictorial representations of a scream*."[35]

In his two-volume *Francis Bacon: logique de la sensation* [Francis Bacon: Logic of Sensation], Deleuze is concerned with explaining Bacon's scream as much more than a simple representation, even one of an extreme psychological state.[36] This stands in contrast to Dolar's reading of Edvard Munch's 1893 painting *Der Schrei der Natur* [The Scream of Nature] as a limit instance of the scream: "We see the void, the orifice, the abyss, but with no fetish to protect us or to hold on to."[37] Deleuze instead traces the scream to the logic of painting itself, specifically to the relation of field and Figure, and to the rhythm that is created between them. Bacon's paintings are characterized by large, shallow fields of color (red, black, orange, ochre), against which human figures, "ordinary bodies in ordinary situations of constraint and discomfort"[38] are superimposed. Much of the drama of a given image centers around the ways in which the pictorial elements of field and Figure encounter each other, usually through some spasm: "loving, vomiting, excreting, the body always attempting to flee *through* one of its organs, in order to rejoin the field [aplat], the material structure."[39] For Dolar, there is a direct relationship between the screamer and the landscape, such that the scream can be read as eddying back into the mouth or, as Munch himself perceived it, as emanating outward.[40] Deleuze identifies a much more violent operation in Bacon. The shadows cast by his figures are not to be understood as silhouettes—mimetic figures cut from light—but as the body evading itself: "The scream . . . is the operation by which the entire body escapes through the mouth."[41] Imbert notes how Bacon's "body seems to get longer, flatten down and stretch out, as if it were contracting itself to pass through a hole."[42] Even objects lend themselves to this great tumultuous spasm between Figure and field: sinks, umbrellas, chairs, puddles of water, and paint are all equipped with "exaggerated points"[43] through which the body tries to flee.

As far as I can ascertain, the poet and the painter have only ever been compared on one occasion, in passing, by Abderrahman Tenkoul, who notes: "Like painter Francis Bacon, whom Michel Leiris describes as an 'outlaw,' Khaïr-Eddine 'grabs and in a way rapes that which he wants to represent.'"[44] I propose to linger within the bounds of this rare comparison. Where previous models of reading Khaïr-Eddine have struggled to account for the detail, breadth, obscurity, and insistence of his poetic diction, particularly at those points—and there are many—where the reader is taken beyond transparent references to the real, Deleuze's reading of Bacon's painting provides a guide to the complex interplay of body, voice, violence, rhythm, and art that may allow us to draw out some of the hidden dynamics of Khaïr-Eddine's secret music. More than that, Bacon provides the alternative milieu, the other code, the counter-rhythm against which a new rhythm—a new secret music—might come into audition.

The following untitled poem was first published in *Soleil arachnide* [Arachnid Sun]. It contains few clear references to a historical moment, to an ideology, or even to a particular place. As with other such poems by Khaïr-Eddine, critics have passed over it in silence. In three brief sections, I explore the poem for traces of Khaïr-Eddine's secret music, noting that these "do not reveal three successive movements in an evolution"[45] so much as three possible aspects of his poetics:

et qui rampe à mon nombril de torrents ocres
et décapite mes cols de tonnerres fascinés
hache autrefois rire
ce ciel sans ange a retrouvé toutes ses griffes
mais ce ramassis de chanvre occulte
tourne mal à la base même du mur d'affres
qui rampent à mon nombril de terreurs ocres

tranchez donc mes oiseaux seuls
je parle d'un œil versé dans chaque gramme
d'ambre amer
fumé craché sur cette publicité d'astres où tombe
pygmée ma voix noire de sangsue
tranchez donc mes oiseaux seuls

voici criée sans virgule la menace
par je sais quels clous coupés en sacres
le hasard veut qu'un chemin
gîte ici
et les cous d'enfants vantés par le sexe gros du seigle
et du sommeil
voici criée sans virgule la menace

lorsque ses ongles s'incrustent dans la chair bleue du sabre
toujours hurler quoi pleurer qui
trompé de silences obtus ivre nuit sans matrice
où vole l'insecte ma femme
à moins d'une barque dont la mer se souvienne
lorsque ses ongles s'incrustent dans la chair bleue du sabre

dossiers de tous les météores du cuivre halluciné
cette affaire punique me jonche vaste
et dévaste mon ombre de vin rouge
par le cri femelle de l'oiseleur
mais comme le soleil est un fruit très gâté
ombre notoire
cette ombre et son fil s'insinuent dans ma peau
dossiers de tous les météores du cuivre halluciné

et je pars avec ce qui me reste de moi hurlé
à ras du trottoir

et je trinque avec mon défi luisant sable
sous l'arbre dru où mes serpents tornades
brisent les flûtes
et je danse ma fascination
sur l'épine malhabile de tes prunelles
et je pars avec ce qui me reste de moi hurlé

j'écume de poèmes censurés et d'absinthes
ineffacées d'un vol de genoux dérapant
et j'insulte le mollusque de cette conque
blanche où l'habitude a fixé ses barreaux
qui me nomment lion giclant à vareuse inédite
d'audaces connues du marais haut placé
j'écume de poèmes censurés et d'absinthes

maintenant je vous lance mes poumons cerfs-volants
dans la rigueur où se mouille mon espace
et je dis
le printemps n'existe pas il s'est rompu l'échine
contre la rafale sourde (palmier-prison
qui t'écris toi-même et t'étonnes)
maintenant je vous lance mes poumons cerfs-volants[46]

---

and who crawls into my navel of ocher torrents
and beheads my necks of mesmerized thunder
[axe] erstwhile laughing
this unangeled sky has found its claws again
but this heap of arcane hemp
loses its way at the base of this wall of cramps
who crawl into my navel of ocher [terrors]

butcher then my solitary birds
I mean the eye poured into every gram
of bitter amber
smoked and spit onto the advertisement of stars
from which falls my leech-black pygmy voice
go on then butcher my solitary birds

here without commas the threat is announced
by a couple nails I know cut into blessings
chance wants a path

to bivouac here
and the necks of children exalted by the fat sex of rye
and sleep
here without commas the threat is announced

once its fingernails are embedded in the saber's blue flesh
always yelling what weeping who
deceived by obtuse silences drunken moldless night
in which my wife the insect hovers
at least one boat the ocean remembers
once its fingernails are embedded in the saber's blue flesh

files for all the meteors of hallucinated copper
this punic affair strews my debris widely
and unwinds my red wine shadow
with the birdcatcher's female call
but as the sun is a highly spoiled fruit
incontrovertible shadow
this shadow and its wire thread themselves into my skin
files for all the meteors of hallucinated copper

and I am leaving with what remains of me screamed
down as low as the curb
I toast with my glittering defiance sand
beneath the hearty tree where my tornadic snakes
shatter flutes
and I dance my fascination
on the incompetent thorn of your pupils
and I am leaving with what remains of me screamed

I froth with censored poems and absinthe
unerased by a flight of skidding knees
and I insult the mollusk of this conch shell
white in which habit has screwed the bars
which call me surging lion of the unprecedented peacoat
with known audacities from a highly placed swamp
I froth with censored poems and absinthe

now I launch at you the kites of my lungs
in the rigor that wets my space

and I say
spring does not exist it has broken its back
on the wind's deaf edge (palm tree prison
writing to and astonishing yourself)
now I launch at you the kites of my lungs[47]

(I) EXCAVATION OF A SCREAM

I trace a first element of Khaïr-Eddine's secret music to a simple formal device. With the exception of the first stanza, each stanza begins and ends with an identical line.[48] These liminal lines not only serve to create a verbal frame, stalling any promise of continuity between stanzas; they also create an uneven rhythm, in which the first line of each stanza, enounced in isolation, recurs amid the noise of the intervening lines. Relatively straightforward (if unusual) acts, statements, imperatives, observations—"tranchez donc mes oiseaux seuls" [butcher then my solitary birds] and "dossiers de tous les météores du cuivre halluciné" [files for all the meteors of hallucinated copper]—are complicated through the course of each stanza. The difference between the first and last line might be compared to the examination, through a microscope, of some cellular phenomenon in a weightless vacuum (first line) and of the same in the noise of gravity and atmospheric pressure (final line). Between the repetition of the same, each stanza reveals the difference that was always there, hidden, bubbling away, baroque, as Édouard Glissant might say, not as a reaction but as a "naturality" [une parole de naturalité].[49] It is an example of how a simple rhythm—that of repetition between the first and final lines of a fragment of text—becomes expressive, how it harnesses the chaos it contains to become a territory.

Our understanding of the form and function of Khaïr-Eddine's rhythmic territorializations can be enhanced by considering two related scenarios. First, Deleuze perceives something like this excavation of the invisible in Bacon's painting. He tracks it back to the expressive geometry of Paul Cézanne, whose paintings demonstrate that "rocks only exist through the forces of folding that they harness, landscapes through magnetic and thermal forces, apples through forces of germination: all nonvisual forces that have been made visible."[50] For Bacon, Cézanne opens up a route beyond the illustrative and the figurative, past the abstract, and onto the way of the Figure, a way sometimes called "sensation."[51] For Khaïr-Eddine, Cézanne may enable us to better see, unpick, and experience in its uneven rhythms the cry incrusted in the landscape of Azro Wado. With each successive line of verse, the reader descends deeper into the initial line of verse, like an archeologist of sensation, until they bump up against the same verse with which they started, but which has—in the time of reading—become radically different.

Second, Khaïr-Eddine's stanzas recall a formulation deployed by Bacon in the first of a series of three interviews with the poet Michel Couturier, broadcast on *France Culture* six months before Khaïr-Eddine's interview with Finas. There, Bacon speaks—in faltering French—about painting the mouth:

> Même si on veut faire la bouche, on peut faire la bouche . . . ou même, ou même faire un Sahara de la bouche. Vous savez. On peut aller très loin, presque autour de la tête. . . . Si on a [de] la chance, au même temps ça vous donne, ah, l'apparence au même temps, du sujet.
>
> Even if you want to make the mouth, you can make the mouth . . . or even, or even make a Sahara of the mouth. You know. You can go very far, almost around the head. . . . If you are lucky, at the same time, it gives you, ah, the appearance, at the same time, of the subject.[52]

To "make a Sahara of the mouth" is to extend the mouth as far around the head as it is possible to go, much as each of these stanzas is stretched to include the chaos of the intervening lines. Elsewhere, Bacon calls this stretching a "graph" or a "diagram." Deleuze extends these images further:

> It is as if a piece of rhinoceros skin, viewed under a microscope, were stretched over it; it is as if the two halves of the head were split open by an ocean; it is as if the unit of measure were changed, and micrometric, or cosmic, units were substituted for the figurative unit. . . . It is as if, in the midst of the figurative and probabilistic givens, a *catastrophe* overcame the canvas.[53]

Deleuze insists that painting is the art that necessarily—"hysterically"—integrates its own catastrophe.[54] But in each of these stanzas, Khaïr-Eddine's writing also seems to "pass through the catastrophe," to "embrace chaos,"[55] attempting to emerge from it, in the final stanza, on kites made not of stretched rhinoceros skin, nor of a head split by the ocean, but of exposed lungs: "maintenant je vous lance mes poumons cerfs-volants" [now I launch at you the kites of my lungs].[56]

Each of Khaïr-Eddine's stanzas might therefore be considered a "diagram," specifically a diagram of the open mouth, probably as it screams. The identical line that begins and ends each stanza represents the limits of the mouth, its lips, its edges, of that which in Arabic is "شَفَة" [shafah]. The Hebrew cognate "שפה" [śafah] is, not coincidentally, also the word for "language," which is always a matter of lips and edges, of ends and borders, of indiscretions and limits, of stretchings, translations, and slippages. The intervening lines are a Sahara, stretched rhino skin, lung-kites, the extent to which the mouth can be extended—distorted, defaced—and still remain a mouth. Like Bacon's diagram, each of these stanzas is "a chaos, a catastrophe," even as each contains "a spark [un germe] of order or rhythm."[57] But beyond any comparison, each stanza also invites us to explore the extent to which a poem can wander, divagate, lose itself, while still remaining a poem.

(II) THREE BEATS

A second element of Khaïr-Eddine's secret music can be traced to the rhythms that animate his poetic language. Deleuze identifies three basic rhythms at work in Bacon's triptychs and more generally across his paintings: "one steady or 'attendant' rhythm, and two other rhythms, one of crescendo or simplification (climbing, expanding, diastolic, adding value), the other of diminuendo or elimination (descending, contracting, systolic, removing value)."[58] The psychoanalyst Pierre Fédida, who studied under Deleuze, deploys a similar model to define the essence of subjectivity, a "being out of being that is signified by a pulsive time (systole-diastole) of recollection and projection [de recueillement et de bondissement]."[59] For Fethi Benslama, this ligated movement captures the dynamic of reading, which "conceals an energy of gathering within oneself, and launching outside oneself, an alternating movement (*dam-ilqā'*) comparable to the beating of the heart. To read is then to install a heart, a rhythm between dislocated things."[60] In Bacon's work, though, as Deleuze stresses, the nature of any such beat is perhaps not predictable enough to create bodily organs. In a given figure, one rhythm might dominate but not without the "attendant" presence of another rhythm. Even as Deleuze presents this typology of rhythms, he warns against any overly conscious application of it. They are part of "this irrational logic, . . . this logic of sensation that constitutes painting."[61]

In Bacon's triptych *Three Studies of the Human Head* (private collection, 1953) (fig. 5), the figure bearing a creepy grin in the leftmost panel might be

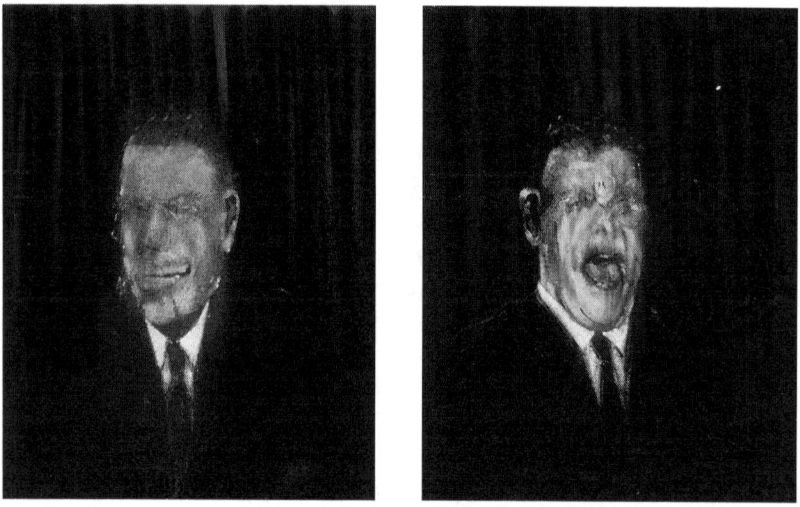

FIG. 5. Francis Bacon, *Three Studies of the Human Head*, oil on canvas, 1953, each panel 61 × 51 cm. Private collection.

said to represent a steady rhythm, a pacemaker, so to speak; the screaming mouth in the central panel may be considered a crescendo, an extreme of simplification; and what remains of the mouth and eyes, smudged beyond recognition in the panel on the right, is a sudden diminuendo or contraction.[62] Even as basic rhythms are ascribed to each picture, they interfere with one another, denying the apparent isolation of each picture. There are hints of the scream in the smile, of the smile in the scream, and of both the smile and the scream in the devastation of the face. This is what Deleuze calls, with muffled echoes of Augustine, "the distributive unity of the three."[63]

Evidence of these three rhythms can be found throughout Khaïr-Eddine's poem. Consider the first two lines of the opening stanza. It is hard to draw any clear idea of what, if anything, is being evoked, even as the syntactic parallels and semantic differences of the two lines create a mini crescendo, a sudden expansion, a poetic manifestation of the diastolic:

> et qui rampe à mon nombril de torrents ocres
> et décapite mes cols de tonnerres fascinés
>
> and who crawls into my navel of ocher torrents
> and beheads my necks of mesmerized thunder

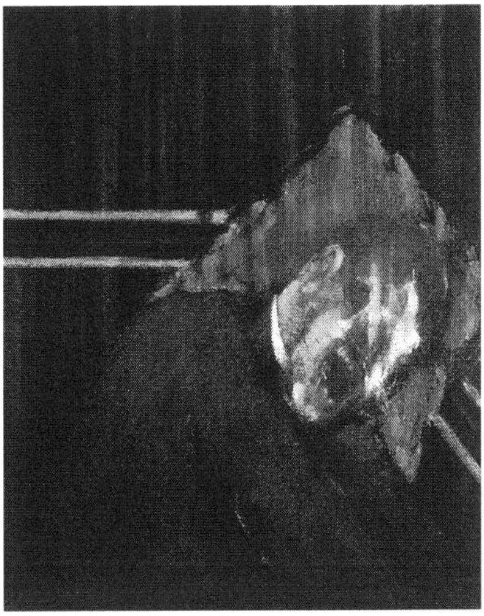

From one line to the next, the action of the singular verb shifts from "ramper" [climb], to "décapiter" [behead]. The direct object moves from the body—"mon nombril" [my navel]—to "mes cols" [necks or cervices], which, although part of the body in the singular, cannot apply to any usual human in the plural. This, in turn, allows for a geographical definition to emerge (as mountain passes, cols, or saddles), unexpectedly translating the body to the landscape. In the acoustic shift from "torrents" to "tonnerres," there is not only a metathesis of the internal consonants (/n/ to /r/ and /r/ to /n/) but also a semantic escalation, from gravity-bound flows of water to the unpredictable realm of electric skies. More subtle traces of the diastolic are evident in the proliferation of the conjunction "et" [and] ("et qui rampe," "et décapite," "et les cous d'enfants," "et dévaste mon ombre," "et je trinque," "et je danse," "et j'insulte," "et je dis," and, on two occasions, "et je pars"), pointing to a logic of accumulation, perhaps of excess, or as Deleuze might say, of "hysteria."[64]

Although these lines precede the remainder of the text, there is no sense that they begin the poem in any significant way. Rhythms do not need to follow the conventions of reading or of looking but can begin anywhere and can continue to be developed at any other point in the text. If we read the poem with an ear for its most expressive rhythms, we might identify the opening line of the third stanza as the fragment that most clearly inaugurates the poem:

> voici criée sans virgule la menace.
>
> here without commas the threat is announced

As an invariable, impersonal, unimodal, and unitemporal verb, "voici" stands apart from other verbal units in the poem, drawing the sort of attention to the line that might more usually be associated with the opening of a poem. The subject of this cry is "la menace" [the threat]. It stems from the Latin "minae" [threats], which is thought to have once designated the protruding parts of a wall.[65] The threat is "criée" [cried], which is to say that it is an acoustic protrusion, an aural equivalent of the spikes, sharpened objects, and tunneling body parts in Bacon's iconography. It is through these increasingly exiguous passages that the field flows into the Figure, and the Figure into the field, and that the body pours itself into its own shadow.

If the central panel of Bacon's triptych shows the threat as an unpunctuated scream ("voici criée *sans* virgules la menace"), then the left panel might display a punctuated scream, a potential scream, currently poised in the creepy grin ("voici criée *avec* virgule la menace"). The panel on the right realizes the full force of Khaïr-Eddine's verse, as the indistinct background with vertical lines of black paint becomes a wall with painted yellow tramlines ("mur d'affres") and a protrusion that causes some physical harm to the figure. The tramlines turn at an obtuse angle right behind the figure's head (echoing the "silences obtus" in the fourth stanza), as if it is the angle of the yellow lines that become protrusive, knocking the figure down, exiling the figure from the realm of the figurative, and blocking the scream from the domain of sound. Bacon's right panel might be compared to works by the Algerian painter M'hamed Issiakhem (Azeffoun, 1938–Algiers, 1985), such as *La mère et la main coupée* [The Mother and the Lacerated Hand], in which the mother's mouth is painted over and silenced.[66] It may even be that the hidden logic of the panel is primarily verbal, as "obtuse," which geometrically defines a plane angle of greater than ninety but less than one hundred and eighty degrees, comes from the verb "obtundere," meaning "to beat against," "to blunt," "to deaden," or "to deafen"—all of which capture the ways the figure's torso is made to disintegrate before our eyes.

(III) FLUTES

> tout en quittant la fin de leur soif
> les meilleurs jours refont surface
> pour accompagner la cigale en guise de flûte[67]

A third element of Khaïr-Eddine's secret music pertains to musical instruments. Throughout his poetry, the sound of the flute is subject to interruption. It is obliterated by sand and eaten by impatience in *Ce Maroc!*:

> le son de flûte que le sable oblitère

> the sound of the flute obliterated by sand[68]

un air de flûte rongé d'impatiences

a flute melody eaten at by impatience[69]

Its song is unsteady in *Résurrection des fleurs sauvages*:

le sang siffle la précaire
flûte de ces bergers sicaires

the blood hisses the precarious
flute of these Sicarii shepherds[70]

And in *Soleil arachnide*, flutes are destroyed:

sous l'arbre dru où mes serpents tornades
brisent les flûtes.

under the thick tree where my tornado snakes
break the flutes[71]

Athena is often cited as the creator of the flute. In Ovid's *Fasti*, she carves a flute out of boxwood, but throws it away when she realizes how her "virgin cheeks" puff up in order to play it:

ars mihi non tanti est; valeas, mea tibia

I value not the art so high; farewell, my flute[72]

Marsyas comes across the flute, teaches himself how to play, and challenges Apollo—god of poetry and music—to a contest. In a curiously open—Baconian if not Khaïr-Eddinian—turn, they agree that the winner of the contest "should work his will on the vanquished."[73] Diodorus Siculus records that the judges were "amazed" by the "strange music" of the pipes, which "in their opinion far excelled, by reason of [its] melody," Apollo's lyre.[74] There are differing accounts of what happens next. Apollodorus says that Apollo then impressed the judges by playing his lyre upside down, which Marsyas could not do with his flute. Diodorus says that Apollo went on to sing and play at the same time. Apollo then "attends" to Marsyas, hanging him from a tall pine and flaying him until his skin comes apart from his flesh.[75]

Of the many versions of this myth, only Ovid pauses to—let's say—excavate the scream, to take a measure of its uneven rhythms. Ovid alone takes the time to inspect, like a haruspex, the satyr's innards. In a phrase that captures how Deleuze perceives Bacon's cry, Marsyas says:

> "quid me mihi detrahis?" inquit;
> "a! piget, a! non est" clamabat "tibia tanti"
>
> "Why do you tear me from myself?" he cried.
> "Oh, I repent! Oh, a flute is not worth such price!"[76]

In light of Bacon, this question becomes an image of the body's emerging shadow, the scream dragging the body out of itself through the mouth. As Marsyas continues to scream, the skin is stripped from his limbs ("clamanti cutis est summos direpta per artus"[77]) until he is nothing but a wound ("nec quicquam nisi vulnus erat"[78]). Blood flows from all sides ("cruor undique manat"[79]), the sinews lie bare ("detectique patent nervi"[80]), his veins throb and quiver without any skin to cover them ("trepidaeque sine ulla / pelle micant venae"[81]) to the degree that one might count the fibers in his chest ("salientia viscera possis / et perlucentes numerare in pectore fibras"[82]). Even as the satyr screams through his mouth, the mouth extends to the rest of the body, revealing the body's ongoing, usually hidden, functions—its own secret music. Ovid's depiction of Marsyas flayed is resumed in Deleuze's description of Bacon's *Fragment of a Crucifixion* (Stedelijk Van Abbemuseum, Eindhoven, 1950) as a painting "où toute la viande hurle" [where all the meat screams][83] (fig. 6).

Both Ovid's and Deleuze's texts resonate with Khaïr-Eddine's poem. There are not only screams ("voici criée sans virgule la menace" [here without commas the threat is announced],[84] "toujours hurler quoi pleurer qui" [always yelling what weeping who], "ce qui me reste de moi hurlé" [what remains of me screamed]) and expressions of pain associated with parts of the body ("mon nombril de torrents ocres" [my navel of ocher torrents]). The stripping of skin from the body unveils new possible forms of action. The speaker adopts verbs normally associated with the elements ("j'écume de poèmes censurés" [I froth with censored poems]). He projects his body out of itself ("je vous lance mes poumons cerfs-volants" [I launch at you the kites of my lungs]). Organs are no longer restricted in number or function, but spread and proliferate, or disappear altogether ("nuit sans matrice" [wombless night]). It is perhaps with this grotesque imagery in mind that Rachida Saïgh Bousta calls Khaïr-Eddine "the infinitely visceral man."[85] And much as the eyes of Bacon's bodies become polyvalent and transitory organs—"Painting gives us eyes all over," as Deleuze says, "in the ear, in the

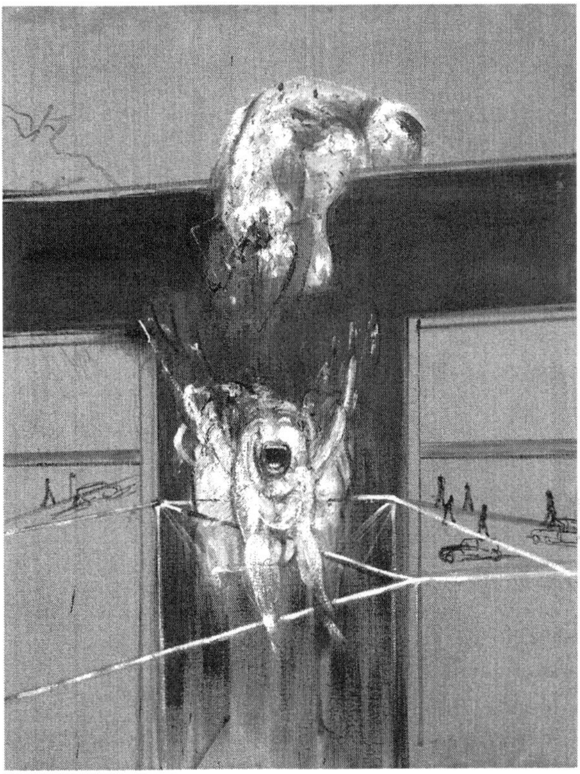

FIG. 6. Francis Bacon, *Fragment of a Crucifixion*, oil and cotton wool on canvas, 1950, 140 × 108.5 cm. Stedelijk van Abbemuseum, Eindhoven. Copyright © The Estate of Francis Bacon. All rights reserved. DACS, London / ARS, NY 2023.

stomach, in the lungs"[86]—the eyes of Khaïr-Eddine's body are omnipresent: "un œil versé dans chaque gramme" [the eye poured into every gram].[87]

Further evidence of Apollo's torture and murder of Marsyas is present in references to decapitation ("et décapite mes cols"), slicing ("tranchez donc"), tearing ("ses ongles s'incrustent dans la chair bleue"), bone-breaking ("il s'est rompu l'échine"), and the axe that used to be a laugh ("hache autrefois rire")—a sinister metamorphosis worthy of Bacon's dark imagination. In "cette ombre et son fil s'insinuent dans ma peau" [this shadow and its wire thread themselves into my skin], we find not only the threads or strings of the god's lyre but their tortuous insinuation into the speaker's body.[88] Apollo's dull amorality, and more generally the immanence of the pagan, is confirmed in "ce ciel sans anges a retrouvé toutes ses griffes" [this unangeled sky has found its claws again] and "le hasard veut qu'un chemin / gîte ici" [chance wants a path / to bivouac here]. The shallow field on which Bacon's detached figures wrestle comes into focus in "à la base même du mur d'affres" [at the base of this wall of cramps]. Where the acoustic remnants of Marsyas's name appear, appropriately defaced and disseminated, in syntagmas such as "mais ce ramassis," "la menace," "d'audaces . . . du marais," and "mouille mon espace," Apollo—often conflated with the sun Helios—is more readily visible as both a notorious shadow ("ombre notoire") and a very rotten fruit ("un fruit très gâté").

It may also be possible to see in Khaïr-Eddine's sun critical glints of Sartre's September 1961 preface to Fanon's *Les damnés de la terre* [The Wretched of the Earth], discussed in the previous chapter, where he protests, "Today, the blinding sun of torture is at its zenith [l'aveuglant soleil de la torture est au zénith]; it lights up the entire country: under this light, there is no laugh that rings true, no face that is not made up to mask its anger or fear, no act that does not betray our disgust and our complicity."[89] Jacques Rancière (b. Algiers, 1940) will counter, with reference to events that took place in the month following Sartre's composition, on October 17, 1961, when demonstrations organized by the FLN in Paris were violently repressed by the French police: "Now, the truth is that this blinding sun never lit up anything. Marked and tortured bodies do not light up anything."[90]

ARRHYTHMIC

> Arythmie: dissymétrie initiale, perte de mémoire, errance dans la solitude, désert sans traces. Étrange la fin de toute vie.[91]

When asked by Lucette Finas why he shouts his poems, Khaïr-Eddine insists, "This theater could only be shouted [hurlé]. All the terms that make up this writing could only be said by being shouted aloud."[92] But what this poem from 1969 and the recital of poems on the radio in 1975 demonstrate is that Khaïr-Eddine's shout is only one rhythm in his poetics. The other is more musical, more lyrical even, although it is a music that is often dismissed as obscure. Marsyas provides a model for understanding the origin and interplay of these two unequal rhythms. Both of these rhythms stem from a physical, acoustic understanding of language. More than any stringed instrument, the flute imitates the human voice, but as it does so, it also prevents the voice from speaking or singing. Khaïr-Eddine's poem evokes the poet's own "voix noire de sangsue" [black-leech voice]—speech that takes place so close to the instrument that it is hard to make out the distance, between the lip and the mouthpiece, that would enable us to hear what the poet is saying. As Philippe Monbrun puts it, "The *aulos* tends to marginalize the *logos*."[93]

When Finas questions Khaïr-Eddine's shout, we see in nuce the same conflict between Apollonian propriety and Dionysian wildness dramatized in the myth of Marsyas. The fifth century B.C.E. saw a debate not only on the value of music produced by the flute, compared with that produced by the more established lyre, but also on whether melodies and rhythms should follow or distort the words they accompanied. Plato opined that "melody and rhythms must follow the words"[94] and reserved the lyre and zither for the ideal city, leaving the pipes or aulos to the shepherds in the country. There is no reason to be taken aback by the philosopher's conservatism. Apollo's citharody is the supreme manifestation of what Deleuze and Guattari call territorialization. It contains the roots of self and other, of dialogue, of the chorus, of democracy, of the colony. Marsyas's new music is "incompatible with the citizen's moral education"[95] but has a much greater ability to move its listeners. The flute is the instrument of intense earthly sensations—pleasures as well as pains. It is verve, genius, hubris, the individual, the Romantic, the decolonial. Much like Bacon's painting, it seems not so much to "pass through the brain" as to "act immediately upon the nervous system."[96] In Khaïr-Eddine's poems we encounter, among other things, a relationship to sensation not all that far removed from Marsyas's flute and Bacon's canvas.

The expressiveness of this poem is by no means exhausted by this brief exploration of three aspects of Khaïr-Eddine's secret music, namely the form of its stanzas; its diastolic, systolic, and attendant rhythms; and its fragments from the myth of Marsyas. Any coherence is intended to be as ephemeral as it is enlightening. By tracing elements of Khaïr-Eddine's secret music, I hope not only to identify and perpetuate the dislocation between shout and poem that is audible in the 1975 recording of the poet's voice, but to articulate the nature of this gap and to explore its depths. Despite claiming to be a proponent of "linguistic guerrilla warfare," Khaïr-Eddine is a poet not primarily of extremes, nor of violence or iconoclasm, but rather of uneven rhythms. We find his music somewhere between that of Athena, who rejects the flute she has invented because it "disfigures her face,"[97] and Marsyas, who does not stop playing the flute in time to (literally) save his skin. Khaïr-Eddine's combat has much in common with that of Bacon, for whom physical struggle, be it with man or bull or some other dark force, is always also an act of love. When, in April 1979, this "genial prospector and demanding critic" [génial prospecteur et sacqueur][98] returned to Morocco after fourteen years of voluntary exile in France, he was briefly arrested. He explained then that his guerilla warfare had never been meant politically but was a matter of language, of "scriptural labor, of writing itself."[99] Without the uneven rhythm of Khaïr-Eddine's shout, there would be no secret music, but his shout may also have distracted us from much of what Khaïr-Eddine's poems still have to say.

CHAPTER 4

Berber Spider

Tahar Djaout, Arachne, and the Afterlife of Oral Poetics

Je sais que dans vos mains
se tissent tant de soleils.

Certes, je ne suis qu'un Barbare.

NIGHTWATCHING

One could be forgiven for thinking that writing poems was one of Tahar Djaout's youthful indiscretions. A glance at a chronological list of the Algerian writer's publications will show how early poetry collections—from *Solstice barbelé* [Barbed Sunstead] in 1975 to *L'arche à vau-l'eau* [The Ark Downstream],[1] *Insulaire & cie.* [Insular & Co.],[2] *L'oiseau minéral* [The Mineral Bird],[3] and *L'étreinte du sablier* [The Grip of the Hourglass][4]—soon give way to a series of novels and a collection of short stories. As we read in his first, highly poetic and digressive novel *L'exproprié* [The Dispossessed], published in 1981,

> *. . . j'étais poète dans le temps et je faisais faire à mes neurones le tour de tous les points d'interrogation logés dans des crânes adipeux j'étais poète dans le temps et je n'eus jamais peur de pisser mon encre cireuse à la face des iconolâtres des dévôts et des blanches académies repeintes dans l'attente des miracles maints temples corrodés par mes poèmes partaient à la dérive d'une canicule complice j'étais poète dans le temps avant de découvrir les acrobaties rauques d'une mathématique complètement étanche . . .*

> *. . . I used to be a poet and I would make my neurons do the rounds of all the question marks lodged in fatty skulls I used to be a poet*

> *and I was never afraid to piss my waxy ink in the face of iconolaters the religious and white academies repainted while waiting for miracles many temples corroded by my poems drifted away from an accomplice heat wave I used to be a poet before discovering the raucous acrobatics of a completely watertight mathematics . . .*[5]

Subsequent works in prose include *Les chercheurs d'os* [The Bone Searchers],[6] *Les rets de l'oiseleur* [The Nets of the Bird-Catcher],[7] *L'invention du désert* [The Invention of the Desert],[8] and, in 1991, a heavily modified version of *L'exproprié.*[9] The novel *Les vigiles* [The Vigilantes] appeared two years before Djaout was assassinated outside his home in late May 1993.[10] The posthumous publication of *Le dernier été de la raison* [The Last Summer of Reason]—an unfinished novel found among Djaout's papers—reaffirms the evolution of the poet into a novelist.[11] Dominique Fisher is one of the rare critics to maintain that, even as Djaout turned to the novel, he did so "without abandoning the principles of poetry."[12] But, as the late Eric Sellin puts it, although Djaout embarked on his literary career as a poet, it was in fiction that he was "to make his mark."[13] Djaout's progression toward prose was increasingly underwritten and informed by the social and cultural commentary that was the basis of his journalism, first at *El Moudjahid*, then at *Algérie-Actualité* (both state-sponsored publications), and finally at *Ruptures*, a weekly magazine founded independently by Djaout, Arezki Metref (b. Sour El-Ghozlane, 1952), and Abdelkrim Djaad (Ighil Ali, 1950–Paris, 2015) in January 1993.[14]

As a poet, Djaout was quick to catch the eye of readers. Before he had any published collections to his name, samples of his fearless teenage iconoclasm, published in literary journals, were noticed by Rachid Boudjedra, who in 1971 had been invited by the Syrian poet Adonis to provide a selection of works by contemporary francophone poets from the Maghreb in Arabic translation for the journal *Mawāqif.*[15] As Boudjedra recalls, "I had this intuition and this honor [of identifying Djaout] when he was still a math student and totally unknown."[16] When challenged on his relation to poetry, Kateb Yacine would often insist, "I am a poet [Je suis poète]. I possess an irreducible and natural inclination to poetry, which has driven me since I was very young. I admit that there are some who do not situate poetry at the center of their concerns when it comes to literature, but for me, there is no question: everything began with poetry [tout a commencé par la poésie]."[17] These are words that Djaout often echoes, as in his conversation with Hamid Abdelkader (b. Algiers, 1967): "I like to work on language and the symbolism of words. I am above all a poet, constantly caught up in his poetic world, trying to insert this world into his novels. I could never betray poetry."[18] Or, as he comments to Isaac-Célestin Tchého in 1987: "The poem, for me, is the essential part, the pinnacle of expression. You can cheat a little with a work in prose, but the poem does not forgive."[19] Poetry is "the first word and the last word too . . . , the crowning achievement of all writing."[20]

Despite Djaout's significant creative and emotional investment in poetry, and his early success, little critical attention has been paid to his poems. The exception to this is a short study from the late 1990s by Youcef Merahi (b. Tizi Ouzou, 1952), which deliberately overlooks the intimately personal in the poems, preferring to see a searing social and political critique of contemporary Algeria: "His nightmares do not come from some internal drama but are the direct and problematic consequence of a particular social schism."[21] By contrast, the purpose of this chapter will be twofold: to examine one of Djaout's last novels, *Les vigiles* (1991), not from a sociological, political, historical, or narratological perspective but from a poetological perspective, that is, for what the novel tells its reader about the continuing significance, urgency, and specificity of poetry in modern Algeria; and, in light of that reading, to examine a cycle in Djaout's earliest collection of poems, *Solstice barbelé* (1975).

Although the country is never explicitly named, *Les vigiles* describes in parallel the fates of two men in independent Algeria.[22] Menouar Ziada, a veteran of the War of Independence and an inhabitant of a suburb of the capital, Algiers, notices that a long-abandoned building is being used at night and reports it to his former colleagues-in-arms, now nightwatchmen, who work in close cooperation with the municipal authorities. These are the "vigiles" of the novel's title—modern versions of the "vigiles urbani," the vigilantes who used to police ancient Rome. A thirty-four-year-old teacher of mathematics by the name of Mahfoudh Lemdjad has been using the building, with the permission of its landlord, to design and construct a new type of loom. The first part of this two-part novel recounts the bureaucratic obstacles Lemdjad encounters when he attempts to patent his invention and apply for a passport that would enable him to travel to an international inventors' fair in Heidelberg. The difficulties continue into the beginning of the second part, when Lemdjad—whose device wins first prize at the fair—returns to Algeria and attempts to retrieve his loom from customs. When his success is reported in one of the newspapers, the authorities realize that the individual they previously persecuted has become a national hero. He is suddenly fêted by the same bureaucrats who had hitherto done everything to thwart his administrative requests. The vigilantes, aware that they are in large part responsible for Lemdjad's difficulties, choose a scapegoat to save them and their post-Independence privileges. Skander Brik, the leader of the group, informs Ziada that he must kill himself as a final service to his country, in the spirit of their fallen comrades. The novel concludes with a description of Ziada's suicide by hanging.

Les vigiles provides a satirical critique of the police state, of excessive and corrupt bureaucratic practices, of modern society's tendency toward totalitarianism, of the disproportionate power and privilege of the generation that fought for and won independence, of a narrow understanding of nationalism, and of nascent Islamic extremism.[23] Phillip Naylor points to *Les vigiles* as a product of a brief period of creative freedom in Algeria—between the inauguration of a multiparty system in July 1989 and the coup against President Chadli Bendjedid in January 1992—during which "the country genuinely engaged and experienced itself, and explored the reality of its social, cultural, and historical pluralism."[24] Raji Vallury sees the novel as charged with a political project—that of "wresting the space of the nation from the despotic territorializations of the state in order to chart out space that allows for the expression of creative flows and desires"[25]—and perceives the loom as a privileged symbol of this operation: "To the police logic that assigns forms, functions, and tasks to those who form part of the community, which decides what one can do, and when, where, and how, Lemdjad's weaving machine, created in the dark of night, opposes the free expression of a productive desire."[26]

None of these valuable readings notes how underwhelming the loom initially appears as the motive for a modern novel.[27] When, in 1861, Charles Baudelaire evaluated the work of his contemporary, the poet Auguste Barbier, he lambasted him specifically for writing about looms: "Here, to put it plainly, all the madness of the century is revealed, bursting out in its unsuspecting nakedness. Under the pretext of writing sonnets in honor of great men, the poet sang of the lightning rod and the loom. You can guess to what prodigious ridicule this confusion of ideas and functions might lead us."[28] When Vallury, for instance, perceives Djaout's loom as an allegory for the space between the political and the aesthetic—as identified and explored by Jacques Rancière and Gilles Deleuze—she overlooks the narrative's insistence on the loom's simplicity. The machine that Lemdjad invents in the disused building in the suburb Sidi-Mebrouk is neither a machine, nor an invention:

> Il fait corps avec cette machine qui n'en est pas une, avec cette invention qui ne le consacrera pas inventeur car elle ne fait que perpétuer une pratique immémoriale qui ne lui est pas vraiment familière mais qui l'avait séduit, voire fasciné dès la première

> fois où il l'avait observée, adolescent, à l'occasion de vacances de printemps passées auprès de sa grand-mère.
>
> He is at one with this machine which is not one, with this invention which will not make him an inventor because it only perpetuates an immemorial practice which is not really familiar to him but which had seduced him, even fascinated him, from the very first time he ever observed it, as a teenager, during spring holidays spent at his grandmother's.[29]

Unlike the self-destructive writing machine in Franz Kafka's "In der Strafkolonie" [In the Penal Colony], an important intertext, the device is not "ein eigentümlicher Apparat" [a peculiar apparatus].[30] Rather, "it is a small machine, a modest loom" [C'est une petite machine, un modeste métier à tisser].[31] So modest, that when Lemdjad returns to the port of Algiers after his triumph in Heidelberg, the customs officer mistakes the packed loom for "a dismantled puppet" [une marionnette désarticulée][32] and does not hide his disappointment:

> . . . je m'attendais à trouver une vraie machine: un astronef miniature, un robot ménager ou un ordinateur. Finalement, vous avez inventé un métier de vieille femme. Vous ne vivez donc pas ici? Vous ne savez que notre pays est résolument engagé dans la voie du modernisme? Sortez donc un jour dans la rue au lieu de rester cloîtré chez vous et regardez les jeux électroniques, les téléphériques, les journaux lumineux. Cela vous donnera peut-être des idées pour d'autres inventions.
>
> . . . I expected to find a real machine: a miniature spacecraft, a food processor, or a computer. It turns out all you have invented is an old woman's loom. Don't you live here? Don't you know that our country is resolutely committed to the path of modernism? One day get outside into the streets instead of staying cloistered up at home and look at the pinball machines, the cable cars, the LED messaging boards. This might give you some ideas for future inventions.[33]

Lemdjad, and Djaout's novel more broadly, is not concerned with ephemeral products of the contemporary. The loom is the privileged vehicle of an ancient practice, considerably more ancient that writing itself. Whereas writing is thought to have been invented with cuneiform in Mesopotamia around five and a half millennia ago, weaving is believed to be at least twenty-seven thousand years old.[34] And whereas a poet like Stéphane Mallarmé, in his 1889 speech on Auguste Villiers de l'Isle Adam, describes "écrire" or "writing" as "une ancienne et très vague mais jalouse pratique, dont gît le sens au mystère du cœur" [an ancient and very vague but jealous practice, whose meaning lies in the mystery of the heart],[35] Djaout's character traces this mystery to the archaic motions of the loom and to his own memory of watching his grandmother weave:

> Quand la grand-mère s'asseyait derrière son métier à tisser, elle devenait une femme vraiment hors du commun. L'enfant qu'était Mahfoudh Lemdjad suivait, obnubilé, les mouvements des longues barres en bois qui se levaient et s'abaissaient tandis que le tapis s'allongeait et que des figures géométriques naissaient comme par enchantement.
>
> When his grandmother was seated at her loom, she became a truly extraordinary woman. The child that was Mahfoudh Lemdjad followed, bewitched, the movements of the long wooden bars, which rose and fell while the carpet grew longer and geometric figures were born as if by magic.[36]

It is only when Lemdjad returns to the village as an adult and discovers that the loom is no longer used by the community that he decides to resuscitate it "en l'allégeant, l'agrémentant et le simplifiant" [making it lighter, more dynamic, and simpler].[37] He thereby aims to revive and perpetuate this immemorial, mostly unfamiliar, feminine practice.[38] The main thing, he states, "est de trouver le modèle le plus esthétique, le moins encombrant et le plus opérationnel" [is to find the most aesthetic, least cumbersome, most operational model].[39]

In this chapter, *Les vigiles* is examined for what it says about poetry and literature, about oral and written expression, and about the constellation of Amazigh (or Berber), Arabic, and francophone cultures particular to modern Algeria. Djaout's insistence on the geometric figures that come to life "as if by magic," as well as on his grandmother's "enchanting gestures," encourage us to hear the "chants" [songs] that would have accompanied the act of weaving. As Walter Benjamin explains in his essay "Der Erzähler" [The Storyteller], weaving is "the web in which the gift of storytelling is cradled."[40] The art of repeating stories has been lost in the twentieth century, he teaches, "because there is no more weaving and spinning to go on while they are being listened to. . . . [Storytelling] is becoming unraveled at its ends after being woven thousands of years ago in the ambience of the oldest forms of craftsmanship."[41] Djaout's loom is also designed to recall a practice that runs parallel to, if it is not intertwined with, weaving, namely orality—whether of song or storytelling, and especially as practiced by women. *Les vigiles* therefore invites us to reflect on the production of modern literature in Algeria and its relation to ancient oral traditions.

LOOM AND SONG

Chaque poète rêve à une géométrie de l'esprit.[42]

Mouloud Mammeri (Taourirt Mimoun, 1917–Aïn Delfa, 1989) was an author, anthropologist, and linguist specializing in Berber languages and cultures. He published the first Tamazight grammar written in the language, *Tajeṛṛumt N Tmaziyt: Tantala Taqbaylit*,[43] later republished as *Précis de grammaire berbère (kabyle)* [Handbook of Berber (Kabyle) Grammar],[44] and founded *Awal*, the first journal devoted exclusively to Amazigh studies. He was the author of novels such as *La colline oubliée* [The Forgotten Hill],[45] *Le sommeil du juste* [The Sleep of the Just],[46] and *L'opium et le bâton* [Opium and the Stick],[47] as well as of articles against French colonization, including a speech presented to the United Nations during the Algerian War of Independence.[48] Mammeri, whose nom de guerre was Si Bouakaz, would notably refuse the material and symbolic benefits afforded to many of those who had secured independence, represented by the vigilantes in Djaout's novel.[49]

In 1980 Mammeri published a critical anthology of Berber poetry from Kabylia entitled *Poèmes kabyles anciens* [Ancient Kabyle Poems].[50] He undertook this project conscious that by transcribing these songs into Latin script, and by presenting the Kabyle transcription alongside a translation into French, he would fail to fully convey their specifically oral qualities: "Many of these pieces, which I present here as lifeless documents, have come to me magnified, inscribed in the dense context of a culture outside of which they become mutilated and extinguished."[51] Linguist Claude Hagège (b. Tunis, 1936) perceives oral style, or "orature," as a literary genre in and of itself,[52] whereas Susan Petrilli and Augusto Ponzio prefer the term "oraliture" to designate instances of transcribed orality that possess the same validity as writing.[53] Mammeri seeks just this type of validity for his own transcriptions but acknowledges that the anthology is an instance of "mitigated" orality, in which the "substance" of the songs and "all the harmonies of their living transmission" have been lost.[54]

Although not the first anthology of Kabyle poetry translated into French, *Poèmes kabyles anciens* is the first anthology to articulate, in a lengthy introduction, the role that publishing and distributing poetry might play in the search for official recognition of Kabyle language and culture.[55] Mammeri's anthology records traces of oral poetry as produced specifically by Berber sages, or "imusnawen" (sing. "amusnaw"). His father, Salem Aït Maamer (1871–1972)—thought to have been one of the last practicing "imusnawen"—had recently died, so the anthology appeared at a watershed moment for Kabyle oral culture. In contrast to the "مرابط" [murābiṭ] or marabout—a Muslim religious leader and teacher, interpreter of the Qur'ān and of Islamic law—the amusnaw was the source of secular knowledge, or "tamusni," and was often also a poet.[56] In conversation with Mammeri, Pierre Bourdieu compares the amusnaw to the Greek "σοφός" [sophos], "the master of a technique that is very practical, as opposed to an abstract and gratuitous wisdom."[57] While Bourdieu draws parallels between Greek and Kabyle cultures, Mammeri stresses the antagonism between Kabyle and Islamic epistemologies, claiming that the tradition of tamusni never had the opportunity to develop autonomously, "without trauma, without the imposition of an external authority." He states with regret that "the *imusnawen* did not have the possibility of making the transition to writing without having to reckon with a kind of competition or domination coming from without."[58] He then concludes, "Islamic culture, despite all its qualities, is very fundamentalist, it does not admit variation; it bases itself on the authority of God, it has been revealed, it is in the text of the Qur'ān. It is complete, and there is nothing else to do than comment on it."[59]

There has been some resistance to this definition of tamusni in recent years. Alain Mahé rejects any claim of a substantive historical distinction between the epistemology of the amusnaw and that of the marabout.[60] Kamel Chachoua goes so far as to assert that Mammeri's presentation of the amusnaw as an equal to, and a competitor with, the marabout is a fabrication, an attempt to resurrect a "mythical and mythological figure."[61] Given that the amusnaw is "a peasant who 'despises' himself and who is ashamed of what he is," he is necessarily dominated by "the charisma, the whiteness, and the finesse" of the marabout, whom he strives to resemble.[62] For Mohamed-Amokrane Zoreli, though, Mammeri's distinction remains valid and is evidence of his determination to formulate a specifically Kabyle epistemology,[63] in much the same way that, more recently, Boaventura de Sousa Santos has argued for the urgent significance of epistemologies of the South.[64]

Mammeri intended the publication of these Berber songs to have political and social, if not religious, significance and to contribute to the nascent popular movement for greater recognition of Kabyle language and culture by the Algerian state:

> What is true culture if not an instrument of liberation? For contemporary Berber culture to be an instrument of emancipation and of real disalienation, all necessary means for its full development should be provided. It cannot be an "Indian reserve" culture [une culture de réserve indienne], nor a marginal undertaking, more tolerated than embraced. No domain should be considered outside its grasp or ambition.[65]

The overtly political nature of this poetic project would create difficulties for Mammeri and for the Amazigh cultural movement more broadly. In March 1980, shortly before he was scheduled to give a talk introducing his new anthology at Hasnaoua University in Tizi Ouzou, Mammeri was prevented from doing so by the local authorities.[66] The cancellation sparked more than two months of civil unrest now known as "Tafsut Imazighen," or the "Berber Spring," commemorated to this day every April 20. Kateb Yacine described the ban as "the unbelievable blunder of a 'wālī' who dared to prohibit a conference on the ancient poetry of the Kabyles."[67] In an open letter written after Mammeri's death in a car accident in February 1989, Djaout recalled, "Who can forget the start of 1980? Men who denied a portion of the culture of this people . . . forbade you from giving a lecture on Kabyle poetry. From all over, from Béjaïa, Bouïra, and Tizi Ouzou, Kabylia rose to defend its poets."[68] Djaout then drew a line between this event and the protests of early October 1988 against the country's economic hardships and the government of Chadli Bendjedid more generally: "And eventually all of Algeria, little by little, year by year, will reject the suppressions, the exclusions, the intolerance, the mediocrity, until the day in October when the country will take to the streets to affirm itself by once again pouring out its blood."[69] The "Black Spring" [Tafsut Taberkant], during which one hundred and twenty-six people were killed and thousands of others were injured and arrested, began in April 2001.

Mammeri's broader cultural project, the publication of his Berber anthology, and the civil disturbances that the interdiction of his lecture caused in the spring of 1980 and beyond should be understood as part of the background to Djaout's *Les vigiles*. Although there is no explicit reference to Lemdjad's ethnicity, his rural origins and perhaps his name allow the reader to imagine that he might be Kabyle. It is therefore possible to envision that when Lemdjad sets out to resurrect the ancient art of weaving specifically as his grandmother practiced it, it is an Amazigh—and more specifically Kabyle—tradition that he seeks to retrieve and perpetuate. Lemdjad's project could then be perceived as similar in kind to that realized by Mammeri—of making available to the present an immemorial practice that would otherwise disappear. Lemdjad is haunted by the project for five years before he does anything about it: "Puis, un jour, il avait pris son carnet. Et les gestes majestueux, qui faisaient jadis danser les fils de laine, s'étaient mis à le guider, à tracer un sillon de clarté, à lui dicter secrètement des schémas et des équations" [Then, one day, he had taken his notebook out. And the majestic gestures, which once made the woolen threads dance, began to guide him, to trace a furrow of clarity, to secretly dictate to him diagrams and equations].[70]

The impossible translation of his grandmother's mesmerizing gestures, of what is nonverbal and uninscribable, into written form may be compared to Mammeri's transcription of acts of orality into "dead documents." But the thrill Lemdjad experiences might better be correlated with that recorded by Malek Ouary (Ighil Ali, 1916–Argelès-Gazost, 2001) in his transcription of Berber songs in the 1940s and 1950s: "Each time I noted down a song, I felt an intense joy: the joy of a bird catcher who has managed to catch gleaming birds in his nets and put them in his cage, to admire them more closely and better, at his leisure, birds that up until then came to him and then vanished without him knowing if he would ever see them again."[71] Ouary repeatedly describes his undertaking as that of a "oiseleur," or "bird catcher," requiring the same guile, patience, and eye for the unusual. He also remains aware of the price of this kind of capture: "But all in all, isn't it better for a bird to be alive in a cage than gone forever in the wild, in other words, dead?"[72] Perhaps not coincidentally, Djaout's sole collection of short stories will be called *Les rets de l'oiseleur* [The Nets of the Bird Catcher].[73] Ouary himself claims that he could have entitled his translated collection of Kabyle songs "La cage aux oiseaux" [The Bird Cage].[74]

In *Les vigiles*, Djaout stresses an important distinction between the otherwise analogous projects of Lemdjad and Mammeri. The oral heritage described and presented by Mammeri is exclusively masculine. Setting the singing associated with weaving alongside the mostly spoken expression of the male imusnawen enables Djaout to correct Mammeri's account of Berber cultural history by affirming the central presence of women. When, toward the close of the novel, the municipal authorities of Sidi-Mebrouk stage a public celebration for the "inventor" of the loom, it is an exclusively male event. Lemdjad uses his short speech to draw attention to the omission of women from the gathering:

> Quant à ma modeste machine qui reçoit ce soir des hommages un peu démesurés, je rappellerai seulement tout ce qu'elle doit aux autres, en particulier aux femmes qui sont absentes de nos célébrations, mais qui se sont attelées des siècles durant à des travaux éprouvants pour tisser brin à brin notre bien-être, notre mémoire et nos symboles pérennes. À travers un métier où elles se sont usé les yeux et les mains et que je réinvente aujourd'hui qu'il a presque disparu, je leur exprime toute ma reconnaissance et je leur restitue une part infime des multiples choses qu'elles nous ont données.[75]

> As for my modest machine, which has received somewhat excessive tributes this evening, I would like to remind you of all that it owes to other people, in particular to the very women who are absent from our celebrations, but who have toiled away for centuries to weave, strand by strand, our well-being, our memory, and our perennial symbols. By means of this loom, on which these women wore out their eyes and hands and which I have reinvented, given its almost complete disappearance, I express all my gratitude to them, and hope to give back a small token of the many things they have given us.

This is to repeat and confirm, albeit in less antagonistic and more constructive terms, the close relation between women and weaving that Sigmund Freud identifies in his new introductory lectures on psychoanalysis from the early 1930s.[76] While for Freud, weaving is an invention bound up with women's "genital deficiency,"[77] for Djaout, its resuscitation by means of a modernized loom is a way of addressing a gender deficiency in modern Algerian society, as evidenced not only by the male-only gathering in the novel, but also by the male-only account of Berber orality in Mammeri's anthology. Djaout's corrective is echoed by Ouary, who stresses the role of singing in the female workplace: "While turning the hand mill, cradling a child, or weaving on the loom, women sing: this is how they confide in each other and console each other."[78] And, as will be seen in the next chapter,

Abdelkébir Khatibi acknowledges throughout his poetic works the importance of female traditions: "Since childhood, this angel has walked toward him, in the guise of mothers, aunts, and sisters weaving secret laws and transmitting them."[79] Assia Djebar addresses an outstanding lacuna in this discussion of orality when she notes that "the Maghreb possesses one of the oldest written cultures, with women as privileged practitioners of writing, namely the tifinagh alphabet of the Tuaregs."[80]

AMAZIGH ARACHNE

If Lemdjad's loom comments on the transformation of Amazigh oral traditions into published texts in Latin script, and if poetry is "the pinnacle of expression," as Djaout claims above, then we might expect to find instances in his oeuvre—and especially in his neglected poetic works—that explore the tropes of orality, inscription, femininity, and weaving. *Solstice barbelé* is Djaout's first published collection of poems.[81] It comprises five sections, the second of which is entitled "Arachné" and includes five poems.[82] In Greek mythology, Arachne is the name of the mortal weaver transformed into a spider by Pallas Athena, as described most famously in book six of *Metamorphoses*. According to Ovid, "tantus decor adfuit arti" [so great was the splendor of her skill][83] that the divine nymphs come not only to look at the clothes once they have been made but to watch them as they are being woven, much as Lemdjad would marvel at his grandmother. Besides being the goddess of war, Athena is also the goddess of weaving, as Homer reminds us when he recalls how she takes off "her soft robe, richly broidered, that herself had wrought and her hands had fashioned."[84] When it is suggested that Arachne has been instructed in weaving by the goddess, she refutes this and instead challenges Athena to a contest.

Athena depicts herself in competition with Poseidon to name the city that will become Athens. In the margins of her tapestry, she incorporates four miniature scenes, each of which illustrates the fate of female mortals who challenge the authority of the gods. Arachne, for her part, depicts twenty-one discrete scenes, in each of which a male god exploits his divine power to force himself upon a female mortal. Arachne's creations are so lifelike that the narrator is able to discern Europa looking back at the land she has left behind, drawing her feet up, afraid of being splashed with seawater. Whereas Athena's composition is restrained, static, and symbolic, Arachne's is dynamic, appealing not only to the most subtle visual accents but also to the sound of the shout that Europa directs toward the companions she has left behind. It is a scene that the painter Diego Velázquez (discussed later in this book) portrayed in 1655, foregrounding the labor of the lowly wool spinners and relegating the weavers to the brilliant background, where a reproduction of Titian's *Rape of Europa* (1560–62) as a hanging carpet can be discerned (fig. 7).

Unlike most mortals who challenge the divine order, Arachne succeeds in surpassing the goddess: "Neither Pallas, nor Spite, could criticize the work."[85] What happens next is recounted with extreme narrative economy. The goddess tears at the tapestry—this is what Shakespeare, in *Troilus and Cressida* (1609), describes as "Ariachne's broken woof"[86]—and hits Arachne on the brow "three or four times" with a boxwood shuttle.[87] Arachne cannot suffer "this"—although what "this" intends is never made clear—and hangs herself. Pallas then takes pity on her and raises her up, saying, "uiue quidem, pende tamen, improba" [Live then, but hang, presumptuous girl],[88] and sprinkles her with the juice of herbs from the underworld:

> . . . et extemplo tristi medicamine tactae
> defluxere comae, cum quis et naris et aures,
> fitque caput minimum, toto quoque corpore parua est;
> in latere exiles digiti pro cruribus haerent,

FIG. 7. Diego de Silva Velázquez, *Las hilanderas, o la fábula de Aracne / The Spinners, or The Fable of Arachne*, ca. 1655–1660, oil on canvas, 220 × 289 cm. Museo Nacional del Prado, Madrid. Copyright © Archivo Fotográfico Museo Nacional del Prado.

cetera uenter habet, de quo tamen illa remittit
stamen et antiquas exercet aranea telas.

. . . and immediately on being touched by the grim drug
her hair dropped off, and with it both nose and ears;
her head became very small, and indeed her whole body was small,
to her flank slender fingers were stuck instead of legs,
the rest of her was belly, yet from it she gave out
a strand and, as a spider, practiced her weaving as before.[89]

The myth of Arachne has often been evoked in reflections on the nature of the literary text. It is in the background of *Le plaisir du texte* [The Pleasure of the Text], when Roland Barthes points to the common source of "text" and "textile":

> We now accentuate, in the fabric [dans le tissu], the generative idea that the text is made [que le texte se fait], is worked through a perpetual intertwining; lost in this fabric [perdu dans ce tissu]—this texture [cette texture]—the subject is unraveled, like a spider dissolving itself in the constructive secretions of its web.[90]

Just as the spider dissolves into her web, so too does the author disappear into her text. Barthes even goes so far as to suggest that the theory of the text formulated by post-structuralists be called "hyphology," from the ancient Greek "ὑφή" [hyphē], meaning "web."

There has been much resistance to Barthes's not so discreet appeal to Arachne. Naomi Schor once denounced the general development of what she called the "Ariadne complex," in which "the relationship between the 'textural' and the textile is on its way to becoming one of the obsessive metaphors of current criticism." She writes, "Be it vertical, horizontal, or transversal, the Ariadne's thread haunts the texts of Barthes, Derrida, and Deleuze, not in the typically structuralist form—that is, metalinguistic—of the Greimasian isotope, but in a poetic form: the thread ('fil') has become an extended metaphor."[91] More recently, Glenn W. Most has pointed out that the use of the Latin "textus" to mean what we now understand as "text" was extremely rare in classical Latin and that while corresponding terms in ancient Greek—such as "ὕφασμα" [hyphasma], meaning "something woven," or "ὑφαίνω" [hyphainō], meaning "to weave"—could refer to a woven discourse, they were also rare and always poetic. Similarly, although "textus" is sometimes used in medieval hermeneutics, the French "texte" is a product of mid-twentieth-century literary theory.[92]

Nancy K. Miller has also shone light on the prejudices at work behind this Arachnean definition of text: "The productive agency of the subject is self-consciously erased by a model of text production which acts to foreclose the question of identity itself."[93] In response, Miller proposes what she calls an arachnology, "a critical positioning which reads *against* the weave of in-differentiation to discover the embodiment in writing of a gendered subjectivity: to recover within representation the emblems of its construction."[94] As Miller writes, "To remember Arachne as the spider, or through the dangers of her web alone, is to retain the archetype and dismember, once again, with Athena, the subject of its history: to underread."[95] Instead, Miller asks us to "overread": "The goal of overreading, of reading for the signature, is to put one's finger—figuratively—on the place of production that marks the spinner's attachment to her web. This is also, as luck would have it, to come closer to the art of natural spiders: the logic of reference may allow us to refuse and refigure the very opposition of the spider and her web."[96]

Although the quintet of poems in Djaout's "Arachné" initially appear to bear little resemblance to Ovid's model, they are examples of Djaout's preliminary exploration of the themes of orality, femininity, and weaving—the same themes that will come to constitute the obscured undercurrents of *Les vigiles*. To echo Miller, we might say that they are an instance of Djaout overwriting the myth of Arachne. By this, I not only mean that he rewrites the myth, perhaps as it comes down to us from Ovid, as a sort of palimpsest. I also mean that he writes the myth to excess, such that the myth begins to take on proportions and dimensions that surpass the myth itself.[97] In so doing, he takes his example from the tapestry that Arachne weaves in Ovid's version, whose plethora of discrete scenes have no structure except that of proliferation and protest. This contrasts with Athena's proportioned composition of self-glorification. It is by overwriting—and not just by overreading—that Djaout is able to, as Miller formulates it, "recover the figurations of Arachne's tapestry."[98]

Contra Barthes, Djaout does not allow Arachne to dissolve into her web, although the Arachne of *Solstice barbelé* will still be unfamiliar to many of us. It is a case of what Khatibi—speaking of Louis Aragon's anamnesis of ancient poetic forms in French and Arabic, or the writing of Jean Genet—calls a "re-rêve" [re-dream],[99] "le rêve du rêve" [the dream of the dream],[100] a poetic recasting of myth. In the opening poem—the only poem to mention Arachne by name—the speaker invokes the figure's clemency, much as one would speak of a goddess:

1.
Pleuvent les sombres abysses
sur mes yeux cryptogames
Et pendant que s'enchevêtrent
les derniers phantasmes
des champs constellés
j'invoque ta clémence
Arachné
Je te conjure de dissoudre
le Rêve Rouge
qui bientôt prendra possession
des terrains vagues
de mes pensées en débandade

Je sais Arachné
que le Soleil
lassé des encensoirs que chaque matin
parfume mon rêve de kif inaccompli
va bientôt secouer son pourpre abyssin
et me précipiter
dans les sillons stériles de la Désillusion

Je t'invoque Arachné
pour maintenir encore ce vague horizon
d'inceste solaire
où dans l'incertaine limite
des rayons enchevêtrés
se faufile quelque rêve hybride

1.
The somber abysses rain
on my cryptogamic eyes
And while the final
phantasms of the
starry fields are tangled
I invoke your clemency
Arachne
I entreat you to dissolve
the Red Reverie
that will soon take possession

of the wastelands
of my stampeding thoughts

I know Arachne
that the Sun
weary of the censers that every morning
perfume my unrealized dream of hash
will soon shake her Abyssinian purple
and rush me
into the sterile furrows of Disillusion

I invoke you Arachne
to maintain this vague horizon
of solar incest
where in the uncertain limit
of entangled rays
some hybrid dream might slip in[101]

This first poem in the cycle might be considered a hymn to Arachné, especially if we take into account the etymology proposed long ago by the philologist Georg Curtius. Curtius perceived the Greek "ὕμνος" [hymnos] as sharing a root with "ὑφάω" [hyphaō], to weave, and "ὑφὴ" [hyphē] or "ὕφος" [hyphos], that is a web or fabric, a connection he traced to "the time when writing was still unknown" and most words relating to poetic compositions "had to be borrowed from the art of the weaver."[102] For Djaout, Arachne is not so much the "improba"—the "one who is disproved of" for her temerity and maybe also for her naivete—nor is she "the presumptuous damzel" identified by Edmund Spenser.[103] Instead, Arachne is a goddess, who no longer receives clemency—as she did from Athena in Ovid—but who bestows clemency on the other. Arachne has become muse and model for the poet, a fellow weaver of "hybrid dreams."[104]

Throughout the five poems—with the exception of the short third poem, composed of only six lines—extremes are shot through with hyperbole. The second poem reads as follows:

2.
Inextinguible succion
sur les yeux boursouflés
de mille Pensées éteintes
là sous les grabats vermoulus

dans l'espace clos
offert à mes possessions noctambules

Meurt la dernière luciole
veillant les escapades agrestes
d'un Rêve gavé de boulons

Se tisse la nuit réticulaire
(Toujours cette impression
de circuler dans les spermiductes
d'une casbah radoubée)
et partout à l'horizon
TENTACULES ARACHNÉENNES

2.
Inextinguishable suction
on swollen eyes
of a thousand extinguished Thoughts
there under the worm-eaten pallets
in the confined space
offered to my noctambulant possessions

The last firefly dies
watching over the rural escapades
of a Reverie stuffed with bolts

The reticular night is woven
(Always this impression
of circulating in the spermatic ducts
of a refurbished kasbah)
and everywhere on the horizon
ARACHNIDIAN TENTACLES[105]

Djaout's textual dreams—such as this one stuffed with bolts—are structured on the principle of the plural: cryptogamic and swollen eyes, somber abysses, final phantasms, sterile furrows, tangled rays, a thousand extinguished Thoughts, moldy rags, noctambulant possessions, rural escapades, the spermatic ducts of a refurbished kasbah, and perhaps most strikingly the ARACHNIDIAN TENTACLES with which the second poem ends. These capital letters recall the typography of a verse in the twenty-ninth sura of the Qurʾān, "The Spider," as translated by Albin Kazimirski de Biberstein:

> Ceux qui cherchent des protecteurs en dehors de Dieu ressemblent à l'ARAIGNÉE qui se construit une demeure; y a-t-il une demeure plus frêle que la demeure de l'araignée? S'ils le savaient!
>
> Those that seek protectors besides God are like the SPIDER who builds a dwelling-place; is there a dwelling-place frailer than the spider's dwelling? If only they knew![106]

The Qur'ānic spider provides a metaphor for someone who devotes their life to ephemeral things instead of to God, just as in Matthew's Gospel the foolish man builds his house upon the sand.[107] However, in one of the ahadith, or sayings, of the Prophet, a spider is credited with weaving a web across the entrance to the cave in which Muḥammad hid from his persecutors after fleeing Mecca. It is for this reason that, in some Moroccan traditions, white spiders should not be killed—unlike malevolent black spiders, about which it is said, "If one of them passes over the eye of a sleeping person it will make the eye swell."[108] The undecidability of the spider's significance is characteristic of all these plural nouns, which combine to create the "hybrid dream" of the first poem and the "reticular night" of the second. Only in the third poem is there any indication that the dream might be too much for the text-web to hold, when the memory of a "Rêve-Mégot" [Dream-Stub] burns up "au contact de mes chimères" [when it comes into contact with my chimeras].[109]

In the fourth poem, which celebrates Arachne's brother, Djaout overwrites Arachne's myth by turning away from Ovid altogether:

> 4.
> Mon frère a la barbe délavée d'un clochard
> le regard crédule d'un enfant chétif
> et la démarche bénigne
> d'un homme qui a peur
> de lacérer le rêve des autres
>
> Il est très doux mon frère
> fumant ses cicatrices
>
> Mon frère n'aime pas la guerre
> (on l'accuse de lâcheté)
> et il pleure à chaque suicide du soleil
> —mon frère piètre chasseur

Il est si étrange mon frère
avec ses doigts noueux
fouilleurs de détritus
avec ses yeux perdus
qui vrillent les canons
avec sa main ouverte
au-dessus des ténèbres

Il est si étrange
mon frère le poète vanneur du blé des pauvres

4.
My brother has the faded beard of a vagrant
the gullible gaze of a sickly child
and the benign gait
of a man who is afraid
to lacerate other people's dreams

He is very sweet my brother
smoking his scars

My brother does not like war
(they accuse him of cowardice)
and he cries with every suicide of the sun
—my brother pitiful hunter

He is so strange my brother
with his gnarled fingers
rummaging in rubbish
with his lost eyes
which can pierce canons
with his open hand
above the shadows

He is so strange
my brother the poet winnower of the wheat of the poor[110]

In this poem, Djaout's aim may be to evoke Jean Sénac, whose late poetry is explored in an earlier chapter and who was stabbed to death at age forty-six in his basement in Algiers at the end of August 1973. *Solstice barbelé* concludes with a series of three poems that explicitly celebrate Sénac's life.[111] But Djaout's poem might also be read alongside a lesser-known Attic iteration of the Arachne myth, as recorded in the scholia to Nicander of Colophon's *Theriaca*, an extended poem in hexameters, which describes venomous spiders, snakes, and scorpions; the wounds they inflict; and ways to remedy their bites. According to the scholia, Arachne's transformation occurs when she commits incest with her brother:

> Phalanx had received Athena's teaching in the domain of war, and Arachne in that of weaving. But they were united in incest, which made them hateful to Athena. The goddess transformed them into animals that crawl, destined to be devoured by their children.[112]

Where Nicander's scholiast speaks of Phalanx as a warrior-brother, Djaout's brother is awkward and weird: "My brother does not like war / (they accuse him of cowardice)." He is instead a poet: "my brother the poet." Bourdieu reminds us in his conversation with Mammeri that "asefru," the Kabyle word for "poem," is related to the verb "fru," or "to winnow grain"[113]—a coincidence that informs the poem's closing line. Arachne's brother and lover—the Kabyle poet—is a "winnower of the wheat of the poor."

In contrast to the preceding poems in "Arachné," which are in "vers libre" [blank verse], the fifth and final poem is made up of thirteen sentences in prose. It marks the densest part of the cycle, where the figures and motifs we are used to identifying in the Arachne myth are largely obscured:

> 5.
>
> Le corps scindé en deux, elle sentit encore naître en elle cette envie de guillotiner la mer.
>
> Et possédée à en mourir par une odeur de plage, elle crut reconnaître l'Aurore dans les vibrations de la stature glabre et déchue. Mais lorsque l'extase rampait vers la négation, le corps, sourd comme le péché, cessait de résonner. Et les rivages de la sanctification s'estompaient de nouveau.
>
> Vingt ans. Ses lèvres arboraient la dorure des sables. Vingt ans: diviniser la chair. Vingt ans et elle se sentait mourir sous le piétinement farouche des cavales échevelées,—leur trot rongeur de rocailles sur ses seins fleurs de grenadier. Et ses yeux, sa chevelure exhalaient le relent sexuel de Tigzirt . . .

Livide et tentaculaire, la main asexuée se noya encore dans une soif de lacération. Et l'orgie de sang recommença aux accents lascifs de la nuit. Lorsqu'une aube fœtale se leva, le corps recouvert d'échancrures mais exhalant encore la nacre et l'encens se ramassa dans un soubresaut de déchéance et de gloire . . .

. . . Et drapé dans l'oriflamme le corps glabre et meurtri.

5.

Her body cleaved in two, she still felt this urge to guillotine the sea well up inside her.

And possessed to death by the odor of the beach, she thought she recognized Aurora in the vibrations of her hairless, fallen stature. But when ecstasy crept into negation, the body, deaf as sin, ceased to resonate. And the shores of sanctification faded away once more.

Twenty. Her lips bore the gilt of sands. Twenty: to render flesh divine. Twenty and she felt like she was dying under the fierce trampling of tousled mares—their trot gnawing stony ground on her pomegranate flower breasts. And her eyes, her hair exhaled the sexual stench of Tigzirt . . .

Livid and tentacular, the asexual hand drowned itself in the thirst for laceration. And the orgy of blood began again with the lascivious accents of the night. When a fetal dawn rose, the body covered with indentations but still exhaling mother-of-pearl and incense drew itself together in a spasm of decay and glory . . .

. . . And draped in the oriflamme the hairless and bruised body.[114]

There is little in the poem to suggest that Arachne is a gifted weaver. Instead, Djaout presents her as a twenty-year-old, with "pomegranate blossom breasts," whose lips bear "the gilt of sands" and whose eyes and hair exhale "the sexual stench of Tigzirt."[115] The black-and-white illustration by Denis Martinez that accompanies this cycle of poems, entitled "Arachné" (fig. 8), is informed by the opening lines of this poem.[116] A third of the way up from the bottom of the picture—perpendicular to the vertical white strip—two naked torsos of the same young woman meet at the head, as if welded together, the spider rising vertically between them. Djaout's Arachne is no longer from Hypaepa, in the mountains of Asia Minor, but from a town in coastal Kabylia, east of Algiers. Her metamorphosis—which the poem appears to describe—will not result in a new afterlife as a spider but in death, as the image of a bruised and hairless body draped in a red banner seems to suggest. Nor is the agent of this transformation one we will recognize as Athena. The ability of

FIG. 8. Denis Martinez, "Arachné / Arachne." Reproduced in Tahar Djaout, *Solstice barbelé: 1973–1975* (Sherbrooke: Naaman, 1975), 22. Reproduced by kind permission of Denis Martinez.

the goddess to change both Arachne's shape and her own is never in question in Ovid, but in Djaout's poem, agency is much less certain: "she thought she recognized Aurora in the vibrations of her hairless, fallen stature."[117]

Let us suppose that Djaout draws the agent of Arachne's transformation from Kabylia, and specifically from the figure of the ogress that populates its oral culture. She could be a "tteryel"—also known as a "tsériel" or "tagrod"—a fairy who can be malevolent or benevolent, fecund or sterile, constructive or destructive.[118] For Nabile Farès, the ogress of Berber oral culture resists positive definition and oscillates between the marvelous and the fantastical.[119] She is variously the antithesis of the founding ancestor, the antinomy of the phallus, and the manifestation of the "vagina dentata," a figure that Djaout references on more than one occasion.[120] The agent of Arachne's metamorphosis might also be Yemma-t n dunnit, "First Mother of the World," who is responsible for creating such phenomena as the stars and the solar eclipse and whom Camille Lacoste-Dujardin describes as the "initiator of death."[121] Similarly to Athena, Yemma-t n dunnit is credited with giving animals their distinctive features. The tortoise was originally a bull at which Yemma-t n dunnit threw two grinding stones from her hand mill, striking it on the back and on the chest.[122] Sheep were created out of dough from Yemma-t n dunnit's hand mill, their black heads coming from the soot she could not wipe from her hands.[123] But whoever the agent of Arachne's metamorphosis in Djaout's poem is, whether Tteryel or Yemma-t n dunnit, she is a mostly malevolent figure: "Livid and tentacular, the asexual hand drowned itself in the thirst for laceration. And the orgy of blood began again with the lascivious accents of the night."

The reimagination of both Arachne and Athena in this five-poem cycle not only displaces a seminal Greek myth into Kabyle mythology; it also reaffirms the shared pagan past of these two Mediterranean cultures. Despite Djaout's Muslim upbringing, the poetics of the Qur'ān—and of Islam more broadly—does not inflect his poetic imaginary as it does that of Khaïr-Eddine, Tengour, or Meddeb, among others discussed in this book. When Djaout comments on religion, he often does so under the cover of fiction, as in *Le dernier été de la raison*: "The verses that trace the path to Paradise seem to him too peremptory; they intimidate the imagination, clip the wings of dream."[124] A similar critique can be found in *L'invention du désert*, when the Qur'ān is evoked as follows: "The Text that muzzles the world with its intransigence, its beauty—that tolerates only acquiescence. The jealous, tyrannical Text that admits of no other word, no other signifying figure. A relay of nothing more than recurrence and sequence in the mechanics of the Perfect. The Text has crossed out existence by sublimating it once and for all. Collapse of the carnal and desiring world."[125] It is this carnal, desiring, pre-Islamic, pre-Christian world, this world of dream and imagination, that Djaout's cycle of poems seeks to resurrect.

ARACHNOID AFTERLIVES

> J'abandonne ma poésie arachnéenne à la quête d'une vie équatoriale.[126]

Arachne is never mentioned explicitly in *Les vigiles*, although traces of her presence in this novel about a loom should not surprise us. When Skander

Brik—whose first name contains an imperfect anagram of Arachne[127]—goes to inform Menouar Ziada that he is to "disappear" for the good of his colleagues and of the country, he waits for him outside Ziada's house early in the morning, "comme s'il avait attendu des heures durant avec la patience de l'araignée" [as if he had waited for hours with the patience of a spider].[128] In Ovid's narrative, the name Arachne becomes associated—through frequent repetition—with the adverb "tamen" [however, nevertheless, yet still]. Her metamorphosis is confirmed by the text when "tamen"—which appears for the final time in the penultimate verse, as recorded above—acquires an initial letter "s" in the final verse and becomes "stamen" [thread, warp of a loom].[129] Once seated with the victim, Skander's own "stamen"—his "ligne de pensée" or "line of thought"—"starts to unravel" [commence à se dévider].[130] Whereas Ovid's narration accelerates to such a degree that the motives for Arachne's suicide are never made clear, Djaout's slows down to again create a curious overwriting of the myth. Brik assures Ziada that his suicide will not be in vain. While in Ovid it was not clear whether Arachne killed herself from shame at her act of hubris, from frustration at her unadvised decision not to listen to the old woman who came to warn her, from anger that her tapestry had been destroyed, or from the injustice of having her victory overruled—or simply from the onset of madness—here the reasons for Ziada's suicide are explained to him:

> Ton suicide sera présenté comme un geste de remords, comme un acte de profonde lucidité, le rachat à prix d'or d'une malencontreuse erreur commise à l'adresse d'un grand inventeur.
>
> Your suicide will be presented as a gesture of remorse, as an act of profound lucidity, redemption, albeit at great cost, for an unfortunate error committed against a great inventor.[131]

In turn, this invites readers of Ovid's account to imagine that Arachne is ordered to kill herself for the sake of the goddess's reputation, thereby reaffirming the static hierarchy upon which Greek mythology depends and which Athena depicted in her tapestry. It is only when this unequal power structure is reestablished that Athena intervenes to transform Arachne into a spider.

Other traces of Ovid's Arachne in *Les vigiles* are less obvious but still in evidence. Brik claims that as a result of the suicide, Ziada's name and that of the town Sidi-Mebrouk will be forever associated with Lemdjad's invention, although there is no reason why either name should be anything more than an ephemeral footnote in an obscure history. The notion that someone who suffers a transformation because of some misfortune will then become synonymous with that transformation—in the same way that Arachne gives her name in Greek, "ἀράχνη" [arachnē], to both the spider and its web—may be understood as traces of Ovid's logic, of long-abandoned narrative cobwebs that persist in the corners of Djaout's text. There are also remnants of Djaout's own version of Arachne, as presented in *Solstice barbelé*. Once Brik has finished informing Ziada of his fate, he takes a swig of coffee and produces "une sorte de succion érotique" [a sort of erotic suction][132] with his lips, echoing the "Inextinguible succion / sur les yeux boursouflés" [Inextinguishable suction / on swollen eyes][133] that begins the second poem of Djaout's "Arachné" cycle.

Les vigiles concludes with an extended passage in which Ziada returns home and prepares to kill himself. As he does so, he ponders whether this life is followed by an afterlife. The peasants of the village in which he was born and raised spoke of heaven and hell in vibrant and familiar detail, as if they were hamlets on the other side of the mountain—and their own village, a branch of purgatory. As Goethe writes in the cycle "Buch des Paradieses" [Book of Paradise] in *West-östlicher Divan* [West-East Diwan], quoted in French translation by Abdelkébir Khatibi,

> Der echte Moslem spricht vom Paradiese
> Als wenn er selbst allda gewesen wäre . . .
>
> The faithful Muslim speaks of paradise
> As if he had himself already been to this place . . .[134]

Ziada's sterility means that he and his wife are unable to achieve the promise of earthly perpetuity—a situation rendered somewhat ironic by the fact that in Algerian Arabic, his name means "birth."[135] In his half sleep, Ziada hears the muezzin, "mélodieux, émouvant, avec quelque chose de lénifiant et de déchirant à la fois" [melodious, moving, with something soothing and heartbreaking at the same time].[136] He wonders whether the paradise promised by Islam is as soft and musical as this call to prayer. As evening falls, the insects start to sing, which causes Ziada to reflect on whether insects go to paradise when they die. More specifically, he would like to know whether an insect afterlife is available to him: "Menouar Ziada aurait aimé que lui poussent comme à elles des antennes, des élytres chantants comme des lyres, une carapace" [Menouar Ziada would have liked to grow antennae just like theirs, elytra singing like lyres, a shell].[137] He thereby spells out what in Ovid's version of the myth is only implied, namely that Arachne's metamorphosis represents an afterlife. Certain things, although not all, will continue beyond death.

Even as Skander Brik is explaining to Ziada how he should execute his imminent fate, a transformation has begun to take place: "Tout en lui—la tête, les membres, les doigts en forme d'appendices osseux, la charpente effilée—évoque un insecte" [Everything in him—his head, limbs, fingers in the shape of bony appendages, his slender frame—was reminiscent of an insect].[138] And yet when Ziada carefully knots the rope, climbs onto the chair, rocks "almost grotesquely" backward and forward before imperfectly kicking the chair away, the hoped-for translation into an insect—perhaps into the spider that Arachne becomes—is not realized. Instead, Ziada feels as though he has been torn apart: "Un serpent s'enroule autour de lui, empêche son sang de circuler. Une bête écailleuse, volumineuse et blessante a élu domicile dans sa gorge, a décidé de rester là jusqu'à son étouffement" [A snake coils around him, prevents his blood from circulating. A scaly, voluminous, wounding beast has taken up residence in his throat, has decided to stay there until he suffocates].[139] Athena does not come to his aid and—much like the Officer who perishes in Kafka's writing machine in "In the Penal Colony," and much like Djaout's version of Arachne—he does not appear to achieve the desired transfiguration. As Kafka writes, "Kein Zeichen der versprochenen Erlösung war zu entdecken" [No sign of the promised salvation could be detected].[140]

Although Ziada does not attain an afterlife, the final pages of the novel appear to contain signs of an afterlife for Berber orality. When recalling his childhood, Ziada remembers a simple song that could be heard every morning emanating from the house of the widow Khadra:

> C'était une chanson qui remplissait le village et tout le crépuscule du monde:
>
> *Épargne le soleil torride*
> *Au travailleur vaillant*
> *Qui trime loin de moi.*
>
> Cette chanson banale ouvrait pour Menouar des horizons insoupçonnés, évoquait des matins euphoriques, des voyages rudes mais pleins d'agréments, des chantiers grouillant de travailleurs.

> It was a song that filled the village and all the twilight of the world:
>
> *Save from the scorching sun*
> *The valiant worker*
> *Who toils far from me.*
>
> For Menouar, this banal song opened up unsuspected horizons, evoked euphoric mornings, hard journeys packed with small pleasures, construction sites teeming with workers.[141]

Walid Bouchakour identifies the widow's song as a French translation of "Arras thili," a song famously interpreted by singer El-Djida Tameqrant (née Mhenni Mebrouka; Ras-n-Tala, 1912–Algiers, 1992) and later by Matoub Lounès (Aït Mahmoud, 1956–Thala Bounane, 1998) and Idir (né Hamid Cheriet; Aït Lahcène, 1945–Paris, 2020). The refrain reads as follows:

> Ih arras thili
> Arras thili
> I win ikhedmen felli
>
> Give shade
> Give shade
> To the one who toils for me.[142]

It is an instance of "aḥiḥa," a traditional Kabyle song originally sung by women at family celebrations or as they worked in the fields, which Kouceila Tighilt, writing in the Algerian newspaper *Liberté*, called a "song of freedom" that historically "liberated" the voices of otherwise voiceless working women.[143] For Ziada, it is a song that conveys the heat of the summer. It has an odor—perhaps of sweat, perhaps of raindrops on the earth, perhaps of cigarette smoke. And yet it remains impossible to explain why the song has such a powerful effect on him: "Les mots étaient-ils très suggestifs? Ou alors toute la magie venait-elle de la voix de la chanteuse?" [Were the words particularly suggestive? Or did all the magic come from the voice of the singer?].[144]

This fictional scene rehearses a topic that has often confronted poets writing in French in the Maghreb, namely how to ensure the perpetuation of orality—here Amazigh orality—and its particular power in modern literature. In an essay first published in 1958, Jean Amrouche spoke of his native village as the place where he heard, for the first time, "a melody of human language that, in the depths of memory, constitutes the archetype of all music, of what Spain admirably calls cante jondo."[145] Federico García Lorca describes this deep song as "teñido por el color misterioso de las primeras edades de cultura" [imbued with the mysterious color of primordial ages].[146] It is "un perfecto balbuceo, una maravillosa ondulación melódica, que rompe las celdas sonoras de nuestra escala atemperada, que no cabe en el pentagrama rígido y frío de nuestra música actual y quiebra en pequeños cristalitos las flores cerradas de los semitonos" [a stammer, a wavering emission of the voice, a marvelous buccal undulation that smashes the resonant cells of our tempered scale, eludes the cold rigid staves of modern music, and makes the tightly closed flowers of the semitones blossom into a thousand petals].[147] Djaout asks us to hear something of this cante jondo in simple compositions, such as the widow Khadra's song, whose most striking characteristic is, as Amrouche puts it, "wealth in austerity" [la richesse dans le dépouillement].[148]

Amrouche, Mammeri, Ouary, and others have all sought to secure, through inscription, traces of an oral culture close to vanishing for all time, just as El-Djida Tameqrant, Matoub Lounès, and Idir have done in recorded performances. Djaout perceives his task differently. Not satisfied with anthropological, cultural, or literary archivization, or musical restoration, Djaout instead implicates his writing in a continuing oral tradition. Much as Arachne continues to weave in her afterlife as an arachnid, so too this Amazigh poet—who first spoke Kabyle and later learned French—admits the transformation of his person, of his language, of his culture, and maybe even of his preferred genre, but continues to weave as before. Kateb Yacine asserts that "our use of French can become a weapon" and that "I write in French to tell the French that I am not French."[149] For Djaout—perhaps less combative and more concerned with bringing the various ethnic and linguistic strands that make up modern Algeria to light in contemporary French—to write in French as an Algerian and as a Kabyle is to "live then, but hang," to continue to live and write, but to do so in another form and under different conditions.

The loom, the spider, and the spider's web—and by extension Arachne—are therefore figures that combine in Djaout's work to form what Bernadette Rey Mimoso-Ruiz calls "a silent claim to Amazighity,"[150] that is, the continuing presence of Kabyle oral culture in modern francophone Algerian literature. For Djaout, the monstrous—but also felicitous—transformation is to write in French prose, where once the Berber sang without inscription. Djaout sees Nedjma and Kahina as the two female figures at the center of

Kateb Yacine's poetics—"both real and mythical, loaded with experience and symbols"[151]—but it is Arachne who inhabits the center of his own creative web. In the same way, the fine, sometimes invisible weft of Djaout's writing—the *mythos* of his poetry that informs the *logos* of his novel—is Amazigh orality.

Djaout proposes a concept of orality that does not entirely coincide with major recent theorizations. Paul Zumthor, for example, perceives orality as "the functioning of the voice as the bearer of language."[152] "This is why," he explains elsewhere, "most poetic performances in all civilizations have always been sung."[153] What Djaout's late novel and early cycle of poems reaffirm is that orality was never just voice, nor was it only sung. It was also bound up with the bodily activity that accompanied it: the creation of visual patterns in wool, the gestures of those working the loom, and the community of working women in which poetic performances took place. As Lemdjad puts it, it was above all the "bewitching" or "enchanting" face and gestures of his grandmother—or what Zumthor calls the "irreducible unity of body and gesture"[154]—that provoked him into reinventing the loom for the present. *Les vigiles* reminds us that weaving contains the gestural traces of an ancient and otherwise mostly lost orality. It is this lost orality that Djaout attempts to retrieve and perpetuate in a literary afterlife, not only in "Arachné" but throughout his poetic and novelistic oeuvre. Djaout's unmistakable shift away from poetry and toward the novel should perhaps therefore be understood as the weaving of text that seeks—increasingly—to both obscure the absence of Amazigh orality and to compensate for that very absence through the creation of new bodies, voices, looms, webs, and weavers.

CHAPTER 5

The Hustle

Virginity, Syntax, and Other Scruples in the Writings of Abdelkébir Khatibi

"IQRA'," OR GABRIEL'S IMPERATIVE

The first word revealed to the Prophet Muḥammad by the angel Gabriel, and to which he would submit himself for the next twenty years, was the command "اقرأ" [iqra'].[1] This could mean "recite," but it could also mean "read," which would suggest, as Fethi Benslama and others have argued, that the sacred text had already been written when it was handed down to the Prophet.[2] The oeuvre of Abdelkébir Khatibi challenges anyone who encounters it with a similar imperative. As Khatibi repeatedly insists, "Read the world of signs and images, read what you see and what you hear. This reading is absolute."[3] For Khatibi, everything is preceded by reading, even religion: "Doesn't the word Qur'ān also mean reading? . . . Before being a believer, you are first of all a reader."[4] The dream of the written text—its primary task and responsibility—is therefore to create its reader: "Any text, sacred or profane, is driven by the desire to invent the reader who comes to it. This is its dream of eternity."[5] Whereas Muḥammad castigated the "shuʿarā'" [poets] for "wandering in every wādī and saying what they do not do,"[6] Khatibi is driven by the desire to rehabilitate the poet as "a claimant to both paradise and incarnate love,"[7] that is, as a guide to both the material and immaterial realms.

This does not mean that reading Khatibi is easy. The reader of Khatibi's poetic texts—from *Dédicace à l'année qui vient* [Consecration to the Year That Comes][8] to "Notes de mémoire pour les femmes" [Memory Notes for Women] and "Notes de mémoire pour les hommes" [Memory Notes for Men] in *Par-dessus l'épaule* [Over the Shoulder],[9] to *Le livre de l'aimance* [The Book of Lovence][10] and *Aimance* [Lovence],[11] among various other publications—will attest that there is much in them that is sensed more than it is grasped. Words shimmer with the brief promise of communion, before meaning drifts away. There are moments when reading will not be enough, when the reader will be required to reach in spirit beyond the foundational Qur'ānic imperative to Isaiah: "Read this (קרא נא זה [ḳera' na' zeh]), I pray thee: and he saith, I cannot; for it *is* sealed (כי חתום הוא [ki ḥatum hu']).''[12] And yet, Khatibi repeatedly affirms that the principles for reading his sometimes hermetic poetic texts are not different from those he teaches us to deploy in reading other cultural phenomena. The text can be a poem, or a tattoo, or a carpet, or a piece of jewelry. In each instance, the reader will have to take risks, often leaping between different semiotic systems. Khatibi will tell us that this is where the thrill of reading inheres: "The intersemiotic gesture is an erotic transport, a production of rotating meanings from a modest geometric sign, or color, or gesture."[13] For there to be such a transport, there must also be the possibility that reading might not succeed. Failure, in fact, will prove to be a necessary part of poetic reading: "Loss of meaning is always a risk in a profession (here writing) often engaged in dazzling momentarily through the introduction of an inscribed trace."[14]

Khatibi's poetry might therefore be described as participating in a tradition of modern mystical literature, a tradition that includes texts as diverse as Johann Wolfgang von Goethe's *West-östlicher Divan* [West-East Diwan] (1819, rev. 1827), itself inspired by a German translation of the Persian poems of Ḥāfeẓ (Shiraz, ca. 1325–Shiraz, 1390), and Rainer Maria Rilke's *Duineser Elegien* [Duino Elegies] (1923), as well as the poetic hermeticism of Stéphane Mallarmé. Although Khatibi draws extensively from the tradition of Sufi poetry in Arabic—as has been demonstrated by Réda Bensmaïa and Yasser Elhariry, among others[15]—his poetry resembles the late work of the twentieth-century Swedish poet Gunnar Ekelöf (Stockholm, 1907–Sigtuna, 1968) as much as it does the work of al-Ḥallāj (Fars, ca. 858–Baghdad, 922) or Ibn ʿArabī (Murcia, 1165–al-Salihiyyah, 1240). These poets are all creators of what Khatibi calls "la grande poésie,"[16] a poetry that aims for "the essential, the crystal, the magnetic, the vertigo of the absolute purity of sounds and words, torn from the ecstasy of the moment," in other words, "the rhythm, the song, the line of force that gives [poetry] tone and breath."[17] Goethe says that, much like the prophetic word, the poetic word "expresses a desire for eternity and immortality," a desire that "only prolongs the love of life and its worship. . . . As soon as we are born, we desire and demand eternity."[18]

Accordingly, each of these poets attempts to create what Khatibi calls a spiritual country—"un pays légendaire"[19]—and to there elaborate "a grand myth that unleashes [the poet's] spirit of invention,"[20] but which also risks exiling the poet from everyday communication. As Khatibi notes in an essay on Ekelöf's "interior Orient," this kind of poetry entails certain dangers: "Any poet who risks, in the fierce love of solitude, measuring herself against the powers of silence that bewitch her, is to some degree lost to the living."[21] Khatibi points to the image—as recounted by the Greek-Irish orientalist Lafcadio Hearn (Lefkada, 1850–Tokyo, 1904)—of the blind musician in "The Story of Mimi-Nashi-Hōïchi," who plays his "biwa," or lute, at night, as requested by a company of strangers, but who does not know that he is playing for the dead.[22]

Khatibi's own "legendary country" is marked by a number of features, not least the poetic concept of "aimance"—"a secret word"[23] for which Khatibi provides fleeting definitions throughout his poetic and theoretical writings.[24] In the opening pages of *Par-dessus l'épaule*, we are told in passing and in parentheses that it is "quite a different notion from that of Love [l'Amour]."[25] "Aimance" is lighter than love, less binding, sometimes reckless, allowing for incoherence, even infidelity, "against all notion of wisdom"[26]: "Aimance is only given to partners in fragments, between the force of one's life and the oblique gesture of one's decline."[27] Whereas the traditional code of love is bound up with theological codes through their shared pursuit of absolutes such as "God, the Beloved, the forbidden Woman,"[28] "aimance" allows for a more incidental, accidental, noncommittal love. It appears, with deliberate echoes of Mallarmé's exquisite later sonnets, like "une pensée en dentelle,"[29] a sort of lacework of thoughts for the other: "'Nothing more than the desires that surround thinking.' Something to be nuanced, one day at a time, provided you have a taste for detail."[30]

It is unclear whether Khatibi initially believes himself to have invented the term "aimance," but it is clear that he would like his reader to think of him as its inventor. In *Par-dessus l'épaule* and *Le livre de l'aimance*, he even states, "This is why I invented Aimance."[31] Similarly, in *Dédicace à l'année qui vient*:

> Et toi, Aimance Aimance
> N'es-tu pas mon emblème chiffré?
> Le seul mot que j'aie inventé
> Dans la phrase de ma vie?

And you, Aimance Aimance
Are you not my ciphered emblem?
The only word I ever invented
In the phrase that is my life?[32]

When these lines are later repeated in *Aimance*, Khatibi swaps out "inventé" [invented] for "réinventé" [reinvented][33] because the word does, in fact, predate Khatibi's use of the term. In his stymied desire to be the creator of "aimance," Khatibi resembles a young Mallarmé, who once asked his friend Eugène Lefébure, in hope rather than expectation, to confirm that the word "ptyx"—a key rhyme in the sonnet that begins "Ses purs ongles . . ." [Her pure nails . . .]—did not exist.[34] Although Mallarmé wanted to be able to point to a word brought into being by the demands of prosody alone—there being in French not enough rhymes on "-yx" to construct a sonnet—he probably knew that it had been used before, as the singular from of "diptych," from the Ancient Greek "πτυχή" (ptychē), meaning "fold."[35] Similarly, Khatibi toys with what we know of the genealogy of "aimance." Appearing in a radio broadcast in conversation with Pascal Amel in 1993, he claims to have recovered "aimance" for the present: "'Aimance' is an ancient word, but it has fallen into disuse. I have taken it back."[36] And yet even this is only partially accurate. The word "amance," without an "i," comes from the Latin "amare" and means "affection" or "love." A homophone of "amance" stems from "exmagare," "to deprive of strength, disable," and describes "dismay" or even "shame." Another homophone, "amence," from the Latin "amentia," means "mindlessness" or "madness." But "aimance" per se does not appear to exist in Old French. To find an approximation of the initial syllable of "aimance" in French, we have to look at derivations of the Latin "adamas, adamantis," which means "iron," from the Greek "ἀδάμας" [adamas], "invincible," from which the French "diamant" [diamond] comes. We might also ponder the "pierre aimantée," or what Socrates, in Plato's dialogue *Ion*, calls "the stone which Euripides called Magnet, but most people call Heraclean"—a stone that "not only attracts iron rings but also puts power in the rings so that they also have power to do the same thing the stone does and attract other rings."[37] "Aimance" might therefore also be a figure for divine inspiration: "For a poet is a delicate thing, winged and sacred, and unable to create until he becomes inspired and frenzied, his mind no longer in him."[38] The shift from "amance" to "aimance" is perhaps similarly inspired and not as straightforward as Khatibi would have us believe.

Notwithstanding its contested origins, "aimance" is deployed in modern French by twentieth-century psychologists to describe stages in a child's affective development. Édouard Pichon explains how a baby first consumes "aimance captative," that is, the pleasure of being loved, before passing to "aimance oblative," that is, the pleasure of loving another.[39] A decade later, Emmanuel Mounier will summarize "aimance" as "the period of great childish and sentimental loves."[40] Étienne Balibar identifies the term as describing object attraction that does not carry the overtly sexual connotations of Sigmund Freud's "libido" and sees its coining as a symptom of the French resistance to the German tendency to hypersexualize psychoanalysis.[41] Initially, Khatibi overlooks these specialist applications, acknowledging them explicitly only later, notably in an essay published a year before his death entitled "L'aimance et l'invention d'un idiome" [Aimance and the Invention of an Idiom].[42]

Khatibi may not even be the only one to rediscover "aimance." In a footnote to *Politiques de l'amitié* (1994), Jacques Derrida claims to arrive at the term independently of his friend and defines it as neither love nor friendship but "a third or first voice, the so-called middle voice, beyond or below loving (that of friendship or of love), activity and passivity, decision, and passion."[43] For his part, Khatibi emphasizes its sexual potential: "I call *aimance* this other language of love that, while naming this opposition, affirms a more active affinity between beings, which may give form to their desire and their mutual affection, even in its incompleteness. I think that such an affinity between lovers [entre les aimants] can liberate a certain inhibited zone of their 'jouissance.'"[44] Or, as he puts it elsewhere, "You might also say that sex is what comes to Aimance as its grace."[45] More recently, in an important collection of critical essays in English on Khatibi's life and work, Jane Hiddleston summarizes "aimance" as "a form of friendship open to contingency and recreation," as well as "an ethical interaction" that "eschews domination and mastery and remains sensitive to the unfamiliarity of the other."[46] In the same volume, Khalid Lyamlahy allows for the carnal aspects stressed by Khatibi himself when he calls it "a form and a language of love that liberate pleasure and bring together the affinities and contradictions of loving relationships."[47] Laurent Dubreuil appears to fault "aimance" for trying to re-create, solecistically, what cannot be re-created, namely "amour," when he dubs Khatibi's ambiguous deployment of the familiar second-person pronoun "tu" and the more formal "vous"—in phrases such as "Si je te vouvoie" [If I say "you" [formal] to you [informal]]—as instances of "enallage," that is, the erroneous substitution of one form for another, from the Greek ἐναλλαγή [enallagē], meaning "interchange."[48]

VIRGIN OF NOWHERE

> Par-dessus l'épaule d'une femme, que voit-on? —une autre femme, répond-elle.[49]

I examine here a recurrent feature in Khatibi's poetic writings, namely the concept of female virginity and more specifically the figure of the female virgin. As Khatibi explains in conversation with Amel, he conceives of "aimance" as enabling an alternative, feminine poetics: "I wanted to graft my text onto a particular sensible relationship to the world, one close to feminine sensibility."[50] As such, "aimance" is meant to evoke the so-called feminine arts: "Carpets (the feminine art par excellence in Morocco), the art of jewelry, tapestries, weaving in general. But also the way of singing or of being in music."[51] Given the prominent role played in "aimance" by sex, it is less clear how the virgin participates in the erotic and poetic economy of Khatibi's texts. I therefore approach this question in two movements—the first devoted to what Khatibi calls "la Vierge de Nulle Part," or "the Virgin of Nowhere," and the second to Khatibi's poetic treatment of the doctrine, familiar not only to Christianity but also to Islam, of the Immaculate Conception.

Consider the following double page spread from *Dédicace à l'année qui vient*, on one side of which we read,

> La vierge de nulle part
>
> The virgin of nowhere[52]

And on the other, noting the acoustic ghost of "aimance" in "hymen scellé,"

> Sur quel hymen scellé
> Annoncer la Louange?
> Avec quel chiffre magique
> Invoquer
> L'augure pré-nuptial?
> La Vierge de nulle part
> Dans l'arrière-pays tout proche
> Portée par le vent et l'Océan
> La Vierge dicible à la cheville tressée
>
> Announcing Praise
> On which sealed hymen?

With which magic cipher
Invoke
The pre-nuptial omen?
The Virgin of nowhere
In the hinterland close by
Carried by the wind and the Ocean
The speakable Virgin with the braided ankle[53]

Discourses as disparate as Talmudic commentary, Mariology, psychoanalysis, forensic medicine, and erotic literature all vest power in the "hymen," what Giulia Sissa dubs "this material token of female intactness, which makes it possible to conceive of a woman's first act of sexual intercourse as a definite, recognizable wound."[54] The presence of "hymen scellé" [sealed hymen] suggests that the virgin evoked here is to be understood as a girl or a woman who has not had sexual relations. Of course, virgins are not always distinguished in this way. Claude Calame notes how the Greek "παρθένος" [parthenos] [virgin] "conveyed a concept of virginity quite different from the one impressed upon our culture by twenty centuries of Marian piety," as it referred to "the young woman who, though pubescent, is not yet married."[55] Similarly, when Isaiah says, "Behold, a virgin shall conceive, and bear a son"[56]—a verse thought to prophesy the birth of Christ—the Hebrew word commonly translated as "virgin," "עַלְמָה" ['alemah], stems from a triconsonantal root conveying a sense of strength or vigor, and also refers to a young woman of child-bearing age. And yet the distinction made here by Khatibi between "vierge" on one side of this diptych of pages and "Vierge" on the other appears to support the notion of a virgin as differently marked, as set apart, as hypostatized—here from a lowercase "v" to an uppercase "V." Accordingly, the Hebrew for a woman who has not had sexual relations is "בְּתוּלָה" [betulah], which is related to the verb "בתל" [batal], meaning "to separate." Similarly in Arabic, the verb "بتل" [batala], to "cut off, sever," gives "البتول" [al-batūl], that is, the Virgin Mary.[57]

When quizzed specifically about the "vierge de nulle part," Khatibi concedes that she is a mythical figure of his own invention: "Yes, it's an image and a thought at the same time. Or rather, a reverie. A Reverie on the nubile body. On the trace and the wound."[58] Khatibi also stages this invention within the poetic texts themselves. As we read in "Notes de mémoire pour les femmes" in *Par-dessus l'épaule*,

> Il inventa cette figure mythique: la vierge – de – nulle – part. A-t-il pris le temps d'en déchiffrer la première syllabe? d'en accueillir l'offrance?[59]

> He invented this mythical figure: the virgin – of – no – where. Has he taken the time to decipher its first syllable? to welcome its offrance?

Despite Khatibi's claim to have invented "la vierge de nulle part," two major sources of inspiration can be determined.

First, this figure appears to stem in part from Khatibi's reading of *Le fou d'Elsa* [Elsa's Madman] (1963), in which Louis Aragon models a poetic reimagination of his wife Elsa Triolet on the figure of Laylá in the ancient Arabic story "Majnūn Laylá." The story tells of the love of the seventh-century Bedouin poet Qays ibn al-Mulawwah for Laylá bint Mahdī, which turns into an obsession for Qays when Laylá's father prevents the lovers from marrying. As Khatibi explains, this absolute love destroys all the usual parameters of human relations: "But we know that Majnūn does not love Laylá. He does not love her presence. Nor her absence, because once absent she could return. Nor her death, because she could rise again in the core of my most affectionate words. So where is she, this virgin of nowhere, in the most beautiful and the purest word? [Où est-elle donc, cette vierge de nulle part, dans le mot le plus beau et le plus pur?]"[60]

Aragon's conceit is to pretend that Elsa exists only in his inscription of her name, which is traced beyond the Arabic approximations of its first two letters—"alif" and "lām"—to the "حروف مقطعات" [ḥurūf muqaṭṭaʿāt], or "disconnected letters," that open a number of the suras in the Qurʾān, as well as to one of the few pre-Islamic Arabian goddesses included in the Qurʾān, namely al-ʿUzzá, whose name means "the most mighty."[61] As Khatibi explains, "You could follow the genealogical wake of the phonetic decomposition of the sacred in the mystique of monotheism (or rather, monotheisms), one next to the other, in their asymmetrical progression toward the Virgin of Nowhere [dans leur procession dissymétrique vers la Vierge de Nulle Part], one of the secret vaults of all courtly love and of the law in its feminine form."[62] The Virgin of Nowhere therefore manifests in Khatibi's critical writings as the telos of a series of acoustic variations on the letters "alif" and "lām." Khatibi says that Elsa becomes "a mosque to [Aragon's] madness, a crypt of courtly love" [une mosquée à sa folie, une crypte de l'amour courtois],[63] and the same might be said of Khatibi's utopian virgin.

Second, the figure with whom Khatibi's placeless virgin is perhaps most usefully approximated appears in *Dīwān*, a trilogy of poetry collections composed by the Swedish poet Gunnar Ekelöf in the final years of his life,[64] and translated into French by Carl Gustaf Bjurström and André Mathieu.[65] The first volume, *Dīwān över Fursten av Emgión* [Diwan on the Prince of

Emgión], opens with the exclamation "Jungfru!" [Virgin!][66] and includes the following lines:

> Jungfru
> du som är den rikaste
> på kyskhet, på okyskhet
> rikast på skönhet, samvaro, rikast på ensamhet
> Jungfru.
>
> Virgin
> you who are the richest
> in chastity, in unchastity
> richest in beauty, in togetherness, richest in loneliness
> Virgin.[67]

Ekelöf's virgin is a paradox, somewhat like Baudelaire's "vierge inféconde" [infertile virgin] in the poem "Allégorie"[68] or his description of God in "Mon cœur mis à nu" as "the most prostituted of beings . . . since he is the common, inexhaustible reservoir of love."[69] Ekelöf's "Jungfru" is both chaste and unchaste or, more specifically, chaste because unchaste, with virginity the result of excessive promiscuity, as we read in the eleventh section of *Vägvisare till underjorden* [Guide to the Underworld], which begins with the reimagining of a quotation from Petronius:

> Ita! Ita! Cur non devirginatur nostra vita?—Jungfrun
> måste devirgineras för att på nytt bli jungfru
> Därför är könet inte till bara för samlag! Högre
> än Oskulden står hon som Ödet gjort till en renad.
> . . .
> Jag vill att dessa anammar Kärleken, som kan vinnas
> om man förlorar sig själv i en annan, om man ger avkall
> på sin fromhets linssoppa, och om man inte är alltför luden!
> Detta är renare än det oskrivna bladets renhet . . .
>
> Yes! Yes! Why is our life not de-virgined?—The virgin
> must be de-virgined to become virgin again
> This is why sex is not just for making love. Higher
> than Innocence stands she whom Fate has purified.
> . . .
> I want these people to convert to the Love that can be won

> by losing oneself in the other, as long as you give up on the lentil soup
> of your piety, and if you are not too hairy!
> This purity is much purer than that of the unwritten page . . .[70]

Ekelöf began writing the *Dīwān* in Istanbul, highly conscious not only of Turkish forms of Islamic spirituality but also of the region's Byzantine past. In the first volume, the anonymous virgin is a "barnlösa moder / åt oss alla" [childless mother / for us all][71] and "Moder åt alla / därför åt ingen / Bröst har du som räcker åt alla"[72] [Mother to all / Therefore to no one / Whose breasts are sufficient for all],[73] with echoes of the multiple breasts of the Ephesian goddess Artemis, or Diana, who, horrified by the prospect of childbirth, obtained eternal virginity from Jupiter.

In the second part of Ekelöf's trilogy, the female figure is dubbed Fatumeh. She is sold into prostitution by her mother, then purchased and impregnated by a man who sees her at a window. The man disappears, her child dies, and she enters the harem of Erechtheion in Athens. As Khatibi explains in his essay on Ekelöf, "Fatumeh is at one and the same time an angel and a prostitute; one soars up to heaven, the other tumbles into bed, then onto the surface of the earth, nailed like a butterfly to a black sheet, watching itself—under the eye of the poet—branching out into the figure of a corpse."[74]

In the final volume of Ekelöf's trilogy, the figure of the virgin is assumed by "the young novice of Split" or "Spálato," who is pursued by a fallen archangel. More than Khatibi's, Ekelöf's virgin can be traced to the figure of Hérodiade in Mallarmé's unfinished project of the same name.[75] In her pursuit of sterile beauty, Hérodiade admires her own reflection in a mirror and objects to being touched by her milk nurse:

> Arrête dans ton crime
> Qui refroidit mon sang vers sa source, et réprime
> Ce geste, impiété fameuse:
> . . .
> Ô mon cœur, cette main encore sacrilège,
> Car tu voulais, je crois, me toucher . . .

> Cease in your crime
> Which freezes my blood back to its source, and repress
> This gesture, famous impiety:
> . . .

Oh my heart, this still sacrilegious hand,
For you wished, I fancy, to touch me . . .[76]

In a similar vein, the angel in *Dīwān* refuses to touch the "novice de Spálato":

Jag . . . vill dig intet
Jag vill bara se dig i din spegel
Jag vill spegla mig i dig
Jag skall inte röra dig
Men du, rena, skall förstå mig
Jag skall älska dig med mina ögon
Jag skall bestråla dig
så att din renhet framstår skönare

I . . . do not want you
I just want to see you in your mirror
I want to reflect myself in you
I'll not touch you
But you, pure, will understand me
I will love you with my eyes
I'm going to irradiate you
so that your purity appears more beautiful[77]

While Mallarmé's Hérodiade performs her virginity in her absolute self-reflection, unsullied by the external world, Ekelöf's concept of virginity is obtained through total communion with the Other such that one loses one's Self.[78]

Although Ekelöf acknowledges the "reluctant" acceptance of Mariology into Christianity, his virgin is no mother of God, no "theotokos."[79] She is instead "Átokos,"[80] a nonproducer, a nullipara, the "neutral," and, like the goddess Diana, an eternal virgin or "Aeiparthenos."[81] Ekelöf's "nullipare"[82]—what we might call his "vierge nullipare" [nulliparous virgin]—brings us into such acoustic proximity with Khatibi's "vierge de nulle part" [virgin of nowhere] that the primary meaning of Khatibi's syntagm begins to distort, as if suffering from magnetic or atmospheric interference. To pass from "nulle part" to "nullipare" requires a semantic shift from "pars, partem," the Latin for "part," "fraction," or "fragment," to "partus," "a bodily bearing or bringing forth," from the verb "parire." In light of Ekelöf's nulliparous virgin, Khatibi's virgin moves from the fragmentation and disconnection associated with "nulle part" toward the logic of generation and genealogy expressed in "nullipare," even as this logic is denied. The presence of "nullipare" in "nulle part" allows not only for the possibility of conventional generation through the loss of virginity but also, beyond Ekelöf, for the possibility of a paradox that Tertullian (Carthage, 155–Carthage, 220) calls "monstrous"[83]—that of a virgin birth, of a birth without intercourse, of an immaculate conception.

MEDITERRANEAN MATRIX

> (ou l'ange Gabriel
> volant vous faire
> un enfant dans le
> dos.[84]

Unlike Ekelöf, who is actively hostile to the Christianity of his upbringing in Sweden, Khatibi is intrigued by religious appropriations of the virgin and allows these to contaminate his poetic imaginary. There are hints of Khatibi's openness to religious discourse in his use of devotional vocabulary, including "sacrement du Poème" [sacrament of the Poem],[85] "Louange" [Praise],[86] "l'Alliance" [the Covenant],[87] "sainte détresse / habillée de prières" [holy distress / clothed in prayers],[88] "aux frontières d'une prière" [at the borders of a prayer],[89] "*fleurs éphémères d'un sacrifice*" [ephemeral flowers of a sacrifice],[90] and so on. In the following fragment, first published in *Par-dessus l'épaule* (1988) and republished unaltered in *Le livre de l'aimance* (1995) and *Aimance* (2003), the Virgin Mary is presented through the medium of ekphrasis, that is, the verbal representation of a visual work of art:

> En admirant "l'Immaculée Conception" (l'original) de Velasquez, il nota ceci: Elle est entre ciel et terre, sur fond de nuages lumineux. Elle baisse les yeux. Les pieds couverts par les franges de la robe. Le drapé: beauté du manteau, en mouvement dans le cœur des nuages, y dansant discrètement. Une couronne d'étoiles autour de la tête. De nouveau, le drapé cache les formes, les seins.
>
> La jouissance n'est-elle pas cette force d'appel entre le ciel et la terre? et leur attraction de seconde main? Un drap s'enroule sur ses plis de mémoire feutrée.
>
> While admiring the *Immaculate Conception* (the original) by Velázquez, he noted this: She is between heaven and earth,

against a backdrop of luminous clouds. She lowers her eyes. Her feet covered by the fringes of her dress. The drapery: beauty of the mantle, moving in the heart of the clouds, dancing discreetly. A crown of stars around the head. Again, the drapery hides her forms, her breasts.

Is pleasure not this force of appeal between heaven and earth? and their second-hand attraction? A drape wraps around its folds of felted memory.[91]

Inmaculada concepción (fig. 9) was painted in Seville around 1618 by a then still teenage Diego Velázquez (Seville, 1599–Madrid, 1660).[92] The rectangular image depicts the Virgin Mary on a semi-translucent lunar orb, emerging from a break in the clouds over a coastline. She is dressed in a purple robe

FIG. 9. Diego de Silva Velázquez, *Inmaculada Concepción / The Immaculate Conception*, oil on canvas, 1618–1619, 135 × 101.6 cm. National Gallery, London, bought with the aid of The Art Fund, 1974, inv. no. NG 6424.

and dark-blue cloak, whose "autonomous, always multipliable folds"[93] cover her entire body except for her bare head and her wrists and hands, which are placed together as if in prayer. The eyes are turned downward, and her brown hair hangs loose about the shoulders. Velázquez had trained in the studio of Francisco Pacheco[94] and painted this picture at around the time that he married his master's daughter, Juana (Seville, 1602–Madrid, 1660), who may have been the model for Mary.[95] Although one of Velázquez's most iconic paintings, it is not an original composition, but instead draws on similar works that could be seen in Seville at the time—specifically *Inmaculada* (Palacio Arzobispal, Seville, 1589), one of the very few known works of Cristóbal Gómez, who was active in the late sixteenth century, as well as various polychromed wood statues by the sculptor Juan Martínez Montañés (Alcalá la Real, 1568–Seville, 1649).[96]

The notion of Mary's immaculate conception enjoyed great popularity at the time of this painting's creation, especially in Seville, despite having no basis in sacred, that is, recognized Christian scripture.[97] The myth is usually traced to the account of Mary's miraculous birth in the *Protoevangelium* of James the Less, an apocryphal gospel written around the middle or second half of the second century that focuses on the life of Mary and the infancy of Christ.[98] An angel appears to the childless Anne while she is praying underneath a laurel tree in which sparrows are nesting to announce that she will give birth. Anne promises to offer the child as a sacrifice to God. At the same time, another angel appears to Joachim, announcing the same news. The description of the meeting between Anne and Joachim at the Golden Gate in Jerusalem after this split annunciation has been the focus of many paintings, including a panel from 1305 by Giotto di Bondone in the Scrovegni Chapel in Padua. Curiously, and despite his avoidance of Christian themes in his poetry, Ekelöf's *Dīwān* also includes a poem on this conjugal encounter.[99]

The need to elaborate a myth of the immaculate conception stems in the first place from the doctrine of the Incarnation. For Christ to have been fully divine as man, he would have to have been conceived without sin, and for this to have occurred, the woman who bore him would have to have been not only virgin "in partu" (i.e., in the act of giving birth) but also herself born without sin. Although the early fathers of the Church agreed on Mary's sinlessness and holiness, and although some of them were familiar with James the Less's gospel, none embraced the notion of her immaculate conception explicitly. This is true of Origen in the third century, even as he called Mary "the one most suitable to bear God's Son."[100] In the fourth century, Ambrose, much invested both in the theology of virginity and Marian devotion, discussed neither Mary's conception nor her assumption.[101]

Later, Thomas Aquinas expressly opposed the idea of Mary's immaculate conception, although he allowed for the sanctification of Mary in the womb and the prenatal gift of grace and liberation from guilt.[102] By contrast, John Duns Scotus, the so-called "Doctor of the Immaculate Conception," argued that Mary's birth was a "praeredemptio" and that she could be considered, recursively, free from sin.[103]

In early seventeenth-century Spain, when Velázquez was still a trainee in Pacheco's studio, Philip III responded to popular pressure by sending two embassies to Rome to request a papal decree confirming the miraculous circumstances of Mary's conception. An apostolic constitution published by Paul V in 1617 prohibited preachers from publicly denying the doctrine.[104] In December 1661, in the dying days of the reign of Philip IV and months after Velázquez's death, Alexander VII issued the bull *Sollicitudo omnium ecclesiarum* [The Care of All Churches], which taught that the Virgin had been conceived without original sin. These texts would largely provide the justification for *Ineffabilis Deus* [Ineffable God] (1854), in which Pius IX officially established the Virgin Mary's immaculate conception as dogma.[105]

Velázquez's painting was likely commissioned for the local Convento del Carmen Calzado, Nuestra Señora del Carmen, alongside the painting of St. John the Evangelist on the island of Patmos (National Gallery, London, 1618–19), which includes a miniature apparition of the Virgin in the top left. The Carmelites trace a prefiguration of the Virgin to a passage in the first book of Kings that tells of the prophet Elijah on Mount Carmel, looking down at the sea from where "there ariseth a little cloud . . . like a man's hand,"[106] presaging the arrival of rain and the end of the drought.[107] In the Hebrew text, the cloud is "עב" [ʻav]—related to "עבי" [ʻavi], meaning "thick"—and properly intends a dark or dense envelope. Velázquez presents Mary accordingly, as if she were emerging from a fold in a troubled sky. But despite the topic of the painting, and the general fervor around this devotion at the time, there is little to suggest that Velázquez himself was much interested in questions of theology. On leaving Seville for the court of Philip IV in Madrid in 1623—at the invitation of his fellow Hispalian Count Olivares—he was no longer bound by market preferences and largely ceased to paint pictures on religious themes.[108]

In a preliminary reading of this fragment by Khatibi, we might surmise that the Moroccan poet is similarly disinterested in the theological implications of the Immaculate Conception. His presentation of Mary between earth and sky, and his pleasure at seeing her thus suspended, identifies Mary as a poetic figure. In his writings on the Austrian poet Rainer Maria Rilke, Khatibi identifies this same suspension as a function of the poet's necessary solitude: "He seems to float in transparency and weightlessness" such that he is able to identify himself with any feature of his "féerie," his imagined universe, "from a state of petrification to the stellar dance of an angel or a magic bird."[109] Khatibi's presentation of Mary also echoes Mallarmé's "Ballets," a text Khatibi knew well, and which begins, "La Cornalba delights me, she dances as if undressed; . . . she appears, called into the air, to sustain herself there, by the Italian fact of the voluptuous tension of her person [elle paraît, appelée dans l'air, s'y soutenir, du fait italien d'une moelleuse tension de sa personne]."[110] Whereas for Mallarmé, the ballerina becomes "poème dégagé de tout appareil du scribe" [poem liberated from any apparatus of the scribe], for Khatibi, Mary operates as "intersigne."[111] She is an intermediary between realms—"Elle est entre ciel et terre"—and hovers between heaven and earth, between word and image, between one trace and another, but also between the sexes.

By means of this ekphrasis, Mary becomes for Khatibi what Elsa is for Louis Aragon, what Arachne is for Tahar Djaout, and perhaps above all, what Nedjma is for Kateb Yacine. This is not because Mary is burdened with the heavy metaphor of a nation—the historical period in which Khatibi operates as well as the cultural frames of reference he chooses to reflect on are different from Kateb's—but on account of the Arabic word from which Nedjma's name comes. The Arabic nouns "نجمة" [najmah] or "نجم" [najm] mean "star," but the verb "نجم" [najama] properly denotes that which appears, rises, breaks forth and comes toward us—like a constellation in the heavens, or like a new nation from under colonial oppression, or like Velázquez's virgin, pictured emerging from a slit in the sky. As Khatibi writes in *Aimance*,

> Le corps désiré: lustration, draperie, parure, déploiement d'une apparition qui va et vient: vous-même.
>
> The desired body: lustration, drapery, adornment, deployment of an apparition which goes and comes: you, yourself.[112]

Kateb establishes Nedjma on the banks of "the Great River, the Oued El Kebir, in memory of the other, lost river, the Guadalquivir, which the Moors, driven out of Andalusia, had to leave behind,"[113] noting the onomastic and mythical, if not actual, confluence of these two Mediterranean streams: "Guadalquivir, Oued El Kebir, the river abandoned in Spain was found beyond the Strait but vanquished this time; hunted under the rock."[114] Here, the Immaculate Conception floats above the first of these rivers, which, having flowed past Velázquez's native Seville, slides into the Atlantic Ocean at Sanlúcar de Barrameda. Velázquez's virgin is neither a "vierge nullipare," nor a "vierge de nulle part." She is instead, to borrow Nabile Farès's term, "l'Étoile *obscure de l'Andalousie*" [the *obscure* Star *of Andalusia*][115] and establishes a specifically Mediterranean matrix in Khatibi's poetic imaginary.

More than the concept of the "vierge de nulle part," the Immaculate Conception also affords an acute sense of the Muslim dimension of Khatibi's poetic writing. Khatibi often reminds his readers that he is "of Islamic origin"[116] and that the weft of his writing is run through with the texts, mythologies, and practices of Islam. In *Par-dessus l'épaule*, he claims to be intrigued by a "peculiar subterranean rapport between, on the one hand, literature and, on the other, the prophetic word of the Qur'ān."[117] Just such a hypogean relationship between literature and Islam can be identified in this fragment on the Immaculate Conception. Specifically, it asks to be considered in light of three Qur'ānic episodes.

First, Islamic commentators provide accounts of the conception of Mary—called Maryam—that closely resemble that recounted in the second century by James the Less and repeated in the 1960s by Ekelöf. Despite being old and barren, Hannah (not Anna), wife of 'Imrān (not Joachim), saw a bird feeding its young and consequently "felt eager to beget children."[118] Ibn Kathīr (Bosra, 1300–Damascus, 1373) and other commentators plainly state that Maryam's parents had intercourse,[119] but the Qur'ān itself is silent on this delicate point. Instead, in the third sura, "The House of 'Imrān," Anna is reported as saying,

> رَبِّ إِنِّي نَذَرْتُ لَكَ مَا فِي بَطْنِي مُحَرَّرًا
>
> [Rabbi innī nadhartu laka mā fī baṭnī muḥarraran]
>
> My Lord, truly I dedicate to Thee what is in my belly, in consecration.[120]

The Qur'ān does not describe the conception of Maryam as miraculous, let alone immaculate. Instead, the conception is celebrated as a dedication, from the Arabic "نذر" [nadhr] [vow, pledge]—a dedication perhaps echoed in the title of Khatibi's collection *Dédicace à l'année qui vient* [Consecration to the year that comes]. The sense that Khatibi appropriates and reinscribes this myth as part of his "legendary country" is enhanced by the central role played by the "vœu," or "vow," in the following lines:

Ainsi la distance rituelle
Consacre l'accolade
Et de lèvre à lèvre
Le Vœu empourpre tes esprits.
Le Pacte férial
N'unit-il pas tes mains!
Et d'où vient
Cette splendeur de l'Attrait?
A quel ensourcement
De l'irrévélé
Es-tu consécration?

Thus the ritual distance
Dedicates the accolade
And from lip to lip
The Vow flushes your spirits.
The ferial Pact
Doesn't it bring your hands together!
And from where does
This splendor of Attraction come?
To which establishment
of the unrevealed
Are you a consecration?[121]

In addition to the description of Maryam's conception, the Qur'ān includes two distinct accounts of how her own son ʿĪsá, or Jesus, is conceived. In the nineteenth sura, "Maryam"—a matricial chapter in more ways than one[122]—Christ's conception occurs when Maryam is approached by a male figure:

وَٱذْكُرْ فِى ٱلْكِتَـٰبِ مَرْيَمَ إِذِ ٱنتَبَذَتْ مِنْ أَهْلِهَا مَكَانًا شَرْقِيًّا فَٱتَّخَذَتْ مِن دُونِهِمْ حِجَابًا
فَأَرْسَلْنَآ إِلَيْهَا رُوحَنَا فَتَمَثَّلَ لَهَا بَشَرًا سَوِيًّا

[Wa-dhkur fī l-kitābi Maryama idh intabadhat min ahlihā makānan sharqiyyan fa-ttakhadhat min dūnihim ḥijāban fa-arsalnā ilayhā rūḥanā fa-tamaththala lahā basharan sawiyyā]

And remember [Maryam] in the Book, when she withdrew from her family to an eastern place. And she veiled herself from them. Then We sent unto her Our Spirit, and it assumed for her the likeness of a perfect man.[123]

The perfectly formed being is often thought to be the angel Jibrīl, or Gabriel. This is echoed in teachings by al-Ṭabarī (Amol, 839–Baghdad, 923) and al-Zamakhsharī (Khwarazm, 1074–Gurganj, 1143), who explain that "the angel came to her as a young, smooth-faced man with pure countenance, curly hair, and a well-built body, without exhibiting a single blemish in his human appearance," noting that, "had he appeared to her in the form of an angel, she would have fled from him and would not have been able to hear what he had to say."[124]

The other Qur'ānic account of Christ's conception is of greater importance to understanding the role of the virgin in Khatibi's poetics. It occurs in the twenty-first sura, called "The Prophets":

وَٱلَّتِىٓ أَحْصَنَتْ فَرْجَهَا فَنَفَخْنَا فِيهَا مِن رُّوحِنَا وَجَعَلْنَـٰهَا وَٱبْنَهَآ ءَايَةً لِّلْعَـٰلَمِينَ

> [Wa-llatī aḥṣanat farjahā fa-nafakhnā fīhā min rūḥinā wa-ja'al-nāhā wa-bnahā āyatan lil'ālamīn]
>
> And as for she who preserved her chastity, We breathed into her of Our Spirit, and made her and her son a sign for the worlds.[125]

The translation "And as for she who preserved her chastity" does not quite capture the precise sense, perhaps even the bodily shape, of the Arabic text. "والّتي أحصنت فرجها" [wa-llatī aḥṣanat farjahā] literally means "and she who guarded" or "fortified her opening."[126] Although "farj" can obtain an anatomical sense—including the vulva—commentators such as al-Baydawī (Beyda, mid-1200s–Tabriz, 1319) interpret this phrase as meaning that the spirit "was breathed through an opening" of Maryam's shirt or its sleeve.[127] Ibn Kathīr suggests that Gabriel "breathed into the pockets of Mary's mail, and that breath found its way to her vulva causing her to conceive right away just as all women do after sexual intercourse with their husbands,"[128] which exegesis is echoed by numerous Islamic scholars.[129] For some, Gabriel blows into a fold in her gown, or into her sleeve, or into the opening around her neck. For others, her clothing was torn at the breast, and the spirit entered that way. For still others, the spirit passed through her mouth, although al-Qāsimī (Damascus, 1866–Damascus, 1914) insists that the spirit was blown directly into her pudendum.[130] Whatever the mechanics and metaphysics of conception endorsed, all commentators acknowledge the presence of fabrics and the gaps, holes, folds, rips, seams, slits, and tears that alone enable an appropriately chaste conception.[131] The ninth-century Islamic scholar Muḥammad al-Bukhārī (Bukhara, 810–Khartank, 870) advised the faithful to keep their private parts veiled from sight at all times, even during intercourse.[132] As Khatibi reminds us, the Prophet's third and preferred wife, 'Ā'ishah, is reported to have said of her husband, "I never saw his sex, and he never saw mine."[133]

Khatibi's poetics is in part predicated on a similar medley of cloths, drapes, and veils, all "symbol[s] of femininity."[134] In Khatibi's novel *Le livre du sang* [The Book of Blood], the androgynous Échanson is introduced to the reader in folds of silence: "Silence, silence drapé de souffles irréguliers" [Silence, silence draped in irregular breaths].[135] More particularly, Khatibi's poems often include scenarios that appear to reimagine Maryam's encounter with the angel, such as in this passage of *Dédicace à l'année qui vient*, in which the first person adopts the perspective of divine messenger:

> Et si je fais un faux pas sans vous toucher
> Sachez alors que je m'envole doucement
> Sous les nuances de vos bras drapés
>
> And if I should take a false step without touching you
> Know then that I am flying away softly
> Under the nuances of your draped arms[136]

Echoes of this undertaking are also evident in Khatibi's ekphrasis of Velázquez's painting:

> Les pieds couverts par les franges de la robe. Le drapé: beauté du manteau, en mouvement . . . le drapé cache les formes, les seins. . . . Un drap s'enroule sur ses plis de mémoire feutrée.
>
> Her feet covered by the fringes of her dress. The drapery: beauty of the mantle, moving . . . the drapery hides her forms, her breasts. . . . A drape wraps around its folds of felted memory.[137]

And in *Dédicace à l'année qui vient*, he writes,

> Crois-moi: dois-je ainsi jurer
> Par la fente de ta jupe?
>
> Believe me: must I thus swear
> By the slit of your skirt?[138]

Laurent Dubreuil cites these lines as evidence of an "irritating and hackneyed machismo,"[139] but it might be worth bearing in mind that, for Khatibi, "jupe" comes to French via the Italian "jupa" from the Latin "juppum," itself a borrowing from the Arabic "جبة" [jubbah], which is "a long outer garment, open in front, with wide sleeves,"[140] usually worn by men but comparable to Mary's "manteau," the dark-red outer garment depicted in the painting by Velázquez.

Khatibi's ekphrasis of *Inmaculada concepción* can simultaneously be inscribed in a Western tradition of literary representations of well-known works of art and in an Islamic tradition—both religious and secular, pious and erotic—of writings on Maryam, the mother of ʿĪsá.[141] Beyond this double inscription, Khatibi's translation of Velázquez's virgin into text, and his insistence on her drapery, teaches us an important lesson that studies focusing exclusively on "aimance" will not notice. Namely that, in Khatibi's poetry, folds are generative. Gilles Deleuze notes how the baroque fold liberates itself from the simple task of giving form to the body, just as it liberates itself from painting and then from sculpture, to fully unfurl itself in the architecture of the seventeenth-century city. As it multiplies, as if to infinity, the baroque fold acquires "autonomy, scale, *not simply for the sake of decoration* but to express the intensity of a spiritual force that exerts itself on the body."[142] For Khatibi—perhaps seduced more by Velázquez than by Deleuze—the fold becomes the place not only where a spiritual force expresses itself but where conception takes place. This conception is no longer punctual, discrete, but continuous, a conception where gestation is both immediate and repeatedly deferred. Khatibi invites us to look upon this poetics of the fold as a feminine mode of writing, similar to that which he identifies in *Le fou d'Elsa*, where Aragon exploits masculine and feminine rhymes to construct "a musical drape," "a counterpoint by which the feminine drapes the masculine" [le féminin *drape* le masculin]—the feminine being "the asymmetrical supplement of the other, its becoming."[143]

DISSYMMETRIC CONCEPTIONS

> Tatouage chiffré:
> khamsa /vulve /rythme[144]

I now introduce another image that will enable us to set the poetics that Khatibi draws from the figure of the female virgin into sharper relief and to see Velázquez's *Inmaculada concepción* in a new light. The image is reproduced in Khatibi's *La blessure du nom propre*, where it is entitled "Le corps subverti: tatouage" [The Subverted Body: Tattooing] (fig. 10). This illustration, in black and red ink, includes two diagrams of the same naked female body: one seen from the front, the other from the back. It is as if the woman imagined beneath the veils of the "Immaculate Conception" has been uncovered. Her hair still hangs down, parted in the middle, but now her forms, breasts, and tattoos are visible. The hands that Velázquez's virgin presses loosely together are hidden in each diagram to reveal, in turn, the buttocks and the pudenda.

Just as this illustration draws on the visual tropes of Western painting, even as it presents instances of Moroccan tattooing, Velázquez's painting

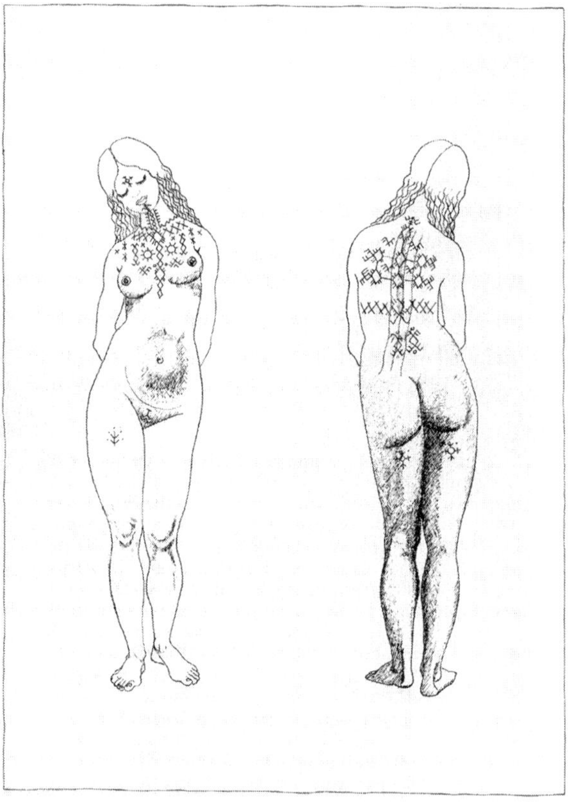

FIG. 10. Anonymous, "Le corps subverti: Tatouage / The Subverted Body: Tattoo." Reproduced in Abdelkébir Khatibi, *La blessure du nom propre* (Paris: Éditions Denoël, 1974), 84. Reproduced by kind permission of Lalla Mina El Alaoui Khatibi.

participates, albeit in obscure ways, in a Maghrebi aesthetic. Consider, for example, the orange fringe that surrounds the edges of Mary's garments, a sort of idealized afterbirth, which calls to mind the orange-brown stain of henna. In traditional Moroccan culture, henna is applied to the bride before marriage to mark the imminent loss of her virginity. The orange-brown stain, whose gradual disappearance serves as a visual register for the first fortnight of new sexual relations, is a central feature in what Khatibi calls "the erotics of henna":[145] "The *red-yellow* color alters according to the rhythm of the days and disappears after between ten and fifteen days. Color *between* the abduction and the legal appropriation, *between* the hymen and the satisfaction of pleasure, henna thus lasts during this nuptial period when coitus is still difficult and laborious."[146] Once set alongside Khatibi's writings, both poetic and sociological, the orange edging around Velázquez's virgin becomes reminiscent of a less-than-immaculate encounter. It marks the pain of preliminary penetrations but also *jouissance*, the development of habits, and the expansion of familiarity. It is a trace, in other words, of the "force of appeal" that inheres between different realms as identified by Khatibi in his ekphrasis—between "sky and earth," between the human and the divine, but also between man and woman.

The residual traces of Moroccan culture in Velázquez's picture may call for a more precise historical contextualization. Beginning in 1609, a decade before this painting was executed, Philip III signed a series of decrees ordering the deportation from Spain of Muslim converts to Catholicism, sometimes called "Moriscos." This was the last act of what Fernand Braudel calls "the slow shipwreck of Iberian Islam"[147] that had begun with the surrender of Abū ʿAbd Allāh Muḥammad XII (Granada, ca. 1460–Fès, 1533), better known as Boabdil, to Ferdinand II and Isabella I outside Granada in 1492.[148] Between 1609 and 1614, thousands of Moriscos were deported from Iberia to cities on the north coast of Africa, such as Algiers, Tunis, and Salé, taking with them what one historian calls "the last vestiges of medieval Spain's religious pluralism."[149] Philip IV—the so-called "rey planeta" [planet king] and Velázquez's champion—considered this mass deportation to be the conclusion of the "sacred reconquest" of the Iberian peninsula from the Islamic "invaders" and his father's only notable achievement.[150] A painting contest was held at El Escorial in 1627 to mark the expulsion, which the young Velázquez won, beating a number of older and more established painters at the court.[151] This sudden success transformed Velázquez's career. He was rewarded with the position of gentleman usher in the king's household, introducing what José Ortega y Gasset describes as a terrible ambiguity into the painter's vocation: "Was it to be the life of a painter or that of a courtier?"[152] Velázquez turned out to be as much a prodigal but reluctant painter as he was an ambitious and enthusiastic nobleman. The painter Antonio Palomino (Bujalance, 1655–Madrid, 1726) plainly asserts that Velázquez's employment at court deprived the world of "many more proofs of his rare skill."[153]

It should be noted in passing that in Pacheco's variations on the Immaculate Conception—created around the same time as his former student's famous piece—traces of the Maghreb and of Islam are much more clearly in evidence.[154] One version (fig. 11) depicts the palm tree under which Maryam is said, in the Qur'ān, to have given birth to Jesus, alone in her eastern exile: "And the pangs of childbirth drove her to the trunk of a date palm. She said, 'Would that I had died before this and were a thing forgotten, utterly forgotten!' So he called out to her from below her, 'Grieve not! Thy Lord has

FIG. 11. Francisco Pacheco, *Inmaculada con Miguel del Cid / The Immaculate Conception with Miguel Cid*, oil on canvas, 1619, 179 × 108 cm. Cathedral of Seville. Courtesy of the Chapter of the Cathedral of Seville.

placed a rivulet beneath thee. And shake toward thyself the trunk of the date palm; fresh, ripe dates shall fall upon thee.'"[155] It also shows La Giralda, the cathedral tower, built in 1198 as the minaret of the main mosque in Seville and intended to resemble that of the Koutoubia Mosque in Marrakech. All remnants of a recently obliterated Muslim Maghrebi past in Andalusia that, in contrast to his father-in-law, Velázquez does little to retain.

The other effect of the approximation of Khatibi's diagrams and Velázquez's painting, more closely related to the argument of this chapter, is that it invites us to reflect on the different ways that the tattoo and the fold create meaning. As the epigraph quoted at the head of this section appears to summarize, the tattoo has a double function, drawn from pre-Islamic pagan traditions—namely, to repel evil and to provoke desire. If, as Khatibi argues, "symmetry is regulated by the divine order"[156] and is the mark of Islamic art as much as of its theology, then the tattoo is by contrast inherently unstable and unsettling: "Inscribing on the body goes back to an archaic type of writing that predates divine symmetry. The tattoo allows for this erotic duel between symmetry and asymmetry, this lively economy of amorous expenditure and of a split, dramatized desire."[157]

Depictions of the Immaculate Conception, such as those created in the early seventeenth century by Velázquez, Pacheco, and others, also appear to privilege visual symmetry, with the virgin placed centrally, thereby reflecting toward the viewer the brilliant, unhindered light of doctrine. When we consider the degree to which Christ's conception is bound up with his mother's, both needing to be immaculate, then the notion of their perfect symmetry, of the immediate reflection of one in the other, is only enhanced.[158] But the juxtaposition of Velázquez's veiled virgin with the tattooed body in Khatibi's book alerts us to a common troubling of the symmetrical and the orders it represents, and it is in these interstices that we are invited to read. As Khatibi asserts in *La blessure du nom propre*, "The *doxological* body"—that is, the body that "glorifies" God (from the Greek "δόξα" [doxa], meaning here "glory"), perhaps even the body that literally bears the "word" of God (from "λόγος" [logos], meaning "that which is said")—"should be read like an intersemiotic score."[159]

In both the sacred and the profane image, the model stands with her weight on one leg, in a modest contrapposto, right shoulder dipped, as if in the process of shrugging off the designs of another, be they divine or mundane. The slight inflection of the knee, the bent neck, the head tipped sideways, are all subtle indications of resistance, and of the participation in the erotic duel between symmetry and its imperfections. Khatibi further amplifies these gestures by inverting the conventional norms of propriety. For

Khatibi, it is the tattooed woman who is covered, and the veiled virgin who is naked. The tattoo is a "vêtement écrit,"[160] an inscribed garment. As he puts it, "Let's call the totality of drawings decorating the body a 'fabric' [*tissu*]," before concluding, "The back, the thighs, and the buttocks are now united with the text."[161] The purpose of Khatibi's ekphrasis, on the other hand, is to reveal the "forms" and "breasts" that Velázquez's painting conceals.[162]

The tattoo and the fold, both visual forms of rhythm, share a logic of dissymmetry with inscribed language. It is what Mourad Yelles, in conversation with Habib Tengour, calls—in reference not only to Tengour's name but to the pitching of the ship in the opening poem of Mallarmé's *Poésies*—"tangage."[163] Or as Khatibi writes, "There is dissymmetry between the two, fold, veiling, scansion, and loss of meaning—this is inevitable."[164] Much like that of the tattoo and the fold, the purpose of Khatibi's poetry is to repeatedly create a sense of imbalance, to catch the reader midstep, to cause them to stumble, to require them to read again. Mallarmé describes the reader's progress succinctly in "Un coup de dés" [A Toss of the Dice] in a fragment that reads: "selon telle obliquité par telle déclivité" [according to such obliquity by such declivity].[165]

There is, though, one important way in which the tattoo and the fold differ, and where the analogy of veiled virgin and tattooed prostitute diverges and becomes untenable. It is that the tattoo has signs but no syntax. The tattoo enables punctual, discrete, disconnected readings, constellated expressions of novel thought. The operative function of the fold, on the other hand, is fundamentally intermediary. The fold is the part of Velázquez's iconography that comes closest to being verbal. It belongs to the visible world but refuses to be fully visual. It lends itself to and resists representation. It conceals forms and takes on no definite form itself. It is infinite in its possible modulations. If Islam joins with Christianity in believing Maryam to have received and given birth to God's Word or "كلمة" [kalimah],[166] then Khatibi, drawing on Velázquez, shows us that the Word is manifest not as man born to a virgin, not as incarnation, but in the reader's encounter with the folds of the virgin's dress, the "ḥijāb" or "veil" that Mary draws between herself and the outside world to give birth in her eastern exile, or what Mallarmé called, after an evening watching ballet, "le dernier voile qui toujours reste" [the final veil that always remains].[167] If conception can be said to take place, it occurs in passing, in the parerga, not in an immaculate body at all, but around a concealed body: "C'est, voyez-vous, la manière de draper son corps, ses plis couverts" [It is, you see, the way she drapes her body, her covered folds].[168] Velázquez and the Qur'ān each displace the Incarnation from the body to the folds that surround the body. It is this crucial displacement that Khatibi appropriates and develops throughout his poetic writing, specifically through his handling of syntax. Only syntax can approximate the articulations of the fold. This is why Derrida, with reference to Mallarmé's late essay "Crisis of Verse," can speak of "the syntax of the curtain, of the screen, of the veil . . ."[169]

SYNTACTIC SCRUPLES

> O frères! si notre syntaxe elle-même
> n'est pas un rouage de la liberté . . .[170]

Few critics have attended to the role that syntax plays in Khatibi's poetics. Barbara Johnson half jokes that it is "not an inherently exciting subject,"[171] echoing what Roland Barthes once called "l'ennui de la syntaxe" [the boredom of syntax].[172] And yet whatever the topic of discussion, Khatibi never leaves syntax untouched. In a short article written in 1997, he confesses, "Syntax is my target . . . , my delight, my passion, my factory of folly, my wiretapping set. And, as Supervielle, this magnificent lyric poet puts it, 'mon oublieuse mémoire' [my forgetful memory]. . . . Syntax expands the space of hospitality where the writer is received in his or her own text as a guest, in the shadow of the reader."[173] He notes that, historically, the French language set itself apart from other altered forms of Latin not by its lexicon but by a syntax that bore the imprint of a particular local idiom: "This is where the initial principle of identity [of the French language] lies . . . and in relation to which we are all inscribed, French as well as francophone, with our languages, our idioms, our cultures, long before colonization and the French Empire."[174] Although the Moroccan form of dialectal Arabic is Khatibi's mother tongue, it is not the only language that invades, pacifically or otherwise, his written French: "I practice, more or less, five languages: Arabic, French, English, Spanish, Swedish, and a few scraps of an idiom commonly called Berber."[175] When he incorporates vocabulary from these languages into his written French, he has "a tendency, in this play of weaving, to disseminate the foreign lexicon throughout the movement of the syntax." It is Khatibi's idiosyncratic deployment of a syntax suited to his "linguistic sensibility"[176] that enables him to inhabit French in a new way, such that French becomes his "demeure," a dwelling that is always in the process of losing and retaking syntactic shape: "To write, to erase, to write again, until the end of days . . ."[177] This is an instance of what Derrida calls "displacement without reversal," which is "always an effect of language or writing, of syntax, never simply a dialectical reversal of the concept (signified)."[178]

Unlike Rimbaud, whose syntax Khatibi considers "unique" if not inimitable, Mallarmé provides him with a model for writing.[179] In an interview with Maurice Guillemot in October 1895, the future "prince of poets" is reported to have said, "You realize then that I am profoundly and scrupulously syntactic [profondément et scrupuleusement syntaxier], that my writing is devoid of obscurity, that my phrase is as it should be."[180] At first sight, "συντάσσω" [syntassō], from "σύν" [syn] [with] and "τάσσω" [tassō] [to arrange], promises an almost martial ordering or construction. But Mallarmé, like Khatibi, knows that the etymological roots of "τάσσω" spread wide and deep, with cognates in Latin ("tango" [to touch]) and Old English ("þaccian" [to touch, to pat]). This explains why, in one of the most famous modern defenses of poetic obscurity, written in response to an attack by the young Marcel Proust, Mallarmé uses the verb "appuyer" [to touch, to press] to describe the way the reading eye meets the written text. As it reads, the eye pushes up against the phrase and mollifies its roughness, finding the sequence of rhythms required to release its tension: "—Appuyer, selon la page, au blanc, qui l'inaugure son ingénuité, à soi, oublieuse même du titre qui parlerait trop haut" [—To press, according to the page, to the whiteness, which inaugurates its ingenuity, to itself, forgetful even of the title, which would speak too loudly].[181] Mallarmé here comes close to describing the tact required for Arabic calligraphy, where the dimensions of the script depend on the correct amount of pressure being applied to the "qalam," or reed. The size of the letter "alif," the unit by which all other letters are measured, is established by a set number of square points made by the tip of the "qalam," and therefore depends "on the way the reed pen is cut and on the pressure applied by the fingers [la pression digitale]. This pressure must be both supple and precise enough to separate the two lips of the tip of the reed."[182]

In *Le corps oriental* [The Oriental Body], Khatibi speaks of touch as "لمس" [lams]: "To palpate, to touch with the hand, to deflower a girl or have fun with her, to ask, to pray to or for someone. This word suggests the body's vulnerability, its fragility, regardless of whether the body is healthy or sick, masculine or feminine, noble or popular, delicate or coarse. A vulnerability that seeks to love, to procure pleasure."[183] As Khatibi indicates, the verb "لمس" [lamasa] tends toward the range of passive modes of touching. It is touch in which the sensation of softness remains, as is evident in its derivatives including "لميس" [lamīs] [soft to the touch], "ملموس" [malmūs] [touched, felt], "تلمّس" [talammus] [search, quest], and even "ملتمس" [multamas] [request, petition, application].[184]

Another verb meaning "to touch," namely "مسّ" [massa], has harsher connotations. It is properly "to finger," "to handle," "to palpate," such as when a teenage Rimbaud describes the poet's task as follows: "Il devra faire sentir, palper, écouter ses inventions" [He will have to make us feel, palpate, listen to his inventions].[185] Metonymically, "massa" can mean to cohabit with a woman, as well as to violate or infringe upon another's space.[186] It is used to define legal sexual intercourse, not least in the Qur'ān. When Maryam asks Gabriel how she can conceive without having touched or having been touched, she uses the verb "massa" to articulate her dilemma: "My Lord, how shall I have a child while no man has touched me [ولم يمسسني بشر (wa-lam yamsasnī bashar)]."[187] As the legal framing of this type of "touching" reveals, it is associated with misfortune or calamity, including encroachment, physical attacks, and unstable psychological states—insanity, madness, frenzy, possession, fever.[188]

The touching Mallarmé and Khatibi require for literature is of the former type: "Writing takes place with approximate strokes [par touches approximatives], with touchings [par tâtonnements], with greater or lesser gaps between the will to write and its shaping, always unfinished, breakable, detachable into fragments."[189] It is with the imbrication of syntax and erotics—as well as the practice or praxis not only of writing and of calligraphy but of reading—that we might more fully understand the significance of Khatibi's presentation of his entire poetic oeuvre as being a treatise on touching:

J'écris pour les aimants
Sur peau-de-gazelle
Et si je vous imagine,
Lectrice et lecteur,
Découper ces feuillets
Avec le chiffre d'or
Et sa double joie de mirage
C'est que je vous confie
De main en main cachée
Un traité du Toucher

I write for lovers
On gazelle skin
And if I imagine you,
Reader and you, reader,
Cutting out these pages

With the golden figure
And its double joy of mirage
It's because I'm entrusting you
Hidden from hand to hand
With a treatise on Touching[190]

The treatise on touching that Khatibi entrusts to us throughout his poetic writings cannot be understood without reference to the figure of the female virgin, the virgin of nowhere, who might also, as per Ekelöf, be the virgin of everywhere: "Where does our pleasure come from? From nowhere, since the virgin has never existed anywhere, except in myth."[191] In poetry, as in religion and mythology, virginity is a trick, a fraud, a hustle. There is no pure origin. There are only beginnings: "The virginal is not found in the virgin [la vierge] but at the beginning of each new encounter."[192] The hustle of virginity is, in Western culture, closely tied to the notion of the Incarnation, that is, the manifestation of God as man, which, in *Maghreb pluriel*, Khatibi identifies as the defining feature of Western metaphysics.[193] Unlike Ekelöf, though, who turns resolutely away from established religions, Khatibi decides to see what can be gleaned from the "theological enclosure"[194] not only of Islam but also of Catholicism. When, in *La blessure du nom propre*, Khatibi asserts that the subordination of Maghrebi culture to the West "calls for a similar decentering"[195] of Western culture, he must also have in mind such fundamental Christian concepts as the Incarnation. His poetic writings therefore continue the work of displacement begun in the Qur'ān, which relegates the conception of Jesus to a serendipitous gap in the fabric covering his mother's body, and in Velázquez's painting, which dislocates conception to the virgin's ample folds. For the Incarnation to be displaced from the French language, the modern poet must continue to dislocate conception to the folds that join pages, lines of verse, phrases, words, and letters. As in the Immaculate Conception, there is no human father, no father to speak of, but there is no mother either. There is no annunciation or revelation, just an infinite series of beginnings, modulated according to the shape of the folds at a given time, and a constantly reinvented reader.

CHAPTER 6

Corporeal Fantasies, False Bodies

Ways of Seeing with Abdelwahab Meddeb

E già iernotte fu la luna tonda.

FALSE BODIES

In an interview to mark the publication of *Phantasia*, Abdelwahab Meddeb's second novel, Tahar Djaout notes, "As was the case with the title of [your first novel] *Talismano*, the reader is immediately confronted with the splintering of meanings, the disorientation of the neologism, and the shock of hybridization. Is *Phantasia* the collision or the articulation of phantasm and fantasia? between phantasm and fantasy? Everything is possible in the Greek-Arabic semantic confluence."[1] The title of Meddeb's *Phantasia* is often thought to refer to the French term "fantasia" and the Arabic "فانتازيا" [fāntāziyā], both colonial expressions denoting "an Arab dance and recitative"[2] or, more specifically, "an orchestrated display of Arab horsemanship and military skill."[3] Jocelyne Dakhlia suggests that the title marks the almost unconscious emergence of the ancient Mediterranean lingua franca, a language that largely died out in the course of the nineteenth century and in which "fantasia" refers primarily "to ostentation, to provocation, to showing off, and to making a fuss and seeking out confrontation,"[4] all senses articulated in Hugo Schuchardt's landmark early twentieth-century study "Die Lingua franca."[5]

But what of the title's particular orthography? When Abdelkébir Khatibi set out to read Meddeb's *Talismano*, he got no further than the first letter of Abdelwahab's name, "ع" ['ayn].[6] The title of *Phantasia* similarly invites its reader to dwell on the significance of its opening phoneme. The transliteration of the letter "ف" [fā'] as "ph" instead of "f" appears to direct the reader's attention from French and Arabic modulations of the word—not to mention "la langue franque"—perhaps to the German "Phantasie," but more likely, and as Djaout suggests, to the Greek letter "φ" [ph] and to the verb "φᾰντᾰ́ζω" [phantazō], meaning "to make visible, to present to (or as to) the eye."[7] "Phantasia" is thus an invitation to explore how the novel "makes visible," how it "presents things" via inscribed language in the reader's imagination.

The implicit problematization of the title recalls Augustine's use of the same term in *De musica* [On Music].[8] There, he writes that he has found no better way in Latin to describe "whatever the memory contains from the motions of the mind brought to bear on the passions of the body" than the Greek "phantasíai."[9] For the mature Augustine (Thagaste [Souk Ahras], 354–Hippo Regius [Annaba], 430), there is the risk that such fantasies—that this foreign term appears to keep at a safe remove—can lead the subject further and further from the phenomenal world: "When these motions react with each other, and boil up, you might say, with various and conflicting winds of purpose, they generate one motion from another . . . like images of images, to which we give the name phantasms."[10] Accordingly, in *Confessions*, Augustine considers the dualistic teachings of Mani, to which his juvenile self had been in thrall, to be not only "falsa corpora" [false bodies] but also "corporalia phantasmata" [corporeal phantasms][11] and "phantasmata splendida" [glittering fantasies].[12] Although it is one thing to find a fantasy *in* the memory and quite another to make a phantasm *out of* the memory, both are to be avoided: "Let us resist them as much we can, nor so fit our mind to them that, while our thinking is on them, we believe we see them with the understanding."[13]

By contrast, Meddeb's *Phantasia* embraces and explores these fantastical and phantasmatic ways of seeing. The narrator explains early in the novel that he is interested not only in what can be seen in the real but also in afterimages as they play out in the mind's eye:

> Mon regard ne se concentre pas sur le réel seul. Le champ de la vision se propage en halo. L'œil est hanté par tant d'images qui proviennent du monde et de ses doubles. Contente-toi de voir le vide qui est dans les choses imprimées sur la rétine.
>
> My gaze does not focus on the real alone. My field of vision spreads like a halo. The eye is haunted by so many images that come from the world and from its doubles. Just look at the emptiness of those things imprinted on the retina.[14]

Throughout the work, the line between what is seen in the real and what is imagined in the mind is confused, as images from multiple sources flow into one another:

> Le réseau mental jette son filet sur la faculté de voir. Le domaine qui s'étend derrière les choses est visité par le fantôme qui en moi veille.
>
> The thinking mind casts its net over the faculty of seeing. The realm that extends behind things is visited by the ghost that keeps watch within me.[15]

The narrator compares this way of looking at the world to the way a calligrapher searches for the figure in the letter, appearing to confirm the implicit invitation in the book's title to look behind its opening phoneme:

> Je regarde derrière les choses comme le calligraphe qui scrute dans la lettre l'image qui lui a donné naissance.
>
> I look behind things, like the calligrapher who scrutinizes the letter for the image that gave it birth.[16]

This chapter seeks a more precise understanding of the visual economy presented in *Phantasia*—that is, of how the novel teaches its reader to see—by examining specifically the interplay of letters and images. The mental images shunned by the mature Augustine are pursued by Meddeb, who ceaselessly exploits the visual appearance of letters, characters, and nonverbal signs for their fantastic, if not phantasmatic, potential. Preliminary indications of this are evident in the repeated recourse to non-Latin scripts, often reproduced without the aids of transcription or translation. This is mostly text in Arabic,[17] but there are also lines in biblical Hebrew,[18] a quotation in Sumero-Akkadian cuneiform,[19] various Chinese characters,[20] Egyptian hieroglyphs,[21] and the Japanese word that is homonymous with the name of his lover, Aya,[22] as well as the "taijitu" and the "aum" symbol.[23] As Christian Jambet writes, "Above all, Abdelwahab Meddeb was a poet, and it was as a poet that he loved language, the Arabic and French languages and those he liked to learn, curious to see them dialogue and peacefully exchange their riches."[24]

Phantasia is also marked by the presence of several descriptions of works of art, which are given a fleeting mental life through the trope of ekphrasis, understood here in James Heffernan's broad definition as the "*verbal representation of visual representation.*"[25] I investigate the interplay of letters and images in *Phantasia* by focusing on the first of its many descriptions of works of art, namely of *The Deposition* by the sixteenth-century Florentine painter

Jacopo da Pontormo (Empoli, 1494–Florence, 1556). Examining the ways we are called to see as we read will also enable us to respond to a striking lacuna in studies of Meddeb's writing. Although recent criticism has focused on the author's relation to Islam, particularly in its Sufi forms,[26] no attention has yet been paid to what, in *Phantasia*, is an extensive engagement with Christian, specifically Roman Catholic, culture, theology, and aesthetics.

"ALIF," "LĀM," "MĪM"

Meddeb establishes the role of letters in his fantasy at the start of the second chapter of *Phantasia*, when his narrator takes up the Qur'ān:

> Je regarde le ciel se découvrir. Entre les nuages, le soleil traîne des pièces de tulle qui reprisent le firmament. D'une main, je tire le rideau. De l'autre, j'ouvre le Livre.
>
> I watch the sky reveal itself. The sun draws bits of tulle between the clouds, as if to darn the firmament. With one hand, I pull the curtain. With the other, I open the Book.[27]

The Qur'ān, as its etymology indicates, and as noted in the previous chapter, is a book to be read. The first five verses revealed to Muḥammad, in Mecca in 610—thought to be the opening verses of the ninety-sixth sura, "The Blood Clot"—issue an imperative: "Recite [or Read] in the Name of thy Lord Who created, created man from a blood clot. Recite! Thy Lord is most noble, Who taught by the Pen, taught man that which he knew not."[28]

Here, the reading of the Qur'ān extends no further than the three Arabic characters—known as "حروف مقطعات" [ḥurūf muqaṭṭa'āt], or "separated letters"—that open the second sura, "The Cow," namely "alif, lām, mīm":

> Je croise la "Liminaire," gravée dans la mémoire, incipit qui excave l'arabesque de ses lettrines dans l'azur et l'or de l'enluminure. En face de la belle page, je suis ébloui par les lettres qui introduisent à la "Vache," la plus longue sourate, classée en tête de Écritures. Initiatiques lettres الم *alef, lâm, mîm,* qui ouvrent cinq autres sourates. Initiales éparpillées, réticentes à former mot. Les soumettrais-je à la souveraineté du sens, entre l'épanchement et la plénitude, la fortune et le blâme? Les sonderais-je en leur mystère?

> I cross the "Threshold," engraved in memory, an incipit which excavates the arabesque of its initials in the azure and gold of the illumination. Facing the beautiful page, I am dazzled by the letters that introduce "The Cow," the longest sura, ranked first in the Scriptures. Initiatory letters الم *alif, lām, mīm*, which open five other suras. Scattered initials, reluctant to form a word. Would I submit them to the sovereignty of meaning, between effusion and plenitude, fortune and blame? Would I probe them in their mystery?[29]

Qur'ānic tradition says that these three letters—written as a word but not pronounced as such—are closed to interpretation. As the eighteenth-century translator Claude-Étienne Savary glosses, "Commentators of the Qur'ān . . . are convinced that God revealed their meaning only to their Prophet, & that they will always be unknown to other mortals."[30]

Instead of reading these letters as components of a mysterious word, the narrator copies the calligrapher and searches within each character for the image that gave it form. This is what Djaout refers to when he speaks of "the propensity of the Arabic letter to incorporate itself, by its movement and its strivings [par son allure et ses élancements], into a plastic work," such as that created by Denis Martinez.[31] In *Dédicace à l'année qui vient* [Consecration to the year that comes], Khatibi evokes something similar, when he writes:

> Implosion
> Que le calligramme saisonnier
> Fixe en son trait rapide
>
> Implosion
> That the seasonal calligram
> Fixes in its rapid stroke[32]

Meddeb's narrator traces each of these three disconnected letters to a different part of the mouth, which together chart the buccal cavity:

> Si l'*alef* est émis du fond de la gorge, le *lâm* s'articule au milieu du palais et le *mîm* par les lèvres.
>
> If the *alif* is emitted from the back of the throat, the *lām* is articulated in the middle of the palate, and the *mīm* by the lips.[33]

The letters not only name the edges of the mouth but bring them into physical resonance:

> Quand tu les prononces, la chair frémit et la pensée pose sa première pierre. En chacune de ces lettres, le verbe s'incarne.
>
> When you pronounce them, flesh quivers and thought sets its first stone in place. In each of these letters, the word becomes flesh.[34]

The closing formulation "le verbe s'incarne"—which could be translated as "the word becomes flesh," "the word is incarnated," or "the word is embodied"—brings the reader closer than they might expect to the Christian doctrine of the Incarnation. This is the doctrine according to which the Virgin Mary conceived a child by the Holy Spirit, and God became man in the person of Jesus Christ. As the evangelist John puts it, "And the Word was made flesh, and dwelt among us" [Καὶ ὁ λόγος σὰρξ ἐγένετο] [kai ho logos sarx egeneto].[35]

At several moments in his oeuvre, Meddeb posits the Incarnation as a problem that should be taken up not only by his reader but by contemporary Islam. In *Instants soufis* [Sufi Moments], a transcription of brief readings broadcast on Radio Méditerranée Internationale (Medi 1) during Ramadan, and first published posthumously, Meddeb is at pains to show how the mystics of Islam's past have explained and even attempted to integrate aspects of the Christian Incarnation. He notes how Ibn ʿArabī believed that it was Jesus's ability to keep vigil and to fast, both "divine attributes," that persuaded Christians that he was the incarnation of God.[36] In *Phantasia*, the narrator evokes one of the most curious artistic representations of the Incarnation ever created, namely *Coronation of the Virgin* (1454) (fig. 12) by Enguerrand Quarton (Laon, 1410–Avignon, 1466). Here, God the Father and God the Son are depicted as identical, save for the folds in their robes and some fine facial differences:

> Quand même le fils serait l'image vivante et parfaite du père, quand même il serait engendré et non créé, quand même il serait consubstantiel au père, il demeure différent en tant que personne.
>
> Even if the son were the living and perfect image of the father, even if he were begotten and not created, even if he were

FIG. 12. Enguerrand Quarton, *Coronation of the Virgin*, Altar of the Charterhouse of Villeneuve-lès-Avignon, tempera on panel, 1453–1454, 183 × 220 cm. Musée Pierre-de-Luxembourg, Villeneuve-lès-Avignon (Gard). Photograph: White Images / Scala / Art Resource, NY.

> consubstantial with the father, he would remain different as a person.[37]

This line—less ekphrasis than exegesis—is then followed by Augustine's definition of the Trinity:

> *Une substance, trois personnes . . . C'est le père qui engendre le fils. Le fils n'est donc pas celui qui est le père. C'est le fils qui est engendré par le père. Le père n'est donc pas celui qui est le fils.*
>
> *One substance, three persons . . . It is the father who engenders the son. The son is therefore not the one who is the father. It is the son who is begotten by the father. The father is therefore not the one who is the son.*[38]

Notwithstanding Augustine's assured explication here, it is fair to say that the reconciliation of mortal mutability and divine immutability remains a profoundly fantastical concept. Only months before his conversion from Manicheism to Christianity in 387, Augustine himself shied away from the idea and, in the words of Pierre Courcelle, "was content with admiring Christ as an eminent man."[39] In an article published in 1995, to which I return below, Meddeb opines that the Incarnation remains "l'impensé islamique par excellence," that is, "the one thing that Islam has not yet formulated."[40] In a 2006 discussion with Marc Semo and Christophe Boltanski about the uncreated Qur'ān, Meddeb draws a parallel between a fourteenth-century Persian miniature showing Gabriel instructing Muḥammad to read (fig. 13)

FIG. 13. Anonymous, *Muḥammad Receiving His First Revelation from the Angel Gabriel*, miniature illustration on vellum, 1314. Reproduced in Rashīd al-Dīn Ṭabīb, *Jāmiʿ al-tawārīkh* [Compendium of Chronicles] (1314), 220. Digital image: © The University of Edinburgh. Original: © The University of Edinburgh.

and the scene of the Annunciation, which appears on two occasions in the Qur'ān, when Jibrīl appears to Maryam to announce that she will give birth to a child. He thereby suggests that the Holy Book is itself a form of incarnation—"Le Livre est donc une forme d'incarnation"—although he admits that this is an idea that contemporary Muslims do not accept.[41]

DEPOSITION

Early in *Phantasia*, the narrative provides a schematic model of how "la vérité islamique," or "Islamic truth," relates to figurative images:

> Elle est à la croisée de la loi mosaïque, qui proclame l'interdit de figurer, et de la légitimité christique, qui glorifie l'icône.
>
> It is at the crossroads of Mosaic law, which proclaims the prohibition of figuration, and of Christic legitimacy, which glorifies the icon.[42]

This is to say that Islamic teaching oscillates between the Christian doctrine that, through the efforts of its clerks (Augustine among them), recuperates and resurrects the styles and habits of the ancients and the Decalogue's prohibition, as recorded in Exodus and reproduced by Meddeb in the original Hebrew:

> לֹא תַעֲשֶׂה לְךָ פֶסֶל וְכָל תְּמוּנָה
>
> [lo' ta'aśeh lekha pesel vekhol temunah]
>
> *Tu ne te feras pas d'image taillée, ni aucune représentation.*
>
> You shall not make for yourself a graven image, nor any representation.[43]

When distinguishing the three monotheistic religions on the basis of people's relation to language, Fethi Benslama notes that in Judaism, the legibility of the divine word to the chosen people requires that the law be inscribed on tablets that are then broken. In Christianity, the incarnation of the divine word in the form of man only becomes effective through Christ's suffering and death. In Islam, "the essential fact seems to take place on the plane of the enunciation of the word of the Law by man, by means of the tongue [au moyen de la langue]."[44] The destruction necessary for the divine word to become legible is in its enunciation, the way it resounds, perhaps signifies, and then returns to silence.

Meddeb forges a similar dialectic when he asserts that it is the Muslim who reconciles the aniconism of Judaism and the iconolatry of Christianity by pursuing the image in the imagination. Here, the image is isolated from the flesh; it is neither didactic nor mass-produced, but rather intimate and elective; it is unrepresentable in the real, existing only in the unreal zone of the imagination, "without being offered for exchange, without being translated into the sensible."[45] Only in the unreal zone of the imagination can God be worshipped as if he could be seen:

> En elle, *adore dieu comme si tu le voyais.* اعبد الله كانك تراه. Dévisage dieu en ton espace mental. Par simulacre, tu allèges le paradoxe.
>
> In it, *worship god as if you were seeing him.* اعبد الله كانك تراه. Stare at god in your mental space. By this semblance, you alleviate the paradox.[46]

Despite situating the Islamic image firmly in the mind's eye, throughout *Phantasia,* Meddeb repeatedly allows the Incarnation to infiltrate the modern Muslim imaginary by exposing the reader to numerous ekphrases of Christian works of art. These include statues by Gian Lorenzo Bernini,[47] Antonello da Messina's epicene saints,[48] the bleeding Sebastian by Andrea Mantegna,[49] Pietro Cavallini's archangels,[50] Noah intoxicated by Paolo Uccello,[51] Michelangelo's Moses,[52] Donato Bramante's Christ at the column,[53] and a Salomé by Domenico di Pace Beccafumi.[54] The first painting to be named, though, is *The Deposition* (fig. 14) by Jacopo da Pontormo—a painting that has hung above the altar of a side chapel in the church of Santa Felicità, in Florence, since its creation between 1525 and 1528.

Asked by Djaout about the presence of painting in this novel, Meddeb responds, "I really love painting. When, as an adolescent in Tunis, I first read Proust, I came to the terrible realization that I lived in a pictorial desert."[55] In response to Djaout's suggestion that *Phantasia* is a "mannerist" work, Meddeb replies,

> Mannerism is one of my favorite schools of painting. In *Phantasia* there are tributes to two Mannerist masters: Beccafumi, the Sienese, with his Madonnas who look as though they have been

FIG. 14. Jacopo da Pontormo, *Deposizione / The Deposition*, oil on panel, ca. 1528, 313 × 192 cm. Capponi Chapel, Church of Santa Felicità, Florence. Photograph: © NPL—DeA Picture Library / Bridgeman Images.

> burned by an inner fire, under the glacis of their garments; and Pontormo, this Florentine who forces his colors toward a neon brilliance, who excessively exaggerates the proportions, with figures who are both tall and slender. I am forgetting a third mannerist who features in the text, namely Il Sodoma. There must be others, too.
>
> What is mannerism as an aesthetics, as a rhetoric? It's a way of going beyond classical form. I have a marked tendency toward confrontation with excess, toward limit-experiences.[56]

In *Phantasia*, Pontormo's altarpiece is evoked after an extended sequence of images that enter the narrator's mind aboard a flight to Paris, each of which barely comes into narrative focus before it slips into the next: an encounter with Rābiʿah al-Baṣrī, the eighth-century mystic and poet; the Kaʿbah; an unknown garden; a Byzantine icon of the Virgin that comes alive as a winged chimera and with whose breasts the narrator enthusiastically grapples; stock images of the avenues of Manhattan (recently visited); Chinese ideograms; and so on. It is a series of reflections that offer nothing more than outlines. As the narrator puts it, "Dans le flux de la pensée, le fragment s'impose" [In the flow of thought, the fragment imposes itself].[57]

The appearance of a named painting marks a significant shift in the type of visuality appealed to in the novel:

> Un bruit aquatique me fait apparaître mon double arpentant, pendant la semaine sainte, le jardin d'une villa florentine, sur l'autre rive de l'Arno. Dans une grotte, un silène bat d'eau la mesure. La pierre prend la forme d'une tortue géante qui crache de sa gueule le jet qui soude les sons de la viole d'amour parvenus de l'église Santa Felicità où brille dans le fondu d'un néon froid, ultramarin et pervenche, ketmie et guimauve, *La déposition* du Pontormo. Les corps, aux proportions étirées, encerclent d'ondulations sinueuses la dépouille du Christ. Le deuil masque les visages. La rhétorique emphatique veille sur un théâtre de lamentation. Orgue, violoncelle et violons endiguent l'hermaphrodite haute-contre qui chante en solo ou avec l'enfant les tercets du *Stabat mater*.
>
> An aquatic sound causes my double to appear before me, during Holy Week, pacing up and down the garden of a Florentine villa, on the other bank of the Arno. In a grotto, a satyr beats time with water. The rock assumes the form of a giant tortoise, which spits from its mouth the jet that fuses the sounds of the viola d'amore coming from the church of Santa Felicità, where, in the fade of a cold neon, ultramarine and periwinkle, hibiscus and marshmallow, shines Pontormo's *Deposition*. The bodies, with stretched proportions, encircle the remains of Christ with sinuous undulations. Mourning masks the faces. The emphatic rhetoric keeps watch over a theater of lamentation. Organ, cello, and violins restrain the hermaphrodite countertenor, who, solo or with the child, intones the tercets of *Stabat Mater*.[58]

Meddeb does not name the Palazzo Pitti, the "villa" built in the 1460s in the quarter of Florence known as Oltrano, here dubbed literally the "other bank" of the river Arno. Its garden, the Giardino di Boboli, includes the Grotta del Buontalenti, in whose third and final chamber stands a gray basin, over the edge of which four satyrs spout water through their mouths toward the dazzling white marble statue of Venus by Giambologna (Douai, 1529–Florence, 1608). The Giardino itself rises behind the palace in terraces, one of which includes a green rectangular pond, the Vasca del Nettuno, in the center of which is a weed-covered rock, much like a "giant tortoise," upon which towers the statue of Neptune by Stoldo Lorenzi (Settignano, 1534–Pisa, 1583), trident raised as if about to stab the surface of the water. Closer to the river, around the corner from the Ponte Vecchio, stands the church of Santa Felicità, rebuilt in the 1730s. On the right-hand side as you enter is the so-called Capponi Chapel. Besides *The Deposition,* the chapel includes a fresco of the Annunciation, also by Pontormo, and a dazzling stained glass window from 1525 by Guillaume de Marcillat (Le Châtre, 1470–Arezzo, 1529), depicting the carrying of Christ to the tomb. In each of the spandrels, there are roundels of the evangelists, one of which appears to be by Pontormo's protégé Bronzino (Florence, 1503–Florence, 1572).[59] Meddeb's fantasy is to move with the speed that only narrative can afford between each of these cultural landmarks, such that they become confused, a grotesque dream sequence that Pontormo's picture suddenly punctures. As Christine Goémé noted in her interview with the author, recorded shortly before his death, "At breakneck speed, the narrator obtains access to all sorts of spaces, eras, names, arts, and, basically, the entire library of humanity. You could say, in this sense, that this really is a novel of freedom [le roman de la liberté]."[60]

Pontormo's *Deposition* ostensibly names the moment in the Passion of Christ when his corpse is taken down from the cross to be buried in time for the Sabbath at sundown. In religious painting, it is a scene that only becomes popular in the later Middle Ages. As Amy Knight Powell has shown, at a time of growing debate around the role of representational images, the Deposition "gave measured form to late medieval iconophobia."[61] Across northern Europe, this fear of the image will culminate in the Reformation's aniconism, if not outright iconoclasm. If Christ is the "image of the invisible God [εἰκὼν τοῦ θεοῦ τοῦ ἀοράτου] [eikōn tou theou tou aoratou]," as Saint Paul (Tarsus, 5–Rome, 64/65) says in his letter to the Colossians—the "imago dei"—then the Deposition depicts the moment after the image has been taken down but before it has been put away.[62] Powell says it is an "auto-iconoclasm, a politicized self-negation,"[63] but it might more simply be termed an "anicon," an image on the point of denying itself, an ostentation that immediately precedes its occultation. The deposition may even prefigure the shift to abstraction in the twentieth century, which comes about, as Meddeb later explains, in part "par réaction à une tradition iconique saturée" [as a reaction to a saturated iconic tradition].[64]

Pontomoro's *Deposition* is the most prominent instance of this Christian trope in *Phantasia*, but it is by no means the only one. The narrator later recalls a painting from 1556 by Tintoretto called *Trafugamento del corpo di san Marco* [Stealing of the Body of Saint Mark], preserved in the Gallerie dell'Accademia in Venice, which shows the martyr's corpse being saved from the pagan pyre during a rainstorm and carried away for burial, which motif clearly echoes Christ's deposition and transportation to the tomb:

> Aux jardins du Palais-Royal, la régularité répétitive de l'architecture t'oblige à revisiter ta mémoire vénitienne, place Saint-Marc, telle qu'elle a été amplifiée par la légèreté fantasmagorique de Tintoretto, à travers la vertigineuse perspective d'arcades peuplées de personnages fuyant dans la précipitation l'orage soudain.
>
> In the gardens of the Palais-Royal, the repetitive regularity of the architecture forces you to revisit your Venetian memory, Piazza San Marco, as amplified by the phantasmagoric lightness of Tintoretto, through the dizzying perspective of arcades populated by figures fleeing in haste from the sudden storm.[65]

Consider also the Deposition scene from 1303–5 known as *Compianto sul Cristo morto* [Lamentation over the Dead Christ], painted as a fresco by Giotto di Bondone in the Scrovegni Chapel, Padua, which, although not named, is visible in the following passage:

> De bleu en bleu, j'aborde l'aube de Giotto, ciel lavé que rongent les lamentations des anges qui tournent au-dessus du Christ mort, entouré par les femmes en pleurs et Jean l'imberbe, tempérant la réserve des hommes. D'un bleu où se profile le paysage urbain qui initiera la peinture au réel.
>
> From blue to blue, I approach the dawn of Giotto, a washed sky consumed by the lamentations of the angels circling above the dead Christ, who is surrounded by the weeping women and a

> smooth-faced John, tempering the men's reserve. A blue that profiles the urban landscape and introduces painting to the real.[66]

In "Hallâj revisité" [Al-Ḥallāj Revisited], an article published the same year as *Phantasia,* Meddeb allows his reader to more fully understand the significance he invests in this painting—and in the Deposition more broadly—by replacing "the inert body of Christ" with "the revived ashes of al-Ḥallāj," such that the fourteenth-century Paduan painting becomes "a cosmic lamentation" for the tenth-century Persian Sufi mystic.[67] He thereby reiterates and seeks to justify a method that is not based on "the exactitude of the quotation," but rather on a "poetics of reminiscence, the poetics of one who hallucinates, who is possessed, who, in contact with the invisible, writes under the dictation of delirium."[68] This method not only describes Meddeb's evocation of Giotto's painting in both his article and his novel—and his self-assured appropriation, translation, and development of al-Ṭabarī's account of the crucifixion, beheading, dismembering, and death of al-Ḥallāj in an extended footnote—but also al-Ḥallāj's fatal identification with the Incarnation.

In the case of Pontormo's altarpiece, it is somewhat unclear whether the painting even portrays a deposition, despite the title by which it is known. Giorgio Vasari, who knew Pontormo in person, said that he "was a man without a firm and steady mind . . . who always went about indulging in fanciful ideas."[69] And the composition is, in fact, striking for the absence of the usual symbols of the Passion. Barring the nondescript green ground at the base of the picture and the blue sky at the top, the only external feature is a cloud in the top left, conspicuous not only by its presence but also by its being lit not from the right (the west), as the figures and the chapel are, but from the left. There is no cross, almost always depicted in scenes of the Deposition, although in the top left of a preparatory sketch for the painting, a ladder, presumably leaning against the cross, can be seen.[70] There is also no tomb, which precludes it from being an entombment. Some call the scene a "Grabtragung" [bearing to the grave], like that illustrated in de Marcillat's stained glass window.[71] Doris Wild specifically traces the model for Pontormo's painting to a sarcophagus panel depicting the death and "Grabtragung" of Meleager,[72] but there is no way of knowing for certain whether Christ is being lifted up or put down, if he is being carried, proffered, or held still. The normal markers deployed in Renaissance painting to indicate the direction of movement, such as a pointing finger or a turned head, are not utilized here. Given that Pontormo probably had Michelangelo Buonarroti's

Pietà (1498–99) in mind—as well as Raffaello Santi's *Pala Baglioni* (1507), which includes the same visual oscillation between the bearing and transporting of the corpse—the painting is perhaps most accurately described as a fractured pietà.[73] Mary, the mother of Christ, is seated to the right as we look at the picture, dressed in ample blue robes, her knees pressed together, while on the left, her near-naked son is borne by two men—one upright, the other crouched—who may in fact be adolescents or even angels. A bareheaded blond woman dressed in pink, red, and pale yellow, brandishing a cloth in her left hand, her back turned toward the viewer, theatrically interposes herself between Mary and Christ, dramatizing the visual caesura.

Within a few phrases of this passage, Meddeb's narrator will refer to the Passion as the "spectacle"[74] of the Incarnation, an event that prepares the ground for Christianity's close alliance with the figurative image, despite a few centuries of "defiance" and "hesitation."[75] But in Pontormo's picture—and in Meddeb's verbal appropriation of it—the focus is not on the Passion but on what happens to the figurative image. The image of God is taken down, not to be hidden away in a tomb but to be carried before our seeing and reading eyes. Christ here is metaphor in the literal sense, as that which is "carried across," from the ancient Greek "μεταφέρω" [metapherō]. It is perhaps no coincidence that the arrangement of the corpse mimics the letter "M"—for Messiah, maybe, but also for metaphor, and perhaps even for Meddeb. Most importantly, Meddeb's brief ekphrasis of the picture represents the translation of the Incarnation—of the Word made flesh—not to the tomb, a precondition for bodily resurrection, but back into words, language, metaphors, verbal images. It is perhaps this translation back into words that Mohammed Khaïr-Eddine intends by the title of his 1981 collection, *Résurrection des fleurs sauvages* [Resurrection of Wild Flowers].[76] The resurrection of flowers marks the poetic moment that succeeds the conventional use of metaphor and the resuscitation of figures considered marginal or inappropriate. Paul de Man says that "the existence of the poetic image is itself a sign of divine absence" and sees "the conscious use of poetic imagery" as "an admission of this absence."[77] But what Meddeb suggests, with help from Pontormo, is that the poetic image always bears marks of the Incarnation and that what appears to be carried away from us in abstraction is always also being brought closer to us as figuration.

I propose that Pontormo's picture captures a process that is central to Meddeb's fantastical, phantasmatic poetics, in which the Incarnation is grasped not to be hidden away but to be continuously carried aloft and passed along. If the Deposition as portrayed by Pontormo provides a model for the image in Meddeb, and perhaps in Meddeb's vision for Islam, then that model is one in which the Incarnation is present but suspended between the descent from the cross and the tomb, deposited in signs but not obscured. Conventional Islam may not tolerate such ambivalence, but Meddeb delights among Catholicism's ambiguities.[78] The narrator's reflections are interrupted by the imminent arrival of the plane at Orly, near Paris, and the concomitant rituals of descent. This landing, which now mirrors the Deposition, if not the Incarnation itself, will be reversed by the ascension that occurs on the escalators at Beaubourg in the fourth chapter of *Phantasia*. This itself is a reiteration, if not parody, of Muḥammad's Miʿrāj, when the Prophet leaps to the heavens on al-Burāq from the Temple Mount in Jerusalem.

SALABA ṢALABA

At the center of Pontormo's *Deposition*, there is an absence of figures and activity. Leo Steinberg says that it "is as though the dead Christ had slipped from his mother's knees," which represent "that voided middle about which all revolves . . . , the widowed center of the design."[79] Meddeb, by contrast, sets the corpse at the heart of his ekphrasis, gently dislocating Pontormo's pictorial geometry, in the following phrase:

> Les corps, aux proportions étirées, encerclent d'ondulations sinueuses la dépouille du Christ.
>
> The bodies, with stretched proportions, encircle the remains of Christ with sinuous undulations.[80]

Just as "dépouille" occupies the focal point of this phrase, so too the term obtains a central place in Meddeb's poetic vocabulary. It appears repeatedly in *Phantasia*, in several of his collections of poetry, in his other novel *Talismano*, and in his theoretical writings on Islam. In his poem "Portrait de l'artiste en soufi" [Portrait of the Artist as a Sufi], the following lines limn Christ's corpse, awaiting burial in Vittore Carpaccio's *The Dead Christ* (ca. 1505) (fig. 15):

> . . . la dépouille
> étendue du Christ dont le visage serein
> jubile sans ostentation discret
> face silencieuse qui retient le sourire
> et le bas soupir

FIG. 15. Vittore Carpaccio, *The Preparation of Christ's Tomb, or The Dead Christ,* oil on canvas, ca. 1505, 145 × 185 cm. Gemäldegalerie, Berlin. Photograph: Joerg P. Anders.

> . . . the laid out
> remains of Christ whose serene countenance
> exults without ostentation discreet
> silent face that restrains the smile
> and the low sigh[81]

In the ekphrasis of Pontormo's painting, the term "dépouille" [remains] both echoes and distorts the verbal form of "déposition" [deposition], stretching the picture as it translates it into words, virtually encircling the painting with a parergon of sinuous textual undulations. Meddeb permits his evocation of Pontormo's *Deposition* to morph into a description of the operatic setting of "Stabat Mater," a poem commonly attributed to the Franciscan Jacopone da Todi (Todi, ca. 1230–Collazzone, 1306) and set to music by Giovanni Battista Pergolesi (Iesi, 1710–Pozzuoli, 1736) as he was dying in a monastery on the Gulf of Naples.[82] It might be claimed that this somewhat anachronistic juxtaposition further disfigures the verbal rendition of the painting.

To understand the importance of "dépouille" to Meddeb's ekphrasis of Pontormo, and more broadly to his pursuit of the Incarnation, we need to turn to an essay by Meddeb published in the inaugural edition of his journal *Dédale*, entitled "L'icône mentale" [The Mental Icon]. In the course of his discussion of إنشاء الدوائر [Inshā' al-dawā'ir] [Production of the Spheres]—a text composed by Ibn 'Arabī in Tunis around 1200—Meddeb reflects on what the Sufi theosoph calls "صفات السلب" [ṣifāt al-salb], or the "attributes of privation":

> . . . le mot *salb*, que je traduis dans le contexte par privation, provient d'une racine dont les formes verbales varient entre arracher de force, piller, dépouiller, voler, tirer, extraire, porter le deuil, être privé d'un membre de sa famille, et pour les femmes et les femelles, de son petit, de son enfant, de son fœtus, et pour les arbres, perdre le feuillage et le fruit, être nu . . .

> . . . the word *salb*, which I translate in this case as deprivation, comes from a root whose verbal forms vary between forcibly uprooting, looting, despoiling, stealing, pulling, extracting, mourning, being deprived of a member of one's family, and, for women and females, of her little one, of her child, of her fetus, and for trees, to lose foliage and fruit, to be naked . . .[83]

Even as he proposes a translation for "سلب" [salb], Meddeb permits alternative meanings to proliferate. The verb "سلب" [salaba] operates much as "dépouiller" does in French; its meanings include verbs such as "to take away, steal, wrest, snatch, rob, strip, dispossess, deprive" and nouns such as "loot, booty, plunder, spoils," as well as additional senses not present in the French, such as the "hide, shanks and belly of a slaughtered animal."[84] What is more—perhaps appropriately for a verb that can signify unlawful dispossession—"salaba" can itself be dislodged and deposed by a verb that is practically homophonous (particularly to a foreign ear), namely "صلب" [ṣalaba], which means "to crucify."

The resemblance of "سلب" [salaba] and "صلب" [ṣalaba] is, I maintain, a crucial element of Meddeb's negotiation of the Incarnation in *Phantasia* and beyond. Despite the apparent promiscuity of what Meddeb calls his "cultes mêlés," or "mixed cults,"[85] it is notable throughout the novel that there are no direct references to the crucifixion, the cross, or other paraphernalia of the Passion, much as is the case in Pontormo's *Deposition*.[86] This is in marked contrast to Khaïr-Eddine, for instance, who openly evokes the crucifixion, including in his first major poem "Nausée noire" [Black Nausea]: "voici donc les crucifixions les plus inattendues" [here are the most unexpected crucifixions].[87] He evokes it in his later work too: "Certains êtres, mêmes les chats, sont si maigres qu'on s'en détourne tant la férocité de leur décharnement rappelle les clous qui fixèrent le Christ à la croix" [Some beings, even cats, are so skinny that you turn your back to them, so much does the ferocity of their emaciation recall the nails that pinned Christ to the cross].[88] In Meddeb's *Phantasia*, the exception—if it can even be called such—occurs in the second sentence of the tenth chapter, when the narrator steps into a taxi at a red light, "between" the gibbous moon in the night sky and a flashing green pharmacy sign.[89]

Meddeb is of course aware that the cross is not limited by its role in Christ's Passion, and that it both preexists and exceeds Christianity's appropriation of it. As Abdelkébir Khatibi reminds us, "It is traced on the arms of pilgrims returning from Jerusalem. A cross is tattooed on the foreheads of Jewish Moroccan babies. It is also reported in southern Oran. This gesture of drawing a cross on an object, to sacralize it by symbolically cutting it into four, is therefore millenary. To make such a gesture in front of another person is to disperse their possible power over you."[90] At first sight, the absence of the cross in *Phantasia* appears to align the text with Islamic teaching, which avoids the cross, and specifically with the Qur'ān, which does not allow for either the death or the crucifixion of ʿĪsá bna Maryam:

> وَقَولِهِم إِنّا قَتَلنَا المَسيحَ عيسَى ابنَ مَريَمَ رَسولَ اللَّهِ وَما قَتَلوهُ وَما صَلَبوهُ وَلٰكِن شُبِّهَ لَهُم
> وَإِنَّ الَّذينَ اختَلَفوا فيهِ لَفي شَكٍّ مِنهُ ما لَهُم بِهِ مِن عِلمٍ إِلَّا اتِّباعَ الظَّنِّ وَما قَتَلوهُ يَقينًا
>
> [Wa-qawlihim innā qatalnā al-masīḥa ʿĪsá bna Maryama rasūla llāhi wa-mā qatalūhu wa-mā ṣalabūhu wa-lākin shubbiha lahum wa-inna lladhīna khtalafū fīhi la-fī shakkin minhu mā lahum bihi min ʿilmin illā ttibāʿa al-ẓanni wa-mā qatalūhu yaqīnā]
>
> And for their saying, "We slew the Messiah, Jesus son of Mary, the messenger of God"—though they did not slay him; nor did they crucify him, but it appeared so unto them. Those who differ concerning him are in doubt thereof. They have no knowledge of it, but follow only conjecture; they slew him not for certain.[91]

The term used in the Qur'ān to express the resemblance that would allow for Christ to appear to suffer death and crucifixion, and yet to survive, is "ولكن شبّه لهم" [wa-lākin shubbiha lahum] [and yet it appeared so to them]. In "L'icône mentale," Meddeb notes how the root of the verb "شابه" [shābaha], "to resemble" or "look like," is associated not only with words such as "شبه" [shibh], "resemblance" or "image," but also with the notion of the equivocal, of the in-between: "شبهة" [shubhah] is "obscurity," "vagueness," "uncertainty," and "doubt."[92] In short, it is a somewhat paradoxical root that acknowledges that for there to be resemblance, there must also be discrepancy. In the Qur'ān, the crucifixion and death of Christ *appear* to occur but do not do so. It is what Augustine—were he Muslim—might name a "false body," a "glittering fantasy," or a "corporeal phantasm." He does as much in *Confessions*, when he recalls his previous Manichean belief that a "phantasm" of Christ had been crucified.[93] For Meddeb, the crucifixion ("ṣalaba") asserts itself only in its acoustic proximity to privation ("salaba"), through the intermediary of "dépouille." This resemblance permits him to approach the Incarnation while resisting the larger soteriological narrative of crucifixion, entombment, resurrection, and ascension.

Naming and representing Pontormo's *Deposition* therefore enables Meddeb to recuperate the Incarnation even as he denies the cross. This is the Incarnation as Deposition, permanently suspended between ostentation and occultation. Despite Meddeb's circumspection here, we can still probably set him alongside the Muslim heretics celebrated in *Phantasia*—those mystics who, knowingly or otherwise, brush up against the Incarnation. These include the two great exponents of "the Sufism of excess,"[94] the Persian Bāyazīd Bisṭāmī (Bastam, 804–Bastam, 874) and al-Ḥallāj, figures who have long been synonymous with their ecstatic statements or "شطحات" [shaṭaḥāt], which, as Meddeb explains, paradoxically invest the human, or "ناسوت" [nāsūt], with the divine, or "لاهوت" [lāhūt].[95] It is al-Bisṭāmī who, in his moment of communion with God, proclaims, "*Louange à moi, que ma gloire est grande*" [Praise be to me, how great is my glory], a translation of "سبحاني ما أعظم شاني" [subḥānī mā aʿẓama shānī].[96] As Meddeb explains elsewhere, "What is usually said in the third person and belongs to the absent God is said in the first person, simply because in a state where the subject is absent to him- or herself, it is God who speaks from their lips." He concludes, "Al-Bisṭāmī pronounces in such a way that divine Pronouncement shakes."[97] Al-Ḥallāj's greatest and most terrible utterance—"أنا الحقّ" [anā al-ḥaqq] or "Je suis le Vrai" [I am the True]—accorded to himself one of the names of God and resulted in his crucifixion for blasphemy in Baghdad.[98] The scholar Louis Massignon attributed his own turn to Islamic mysticism to an encounter with these "theopathetic locutions,"[99] saying in a conference at the Benedictine monastery in Toumliline in 1948 that they "entered his life like arrows."[100]

In spite of the importance of these pronouncements in *Phantasia*, when, toward the end of his life, Meddeb revisits al-Ḥallāj's statement, he softens its fallacious edges, as if trying to save the mystic from himself. Meddeb provides two possible translations rather than the single one in the novel, allowing this heretical statement of embodiment the accommodation of abstraction: "Je suis le Vrai, Je suis la vérité créatrice" [I am the True, I am the creative truth].[101] Meddeb explicitly defines this statement as "an utterance intended to crystallize the doctrine of substantial union (ʿayn al-jamʿ) between God and man,"[102] avoiding the Arabic for "incarnation," namely "حلول" [ḥulūl].[103] He then proceeds to disperse any echoes of Christ's crucifixion and death by evoking al-Ḥallāj's passage "to the gallows, then to the brazier,"[104] and reminding his reader that the mystic's ashes are scattered in the Euphrates river, which would seem to render any bodily resurrection impossible.[105]

But the most important model and guide for Meddeb is Ibn ʿArabī, the inspiration for his later collection *Tombeau d'Ibn Arabi* [Tomb of Ibn ʿArabī]. In *Phantasia*, Meddeb describes him as being "à un cheveu de confirmer la célébration de l'image en chrétienté, à cause de l'incarnation, concept qui sépare" [at a hair's breadth from confirming the celebration of the image in Christianity, because of the Incarnation, a concept that separates].[106] This is an episode to which Meddeb returns, more as philologist than as poet, in his 1995 article.[107] For Meddeb, there is both joy and trepidation in the possibility of this transgression. Toward the end of the novel, the narrator recalls attending a Mass in the church of Saint Julien le Pauvre in Paris, celebrated in Arabic and Syriac by a Greek Catholic priest:

> Je jubilais quand la voix chantait en vérité ce qui m'est blasphème. Quelle inquiétante joie d'entendre l'inouï s'incarner en la glorification du *fils de dieu* ابن الله dans la langue du Coran, qui, dès le berceau, a scellé mes oreilles par l'évidence du dieu *un et impénétrable, qui n'a pas engendré et n'a pas été engendré*!
>
> I was exultant when the voice sang what in truth is blasphemy to me. What disturbing joy to hear the unheard of be incarnated in the glorification of the *son of god* ابن الله in the language of the Qurʾān, which, from the cradle, had sealed my ears with the self-evidence of the *one and impenetrable* god, *who has not begotten and has not been begotten*![108]

QUR'ĀNIC PIETÀ

The significance of Pontormo's painting to *Phantasia*'s visual economy, and to Meddeb's appropriation of the Incarnation, culminates toward the end of the novel, when the narrator is on the subway leafing through a book containing color reproductions of Arabic calligraphy:[109]

> Sur fond floral céladon, les lettres éclatent comme une musique, en des rutilements outremer, carmin. Verticale ou couchée, agressive ou lascive, l'écriture me donne des ailes et m'emporte loin des voyageurs macérés dans le silence et le malheur. Où que j'ouvre le livre, les illustrations resplendissent.
>
> On a celadon floral background, the letters burst out like music, glowing ultramarine, carmine. Vertical or prostrate, aggressive or lascivious, this writing gives me wings and transports me far from these other travelers steeped in silence and misfortune. Wherever I open the book, the illustrations are resplendent.[110]

In these opening lines of the eighth chapter, there are clear echoes of the previous description of Pontormo's altarpiece that "brille dans le fondu d'un néon froid, ultramarin et pervenche, ketmie et guimauve" [shines in the fade of a cold neon, ultramarine and periwinkle, hibiscus and marshmallow].[111] Specifically, the "fond floral céladon" [celadon floral background] of the calligraphy recalls the pale gray-green of the figure at the top right and the cloths at the base of the picture. More generally, the notion of floral colors identifies the colors of the painting. The "pervenche" [vinca][112] has periwinkle flowers not unlike the blue of the garments worn by three of the women in the top half of the picture. "Ketmie" comes from the Arabic "خطمي" [khaṭmī] and is a generic name for the hibiscus or marshmallow.[113] It is most often red or light pink in color, as in the "carmine glowing" or "rutilemen[t] . . . carmin" of the Arabic letters.[114] We see it also in the outer garments of the apostle holding Christ's torso and the female figure on the right, whose back is turned to the viewer. "Guimauve" designates the althaea, closely related to, and often confused with, the preceding plants.[115] The "outremer" that describes the "musical" explosion of the Arabic script is homonymous with the "ultramarin" that Meddeb identifies in Pontormo's painting.[116] The confusion of tones, of colors, and of visual musicality in Pontormo's deposition and in the unidentified calligraphy that opens this chapter may show Meddeb in the act of casting a new Islamic aesthetic. At the very least, the resemblance of these two passages suggests that, far from being antithetical, Christian representations of God's incarnation and decorative Islamic calligraphy can achieve deep imbrication.

Any resonance between the illustrations of calligraphy and of the Incarnation are further enhanced by the descriptions that follow:

> Au gré des feuillets, je tombe par hasard sur des lettres d'or qui ornent un vélin bleu nuit, consonnes archaïques aux arêtes vives, isolées, sans points diacritiques, ni signes vocaliques, dépouillées jusqu'à l'indéchiffrable, astres scintillant dans le métro et pénétrant sous la calotte allumée de mon crâne.
>
> As I go through the pages, I happen across gold letters that adorn a midnight blue vellum, archaic consonants with sharp edges, isolated, without diacritical marks or vocalic signs, stripped to the point of being indecipherable, stars scintillating in the subway and penetrating under the lit cap of my skull.[117]

If the Arabic consonants have been "dépouillées," or "stripped down," to the point that they become indecipherable, they nevertheless provide an alternative, perhaps fantastical but no less legitimate mode of legibility. It is a mode that recalls the disposition of bodies in Pontormo's painting, as given verbal form by Meddeb:

> Les corps, aux proportions étirées, encerclent d'ondulations sinueuses la dépouille du Christ.
>
> The bodies, with stretched proportions, encircle the remains of Christ with sinuous undulations.[118]

Instead of simply establishing an equation between Pontormo's bodies and the Arabic letters, Meddeb's phrase demonstrates that the image breaks down the economy of calligraphy into two parts: first, the encircling undulations of stretched proportions; and second, the representation of God, the Incarnation, the "dépouille" or "salb" of the "déposition" at its center. The consonants bear no vocalic signs or diacritical marks, just as Christ's stigmata are discreet and clean. Neither the letters nor the corpse have any meaning except that which is attributed to them in the viewer's imagination via the inspiration of, on the one hand, vowels, and on the other, faith.

We cannot see the calligraphy evoked at the beginning of chapter 8, but we may not need to. As Khatibi reminds us, "Calligraphy is a delirious rhetoric, which dynamites the linguistic sign. . . . The calligraphic letter is no longer quite a letter, it is rather something between the letter and the musical note."[119] In *Phantasia*, though, the explosion is visual before it is acoustic. The first instance of Arabic script in the novel was related to the narrator's "reading" of the Qur'ān, adumbrated above, in which the three letters "alif," "lām," and "mīm" appeared not as "ألم" [a-l-m] but as .[120] In this transcription, the "alif" is set apart, while the "lām" and the "mīm" are not ligated as usual but instead overlap as if in an embrace. The elongated serif on the "alif" appears to gesture toward the other letters, while its curving tail perhaps recalls the contrapposto of the figure holding Christ on the left of Pontormo's picture. Meddeb concluded above that in each of these unarticulated letters, "le verbe s'incarne" [the word is incarnated].[121] In the painting, the stretched proportions and sinuous undulations of the bodies encircling Christ's corpse strain figuration and reach toward the abstraction of the letter. There is, in the arrangement of these three letters, the same sense of capturing a stately dance in a moment of silence that pervades Pontormo's image. We might even say that the letters bend themselves to create a broken and contested pietà. As such, the "alif," "lām," and "mīm" form a new transcription of the Name. Not a novel Trinity, nor a slimmed down tetragram, but perhaps a "trigram," also unique and unpronounceable, in which the Arabic letters penetrate the body of Christ, just as the Incarnation leaves its mark on the mysteries of calligraphy.

As Meddeb's narrator peruses these reproductions of Arabic script, the underground train comes to a sudden stop, throwing him headlong from his seat. His fall "dans la ténèbre souterraine, entre deux stations" [in the subterranean darkness, between two stations], is arrested by the woman sitting opposite him: "les bras de femme, fins et de noir vêtus" [woman's arms, slender and dressed in black].[122] This is the first encounter between the narrator and Aya, his lover and partner in the erotic episodes recounted elsewhere in the novel. This unforeseen meeting of bodies brings multiple elements of the Passion into fragmented focus. When the narrator falls into the arms of the woman in black, they together repair, albeit momentarily, the fractured pietà of Pontormo's altarpiece. The narrator's subterranean passage through Paris begins to resemble Christ's descent into hell. The halt in the tunnel between two stations—a charged word in Sufism—becomes a novel station of the cross. The narrator thanks the woman "qui s'est interposée pour éviter ma chute" [who intervened to prevent my fall],[123] evoking not only one of Christ's three falls on the way to Golgotha, and the Fall that the Messiah claims to repair, but also the Virgin Mother in her role as intercessor, here interposer. The confusion of mother and lover, of virgin and paramour has already been broached in the context of Quarton's *Coronation* (fig. 12), where we are told that Mary appears more beautiful to the narrator when he thinks of her as the painter's lover: "Cette Marie de chair qui éveille Éros serait l'hymne par laquelle l'artiste aurait célébré l'amante" [This Mary of flesh and blood who arouses Eros is the hymn of praise with which the artist celebrates his lover].[124] Here, Aya becomes a virgin of the flesh, no longer a mother without sin but instead sensuously incarnate.

When the narrator exits the train, he is followed by Aya, leading to an impromptu conversation in the Tuileries Garden on their shared Muslim heritage: "J'aime la calligraphie arabe" [I love Arabic calligraphy], Aya explains, "Bien que cela ne paraisse pas, je suis d'ascendance musulmane" [Although it doesn't look like it, I am of Muslim descent].[125] Although she speaks for both of them in their origin and preference, our reading of *Phantasia* implies that this is only one side of the fold. The narrator is also in thrall to Christian iconography and, although it may not look like it, could be said to be of Christian descent. This is not to say that he is Christian in any conventional sense but that he lives with the descent of the body from the cross, with the deposition of the icon, with the suspension of the Incarnation as captured by Pontormo in Santa Felicità, on the far side of the Arno, in the first decades of the sixteenth century.

The narrator appears to confirm this when he explains that although not a practicing Muslim, he cannot escape from his Islamic origin:

> J'en entretiens la trace à travers des rites et une culture dont je soigne la mutation. . . . Les résurrections ont lieu lorsque les identités se cristallisent dans le sursaut qui s'oppose à l'hégémonie.[126]
>
> I maintain my ties to it in rites and a culture that I try to adapt. . . . Resurrections take place when identities crystallize in the jolt that refuses hegemony.

If, in *Phantasia*, the Incarnation becomes a feature of Meddeb's deft mutation of Islam, then it also announces the possibility of an alternative resurrection. Not of Christ, nor of the faithful dead or even of Khaïr-Eddine's wildflowers, but of a new Islam, an Islam that, among other things, is able to incorporate the phantasms of Pontormo, of Mannerism and the Renaissance, not to mention the reader's own fantasies. As the narrator notes, somewhat arcanely, "Je ne souhaiterais pas demeurer dans la tribu des chrysalides" [I would not want to be stuck in the tribe of the chrysalides].[127]

An awareness of the role played by the Incarnation in *Phantasia*'s visual economy cannot exhaust our understanding of how the novel teaches its reader to see. But it enables us, at the very least, to counter the still prevalent notion that cultural Islam is necessarily aniconic or even iconoclastic. Here, we see how "la vérité islamique," or "Islamic truth,"[128] need not turn away from the figurative but may in fact move decisively, if discreetly, toward it. The interplay of incarnation and calligraphy in Meddeb's prose also allows us to see how the Maghrebi writer in French might reproduce what Hédi Abdel-Jaouad calls "the plastic potential, the materiality that inheres in the Arabic letter," and thereby become "a calligrapher in the language of the other."[129]

Phantasia is Meddeb's second and final novel, after which he turns to poetry with the publication of *Tombeau d'Ibn Arabi*,[130] "reinvent[ing] his literary persona as Sufi poet"[131] even as he remains "both decadent and pious."[132] He has been said to mobilize Sufism "as an aesthetic tradition inseparable from its ethical preoccupations,"[133] confirming Tengour's comment that "there always exists a non(?)-conscious smidgen of Sufism in the Maghrebian writer who is not a clever faker [qui n'est pas un habile faiseur]."[134] Others have noted the imprint of Taoism and Buddhism on Meddeb's thought,[135] to say nothing of the effect of secular Europe. Still others perceive his fiction as translating "Islamic cultural practices from Arabic into French."[136] Future studies may have to take more seriously the ways in which Meddeb's fictional work is unexpectedly dis-orienting, theologically promiscuous, and, at times, deliberately heretical.

CHAPTER 7

Qur'ānic Visions

Arthur Rimbaud and the Artificial Vertigo of Flowers

Les fleurs qui parent les sentiers de la vie sont une épreuve.

ISLAMIC RIMBAUD

In *Soumission* [Submission], Michel Houellebecq's sixth novel—published in 2015 but set in 2022—a surprise result in the French presidential election sees a moderate Islamist installed in the Élysée Palace.[1] Sweeping reforms are rapidly introduced, not least in the national education system, where nevertheless one thing remains largely unchanged. The writings of Arthur Rimbaud, whom the narrator dismisses as "a *bogus topic* if ever there was one" and "the world's most beaten-to-death subject, with the possible exception of Flaubert,"[2] can still be studied and taught at the new Islamic University of Paris on condition that the poet's late conversion to Islam is accepted as fact: "But regarding the most important thing," the narrator tells us, "regarding the analysis of his poems, there had been no intervention to speak of."[3]

We will probably never know if Rimbaud converted to Islam during the almost twelve years he spent working as a trader in the Arabian Peninsula and Horn of Africa between 1880 and 1891.[4] It is clear from Rimbaud's correspondence throughout the 1880s that both Islam and the Arabic language were of interest to him. It is thought that Rimbaud asked his mother for an Arabic dictionary sometime in the second half of 1880, because in early November he wrote to complain that the "Arabic books" he had asked for two months previously had still not arrived.[5] This frustration is echoed in another letter, dated February 15, 1881:

> A propos, comment n'avez-vous pas retrouvé le dictionnaire arabe? Il doit être à la maison cependant.

> Dites à F. de chercher dans les papiers arabes un cahier intitulé *Plaisanteries, jeux de mots, etc.*, en arabe; et il doit y avoir aussi une collection de *dialogues, de chansons* ou je ne sais quoi, utile à ceux qui apprennent la langue. S'il y a un ouvrage en arabe, envoyez; mais tout ceci comme emballage seulement, car ça ne vaut pas le port.
>
> By the way, how have you not found the Arabic dictionary? It has to be at home, though.
>
> Tell F. to look among the Arabic papers for an exercise book entitled *Jokes, Word Games, etc.*, in Arabic; and there should also be a collection of *dialogues, songs*, and so forth, useful to anyone learning the language. If you find a book in Arabic, send it; but send it only as packaging, for it is not worth the postage itself.[6]

It is unclear if Rimbaud ever received these papers, and if so, if they were of any help. According to Alfred Bardey—for whose company Rimbaud worked in Aden and Harar—by the early 1880s, his employee knew enough Arabic to issue commands, which supposedly earned him the respect of the local workers.[7]

Beyond the Arabic language, the letters sent to his mother and siblings also betray his eagerness to learn more about Islam. On October 7, 1883, Rimbaud requested that his family forward a letter to the Hachette booksellers, in which he ordered a bilingual copy of the Qur'ān:

> Je vous serai très obligé de m'envoyer aussitôt que possible à l'adresse ci-dessous (contre remboursement) la meilleure traduction française du Coran, (avec le texte arabe en regard s'il existe ainsi)—et même sans le texte.
>
> I would be most obliged if you could send as soon as possible to the address below (paid on delivery) the best French translation of the Qur'ān, (with the Arabic text facing if this exists)—and even without the text.[8]

The critic Pierre Brunel is by no means alone in dismissing the notion that such a possession could have any broader significance: "And he kept the Qur'ān, which does not mean, as has sometimes been claimed, that he became a Muslim. Maybe, quite simply, [books like these] were hard to sell."[9] Steve Murphy is also skeptical: "Was Rimbaud familiar with the Qur'ān?

There is nothing to suggest that he was, even if nothing prevents us from imagining that he had access to his father's [Arabic] papers."[10] Christopher Miller states categorically that the later phase of Rimbaud's life can have no effect on the way we read his poetry, but admits that it remains "important to read and study the fallacy rather than ignore it."[11] Hédi Abdel-Jaouad goes so far as to ask, "Why shouldn't we speak of Rimbaud's Islamic vocation?"[12]

Various testimonies from people who encountered Rimbaud at the time appear to suggest that his interest in Islam, and in Arabic, was closely tied to his experience of living in the city of Harar, which was a "hub of Muslim dissemination in southern Abyssinia" and of Qādirī Sufism in particular.[13] Léonce Lagarde, the first ambassador of France to Ethiopia, reports that Rimbaud "is said to have considered studying the Qur'ān and that he thought about Islam in some depth, before, naturally, trying to interpret Qur'ānic principles, and sharing his opinions with Muslims he encountered."[14] These attempts appear to have backfired: "It is alleged that his interpretations—considered too personal—provoked some anger, such that one day, somewhere near Harar, a group of fanatics apparently set upon him, beating him with sticks."[15] Lagarde retold this story many years later in a letter to the poet Paul Claudel: "[Rimbaud] struggled on the one hand for his life (what a rough life!), and then dreamed of things that the natives and the Muslim leaders of the emir's entourage at the time did not understand . . . However, they considered him to be divinely inspired, so much so that 'followers' flocked to him, arousing the jealousy and antipathy of the qadis and muftis threatened in their 'affairs' by the new prophet, whom they tried, moreover, to have killed on the spot."[16] The Italian journalist and explorer Ugo Ferrandi, who knew the former poet in Aden and Tadjoura in the mid 1880s,[17] also records that Rimbaud was an Arabic speaker who "explained and expounded the Qur'ān to the locals."[18] But the most persuasive sign of Rimbaud's possible conversion to Islam may be material. A gold seal, found among Rimbaud's effects and with which he stamped his correspondence throughout the 1880s, was engraved with the Arabic motto "Abdo Rinbo," an abbreviation of "'Abd Allāh Rimbaud" [Rimbaud, servant of God].[19] And even as she insisted that Arthur died a repentant Catholic, Isabelle recalls that on his death bed in Marseille her brother kept repeating the words "Allah Kerim," or "God is generous," where "الكريم" [al-karīm], "the generous or noble one," is one of the ninety-nine names of God.[20]

The historical detail of the erstwhile poet's eventual turn to Islam interests me here little more than it does Houellebecq's awkward and lonely narrator, who is, in any case, more concerned with Joris-Karl Huysmans's conversion to Roman Catholicism. I suggest instead that Rimbaud's exposure to Islam, and specifically to the Qur'ān, when he was still a schoolboy and poet, was both more extensive and more decisive than has so far been acknowledged. I propose that traces of Rimbaud's reading of a specific French translation of the Qur'ān can be identified in *Illuminations*, the collection of prose poems left unfinished around 1875 and first published in 1886 through the organizational and editorial efforts of Paul Verlaine.[21] Any confirmation of the poet Rimbaud's encounter with Islam through its central sacred and poetic text may require us to reappraise the way we read and think about his prose poetics.[22]

Preliminary evidence of the young poet's interest in Islam will be familiar to many, so I will limit myself to a handful of examples. Consider, for instance, the possible motivations behind a poem such as the 1871 sonnet "Voyelles" [Vowels], in which a color is ascribed to each of the five vowels, "A noir, E blanc, I rouge, U vert, O bleu: voyelles . . ." [A black, E white, I red, U green, O blue: vowels . . .],[23] which appears to echo the practice of using different colored inks for vowels and diacritical marks in early manuscripts of the Qur'ān. This practice was instituted by the poet Abū al-Aswad al-Du'alī (Hejaz, 603–Basra, 689), who used large colored dots to distinguish otherwise identical consonants from each other ("i'jām" or "nuqaṭ") and to indicate the presence of otherwise unmarked short vowels ("tashkīl"). Although this system was later refined—notably by Abū 'Abd al-Raḥmān al-Khalīl ibn Aḥmad al-Farāhīdī (Oman, 718–Basra, 786), who included different shapes for the diacritical marks, removing the need for distinction by color—manuscripts pointed with colored vowels continued to be inscribed, as can be seen in the eighteenth-century Maghrebi Qur'ān preserved at the Walters Art Museum in Baltimore (fig. 16), among many other examples.[24] Any possible connection between the colored vowels of this sonnet and the Qur'ān may be marginally enhanced when we consider the poet's use of capital letters in the final words of the autograph manuscript, which serve to create a sort of hypostasis: "—Ô l'Oméga, rayon violet de Ses Yeux!" [—O, the Omega, purple ray of His Eyes!][25]

The single-letter title of the prose poem "H"[26]—source of many more-or-less outlandish and sometimes brilliant conjectures—may recall the various suras preceded by "حروف مقطعات" [ḥurūf muqaṭṭa'āt] [disconnected letters], sometimes called "فواتح" [fawātiḥ], or "prefatory" letters. Abdelkébir Khatibi points to these "arbitrary, random letters that exceed the norms of linguistic economy"[27] as markers of "إعجاز" [i'jāz], that is, of the Qur'ān's "inimitability"—the notion that the Qur'ān is uncreated and eternal and could therefore never be created by mankind. The letters "طه" [ṭā hā] that introduce the twentieth sura of the Qur'ān, as illustrated in figure 16, and are devoid of any obvious meaning, become "T. H." in Claude-Étienne Savary's

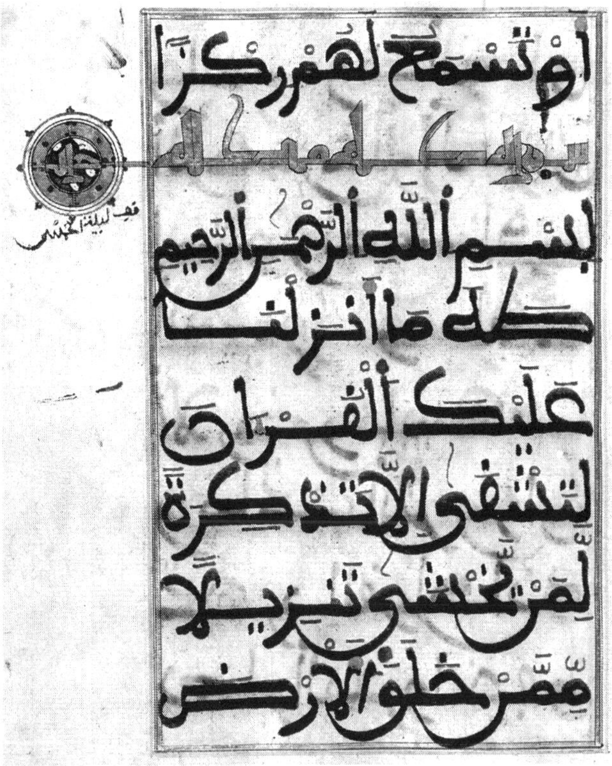

FIG. 16. Illuminated chapter heading for "Sūrat Ṭā Hā," including verses 19:98 (partial) and 20:1–4 (partial), ink and pigments on Italian paper with a watermark of three crescents, Maghreb, eighteenth century C.E., 30 × 21.5 cm. The Walters Art Museum, Baltimore. The illuminated chapter heading for "Sūrat Ṭā Hā" is written in a decorative New Abbasid (Broken Cursive) style in gold ink. The text is written in a large Maghrebi script, with diacritical marks in red, green, and yellow ink. In translation, the page reads: "Or hear from them a murmur? Sūrat Ṭā Hā. In the Name of God, the Compassionate, the Merciful. Ṭā Hā. We did not send down the Qur'ān unto thee that thou shouldst be distressed, but only as a reminder unto one who fears [God], a revelation from He, Who created the earth . . ." (Seyyed Hossein Nasr et al., eds., *The Study Quran: A New Translation and Commentary* (New York: HarperOne, 2015), 786, 789).

translation from the 1780s. Savary notes, in keeping with conventional Islamic teaching, that "all of these characters are mysterious, and God alone understands them."[28] Notwithstanding the identification of "H" with "Hortense," mentioned twice in the poem, a similar mystery encircles this text. As

Rimbaud writes at the end of "Parade" [Sideshow], "J'ai seul la clef de cette parade sauvage" [I alone have the key to this savage sideshow].[29]

In his letter to Paul Demeny from May 15, 1871, Rimbaud speaks of the need for poets to submit themselves to "un long, immense et raisonné *dérèglement* de *tous les sens*" [a long, immense, and reasoned *disorganization* of *all the senses*].[30] When read alongside the translation of the eighteenth sura, "The Cave," undertaken by the francophone orientalist Albin Kazimirski de Biberstein (Korchów, 1808–Paris, 1887), the conventional aspect of Rimbaud's "*dérèglement*" is altered: "Do not obey him whose heart we have made forgetful of our memory, who follows his inclinations, and whose actions are all disorder [et dont toutes les actions sont un déréglement [*sic*]]."[31] In a footnote, Kazimirski identifies "déréglement" as a translation of the Arabic "فرط" [furuṭ], explaining that this word "describes the uncontrolled bolting of a horse, who leaves all others behind and abandons them."[32] In his bilingual, Arabic-French dictionary, however, he attributes a proliferation of possible meanings to "furuṭ," including "1. A very quick horse in racing, who outpaces all the others. 2. An abandoned case that is not pursued. 3. Too much, excess, what is done by surpassing all measures. 4. Iniquity. 5. A very high hill, almost a mountain."[33] All these meanings, once brought to light, attach themselves parasitically to Rimbaud's use of the term, distorting and enriching it in previously unexpected ways, enabling alternative perspectives on Rimbaud's poetics. This is an example of how Qurʾānic Arabic might, through translation, reinvest a French term with new significance, an instance of the "pacifist invasions" that, as per Yasser Elhariry, accelerate the development of a "postfrancophone literature—a literature, ostensibly written in French, that is neither French nor francophone, neither both nor hybrid nor 'between' yet always situated in relation to its pasts, itself, its past selves."[34]

The most unambiguous reference to Islam in Rimbaud's poetic oeuvre is found toward the end of *Une saison en enfer* [A Season in Hell], in the section headed "L'impossible" [The Impossible], in which the poet casts a retrospective eye over the vicissitudes of his adolescent poetic project:

> J'envoyais au diable les palmes des martyrs, les rayons de l'art, l'orgueil des inventeurs, l'ardeur des pillards; je retournais à l'Orient et à la sagesse première et éternelle.—Il paraît que c'est un rêve de paresse grossière!
>
> Pourtant, je ne songeais guère au plaisir d'échapper aux souffrances modernes. Je n'avais pas en vue la sagesse bâtarde du Coran.

> The devil could take the palms of martyrs, the rays of art, the pride of inventors, the enthusiasm of plunderers; I returned to the Orient and to the first and eternal wisdom. This appears to be a dream of vulgar laziness!
>
> And yet, I hardly ever thought of the pleasure of escaping from modern sufferings. I did not have the bastard wisdom of the Qur'ān in mind.[35]

Responding to what initially appears to be a rejection of Islam's holiest text, most commentators have attempted to rehabilitate Rimbaud's comment through interpretation. Valeria Zotti argues that Rimbaud's rejection of the Qur'ān's "bastard wisdom" is specifically a rejection of "the notion of fate," in which "the ego is completely negated,"[36] rather than a rejection of Islam in its entirety. For Claude Jeancolas, the adjective "bâtard" [bastard] means that "this sacred text is not purely oriental" but "also based on the ancient texts of the Bible, upon which Western values are founded."[37] By extension, "bâtard" might be understood as describing the hybrid descendance of a supposedly illegitimate coupling, here of Judaism and Christianity. In much the same way that the syntagma "plante bâtarde" denotes a wild or ungrafted plant,[38] "sagesse bâtarde" might denote the origins of this holy text in the Arabian Desert, as dictated to Muḥammad by the archangel Gabriel, first in Mecca, then in Medina.

Two additional interpretations of "bâtard" should also be considered. First, in calligraphy, "bâtard" indicates script in which liaisons between letters are elaborate and curved, and tails of letters long and somewhat extravagant.[39] It follows that, in printing, a "caractère bâtard" is a type that imitates the calligraphic style.[40] Although usually applied to Latin script, "bâtard" may here describe the cursive aspect of the Qur'ān's Arabic script, or what is properly called "نسخ" [naskh], especially for someone who does not read Arabic. This would suggest not only that the adolescent Rimbaud had seen an Arabic copy of the Qur'ān, but that, far from repudiation, "sagesse bâtarde" conveys his amazement at the visual aspect of this sacred and poetic text—a fascination later shared by the poet Yves Bonnefoy, who speaks of the "hypnotic entanglements" of Islamic script.[41] Of course, the verb "نسخ" [nasakha] means both "to copy a book, a manuscript" and "to efface, make disappear."[42] The coexistence of these mutually preclusive meanings may stem from a deep scholastic practice, as students learn the Qur'ān by heart precisely through such a process of inscription and immediate deletion.[43] It is an exercise recalled by many of the poets discussed in this book, including Tahar Djaout, whose narrator in *L'invention du désert* recalls,

"You think back to your tenacity as a child, who coated then washed—incessantly—the surface assigned to writing. You think back to the Qur'ānic slate; to letters which become blurred, swallow each other, then disappear, leaving thick, slow streaks on the blackened clay."[44] Whereas for Djaout, the Qur'ān's "bastard wisdom" is inscribed to then be erased, for Rimbaud, it is as if this wisdom reverses its premature erasure to reinscribe itself not only in his life but also in his poetry.

Second, there is the possibility that "bâtard" includes the poet's sense of his own interrupted filiation. Frédéric Rimbaud (Dole, 1814–Dijon, 1878) abandoned his wife, Vitalie Cuif (Chuffilly-Roche, 1825–Chuffilly-Roche, 1907) and their four children in 1860, when Arthur was six years old. Frédéric was a soldier in the French infantry and had served in Algeria from 1842 onward, becoming the head of the Office of Arabic Affairs in the village of Sebdou, south of Tlemcen, in 1844.[45] In 1852, he was the coauthor, with the geographer and historian Oscar Mac Carthy (Paris, 1815–Algiers, 1894), of an article entitled "Les sauterelles à Sebdou en 1849" [The Grasshoppers at Sebdou in 1849],[46] in which two verses from the Qur'ān—referenced in a manuscript by a local marabout—are quoted, not in Arabic but in Kazimirski's French translation:

> Les yeux baissés, ils sortirent de leurs tombeaux, semblables aux sauterelles dispersées.
> Courant à pas précipités auprès de *l'ange* qui les a appelés.
>
> With eyes downcast, they will emerge from their tombs, like scattered grasshoppers,
> Running with hurried steps to *the angel* who summoned them.[47]

The author Mohamed Kacimi (b. El Hamel, 1955) notes that the article demonstrates "not only a good knowledge of dialectal Arabic (Rimbaud often quotes the terms of the original language: goutaia, chaouch, chouâf, djerrad) but shows a real attentiveness to the local imaginary."[48] This appraisal of Frédéric's linguistic abilities is in line with research undertaken in the 1890s, when historians Jean Bourguignon and Charles Houin concluded that Rimbaud's father was "a distinguished Arabic linguist." They continued, "His family possesses an Arabic grammar book reviewed and corrected by him, a quantity of French-Arabic documents on expeditions in Algeria, a translation of the Qur'ān with the Arabic text set alongside."[49]

There has been some debate as to the accuracy of such evaluations, as Simon Godchot subsequently demonstrated.[50] But this absent and Arabic-speaking father nevertheless helps to explain the young poet's interest in the so-called Orient and in figures such as 'Abd al-Qādir, who features in Rimbaud's early poem "Jugurtha," written in Latin as part of a school competition at the Douai Academy in July 1869.[51] This relation may also help explain the Carolopolitan poet's vision in *Une saison en enfer*: "Je voyais très franchement une mosquée à la place d'une usine" [I saw very frankly a mosque in the place of a factory].[52] This hallucination in particular has repeatedly captured the imagination of francophone poets in the Maghreb. In his poem "Poubelles précieuses" [Precious Trash], Jean Sénac writes, "Coran Mosquée haut-parleur sapin" [Qur'ān Mosque loud-speaker pine tree].[53] And in an article on al-Ḥallāj, during a Rimbaldian vagabondage on the Brenta river between Padua and Venice, Abdelwahab Meddeb allows himself to daydream: "I see, on the other side, above the Villa Foscari, the Palladian 'Malcontenta,' I see minarets instead of chimney stacks [je vois des minarets à la place des cheminées], as if rediscovering an echo of the Mesopotamian reference, the focal point of my 'immaginativa,' which mimics places and climes, thanks to a transfigured reality, emerging on the page ready to receive the images that arrest me, whether Eastern or Western."[54] The shadow cast by the mosque in *Une saison en enfer*, which extends to Sénac's Algerian cityscape and to Meddeb's passage through northern Italy, is indistinguishable from the shadow cast by Rimbaud's absent father. This is what Mohamed Kacimi calls the "Arabic shadow" that followed Arthur from the start,[55] but we might also call it Rimbaud's "bastard wisdom."

FLOWERS

> La fraîche carnation d'enfant anglais qu'il conserva longtemps avait fait place, dans cet intervalle de deux années, au teint sombre d'un kabyle.[56]

The value of the Qur'ān to a young person interested in poetic writing has been demonstrated on many occasions. Meddeb declares that it was his contact with the language of the Qur'ān that first gave him a predisposition to "poetic reading": "In this way, I privileged a physical relation to language, in whatever form, listening to its scansion, the musical reception provoked by the combination of its vowels and consonants. I succumbed to the irrepressible desire to return the text I had before my eyes to its oral genesis, as if sound trumped meaning. The holy status of language, be it as voice or trace, is achieved as soon as the signifier takes precedence over the signified."[57] Had Rimbaud undertaken to read the Qur'ān at the time he was writing poetry, he would likely have read Kazimirski's translation, either in the edition read and used by his father or in one of several reprints, and it is conceivable that there are traces of any such reading in his poems. If this were the case, then we would need to examine how an Islamic—or, more properly, Qur'ānic—perspective might transform the ways in which we approach the interpretation of Rimbaud's poetic texts, including the following prose poem:

> FLEURS
>
> D'un gradin d'or,—parmi les cordons de soie, les gazes grises, les velours verts et les disques de cristal qui noircissent comme du bronze au soleil,—je vois la digitale s'ouvrir sur un tapis de filigranes d'argent, d'yeux et de chevelures.
>
> Des pièces d'or jaune semées sur l'agate, des piliers d'acajou supportant un dôme d'émeraudes, des bouquets de satin blanc et de fines verges de rubis entourent la rose d'eau.
>
> Tels qu'un dieu aux énormes yeux bleus et aux formes de neige, la mer et le ciel attirent aux terrasses de marbre la foule des jeunes et fortes roses.
>
> FLOWERS
>
> From a terrace of gold,—among the silk cords, the gray gauzes, the green velvets, and the crystal disks that blacken like bronze in the sun—I see the digitalis opening on a carpet of silver filigrees, of eyes, and of hair.
>
> Pieces of yellow gold strewn across the agate, mahogany pillars supporting an emerald dome, bouquets of white satin, and of thin ruby stems, surround the water rose.
>
> Like a god with enormous blue eyes and with forms of snow, the sea and the sky draw, to the marble terraces, the crowd of young and strong roses.[58]

Edward Ahearn notes that from its initial utterance—"D'un gradin d'or . . . je vois" [From a terrace of gold . . . I see]—the poem emphasizes the importance of perspective and vision, designating an eminent point from which everything that follows can be seen by the first person.[59] Despite the poem's title, the object of the vision in this opening phrase is not a flower—the digitalis, or foxglove—but the event of its opening, or what Martin Heidegger calls, in his reading of a poem by Parmenides, "ἀλήθεια" [alētheia], that is, "die Unverborgenheit . . . die Lichtung des Offenen" [unconcealment . . . the uncovering of the open].[60]

The uncovering of this opening, or unconcealment, has provided space for a variety of interpretations. For several critics, the poem describes a decorated interior. Suzanne Bernard specifically identifies a theater, although she concedes—in light of the final phrase—that it could also be a ballet.[61] Bruno Claisse sees "the delirious luxury of the upper social classes of the period"—as represented in certain Second Empire novels, "where all things 'sweated gold, dripped gold'"—and goes so far as to anchor the poem in the historical context of a rise in popularity of luxury beach villas.[62] Others are more sensitive to the way in which the poem appeals to the natural world. Antoine Adam—editor of the first Bibliothèque de la Pléiade edition of Rimbaud's works—sees any reference to the internal decor of a theater as the metaphorical product of a vision of nature.[63] Ross Chambers similarly admits the presence of a theater that is interchangeable with nature.[64] For Ernest Delahaye, companion of Rimbaud's youth, the poet "is lying in sweet, fresh grass, . . . his head stretched out among so many plants that touch it, his eyes seeing details from very close up that his mind then interprets."[65] For Anne-Emmanuelle Berger, it is the "auriferous dominant"—the multiple presence of the acoustic particle "or" [gold]—that "is articulated over vision as the agent and channel of poetic production."[66] Perhaps the most striking reading of "Fleurs" to date is that proposed by Jean-Pierre Richard, who describes it as a "strange poem," Rimbaud's "*floral apotheosis*," and a poem in which "the triumph of the flowers unfolds in three successive movements, where florality in turn reveals itself, consolidates itself, and finally surpasses and destroys itself."[67] Common to almost all these readings—it might be more apt to speak of them as critical visions—is a tendency to imagine what the poet himself saw, either in the real world or in the eye of his mind.

Instead of perpetuating this rich critical tradition, according to which Rimbaud's poems offer privileged explorations of the visual and visuality, I propose to read "Fleurs" in the light of Rimbaud's interest in Islam and Islamic traditions—and especially in the Qur'ān. I begin by evoking one of the few critics to counter the call of the visual in *Illuminations*, namely Jean-Marie Gleize:

> If the spectator wants to get closer to the poem, to try, as Rimbaud says about the skies of his childhood, to "refine his optics," he will have no choice but to confirm that the essence of Rim-

> baud's effort consists not in producing images, in transcribing visions, in describing landscapes, however novel they may be, but in preventing these images from fully forming. Put simply, Rimbaud is not proposing a new spectacle; he does not stop or cause the poem to stop at any vision. As soon as the image, as soon as truth, has been embraced (much more than "seen"), they then "fall" with the subject who embraces them (see "Aube" [Dawn]) and there has to be another departure (see "Assez vu!" [Enough seen!] in "Départ" [Departure]) "through an image-less universe" ("Jeunesse II" [Youth II]; "Sonnet" [Sonnet]).[68]

Rather than concede, with Richard, that "we are, above all, present at the simple miracle of florescence,"[69] we might—in the spirit of Gleize—situate the poem in an Islamic perspective by quoting one of the ahadith of the Prophet, as recounted by his cousin Ibn ʿAbbās (Mecca, 619–Taif, 687): "To a Persian painter who asked [Muḥammad], 'But does this mean I will no longer be able to depict animals? Will I no longer be able to pursue my profession?' he replied, 'You will, but you should decapitate the animals so that they no longer look alive, and try to make them look like flowers.'"[70] Given that the Qurʾān contains no explicit prohibition regarding the production or consumption of representational images, the aniconic practices commonly associated with Islam, particularly in its Sunni forms, can be traced to accounts such as this. When Émile Dermenghem claims that the then almost sixteen-year-old Algerian artist Fatima Haddad (Bordj El Kiffan, 1931–Blida, 1998)—better known as Baya Mahieddine—probably had no thought of any such interdictions when she created her iconic paintings in which figures often effloresce, he allows himself to reinscribe the religious anecdote: "Her women and birds are also flowers, sumptuous flowers, bursting, crawling, walking, dancing in lines and colors of astonishing richness, whose dresses and plumages are of incredible decorative luxuriance, with endlessly innovative patterns."[71]

This hadith and Dermenghem's variation on it invite us to examine more closely what Richard calls "the importance of floral lyricism in Rimbaud and the richness of his floral imaginary."[72] Richard admits that the wealth of this floral imaginary is not a function of the characteristics evoked in the poem: "As varied as they may appear, these flowers nonetheless all possess the same character, an essential trait: they are all 'magic flowers,' powerful but poorly differentiated, almost impersonal . . . purely floral beings."[73] It is unclear whether Richard is aware of the hadith mentioned above, but he nevertheless proposes a reading of Rimbaud's flowers that is remarkably similar to Ibn ʿAbbās's description of the Islamic flower. As Richard continues, the perfect Rimbaldian flower would resemble a stone because "the first attribute of the stone is modesty [pudeur]" and "it is always ready to close in on itself, or to flee into the ground; . . . Stone, skittish flower."[74]

It should come as no surprise that stones and flowers often appear alongside each other in Rimbaud's work, whether it be "Des fleurs presque pierres . . ." [Flowers that are almost stones . . .] in the 1871 poem "Ce qu'on dit au poète à propos de fleurs" [What Is Said to the Poet about Flowers][75] or "Oh! les pierres précieuses qui se cachaient,—les fleurs qui regardaient déjà" [Oh! The precious stones that were hidden—the flowers that were already watching] in "Après le déluge" [After the Deluge],[76] the opening poem of *Illuminations*. Louis Massignon refers to this anecdote from the ahadith to illustrate the characteristics of the metaphor in Islamic poetry. It is a metaphor that is "a kind of inanimation of metaphor," a metaphor that distances itself from the real to make itself unreal. As Massignon explains, "There is a descent of the metaphor. Man is compared to animals; the animal is compared, generally, to a flower, and the flower to a stone: a tulip is a ruby."[77] Paul de Man comes close to Richard's conclusion when discussing the line in Friedrich Hölderlin's hymn "Brot und Wein" [Bread and Wine] that reads, "Nun, nun müssen dafür Worte, wie Blumen, entstehn" [Well, now words, like flowers, must come into existence for it]. He admits that the "effect of the line would have been thoroughly modified if Hölderlin had written, for instance, 'Steinen' [stones] instead of 'Blumen' [flowers]" but maintains that "the relevance of the comparison would have remained intact as long as human language was being compared to a natural thing."[78]

In "Fleurs," the reader is invited to no longer see the flower in poetry as "the poetic object par excellence,"[79] as Jean-Paul Sartre says of a famous phrase in Jean Genet's novel *Notre-Dame-des-Fleurs* (1943): "Le jardinier est la plus belle rose de son jardin" [The gardener is the most beautiful rose in his garden].[80] Instead, the reader is asked to see flowers not only in "la digitale" [the digitalis], "les bouquets de satin blanc" [the bouquets of white satin], "la rose d'eau" [the water rose], and "les jeunes et fortes roses" [the young and strong roses], but in all manifestations of matter: gold, gauzes, velvets, crystal, bronze, silver, agate, acajou, emeralds, satin, rubies, and marble terraces—the last of which are, as Berger astutely notes, "an ideal earth for growing 'flowers that are almost stones, famous.'"[81] Berger sees all of Rimbaud's flowers as wedded to a "hardening, mark of an overinvestment that augments their value as poetic ornaments."[82] In other words, everything is flower in this poem, but the flower itself is no longer flower. To take up a question posed by Jacques Derrida in *Glas*, the poetic flower in Rimbaud's poem reintegrates itself "into the series of bodies or of objects of which it forms a part."[83] Rimbaud's flower is no longer—and perhaps never was—the poetic object par excellence. It is instead haunted by an absent figuration, by an aborted visual representation. If a referential order persists, it is one of decapitated monsters.

BLUE EYES

> . . . la tribu de Rimbaud et de Mohand ou M'hand, d'Hannibal, d'Ibn Khaldoun et de Saint Augustin . . .[84]

When Rimbaud's "Fleurs" is juxtaposed with Kazimirski's translation of the Qur'ān, a number of textual echoes become evident. In the sura called "The Cave"—immediately following the account of the seven sleepers of Ephesus referenced by Rimbaud in "Les déserts de l'amour"[85]—a single verse appears in which a cluster of the terms and images evoked in "Fleurs" can be identified:

> À ceux-ci les jardins d'Éden; sous leurs pieds couleront des eaux; ils s'y pareront de bracelets d'or, se vêtiront de robes vertes de soie forte et de satin, accoudés sur des siéges.
>
> Quelle belle récompense! quel admirable lieu de repos!

> To these the gardens of Eden; under their feet waters will flow; they will adorn themselves with golden bracelets, will dress themselves with green dresses of strong silk and satin, leaning on seats.
>
> What a beautiful reward! What an admirable resting place![86]

Constitutive fragments of this verse reappear—re-motivated, re-positioned, and re-qualified—in Rimbaud's poem. The "soie forte" [strong silk] becomes "cordons de soie" [silk cords]. The "robes vertes" [green dresses] become "velours verts" [green velvets]. "Robes . . . de satin" [dresses of satin] become "bouquets de satin blanc" [bouquets of white satin].

In the fifty-sixth sura, "The Event," the inhabitants of the same "garden of delights" are again seated in richly ornamented chairs:

> Se reposant sur des siéges ornés d'or et de pierreries,
> Accoudés et placés en face les uns des autres.

> Resting on seats decorated with gold and jewels,
> Leaning and seated opposite each other.[87]

The following verse adds that around them "circuleront des jeunes gens éternellement jeunes" [will circle young people who are eternally young],[88] which calls to mind the crowd "des jeunes et fortes roses" [of young and strong roses] drawn by the sea and the sky to the marble terraces in Rimbaud's poem.

Among the possible coincidences of Rimbaud's "Fleurs" with Kazimirski's translation of the Qur'ān, the most intriguing concerns the "dieu aux énormes yeux bleus" [god with the enormous blue eyes] of the final phrase, an image that many critics pretend not to see. In *Une saison en enfer*, Rimbaud appears to describe himself as having inherited "l'oeil bleu blanc" [the white-blue eye] from his "ancêtres gaulois" [Gaulish ancestors].[89] In "Les poètes de sept ans" [Seven-Year-Old Poets], the disgusted soul of the young poet-protagonist is expressed partially in "les yeux bleus" [the blue eyes],[90] unseen by the mother who has "le regard bleu,—qui ment!" [the blue gaze—that lies!].[91] Pierre Brunel notes that in visual records of Rimbaud's eyes, they seem to be not blue but black: "Who to believe? Who is lying? It is perhaps above all important to underline that the poetic text does not possess the status of the raw document. In neither 'Les poètes de sept ans' nor in 'Mauvais sang' is Rimbaud seeking to describe his person."[92] That said, Rimbaud's contemporaries, such as Léon Valade, speak of his "yeux bleus profonds" [deep blue eyes].[93] Verlaine remembers variously "des yeux d'un bleu pâle inquiétant" [disturbing pale-blue eyes][94] and "ces cruels yeux bleu clair" [these cruel light-blue eyes].[95] Ernest Delahaye recalls visiting Roche in 1879, following Rimbaud's return from Cyprus: "Je ne reconnus d'abord que ses yeux—si extraordinairement beaux!—à l'iris bleu clair entouré d'un anneau plus foncé couleur de pervenche" [I only recognized his eyes at first—so extraordinarily beautiful!—with a light-blue iris surrounded by a darker periwinkle-colored ring].[96]

In Kazimirski's version of the following Qur'ānic verse, blue eyes become a problem of translation:

يَوْمَ يُنفَخُ فِي ٱلصُّورِ ۚ وَنَحْشُرُ ٱلْمُجْرِمِينَ يَوْمَئِذٍ زُرْقًا

> [Yawma yunfakhu fī l-ṣūri wa-naḥshuru l-mujrimīna yawma'idhin zurqā]
>
> Le jour où l'on sonnera la trompette et où nous rassemblerons les coupables, qui auront alors les yeux frappés de cécité.
>
> The day the trumpet is sounded we will gather together the guilty, whose eyes will then be struck with blindness.[97]

The Arabic word that Kazimirski translates as "cécité" [blindness] is not "أَعْمى" [aʿmá], or "blind," but "زُرْقًا" [zurqan], which signifies "blue."[98] In its verbal form, the triconsonantal root associated with "zurqan" can mean "to be turned entirely toward someone" and, when applied to vision, describes the eye "when the pupil is directed wholly toward a single object, so that the whiteness of the eye seems to occupy the eye."[99] "Zurqan" therefore also describes the eye as it casts an oblique glance, much like the brown eye of the boy who squints in Rilke's *Duineser Elegien* [Duino Elegies].[100]

We might wonder how in the case of this translation, blue eyes come to be "struck with blindness." The translator provides the following justification:

> The Arabic word *zorkan* (acc. pl. of *azrak*) properly designates those who have blue eyes and can be applied to those who have a cataract or to those who have naturally blue eyes. The Arabs have always had a great aversion to men with blue eyes, a typical sign of the Greeks, their enemies, and Muḥammad could very well have given this mark to the condemned; however, verses 124 and 125 of this same chapter, where Satan is threatened with having to appear blind on the Day of Judgment and where Muḥammad uses the word *a'ma*, blind [aveugle], give to understand that the issue in the verse that concerns us is blindness [cécité].[101]

This is to say that "cécité" [blindness] is not a literal translation of the Arabic, but instead a displacement of the principal meaning of the word, that is then justified by the presence of blinding as a form of divine punishment elsewhere in the same chapter.

Kazimirski is not alone in stumbling over the word "zurqan." In Savary's translation—which Kazimirski initially intended to correct and otherwise improve, before determining to undertake his own translation—the verse reads as follows:

> Le jour où la trompette sonnera, les scélérats seront rassemblés, et leurs yeux seront couverts de ténèbres.
>
> The day the trumpet sounds, the wicked will be gathered together, and their eyes will be covered in shadows.[102]

This translation closely resembles that realized in Latin by Ludovico or Luigi Marracci (Lucca, 1612–Rome, 1700) in 1698:

> Die *quadam* insufflabitur in tubam, & congregabimus scelera-tos: die illa erit hebetudo oculorum.[103]

In addition to drawing from Marracci, Kazimirski also turned to George Sale (Canterbury, 1697–Westminster, 1736), whose translation into English from 1734 reads as follows:

> On that day the trumpet shall be sounded; and we will gather the wicked together on that day, having grey eyes.[104]

Sale also comments on the translation of "zurqan," noting that the word "signifies also those who are squint-eyed, or even blind of a suffusion."[105] In each of these instances of translation from Arabic into Latin, English, and French, the blue aspect of these eyes is suppressed to give eyes that are gray, shadowy, dull, or struck with blindness. The translation of this fragment of the holy text also renders its non-Arabic reader momentarily blind, obscuring the actual meaning of these eyes that do not see.

Let us now suppose that the sea and the sky that draw the crowd of young and strong roses to the marble terraces in "Fleurs" do so "tels qu'un dieu aux énormes yeux bleus" [as a god with enormous blue eyes], that is to say, as a god whose "enormous blue eyes" have lost not only their color but also their ability to see. The presence of the big blue eyes of a divinity that does not see—and that is only revealed once the poem has been juxtaposed with a translation of the Qur'ān—encourages us to further question the poem's appeal to the visual. For instance, in the representation of the god with enormous eyes, we may now perceive an idol that cannot see because it is a human creation, a vain form of poetic matter. It would then be a poetic image, such as those condemned—albeit obliquely—in the twenty-sixth sura, "The Poets":

> Ne vois-tu pas qu'ils [les poètes] suivent toutes les routes comme des insensés? Qu'ils disent ce qu'ils ne font pas?
>
> Do you not see that they [the poets] follow all the roads like madmen? That they say what they do not do?[106]

Despite the plethora of images in the poem, when set alongside Kazimirski's translation of the Qur'ān into French, the image of the blue eyes of a god who does not see invites readers to discern a poetic critique of idolatry and iconolatry.

ARTIFICIAL VERTIGO

> Quant aux fleurs, courtes et de couleurs tranchées, ce sont, n'est-ce pas? des imitations, artificielles, et faites pour jouer la mosaïque.[107]

Given these instances of apparent proximity between "Fleurs" and certain Islamic traditions, we might ask if an Islamic critical perspective can help us reach a more accurate understanding of the ways the visual is manifested and dissimulated in Rimbaud's prose poetry. When, in *Maghreb pluriel*, Abdelkébir Khatibi attempts to define Islamic art and its relation to aniconism, he does so by contemplating a rigorously symmetrical mosaic in the form of a rose.[108] Through his contemplation of this rose-shaped mosaic, Khatibi attempts to reevaluate the ways in which Islam relates to the visual, and specifically to art, by thinking beyond the ideology of aniconism and the culture of calligraphy. His goal is to move away from the notion that Islamic art is a product of the religious protocol and to instead propose religion as a product of art.[109]

According to Khatibi, the "rosace," or rose mosaic, provides the believer with the possibility of dreaming and of being entranced by the stunning symmetrical motifs of the stylized rose, which appear to move ceaselessly between the rose and its representation. It is through the rigorous symmetry of the rose—a figure that naturally denies symmetry—that the spectator is exposed to what Khatibi describes as "a sort of artificial vertigo, necessary for any infinite explanation of art."[110] The contemplation of the mosaic brings about a physical state of exaltation in Khatibi that is evident not only in the content of his text but also in its hesitations and repetitions, producing syntactic folds that evoke the bloom's overlapping petals:

> Comme si, oui comme si, intrigué, bouleversé par le secret d'un paradigme, j'étais invité à m'initier, par un mouvement incessant et alerte, à cette symétrie rigoureuse de ce qu'on appelle les formes et les couleurs, symétrie si stricte assurément qu'elle semble exploser hors de la logique qui la tient du dedans en se dirigeant vers ce centre étoilé de la mosaïque, centre à huit branches, point orthogonal et orange, lequel cristallise toute la construction circulaire tout en la maintenant libérée dans sa grâce, tournant dans son élément rythmique; point où le vide, en quelque sorte, se repose, se contemple à travers l'émerveillement qui se développe en s'y incrustant: dans chaque morceau taillé de la pierre, chaque détour ou jonction d'une parfaite symétrie.

> As if, yes as if, intrigued, shaken by the secret of a paradigm, I was invited to initiate myself, by an incessant and agile movement, into this rigorous symmetry of what are called forms and colors, symmetry so strict, indeed, that it seems to explode out of the logic that holds it together from the inside by moving toward the starred center of the mosaic, a center with eight branches, orthogonal and orange focal point, which crystallizes all the circular construction while keeping it liberated in its gracefulness, turning in its rhythmic element; a point where, you might say, the void rests, contemplates itself through the wonder that reveals itself by encrusting itself in it: in every cut piece of the stone, every detour or junction of a perfect symmetry.[111]

The rotating, turning "movement" of the rose mosaic around the absent center—where the void "rests"—creates what Khatibi calls "this quality of vertigo, vertigo of symmetry"[112] and "the experience of a voluptuousness, of a whirling thought,"[113] or "the artificial vertigo brought about by looking at a rose mosaic."[114] The rose-shaped mosaic tirelessly draws in the spectator's gaze until the spectator ceases to look and becomes lost in their contemplation. For Khatibi, the perfect circularity of the rose mosaic cancels its very circularity and prevents the viewer from seeing it as a stable figure, throwing him or her—as if in a spiral—into the void. The rose mosaic destroys the beauty of the circle contained within itself to create a geometric form that is constantly in the process of opening itself up. It is a phenomenon that can be identified in modern Maghrebi art, too, notably in the painting of the late Mohamed Melehi (Asilah, 1936–Boulogne-Billancourt, 2020), whom Khatibi credits with correcting our "plastic vision" and with transforming the way we look through his marriage of Zen mysticism, the optical art of Bridget Riley, and the power of decorative Arabo-Islamic art.[115] In Melehi's painting there is "no concession to figurative seduction, even if waves appear to emerge in the distance. Nothing trembles here except the sign."[116]

Much like the wave in Melehi's oeuvre, the rose mosaic is a vanishing figure to which Khatibi often returns, not least in his novels: "A dancing geometry: triangles, parallels, circles, and other transfigurations. The erotic arabesque";[117] and "The trembling trace of a rose mosaic, trembling insofar as it gradually fades as the gaze fades away. Rosette surrounded by tight interlacings, which, as it moves toward the center, bursts into a starred polygon—the star of Islam. Turning on itself, the center overflows toward the outside, which accompanies it with measure and rigor."[118] Among Khatibi's fragments on Barthes's late writings, he alludes to the author's "*eu-*

phoric phrase on Japan," which gives "the impression of a pleasure that wavers on itself, by means of an artificial vertigo" and that conjures up "loss, trembling, *vacilar*, the art of dance, gestures of the idea, a calligraphy of the imaginary."[119] As Gleize notes, such whirling is also a dynamic that recurs in *Illuminations*: "It is from the perspective of highlighting a syntax of whirling [une syntaxe de la giration] alone that we ought to reread *Illuminations*. This study will require both a detailed examination of the thematic investment in this seme (turning [tourner]) and a description of the linguistic effects of this strategy. Work in progress."[120]

It is this same form—geometric but also open—that we find in the cursive script of written Arabic, the "bastard" script that—as Massignon puts it—"breaks figures . . . and the habitual concert of these forms open."[121] This same geometric and open form can be seen in Rimbaud's poem in the "rose d'eau" [water rose]. Pierre Lauxerois ventures that the water rose is an image "of a stone rose." He continues, "Covered with a dome and surrounded by pillars, it occupies, in a classical park, the center of a basin. This rose is at the same time a stone flower and a flower in language."[122] Bernard sees a water lily and with it the reinscription of French Romanticism: "The sense of water lily [nénuphar] is quite probable and could well come from Chateaubriand, who, in his description of the 'Meschacebé' [Mississippi] (in *Atala*) speaks of the 'floating islands of pistia and of water lilies, whose yellow roses rise up like little pavilions.'"[123] Christian Pagès identifies a literal translation of the German word for a water lily, namely "Wasserrose."[124] For Brunel, it is important "that the focus of the evocation not be a real flower, and that it be, instead of the mystic rose, a flower that does not exist outside of Rimbaud's flora: a rose that has the transparency of water."[125] The geometric valency of the flower, however, is enhanced and reasserted by the circular figures that surround it: "Des pièces d'or jaune semées sur l'agate, des piliers d'acajou supportant un dôme d'émeraudes, des bouquets de satin blanc et de fines verges de rubis" [Pieces of yellow gold strewn across the agate, mahogany pillars supporting an emerald dome, bouquets of white satin and of thin ruby stems].

In light of Khatibi's reading of the rose mosaic, the reader will become more sensitive to the proliferation of symmetrical and circular motifs in Rimbaud's poem: "les disques de cristal" [crystal disks], "le soleil" [the sun], "Des pièces d'or jaune" [Pieces of yellow gold]. "L'agate" [agate] is a type of quartz that has a concentric structure. "Un dôme d'émeraudes" [An emerald dome] is equally round, as are the "bouquets de satin blanc" [bouquets of white satin] that themselves "entourent la rose d'eau" [surround the water rose]. The "enormous blue eyes" of the god could also—given their extremely large size—be more circular than oval, particularly when we recall that blue was the color juxtaposed with the letter "O" in the sonnet "Voyelles."[126] What is more, something of the geometric motifs of Islam's aniconic decoration can be found in the "tapis" [carpet] decorated "de filigranes d'argent, d'yeux et de chevelures" [with silver filigrees, with eyes, and with hair]—the link between the decorative motifs of the poem and the geometric art of Islam made even more insistent by the phonetic presence of "Dieu" [God] in "d'yeux" [with eyes].[127] In the symmetrical, geometric, decorative, and nonfigurative details of Rimbaud's poem—what Khatibi terms the "trappings of insignificance"[128]—a reader may undergo an ecstatic spiritual experience similar to that experienced by the believer contemplating the rose mosaic, and thereby glimpse the eternal.

Perceiving something of the artificial vertigo that a stone mosaic provokes for Khatibi in Rimbaud's "Fleurs" helps to clarify and develop what previous readers of the poem have already noted. Chambers maintains that the vision in "Fleurs" is "made curiously artificial, struck with immobility," adding that "even the attraction exerted on the crowd of roses by the sea, the sky, and the terraces appears in an eternal present."[129] He suggests that the poet succeeds in saving himself, "fixing" the vertigo at the very moment he is about to be swallowed up in the vision.[130] Khatibi, however, teaches his reader precisely to abandon themselves to intense contemplation of this textual artificiality. If Rimbaud's vegetal "water rose" asks to be exchanged for Khatibi's stone rose, then this would repeat and confirm what Richard perceives in Rimbaud's poetic imaginary: "Around the open flower is the construction of a whole play of architectures of stone or solid wood: rigorous, geometric, arranged to protect, arranged almost in adoration of this tender, blooming heart."[131] Richard opines that in contrast to Francis Ponge's "love of the thing for itself," for Rimbaud the flower and the stone are never discrete entities, but are constantly in flux, one falling into the other in an eternally rotating movement.[132]

Contrary to what Houellebecq's narrator in *Soumission* would have us believe, an Islamic Rimbaud—or at least a hermeneutic approach that is more sensitive to the interlacings of Islamic aesthetics, Qur'ānic linguistics, and Rimbaldian poetics, an approach more suited to the ways that images are avoided even as they submerge the reader, and whereby the flower no longer dominates "the fields in which, however, it still belongs"[133] but instead constitutes a motivating element of a new aniconic poetics—could well change the way that we read and think about *Illuminations*. To read these prose poems for their resonance with Islam—especially as manifested in translations of the Qur'ān into French and in the ahadith—is to become aware of what Khatibi calls "the glory of the invisible."[134] It is to become more sensitive to what remains beyond representational or mimetic language. It is to displace the figurative so as to contemplate the divine in the decorative. As Michel de Certeau tells us in a text he claims to have composed in a single nocturnal sitting, as if in a trance, "The vision coincides with the disappearance of seen things."[135] Bearing in mind that "الإسلام" [al-islām] means "submission," to read the Islamic in Rimbaud is above all to put aside a desire for control and comprehension, and to submit oneself to the artificial vertigo of the poem.

CONCLUSION

A Poetic Genealogy of North African Literature

ZIGZAG

"I think this is the place to break off," writes Sigmund Freud toward the close of the penultimate chapter of *Jenseits des Lustprinzips* [Beyond the Pleasure Principle], "But not without adding a few words of critical reflection."[1] What follows, though, is not what one might expect of the conclusion of a quasiscientific exploration, as Freud asks himself whether and to what extent he is himself convinced of the assumptions he has developed. He insists instead that the affective moment of conviction is not something that should come into consideration at a time of conclusion. Jean-François Lyotard later notes that there is no reason to be alarmed by this absence of "déterminité," that is, "Bestimmtheit" or "resolution." It is not "a 'little' conviction or a *lack* of conviction that the economist of 1920 experiences but an undecidability of affect, a positive power of not knowing whether he believes in his theory or not, a power of affirming that is foreign to the question of belief."[2]

The absence of resolution leads Freud to conclude, in the seventh and final part of his work, with reference to poetry: "In any case, allow a poet to console us about the slow progress of our scientific knowledge."[3] And he quotes the following two verses:

> Was man nicht erfliegen kann, muss man erhinken.
> . . . .
> Die Schrift sagt, es ist keine Sünde zu hinken.
>
> What one cannot fly toward, one must limp toward.
> . . . .
> Scripture says it is not a sin to limp.[4]

These lines are taken from the poet Friedrich Rückert's 1837 German translation of the eleventh-century Arabic text مقامات [Maqāmāt] [Stations] by al-Ḥarīrī of Basra (Basra, 1054–Basra, 1122), a collection of fifty short anecdotes written in rhymed prose called "سجع" [saj'], from the Arabic verb that describes the rhythmic cooing of doves or pigeons.[5] The anecdote or "station" in which these lines appear might not be out of place in one of Habib Tengour's "essayistic incursions"[6] or in Charles Baudelaire's *Le spleen de Paris* [Paris Spleen], which also, by chance, includes fifty short poems in poetic prose.[7] The poem quoted by Freud tells of an impoverished man who limps and who, in return for a gold coin, is able to both sing the coin's praise and condemn it as worthless. The narrator realizes too late that he has been duped—that someone so skilled in rhyme must be a poet, and that the limp must be a conceit. The poet admits his deception and in his defense quotes from "الفتح" [al-Fatḥ], the forty-eighth sura of the Qur'ān, also known as "The Victory" or "The Conquest":

لَّيْسَ عَلَى ٱلْأَعْمَىٰ حَرَجٌ وَلَا عَلَى ٱلْأَعْرَجِ حَرَجٌ وَلَا عَلَى ٱلْمَرِيضِ حَرَجٌ

> [Laysa 'alá l-a'mā ḥarajun wa-lā 'alá l-a'raji ḥarajun wa-lā 'alá l-marīḍi ḥarajun]
>
> There is no blame upon the blind; nor is there blame upon the lame; nor is there blame upon the sick.[8]

The word for lame or limping that Rückert translates as "hinken" is "أعرج" [a'raj]. It shares a root, though not a vocalization, with the verb meaning "to ascend, mount, rise" and with the substantive "معراج" [mi'rāj], meaning "ladder" or "stairs." In Islam, "mi'rāj" describes the midnight journey made from Jerusalem to the seven heavens by Muḥammad on the twenty-seventh day of the month of Rajab. Just as the meaning of this collection of consonants moves from the sublime to the decrepit, from the ascendant Prophet to the halting beggar, from religious conviction to studied duplicity, so can the verb describe the sinuous motion of a zigzag, the bending movement back and forth, the curves and twists of a winding line. Lyotard will explain the difference "between *flying* and *limping*" [entre *voler* et *boiter*][9] that closes Freud's work and that inheres in "a'raj," as being a question not of method but of passion: "Claudication is an affection relating to space and time, it is the tilting extension and the stammering duration, the lame person *does not know if he believes* in time and space, while the one who flies is *convinced* of it."[10] If this book proposes a poetic genealogy of North African literature, it does not seek to provide a flying overview, however inspired, nor a definition of lineages or hierarchies, nor a sense of historical progress. A poetic genealogy proceeds in fits and starts, along broken lines. It is distracted by details, diverted by ruptures and accidents. On impulse, it often halts on fragments of text, mostly unconcerned with drawing definitive conclusions about the whole. It thus develops Michel Foucault's notion of genealogy as that which entertains "the claims to attention of local, discontinuous, disqualified, illegitimate knowledges against the claims of a unitary body of theory."[11] This book puts forward only one such genealogy, developed according to the unique logics of its component parts, perhaps forming the basis of what Lyotard calls "a theory-fiction" [une *théorie-fiction*].[12] If it casts light on an "epistemological moment," it is "one of the imagination, in the work of inventing hypotheses."[13]

As with the "differend," this poetic genealogy is designed to articulate and amplify what the poets—Farès, Amrouche, Sénac, Khaïr-Eddine, Djaout, Khatibi, Meddeb, and Rimbaud—and their texts say, regardless of whether what they say fits into a preestablished framework of expectation. Accordingly, the discussion in these pages often strays from the topics we might more usually associate with the modern Maghreb and its literature in French. This includes a Kabyle's investment in the French poetry of Catholic mysticism; the impact of Jean-Paul Sartre's presentation of Black francophone poetry on a pied-noir supporter of Algerian independence; the juxtaposition of a Moroccan poet and the Anglo-Irish painter Francis Bacon; the poetic inquiries of an Algerian journalist into the links between Greek and Kabyle myth; a Moroccan philosopher's intense and critical engagement with devotional Christianity; and the tentative reconciliation of the Christian concepts expressed in Italian Renaissance painting with certain tenets of modern Islam by a Tunisian author, thinker, and radio presenter. This is a genealogy developed mainly on the basis of poetic texts and on the questions encountered when reading them, rather than on established historical or literary-historical narratives. When Lyotard insists that artists should not be expected to "carry on their shoulders the weight of the world, the seriousness of the same problems that those in charge face and do not know how to solve," he explains that this is not because art is disengaged, gratuitous, for its own sake but, on the contrary, "because art is, like science, only another name for displacement and travel [pour déplaçabilité et voyage]."[14] It is hoped that the theoretical-fictional activity involved in reading and interpreting these poetic texts will subsequently carry "the same power of *wandering* [la même puissance de *wandering*]"[15] that operates throughout this book into broader debates in Maghrebi literature.

MAGHREB

Although the title of this book articulates the presentation of a poetic genealogy of North African literature, within the book reference shifts repeatedly between North Africa and the Maghreb. The former term is more immediately comprehensible for an English-language reader, and is therefore used in the title, but the latter perhaps offers more opportunity for the imaginative wandering advocated here by Lyotard, al-Ḥarīrī, and Freud.[16] When Pascal Quignard looked back at his translation of Lycophron's *Cassandra* from ancient Greek into modern French in the late 1960s, he spoke of the importance of the displacement enabled through the exploration of etymologies: "I traveled. I went to the other world. I descended into lost centuries. I approached the country of the dead. I was looking for etyma in the reeds, among the shadows, in still water."[17] If we travel into the underworld of historical but now obscured meanings of "Africa," via the Latin "Āfrica," we may arrive at "Āfrī"—the plural form of "Āfer," the name of an ancient people who lived to the west of the Nile, in a region that included modern-day Libya and Tunisia. In modern Kabyle, "ifri" or "ifran" can refer to an escarpment or cavern, leading some to suggest that the "Āfrī" were so called after the rocks they inhabited, although there is much here that remains to be ascertained.[18]

The etymology of "Maghreb" and its variants takes us into other dimensions, a world which bears the traces of imagination and realization, of exploration and discovery, of occupation and appropriation. Writing in the mid-1960s, Kateb Yacine recalls that for the Arabs, the Maghreb was initially a place of exile: "*Gharib*, en arabe, signifie étranger. La *ghorba*, c'est l'exil" [In Arabic, *ghārib* means foreigner. Exile is *ghurbah*]. For Kateb, "ghurbah" describes specifically "the poet's wandering and the strange presence of the foreigner," as exemplified by the then recently departed Turkish poet Nâzım Hikmet (Thessaloniki, 1902–Moscow, 1963).[19] The term "Maghreb," though, can be both more protean and more precise. As exile, it projects and comments on the gradual Arabic invasion of North Africa during the seventh and early eighth centuries—sometimes called "الفتح" [al-fatḥ], like the forty-eighth sura quoted above—as the Umayyad Caliphate opens westward toward the Atlantic Ocean. The term "Maghreb" acquires signification in the process of its expansion, before being codified by medieval Arabic cartographers, traders, and explorers.

The three consonants from which "Maghreb" stems are therefore rich in shifting meanings. The verb "غرب" [gharaba] is "to go away, to depart, to absent oneself, to withdraw (from), to leave (somebody or something)."[20] It describes the setting of the sun or the moon or a planet, such that the noun "مغرب" [maghrib] identifies the sunset, the prayer said at that time of day, the state of Morocco, the westernmost Arabic-speaking countries, as well as the west or Occident. As the king in the satirical novel *Moi l'aigre* [Me, the Bitter One] by Mohammed Khaïr-Eddine puts it, "Hé, mais nous sommes aussi des Occidentaux. . . . À n'en pas douter, nous sommes des Occidentaux au même titre que les Américains" [Hey, that means we're also Westerners. . . . No doubt about it, we're Westerners, just like the Americans].[21] The verb "غرب" [gharuba] is to be strange or a stranger, to be "odd, queer, abstruse, difficult to comprehend."

Meanings proliferate as the root lends itself to the various "awzān" (pl. of "wazn") or verbal forms. Besides signifying "to depart" and "to go westward," "غرّب" [gharraba] means "to expel from the homeland, banish, exile, expatriate." The form "أغرب" [aghraba] is "to say or do a strange or amazing thing" or "to exceed the proper bounds, overdo, exaggerate," such as when somebody protests their innocence more than is necessary. To "go to a foreign country, emigrate" or "to become an occidental, become Westernized, be Europeanized; to assimilate oneself to the Western way of life" is "تغرّب" [tagharraba].[22] A similar sense inheres in the form "استغرب" [istgharaba], although here the prefix also gives expression to disapproval, such that this verb can mean "to find someone extraordinary," "to be disoriented, lost," or "to deem something absurd, preposterous, grotesque."[23] Albin Kazimirski de Biberstein defines "اغترب" [ightaraba] as being both "to marry a foreign woman" and "to denationalize oneself" [se dénationaliser].[24] Among its older, equine applications, "أغرب" [aghraba], mentioned above, can also be "to cause a horse 'to run excessively fast, so that it becomes overworked and dies.'"[25] The passive form of this "wazn," "أغرب" [ughriba], denotes a horse that has a white blaze on the forehead or, alternatively, a horse that has blue eyes.[26] The form "غرب" [gharaba] can describe a sheep stricken with illness, and "غرب" [gharuba] is "to be very thin and disappear" or "to hide oneself."[27]

The adjective "غراب" [gharāb] describes something that is very black. And "غرّب" [gharraba] can be "to gather snow or frost so as to eat it."[28]

Much as the meanings of "أعرج" [aʿraj], the Arabic word for "limp," vacillate between the celestial and the terrestrial, the holy and the ridiculous—and much as the poet-vagabond in al-Ḥarīrī's tale reveals himself to be something other than it seemed—so too the root of the Maghreb moves ceaselessly between multiple poles of meaning related to travel, to norms and their dislocation, to extremes and excess, to real and perceived transformations. An awareness of the semantic currents at work in this term may help explain the different Maghrebs imagined through poetry by each of the authors studied in this book. *Le miroir de Cordoue* [The Mirror of Córdoba] by Nabile Farès, a fragmented narrative based on a visit to the Spanish city in 1975, wanders almost timelessly through a myriad of sites both in the author's native Algeria and in Andalusia, a quasimythical space dubbed "la Grande Illusion du Pays d'Al" [the Great Illusion of the Country of Al]—Algérie, Alger, al-Jazā'ir, al-Andalus . . .[29] Toward the end of his life, Mohammed Dib identified the mirror image of Farès's "Pays d'Al" in *L. A. Trip*, a novel in verse based on a period spent in southern California in the mid-1970s.[30] Here, the Maghreb is extended to "West Avenue" and "Sunset et Alvarado,"[31] articulating its westernmost points, as well as the extremes of al-Andalus, before they become oriental, Eastern, the morrow. He thereby takes literally the historian Fernand Braudel's poetic conceit, according to which the strait that divides Tangier from Tarifa is "le Far-West méditerranéen" [the Mediterranean Far West].[32]

In her groundbreaking work on Maghrebi literature, Edwige Tamalet Talbayev encourages us to look not only beyond the "cultural primacy of the French metropole" but also beyond the borders of individual nation-states in North Africa, to what is called "the transcontinental Maghreb," that is, "the transnational deployment of the former North African colonies of Morocco, Algeria, and Tunisia within the millennia-old relation that has materially and culturally bound the region to a variety of sites throughout the broader Mediterranean."[33] The dynamic connections that make up the literary Mediterranean are clearly in evidence in the experiences and works of the poets studied in this book, whether in Amrouche's renewed cognizance of Kabyle poetry through hearing traditional Greek song, or Djaout's juxtaposition of Greek and Kabyle myths, or Meddeb's investment of the Muslim imaginary with paintings from the Italian Renaissance. But when Dib, through poetry, extends the Maghreb to the furthest reaches of America, he reminds us that any transcontinental Maghreb of letters must exceed not only the Maghreb but also the Mediterreanean, which, even in its most capacious definition, is a space that confines.[34] This does not necessarily mean that we are obliged to speak of Maghrebi literature as imbricated in "a globalized, transnational topography"[35] but instead that we must allow the curious logic of literature, the local authority of the literary text, to dictate our search for meaning. This will ensure that any poetic geneaology is alive to the minor, the marginal, the unanticipated, the anomalous, the ill-suited, the inconvenient, the turbulent, the inchoate, the unsettling, the different. This includes what might appear to be the incongruous influence of Patrice de La Tour du Pin or of Jean-Joseph Rabéarivelo on the early poetic development of Jean Amrouche. Or the critical dissonance that may be occasioned by attributing greater importance in the poetic formation of Abdelkébir Khatibi to a twentieth-century Swedish poet, namely Gunnar Ekelöf, rather than to the eminent, not to say legendary, Muslim, Sufi, Arabic-language poets such as al-Ḥallāj or Ibn ʿArabī. If the Maghreb is "a key site of cultural and linguistic syncretism,"[36] as Tamalet Talbayev rightly states—one that cannot be limited to "the parameters of the subject's engagement with the nation and with its restricted models of social agency and collectivity"[37]—then it must also be a site open to the deviations occasioned by the individual preferences, prejudices, displacements, and experiences of those who write. As such, it may sometimes exceed even the generous definition of "a transnational Mediterranean consciousness" defined "across ethnic and confessional lines."[38] It is this realization that leads Yasser Elhariry to conclude, at the close of his dazzling study of Habib Tengour, Edmond Jabès, Salah Stétié, Abdelwaheb Meddeb, and Ryoko Sekiguchi, that their writings "end up being about no community or national imaginary at all, but rather about the lingual: linguistic affinity, the affinity of one language for/by another, and the uncertain future of French and francophone poetry and poetics."[39]

LINGUAL

Just as the poets examined in this book reimagine the Maghreb through their work in often unexpected ways, so too they explore what the French language can do, testing its limits and opening it to new constellations of thought and meaning. The existence of a North African literature in French is now taken for granted, but it is important to remember how young this body of work is and that, in the mid-twentieth century, its future was not assured. As Réda Bensmaïa recalls, "The idea of an Algerian literature written in French was a contradiction in the context of decolonization, and it was believed that political independence would soon be followed by cultural and linguistic independence."[40] In his landmark essays on language politics in the 1950s, Albert Memmi also presumed that French would inexorably give way to Arabic as the language of cultural expression and projection, although he later admitted that French would retain an important role in independent North Africa.[41] On the eve of independence from colonial rule, Malek Haddad described French as his "exile," asserting, "Je suis moins séparé de ma patrie par la Méditerranée que par la langue française" [I am less separated from my homeland by the Mediterranean than I am by the French language].[42] Even such a dedicated practitioner of poetry in French as Jean Sénac initially saw his language as transitional and as inevitably giving way to an Arabic-language literature and culture in a decolonized Algeria—before he conceived of a literature expansive enough to include both these languages and others.[43]

The poets studied in this book are aware of the anomalous place that French occupies in the Maghreb but insist on its necessity. Mohammed Dib identifies French as possessing unique abilities: "Il y a dans le français une *transparence obscure* qui me convient, dans laquelle à tort ou à raison je me reconnais. . . . À écrire en français on côtoie sans cesse un gouffre insoupçonné" [There is in French an *obscure transparency* that suits me, in which, rightly or wrongly, I recognize myself. . . . When writing in French, one constantly rubs up against an unsuspected abyss].[44] In a speech given in Rabat toward the end of his life, Jean Amrouche describes French as "consubstantial" with his being: "Ses rigueurs satisfont un besoin essentiel de mon esprit. Sa souple, sévère, tendre et quasi insensible mélodie touche, éclaire, émeut mon âme jusqu'au fond—ou presque. . . . Je n'emploie pas cette langue, je baigne en elle, j'en suis fait" [Its rigors satisfy an essential need of my mind. Its supple, severe, tender, and almost insensitive melody touches, enlightens, moves my soul to its depths—or almost. . . . I do not deploy this language; I bathe in it. I am made by it].[45] When Mohammed Khaïr-Eddine appeared in an edition of the popular French television show *Apostrophes* in 1984 to discuss the publication of his novel *Légende et vie d'Agoun'chich* [Legend and Life of Agoun'chich], it was suggested to him that writing in French limited his freedom of expression, a notion he rejected out of hand: "On peut fonctionner dans toutes les langues actuellement. La seule condition est la suivante: de savoir le faire" [You can function in any language nowadays. The only condition is this: knowing how to do it].[46] Abdelwahab Meddeb also insists on the need for perspective when it comes to the question of language: "Je crois que c'est bien de calmer le rapport à la langue. Pour ce qui me concerne, l'urgence est ailleurs" [I think we can calm down on the question of language. As far as I'm concerned, the urgency is elsewhere].[47] He goes on to explain that what counts is not only the language one was born with but also the extent to which one learns and cultivates it. As Mourad Bourboune put it, in a debate with Albert Memmi and Jean Pélégri from 1965, "Une langue appartient à qui sait la manier, la briser et la plier aux exigences de la création, la forcer à exprimer son moi profond" [A language belongs to whoever is able to manipulate it, to break and bend it to the demands of creation, to force it to express their inner self].[48]

For many of the poets mentioned in this study, the question of French language in the modern Maghreb is best captured by Mouloud Mammeri, who in an interview given in November 1965 remarked,

> À mon sens, croire que nos passions et nos idéaux sont irrémédiablement liés à l'usage d'une langue, c'est justement tomber dans le piège de ceux qui naguère voulaient nous nier, c'est faire de ce que nous pensons ou éprouvons des réalités d'ordre ethnographique, des objets morts de musées, c'est nous chosifier et nous couper, par là-même, de la grande famille des hommes. Je m'inscris en faux contre une vision aussi rétrograde, aussi peu digne d'une culture véritable, qu'elle soit occidentale, islamique, chinoise ou hindoue. Ce qui arrive de profond aux hommes, en quelque endroit de la terre qu'ils se trouvent, de quelque langue qu'ils se servent, intéresse tous les hommes et, en un siècle de civilisation planétaire, je trouve vain et dérisoire de s'accrocher à des particularités qui, au lieu de nous emmurer dans la prison de nos unicités, devraient être, au contraire, des instruments de notre mutuel enrichissement. La langue française est, pour moi, non pas du tout la langue honnie d'un ennemi, mais un incomparable instrument de libération, de communion ensuite avec le reste du monde. Je considère qu'elle nous traduit infiniment plus qu'elle ne nous trahit.
>
> In my opinion, to believe that our passions and our ideals are irremediably linked to the use of a single language is precisely to fall into the trap of those who once wanted to deny us; it is to make of what we think or experience realities of a purely ethnographic order, dead objects in a museum; it is to objectify us and thereby cut us off from the great family of men. I disagree with such a retrograde vision, so unworthy of a true culture, whether Western, Islamic, Chinese, or Hindu. What happens profoundly to people, wherever on earth they find themselves, whatever

> language they deploy, interests all people and, in a century of planetary civilization, I find it futile and derisory to cling to particularities that, instead of immuring us in the prison of our uniqueness, should, on the contrary, be instruments of our mutual enrichment. The French language is, for me, not at all the despised language of an enemy but an incomparable instrument of liberation and then of communion with the rest of the world. I think that it translates us infinitely more than it betrays us.[49]

In this "century of planetary civilization," a language is not a birthright but a practice to be developed, worked, and fashioned in new and subversive ways. As Jacques Derrida put it, stressing the alienation of all speakers from language, "Il n'y a pas de propriété naturelle de la langue, celle-ci ne donne lieu qu'à de la rage appropriatrice, à de la jalousie sans appropriation" [There is no natural ownership of language; ownership only gives rise to the angry desire to possess, to the jealousy of not possessing].[50] Or as Khatibi—to whose novel *Amour bilingue* [Love in Two Languages][51] Derrida was responding—says, "Cette langue n'est pas une propriété; c'est plutôt le lieu vide d'une identité qui se réincarne" [This language is not a possession; it is rather the empty place of an identity that reembodies itself].[52] A language "appartient à ceux qui l'exercent et l'aiment suffisamment pour la travailler, la transformer" [belongs to those who practice it and love it enough to work on it, transform it].[53]

As is evident throughout this book, the poetic works realized by these Maghrebi authors are invested with a linguistic pluralism that is not limited to that of the Maghreb itself. Elhariry adroitly conceives a corpus of late twentieth- and early twenty-first-century writers whose "love for classical Islamic and Arabic literary cultures and traditions" "progressively, pacifically invade[s]"[54] French language and literature, primarily through instances of translation and intertextuality, and their translingual intertwinings. But as Khatibi reminds us in *Maghreb pluriel*, we are still not close to understanding the translingual entanglements that make up the practice of poetic writing in French: "La langue française n'est pas la langue française: elle est plus ou moins toutes les langues internes et externes qui la font et la défont" [The French language is not the French language: it is more or less all the internal and external languages that make it and unmake it].[55] *A Poetic Genealogy of North African Literature* touches on the German of Kafka, Goethe, Rilke, and Freud; the Swedish of Ekelöf; the Latin of Ovid and Augustine; the Hebrew Bible; the Arabic Qur'ān; and the Kabyle of Si Mohand and a host of now anonymous singers. Even those metropolitan authors who write (almost) exclusively in French unmoor themselves within French through the writing of poetry. As the early twentieth-century French critic Albert Thibaudet says of a poet referenced in this book on several occasions: "Il conviendra de chercher la mesure dans laquelle fut ou non française l'œuvre de Mallarmé" [It will be necessary to work out the extent to which Mallarmé's work was or was not French].[56] Khatibi responds elsewhere by asking about the degree to which he himself might be considered a "hostage" to the French language and its literature.[57]

TEMPORAL

Even as these poets work with, in, toward, away from, and against French, there appears to be a growing cognizance in their writings of some of the underlying theological implications of the French language. When translating the Hebrew Bible into German in the early decades of the twentieth century, Franz Rosenzweig wrote to the philosopher and historian Gershom Scholem and pointed to three figures who, through translation, had contributed in defining ways to the formation of modern German: Notker Balbulus, also known as Notker the Stammerer (St. Gallen, ca. 840–St. Gallen, 912), Martin Luther (Eisleben, 1483–Eisleben, 1546), and Friedrich Hölderlin (Lauffen am Neckar, 1770–Tübingen, 1843):

> Es gibt ja keine bloß sprachgeschichtlichen Tatsachen. Die deutsche Sprache ist, in diesen drei Namen, christliche Sprache geworden. Wer ins Deutsche übersetzt, muß in irgendwelchem Maße ins Christliche übersetzen. In *welchem* Maße, das hängt nicht von ihm ab, sondern (grade wenn er *gut* übersetzt) ausschließlich von dem Übersetzten. Je größer die Nähe ist, in die das Christentum sich die übersetzte Welt herangezwungen hat, um so christlicher wird das Deutsch der Übersetzung sein müssen.
>
> There are no mere linguistic historical facts. In these three names, the German language becomes a Christian language. Anyone who translates into German has to translate into Christian to some extent. To *what* extent does not depend on him, but (especially if he translates *well*) exclusively on what has been translated. The closer the proximity into which Christianity has forced the translated world toward itself, the more Christian the German of the translation will have to be.[58]

I do not propose to identify here those who similarly bring French into existence, through translation or otherwise. Instead, I note that just as Rosenzweig comes to the realization that the language he is translating into is not a neutral language but one that carries the burden of its pasts, the poetic genealogy proposed in this book unexpectedly and increasingly brings to light the historical sacred investments of French.

If we are right to identify Arthur Rimbaud's early interest in the Qur'ān with the inscription of aniconism in his prose poetry, then this may constitute a step away from a French that has grown alongside Christianity and toward an alternative expression preliminarily structured on Kazimirski's translations of Qur'ānic Arabic into French. Jean Amrouche becomes aware of the problematic imbrication of Christianity and French over the course of his rhapsodic career, moving from the devotional and mystical verse of his youth, via "chant" and the Kabyle "asefru," to a more critical understanding of poetry—even as he retains the French language, something of his metropolitan identity, as well as his religious faith. Jean Sénac complained to his mother, Jeanne Comma, that she did not raise him in colloquial Arabic or Tamazight, thereby facilitating his deeply desired integration into Algerian society. His monolingualism, fostered through readings of Louis Segond's French translation of the Bible, is repeatedly dislocated in his poems—not least when he exploits the ambiguities inherent in naming and renaming. Mohammed Khaïr-Eddine often affirms his inability to create literature in any language other than French, although he speaks Tamazight and colloquial Arabic. Nevertheless, the uneven rhythms that structure his difficult poetry seek to alienate French from within. Tahar Djaout, a native speaker of Tamazight, is also aware of the degree to which a language can be burdened by its religious applications, although he prefers to perceive French as a secular conduit away from the sacred inflections of Arabic: "Il y a des choses très violentes que je dis en français que je n'aurais pas dites en arabe ou en berbère. . . . Le français, qui est pour moi une sorte de langue neutre, qui n'a pas d'attache affective, est un merveilleux outil de travail où il n'y a rien de sacré" [There are very violent things that I say in French that I could not say in Arabic or Berber. . . . French, which for me is a kind of neutral language and which has no emotional ties, is a wonderful tool for working with, where nothing is holy].[59]

It is only in the poetic writings of Abdelkébir Khatibi and Abdelwahab Meddeb that the historical sacred investments of the French language are most insistently identified and problematized. Khatibi's poetic oeuvre might best be understood as a lifelong attempt to dissolve the ancient commixture of the French language and Christian theological concepts, and to present in its stead a new, secularized, erotic language of poetry. If Khatibi invokes the Immaculate Conception and the Incarnation, he does so in order to reimagine their relation to French through his poetic exploration of the fold. Meddeb also identifies the Incarnation in French, evoking it repeatedly throughout his poetic, fictional, and nonfictional writings, but he does so as someone who is intrigued rather than repelled, fixing on the compromise of the cross-less Deposition, perhaps concerned not so much with secularizing French than with modernizing Islam, approximating Muslim and Christian theologies in ways that would today still provoke hostile resistance. For a poet writing in the Maghreb in the twentieth and early twenty-first centuries, French is therefore not only a language imposed through the historical injustices of colonization; it is also a language that bears in its very constitution the marks of ancient theological concepts and doctrines. If each of the poets in this study identifies the limits of the liberties this language affords, then each also, in their own way, attempts to pick apart and surpass these limits, transforming French into a poetic language of infinite becomings.

Notes

Book epigraph: Paul Valéry, quoted in Abdelkébir Khatibi, *Figures de l'étranger dans la littérature française* (Paris: Denoël, 1987), 31.

INTRODUCTION

1. Nabile Farès, *L'état perdu, précédé du Discours pratique de l'immigré* (Le Paradou: Actes Sud, 1982), 11.

2. René Char, *Feuillets d'Hypnos* (Paris: Gallimard, 1946), 11. Published in the series "Collection Espoir," directed by Albert Camus.

3. Char, 11.

4. François Fédier, "Qu'est-ce que Dieu?," in *Qu'est-ce que Dieu? Philosophie/théologie: Hommage à l'abbé Daniel Coppieters de Gibson (1929–1983)*, ed. Hélène Ackermans (Brussels: Facultés universitaires Saint-Louis, 1985): 127–37 (133).

5. Jean-Luc Nancy, *La communauté désœuvrée* (Paris: Christian Bourgois, 1986), 124. Quotation from Maurice Merleau-Ponty, *Signes* (Paris: Gallimard, 1960), 156.

6. Nancy, *La communauté désœuvrée*, 126.

7. Friedrich Hölderlin to Leo von Seckendorf, March 12, 1804, in *Sämtliche Werke und Briefe*, ed. Jochen Schmidt, 3 vols. (Frankfurt am Main: Deutscher Klassiker Verlag, 1992–94): 3:471–72 (3:471).

8. Friedrich Wilhelm Joseph von Schelling, *Philosophie der Mythologie*, 2 vols. (Stuttgart / Augsburg: J. G. Cotta'scher Verlag, 1857), 2:139.

9. Nancy, *La communauté désœuvrée*, 157.

10. Farès, *L'état perdu*, 65. See also p. 66, "3. / 4 en arabe" [3. / 4 in Arabic], which refers to the figure for four, or "أربعة" [arbaʿah], in Arabic script: "٤."

11. Nancy, *La communauté désœuvrée*, 162.

12. Réda Bensmaïa, *Experimental Nations; or, The Invention of the Maghreb*, trans. Alyson Waters (Princeton: Princeton University Press, 2003), 18.

13. Bensmaïa, 18.

14. See Olivia C. Harrison, "Transcolonial Hospitality: Kateb Yacine's Experiments in Popular Theater," in *Transcolonial Maghreb: Imagining Palestine in the Era of Decolonization* (Stanford: Stanford University Press, 2016): 41–59.

15. Bensmaïa, *Experimental Nations*, 19.

16. Bensmaïa, 18.

17. Nancy, *La communauté désœuvrée*, 122.

18. Nancy, 123.

19. Bensmaïa, *Experimental Nations*, 23.

20. Edwige Tamalet Talbayev, *The Transcontinental Maghreb: Francophone Literature across the Mediterranean* (New York: Fordham University Press, 2017), 39.

21. Bensmaïa, *Experimental Nations*, 24.

22. Nabile Farès, *Un passager de l'Occident: roman* (Paris: Seuil, 1971), 35.

23. Nancy, *La communauté désœuvrée*, 117.

24. Georges Bataille, "L'absence de mythe," in *Le surréalisme en 1947*, ed. André Breton and Marcel Duchamp (Paris: Maeght, 1947): 65 (65).

25. Nancy, *La communauté désœuvrée*, 119.

26. Bensmaïa, *Experimental Nations*, 26.

27. See also "North African Poetry in French," ed. Thomas C. Connolly, special double issue, *Yale French Studies* 137–38 (2020).

28. Pierre Joris, "About the Author," in *Empedocles's Sandal*, by Habib Tengour, trans. Pierre Joris (Sausalito: Duration Press, 1999): n.p. (n.p.).

29. Gérard Genette, *Introduction à l'architexte* (Paris: Seuil, 1979), 11.

30. Genette, 65. Genette quotes from John Stuart Mill's 1833 essay "Two Kinds of Poetry," which appeared in *The Broadview Anthology of Victorian Poetry and Poetic Theory*, ed. Thomas J. Collins and Vivienne J. Rundle (Peterborough: Broadview Press, 1999): 1220–27 (1223).

31. Arthur Rimbaud to Paul Demeny, May 15, 1871, in *Œuvres complètes*, ed. André Guyaux and Aurélia Cervoni (Paris: Gallimard, 2009): 342–49 (343–44). Although, as Rimbaud concedes a few lines later, "Au fond, [cet avenir] serait encore un peu la Poésie grecque" [When it comes down to it, (this future) will still be a bit like Greek Poetry] (Rimbaud, 347).

32. See Virginia Jackson and Yopie Prins, "General Introduction," in *The Lyric Theory Reader: A Critical Anthology*, ed. Virginia Jackson and Yopie Prins (Baltimore: Johns Hopkins University Press, 2014): 1–8 (1–2).

33. Jackson and Prins, "General Introduction," 4.

34. Ayesha Ramachandran, "Afterword: Lyric Poetics for the Global Renaissance," in *A Companion to the Global Renaissance: Literature and Culture in the Era of Expansion, 1500–1700*, ed. Jyotsna G. Singh, 2nd ed. (Hoboken: John Wiley & Sons, 2021): 447–56 (449).

35. Yasser Elhariry, "Mediterranean Lyric," in *Critically Mediterranean: Temporalities, Aesthetics, and Deployments of a Sea in Crisis*, ed. Yasser Elhariry and Edwige Tamalet Talbayev (Cham: Springer Nature / Palgrave Macmillan, 2018): 241–59.

36. For further work on lyric in French, see Dominique Rabaté, ed., *Figures du sujet lyrique* (Paris: Presses universitaires de France, 1996).

37. Salah Stétié, *Fils de la parole: Un poète d'Islam en Occident; Entretiens avec Gwendoline Jarczyk* (Paris: Albin Michel, 2004), 257.

38. Abdelkébir Khatibi, *La langue de l'autre* (New York / Tunis: Les mains secrètes, 1999), 37.

39. Bensmaïa, *Experimental Nations*, 18.

40. Abdelwahab Meddeb, "Errant et polygraphe," *Dédale* 7–8 (1998): 187–91 (187).

41. Khatibi, *La langue de l'autre*, 37.

42. Stéphane Mallarmé, "Crise de vers," in *Œuvres complètes*, ed. Bertrand Marchal, 2 vols. (Paris: Gallimard, 1998–2003): 2:204–13 (2:211).

43. Johann Wolfgang von Goethe, "Naturformen der Dichtung," in *Werke: Vollständige Ausgabe letzter Hand* (Stuttgart / Tübingen: In der J. G. Cotta'schen Buchhandlung, 1828): 6:119–21.

44. Jean-Marie Gleize, *Poésie et figuration* (Paris: Seuil, 1983), 304.

45. Abdelkébir Khatibi, *Quatuor poétique: Rilke, Goethe, Ekelof, Lundkvist*, ill. Marwan (Neuilly-sur-Seine: Al Manar, 2006), 16.

46. Tahar Djaout, "Lecture interdite," in *Solstice barbelé: 1973–1975* (Sherbrooke: Naaman, 1975): 14 (14).

47. Khatibi, *Quatuor poétique*, 28–29.

48. Gilles Deleuze and Félix Guattari, *Capitalisme et schizophrénie 2: Mille plateaux* (Paris: Minuit, 1980), 598.

49. Farès, *L'état perdu*, 6.

50. Jean-François Lyotard, *Discours, figure* (Paris: Klincksieck, 1971).

51. Jean-François Lyotard, *Discourse, Figure*, trans. Antony Hudek and Mary Lydon, intro. John Mowitt (Minneapolis: University of Minnesota Press, 2011), 5.

52. Lyotard, 5.

53. Lyotard, 107.

54. Michel I. Makarius, review of *Discours, figure*, by Jean-François Lyotard, *L'Homme et la société* 26 (1972): 261–62 (261).

55. "il (idéellement) / s'éloigne du ventre / pour approcher / les signes véritables / de l'interrogation" [it (ideally) / moves away from the stomach / to approach / the true signs / of interrogation] (Farès, *L'état perdu*, 17).

56. "face aux barrières des champs / XXXX derrière / eux sont les hommes / qui offrent leurs récoltes / XXXX aux femmes venues / par lente progression / dans les chemins / printaniers / de l'Ouvert" [facing the fences of the fields / XXXX behind / them are men / who offer their harvests / XXXX to the women who have come / progressing slowly / in the spring / paths of the Open] (Farès, 65).

57. Farès, *Un passager de l'Occident*, 73.

58. Jean-François Lyotard, *Instructions païennes* (Paris: Galilée, 1977); *Rudiments païens: Genre dissertatif* (Paris: Union générale d'éditions, 1977).

59. Martin Heidegger, *Unterwegs zur Sprache* (Frankfurt am Main: Vittorio Klostermann, 1985), 30.

60. Immanuel Kant, *Critique of the Power of Judgment*, ed. Paul Guyer, trans. Paul Guyer and Eric Matthews (New York: Cambridge University Press, 2000), 15; *Erste Einleitung in die Kritik der Urteilskraft, nach der Handschrift*, ed. Gerhard Lehmann (Leipzig: Felix Meiner, 1927), 18.

61. Keith Crome and James Williams, eds., *The Lyotard Reader and Guide* (New York: Columbia University Press, 2006), 12.

62. Réda Bensmaïa, "Les devenirs de Nabile Farès," *Awal* 11 (1994): 69–83; "Nabile Farès, or How to Become 'Minoritarian,'" in *Experimental Nations*, 47–65; "Dif-

fracted Poetics: On Nabile Farès's *L'état perdu*," *Yale French Studies* 137–38 (2020): 46–65.

63. Édouard Glissant, "Le chant profond de Kateb Yacine," preface to *Le cercle des représailles: Théâtre*, by Kateb Yacine (Paris: Seuil, 1959): 7–13 (12).

64. Réda Bensmaïa, "~~Francophonie~~," trans. Alyson Waters, *Yale French Studies* 103 (2003): 17–23 (22).

65. Bensmaïa, "Nabile Farès, or How to Become 'Minoritarian,'" 58.

66. Bensmaïa, 58.

67. Habib Tengour, "Narration et identité 'post-coloniale': de 'L'Épreuve de l'Arc' au 'Poisson de Moïse'," in *Dans le soulèvement: Algérie et retours: jalons: essais* (Paris: Éditions de la Différence, 2012): 163–72 (166). Tengour's *Le vieux de la montagne: Relation, 1977/1981* (Paris: Sindbad, 1983) begins with the following epigraph from Novalis: "La poésie est le réel absolu / Plus une chose est poétique, plus elle est vraie" [Poetry is the absolute real / The more poetic a thing, the truer it is] (12).

68. Charles Bernstein, "What's Art Got to Do with It? The Status of the Subject of the Humanities in an Age of Cultural Studies," in *My Way: Speeches and Poems* (Chicago: University of Chicago Press, 1999): 36–51 (42).

69. Bernstein, 42.

70. See also Beïda Chikhi, "Mohammed Dib, pour une poétique du secret: D'*Ombre gardienne* à *L'enfant-jazz*," *Balises* 3–4 (2002–3): 179–94.

71. Abdellatif Laâbi, "Dib, Poet or, The Art of Unveiling," trans. Donald Nicholson-Smith, *Yale French Studies* 137–38 (2020): 11–21 (11–12).

72. Khatibi, *Quatuor poétique*, 50.

73. Tahar Djaout, "Avertissement," in *Les mots migrateurs: Une anthologie poétique algérienne*, ed. Tahar Djaout (Algiers: Office des publications universitaires, 1984): 3–4 (4).

74. Khatibi, *Quatuor poétique*, 50.

75. Abdelkébir Khatibi, *Figures de l'étranger dans la littérature française* (Paris: Denoël, 1987), 101.

76. Khatibi, 101.

77. Michel Foucault, "Two Lectures," in *Power/Knowledge: Selected Interviews and Other Writings, 1972–1977*, ed. Colin Gordon, trans. Colin Gordon, Leo Marshall, John Mepham, and Kate Soper (New York: Pantheon, 1980): 78–108 (83).

78. Khatibi, *Figures de l'étranger*, 101.

79. Friedrich Nietzsche, *Morgenröte: Gedanken über die moralischen Vorurteile*, ed. Peter Pütz (Munich: Goldmann, 1999), 12.

80. See Jean Amrouche, *Cendres: Poèmes (1928–1934)* (Tunis: Mirages, 1934); and *Étoile secrète* (Tunis: Mirages, 1937).

81. For Amrouche's presentation of the project, see the recording and transcription of his talk "Le roi Midas et son barbier" [King Midas and His Barber], performed on December 10, 1952, at the Centre d'études radiophoniques and first broadcast on March 29, 1954, on Paris M. F (Jean Amrouche, "Le roi Midas et son barbier ou L'écrivain et son interlocuteur devant le micro," in *Les écrivains à la radio: Les entretiens de Jean Amrouche; Études et documents écrits et sonores*, ed. Pierre-Marie Héron (Montpellier: Centre d'étude du XXe siècle, 2000): 13–20).

82. See Héron, *Les écrivains à la radio*.

83. See Louis Massignon and Jean Amrouche, "Des idées et des hommes—Husayn Ibn Mansur Hallaj," 2 parts, first broadcast on *Chaîne Nationale* on October 15 and 22, 1955.

84. Jean Amrouche, *Chants berbères de Kabylie* (Tunis: Monomotapa, 1939).

85. Henri Kréa, *La révolution et la poésie sont une seule et même chose*, pref. Jean Amrouche, frontis. Ferró, ill. Kijno (Paris: Pierre Jean Oswald, 1960).

86. Léopold Sédar Senghor, ed., *Anthologie de la nouvelle poésie nègre et malgache de langue française* (Paris: Presses universitaires de France, 1948).

87. Jean Sénac, *Avant-corps, précédé de Poèmes iliaques et suivi de Diwân du Noûn* (Paris: Gallimard, 1968). On the role of Walt Whitman's *Leaves of Grass* in Sénac's development of the "corpoème," see Delphine Rumeau, *Fortunes de Walt Whitman: Enjeux d'une réception transatlantique* (Paris: Classiques Garnier, 2019): 528–35.

88. Charles F. Peterson, *Dubois, Fanon, Cabril: The Margins of Elite Anti-Colonial Leadership* (Lanham: Lexington Books, 2007), 97.

89. Mohammed Khaïr-Eddine, *Moi l'aigre* (Paris: Seuil, 1970); translated as *I, Caustic* by Jake Syersak (New York: Litmus, 2022).

90. Mohammed Khaïr-Eddine, "Poésie ininterrompue," *France Culture*, October 19, 1975.

91. Mohammed Khaïr-Eddine, "Un homme-poème: Entretiens inédits avec Abderrahmane Ajbour; L''âme aérée'," in *Hommage à Mohammed Khaïr-Eddine*, ed. Jean-Paul Michel et al. (Paris: Préau des collines, 2011): 29–85 (45).

92. Deleuze and Guattari, *Capitalisme et schizophrénie 2*, 384–85.

93. Gilles Deleuze, *Francis Bacon: Logique de la sensation*, 2 vols. (Paris: Éditions de la Différence, 1981).

94. Mohammed Khaïr-Eddine, *Soleil arachnide* (Paris: Seuil, 1969), 54–56.

95. Djaout, *Solstice barbelé*; *Les vigiles* (Paris: Seuil, 1991).

96. Mouloud Mammeri, ed., *Poèmes kabyles anciens* (Paris: François Maspero, 1980).

97. Abdelkébir Khatibi and Mohammed Sijelmassi, *L'art calligraphique arabe; ou, La célébration de l'invisible* (Paris: Chêne, 1976), 198.

98. Khatibi and Sijelmassi, 198.

99. Abdelkébir Khatibi, *Dédicace à l'année qui vient*, ill. Mechtilt (Saint-Clément-de-Rivière: Fata Morgana, 1986).

100. Abdelkébir Khatibi, *Par-dessus l'épaule* (Paris: Aubier, 1988), 11–46, 157–84.

101. Abdelkébir Khatibi, *Aimance*, frontis. and vignettes Gérard Titus-Carmel (Neuilly-sur-Seine: Al Manar, 2003).

102. Abdelkébir Khatibi, *La blessure du nom propre* (Paris: Denoël, 1974).

103. Christian Jambet, preface to *Instants soufis*, by Abdelwahab Meddeb, ill. Hassan Massoudy (Paris: Albin Michel, 2015): 9–27 (25).

104. Abdelwahab Meddeb, *Phantasia: roman* (Paris: Sindbad, 1986; Paris: Seuil, 2003). Subsequent citations refer to the Seuil edition.

105. Abdelwahab Meddeb, "L'icône mentale," *Dédale* 1–2 (1995): 45–66 (63).

106. Abdelwahab Meddeb, "L'islamisme est la maladie de l'islam, mais les germes sont dans le texte," interview by Marc Semo and Christophe Boltanski, *Libération*, September 23, 2006, https://www.liberation.fr/planete/2006/09/23/l-islamisme-est-la-maladie-de-l-islam-mais-les-germes-sont-dans-le-texte_52174/.

107. Habib Tengour, "Le surréalisme maghrébin," *Peuples méditerranéens / Mediterranean Peoples* 17 (1981): 77–81 (80).

108. Sénac, *Avant-corps*, 30.

109. Khatibi, *Quatuor poétique*, 16.

110. Khatibi, 17.

111. Khatibi, 17.

112. Tahar Djaout, *L'invention du désert: roman* (Paris: Seuil, 1987), 71.

113. Rimbaud, *Œuvres complètes*, 306.

114. Kasimirski [*sic*], trans., *Le Koran* (Paris: Charpentier, 1869).

115. George Sale, trans., *The Koran, Commonly Called the Alcoran of Mohammed* (Philadelphia: J. W. Moore, 1856) [1734].

116. Claude-Étienne Savary, trans., *Le Coran* (Amsterdam: Chez les libraires associés, 1786).

117. Ludovico Marracci, trans., *Alcorani textus universus*, 2 vols. (Padua: Typographia Seminarii, 1698).

118. Arthur Rimbaud, *Les illuminations*, pref. Paul Verlaine (Paris: Publications de La Vogue, 1886).

119. Abdelkébir Khatibi, "II. Vertige," in *Maghreb pluriel* (Paris: Denoël, 1983): 227–54.

CHAPTER 1

Epigraph: "I seek an innocent land" (Giuseppe Ungaretti, "Viaggio," in *Allegria di naufragi* [Florence: Vallecchi Editore, 1919], 178 [178]). The epigraph to *Étoile secrète* is a translation of this line: "Je cherche / Un pays / Innocent" (Amrouche, *Étoile secrète*, 12).

1. Beïda Chikhi, "Jean Amrouche, l'intellectuel fantaisiste," *Balises* 1–2 (2000–2001): 151–65 (151).

2. Jean Déjeux, *Littérature maghrébine de langue française: Introduction générale et auteurs* (Sherbrooke: Naaman, 1978 [1973]), 83.

3. Paris: Henri Jouve, 1917.

4. Paris: Les éditions françaises, 1920.

5. Other early works in French include Mohammed Ould Cheikh, *Chants pour Yasmina*, pref. Gaston Picard (Oran: Fouque, 1930); Salah Ettri, *Chants de l'aurore* (Tunis: L'imprimerie de Tunis, 1931); Mohammed Talbi, *Les jardins du soir* (Algiers: Baconnier, 1934).

6. Jean Déjeux, "La littérature nord-africaine de langue française en quête d'un langage authentique," in *Les littératures d'expression française: Écrivains du Maghreb* (Paris: Éditions de la Francité, 1974): 4–9 (5).

7. Déjeux, 5.

8. Djaout, "Avertissement," 3.

9. Jacqueline Arnaud, *Recherches sur la littérature maghrébine de langue française: Le cas de Kateb Yacine*, 2 vols. (Lille: Atelier national de reproduction des thèses, 1982), 1:10; "Jean Amrouche, le précurseur," in *La littérature maghrébine de langue française* (Paris: Publisud, 1986), 129–59.

10. Jules Roy, "Prélude à l'immémorial: El Mouhouv le Superbe, le Généreux," in *D'une amitié: Correspondance Jean Amrouche–Jules Roy (1937–1962)*, by Jean Amrouche and Jules Roy, pref. Marc Faigre (La Calade: Édisud, 1985): 11–12 (12).

11. Guy Dugas, "'Si Amrouche existe, c'est à lui que nous le devons . . .': Jean Amrouche–Armand Guibert, une amitié créatrice," *Expressions maghrébines* 9, no. 1 (2010): 9–25 (18).

12. Déjeux, *Littérature maghrébine de langue française*, 99.

13. Jean Déjeux, "La quête inapaisée: Jean Amrouche et Patrice de La Tour du Pin," in *Jean Amrouche, L'éternel Jugurtha*, by Archives de la ville de Marseille (Marseille: Éditions du quai), 15–28 (16).

14. Albert Memmi, ed., *Anthologie des écrivains maghrébins d'expression française*, pref. Jacqueline Arnaud (Paris: Présence africaine, 1964), 30. The anthology includes a later poem by Amrouche, "Le combat algérien" [Algerian Combat] (31–33), and excerpts from his essay "L'éternel Jugurtha: Propositions sur le génie africain" [The Eternal Jugurtha: Propositions on African Genius] (35–37).

15. Jean Amrouche, "Quelques raisons de la révolte algérienne," in *Un algérien s'adresse aux français; ou, L'histoire d'Algérie par les textes (1943–1961)*, ed. Tassadit Yacine, pref. André Nouschi (Paris: Awal / L'Harmattan, 1994): 23–30 (23). Amrouche's comments were initially pronounced in the Salle Wagram, Paris, on January 27, 1956, at a meeting organized by the Action Committee of Intellectuals against the Continuation of the War in North Africa [Comité d'action des intellectuels contre la poursuite de la guerre en Afrique du Nord] and first published in the journal *Économie et humanisme* (March–April 1956). It might be instructive to consider the life and work of Amrouche alongside that of Léopold Sédar Senghor, who was also born in 1906 under French colonial rule, was also raised Catholic, and also wrote poetry in French, although more prolifically.

16. Amrouche, *Cendres*, 51–52.

17. Réjane Le Baut, *Jean El-Mouhoub Amrouche: Algérien universel: biographie* (Algiers: Chihab, 2014), 79–80.

18. Albert Memmi, *La statue de sel* (Paris: Corrêa, 1953), 178. Le Baut is keen to stress that Memmi's famous portrait does not present a full picture of Amrouche (Le Baut, *Algérien universel*, 67). Memmi later dedicated his collection of poems to Amrouche, "who led me to discover / Al-Ghazālī, Rimbaud, / Milosz and Sa'dī" (Albert Memmi, *Le mirliton du ciel* [Paris: Julliard, 1990], 7).

19. Amrouche, *Cendres*, 67.

20. Amrouche, 67.

21. Amrouche, 68.

22. Amrouche, 35, 66.

23. Amrouche, 96.

24. Amrouche, 73.

25. Amrouche, 55.

26. Amrouche, 73.

27. For further details, as well as an extensive bibliography of critical works on the Malagasy poet, see Moradewun Adejunmobi, *JJ Rabearivelo, Literature and Lingua Franca in Colonial Madagascar* (New York: Peter Lang, 1996).

28. Jean-Joseph Rabéarivelo, *La coupe de cendres* (Antananarivo: G. Pitot de la Beaujardière, 1924). Other collections include *Sylves* (Antananarivo: Imprimerie de l'Imerina, 1927), *Volumes* (Antananarivo: Imprimerie de l'Imerina, 1928), and *Chants pour Abéone* (Antananarivo: Henri Vidalie, 1937). Rabéarivelo also published an anthology entitled *Enfants d'Orphée* (Port Louis, Mauritius: General Printing

and Stationery Co., 1931). A collection of prose poems, *Vieilles chansons des pays d'Imerina, précédées d'une biographie du poète Malgache par Robert Boudry* (Antananarivo: Imprimerie officielle, 1939), was published posthumously.

29. Léon-Gontran Damas, ed., *Poètes d'expression française, 1900–1945* (Paris: Seuil, 1947), 249.

30. Amrouche first met the poet and editor Guibert (Azas, 1906–Saint-Sulpice-la-Pointe, 1990) in Sousse on April 1, 1930.

31. Jean-Joseph Rabéarivelo, *Œuvres complètes*, ed. Serge Meitinger, Liliane Ramarosoa, and Claire Riffard, 2 vols. (Paris: CNRS / Présence africaine éditions, 2010–12), 1:483.

32. Rabéarivelo, 1:515. "Iarive" or "Iarivo" is a diminutive for the city Antananarivo, or Tananarive, forged in the 1920s by Malagasy poets and composers (Liliane Ramarosoa, "Les imaginaires de l'Île à travers la poésie malgache d'expression française," in *L'océan Indien dans les littératures francophones: Pays réels, pays rêvés, pays révélés*, ed. Kumari R. Issur and Vinesh Y. Hookoomsing [Port Louis: Presses de l'université de Maurice, 2001]: 197–212 (198)).

33. Rabéarivelo, *Œuvres complètes*, 1:573.

34. Rabéarivelo, 1:584.

35. Although Amrouche has a fondness for *Cendres*, he will also distance himself from it, as can be seen in a letter to Jules Roy from January 1942: "No, my old man, don't bother digging up this book [*Cendres*], to which I am bound only by sentimental fibers" (in *D'une amitié*, 26).

36. Quoted in Armand Guibert, "Jean Amrouche: images et souvenirs," *Preuves* 137 (July 1962): 68–70 (69).

37. For the agonizing text, see Robert Boudry, "La mort tragique d'un poète," *Mercure de France* (September 15, 1938): 532–49 (547–49).

38. Quoted in Boudry, 544.

39. Déjeux, "La quête inapaisée," 22.

40. Jean Amrouche, preface to *Jean-Joseph Rabearivelo et la mort*, by Robert Boudry (Paris: Présence africaine, 1958): i–iii (ii).

41. Amrouche also published widely in North African literary journals, including *La Kahéna* (Tunis), *Shéhérazade* (Tunis), *Aguedal* (Rabat), *Mirages* (Tunis), *Fontaine* (Algiers), *Cahiers de barbarie* (Tunis), and *La Tunisie française littéraire* (Tunis), which he coedited with Armand Guibert.

42. Milosz was the author of works including *Le poème des décadences* (Paris: Girard et Villerelle, 1899); *Les sept solitudes* (Paris: Henri Jouve, 1906); *Les éléments* (Paris: Bibliothèque de l'Occident, 1911); *Ars magna* (Paris: Alice Sauerwein, 1924); *Les arcanes* (Paris: Librairie Teillon, 1927); and *Miguel Mañara: Mystère en six tableaux*, pref. Armand Godoy (Paris: Bernard Grasset, 1935).

43. "au Poëte, / au Prophète, / notre Maître en vie spirituelle" [to the Poet, / to the Prophet, / our Master in the spiritual life] (Amrouche, *Étoile secrète*, 11).

44. Expressing concern over du Pin's uncertain fate, Mauriac dubs him "the most inspired poet of his generation" (François Mauriac, "Patrice de La Tour du Pin," *Temps présent* 103 (November 24, 1939): 1 (1)).

45. "Patrice de La Tour du Pin est mort" was slated for publication in *La Tunisie française littéraire* on October 30, 1940.

46. Gabriel Audisio, review of *Chants berbères de Kabylie*, by Jean Amrouche, *Cahiers du sud* 218 (1939): 600–601 (600).

47. Jean Amrouche, "Témoignages: Jean Amrouche" in *Ungaretti*, ed. Piero Sanavio (Paris: Éditions de l'Herne, 1968): 261–62 (262).

48. Patrice Arthur Élie Humbert de La Tour du Pin, *La Quête de joie* (Paris: Maestricht, 1933); republished by Armand Guibert in 1935 and Gallimard in 1939.

49. Quoted in Patrice de La Tour du Pin, *Poèmes choisis*, ed. Claude Arnaud, Emmanuel de Calan, and Jean-Matthieu de l'Épinois (Paris: Gallimard, 2010), 221.

50. Jean Amrouche, "La pensée de Patrice de La Tour du Pin," in *Patrice de La Tour du Pin: Avec un poème inédit de Patrice de La Tour du Pin*, with Armand Guibert, Camille Bégué, and A. Denis-Dagieu (Tunis: Mirages, 1934): 81–126 (85). Jean Sénac, the focus of the following chapter, also reads du Pin's *Quête de joie* and writes a poem entitled "La quête inapaisée" (*Afrique* 209 [May–June 1946], 12).

51. Robert Brasillach, *Les quatre jeudis: Images d'avant-guerre* (Paris: Les sept couleurs, 1951), 470. Brasillach identifies du Pin's "brothers" in poetry as Emily Brontë and Edgar Allan Poe (Brasillach, 471).

52. Amrouche, "La pensée de Patrice de La Tour du Pin," 84, 87.

53. Patrice de La Tour du Pin, *Le second jeu* (Paris: Gallimard, 1959), 424. See also "Lettre de carême à des citadins à propos de théopoétique," in *Une lutte pour la vie* (Paris: Gallimard, 1970), 69–88.

54. Toby Garfitt, "Patrice de La Tour du Pin," in *Modern French Poets*, ed. Jean-François Leroux (Detroit: Gale Group, 2002): 271–84 (274). Gauthier offers an altogether more devotional definition: "The flesh of the poet's spiritual experience and the breath of his contact with the great Eucharistic body of the Paschal Christ" (Jacques Gauthier, *La théopoésie de Patrice de La Tour du Pin* [Montreal: Bellarmin / Paris: Les éditions du Cerf, 1989], 81). See also Maurice Champagne, "L'idéologie poétique de Patrice de La Tour du Pin," in *Colloque Patrice de La Tour du Pin: Tenu à la Sorbonne le 21 et le 22 novembre 1981*, ed. Yves-Alain Favre (Paris: Librairie A.-G. Nizet, 1983): 35–45.

55. The poem that closes *Étoile secrète*—"Oraison finale du récitant pour célébrer la mémoire de l'absent" [The Recitant's Final Oration to Celebrate the Memory of the Absent One]—is preceded by a quotation from du Pin (Amrouche, *Étoile secrète*, 97).

56. Brasillach, however, insists, "The mists in which one hears, from the fall onward, the cry of the bird, the call of the hunter, are from France, no doubt. It is at the edge of the French marshes, among familiar reeds, that he has evoked these imaginary creatures . . ." (Brasillach, *Les quatre jeudis*, 471).

57. Du Pin, *La Quête de joie*, 25.

58. Du Pin, 7.

59. Du Pin, 25.

60. Stephen Spender, introduction to *The Dedicated Life in Poetry and The Correspondence of Laurent de Cayeux*, by Patrice de La Tour du Pin, trans. G. S. Fraser (London: Harvill Press, 1948): vii–xix (xv).

61. Du Pin, *La Quête de joie*, 18.

62. Du Pin, 72.

63. Du Pin, 73.

64. Garfitt, "Patrice de La Tour du Pin," 274.
65. Amrouche, *Étoile secrète*, 63.
66. Memmi, "Jean Amrouche," 162.
67. Amrouche, *Cendres*, 78.
68. Amrouche, *Étoile secrète*, 73.
69. Mohammed Khaïr-Eddine, *Ce Maroc!*, ill. Mechtilt (Paris: Seuil, 1975), 53.
70. Amrouche, *Étoile secrète*, 67.
71. Du Pin, *La Quête de joie*, 49.
72. Lyotard, *Discourse, Figure*, 4.
73. Du Pin, *La Quête de joie*, 29.
74. Du Pin, 39.
75. Du Pin, 45, 75.
76. Du Pin, 56.
77. Amrouche, "La pensée de Patrice de La Tour du Pin," 89.
78. Stéphane Mallarmé, *Divagations*, trans. Barbara Johnson (Cambridge: The Belknap Press of Harvard University Press, 2007), 201.
79. See Henry Bauchau, "Jean Amrouche ou la déchirure," *Études freudiennes* 7–8 (April 1973): 193–202. When Khaïr-Eddine commemorates Jean's sister, Taos, he also insists on this semanteme: "je vois / l'aiguille des pics et la honte séculaire! / ils se déchirent sur le champ, ils me déchirent!" [I see / the needle of the peaks and the age-old shame! / they immediately tear each other apart, they tear me apart!] (Mohammed Khaïr-Eddine, "Permanence de Taos Amrouche," in *Résurrection des fleurs sauvages* (Rabat: Stouky, 1981): 47–49 (47). See also Akila Kizzi, *Marie-Louise Taos Amrouche: Passions et déchirements identitaires* (Paris: Fauves, 2019). Note that Marguerite Taos Amrouche was the pseudonym of Marie-Louise Amrouche (Tunis, 1913–Saint-Michel-l'Observatoire, 1976). Marguerite was her mother's baptismal name, whereas Taos approximates the Kabyle word for "peacock."
80. Jean Amrouche, "A propos d'une exécution sommaire," in *Un algérien s'adresse aux français*, 86–91 (90); first published in *Action* (June 1958).
81. Maurice O'Connell Walshe, *A Concise German Etymological Dictionary* (London: Routledge and Kegan Paul, 1951), 192.
82. Du Pin, *La Quête de joie*, 66.
83. Amrouche, *Cendres*, 97.
84. Du Pin, *La Quête de joie*, 47–48.
85. Du Pin, 48.
86. Du Pin, 48.
87. Amrouche, *Étoile secrète*, 66.
88. Déjeux, "La quête inapaisée," 20.
89. Du Pin, *La Quête de joie*, 27.
90. Du Pin, 32.
91. Amrouche, *Étoile secrète*, 70.
92. Jean Amrouche, *Journal: 1928–1962*, ed. Tassadit Yacine Titouh (Paris: Non Lieu, 2009), 70. Gabriel Audisio, who was born in Marseille and grew up in Algiers, is the author of several works of essays and poetry, including *La vie de Haroun-al-Raschid* (Paris: Gallimard, 1930), *Jeunesse de la Méditerranée* (Paris: Gallimard, 1935), and *Sel de la mer* (Paris: Gallimard, 1936). For more on Audisio's concept of the supranational "pays" [country] as "a space of reconciliation and synergy" and its

renewed role in recent Mediterranean studies, see Tamalet Talbayev, *The Transcontinental Maghreb*, 50–58 (53).

93. Amrouche, *Journal*, 70–71.

94. Amrouche, 71.

95. Rainer Maria Rilke, *Duino Elegies: Bilingual Edition*, trans. Edward Snow (New York: North Point Press, 2000), 46–47.

96. Dugas, "Jean Amrouche–Armand Guibert, une amitié créatrice," 21.

97. Le Baut, *Algérien universel*, 115.

98. Jane Hiddleston, *Decolonising the Intellectual: Politics, Culture, and Humanism at the End of the French Empire* (Liverpool: Liverpool University Press, 2014), 165.

99. Hiddleston, 165.

100. Jean Amrouche, "Notes sur la grâce de ravissement en poésie," *Fontaine* 19–20 (1942): 161–67 (162).

101. Tahar Djaout, "Amrouche, *Étoile secrète*, L'enfance de l'homme et du monde," *Algérie-Actualité* 921 (June 9–15, 1983): 21 (21).

102. ". . . song, sprung from a tearing . . ." (Mallarmé, *Œuvres complètes*, 2:156).

103. "The shadow has become / capricious. The song / calls for a clear / phrase" (Nabile Farès, *Le chant d'Akli* [Paris: L'Harmattan, 1981], 9). This collection is dedicated "*To Jean Amrouche / and Abderrahmane Farès, / for their constant / and peaceful friendship*" (Farès, 5). Abderrahmane Farès (Amalou, 1911–Zemmouri, 1991)—Nabile's father—served as president of the Provisional Executive Council between April and September 1962, as arranged by the Evian Accords. For his account of this period, see Abderrahmane Farès, *La cruelle vérité: L'Algérie de 1945 à l'indépendance* (Paris: Plon, 1982). As president, Farès writes to Suzanne Amrouche upon her husband's death, "Deeply saddened by the cruel loss you have suffered, I sincerely share your pain and will never forget the memory of Jean and his work to make Algeria a living reality" (quoted in Amrouche, *Un algérien s'adresse aux français*, 350).

104. Jean Amrouche, *Chants berbères de Kabylie* (Paris: Charlot, 1947). Published in the series "Poésie et théâtre," directed by Albert Camus. Republished by L'Harmattan in 1986 and 1988 with transcription of Kabyle texts by Taos Amrouche. Subsequent citations refer to the Charlot edition unless otherwise noted.

105. Marcelle Schveitzer-Lagleyze, "En route . . . (avec Guibert et Amrouche)," *Les carnets de l'exotisme* 9 (1992): 73–75 (73). The group also vacationed together during the summer of 1936, when they visited Germany, Czechoslovakia, Austria, and Hungary, and in 1938, when they went to Spain and Portugal. There, they met the South African poet Roy Campbell (Durban, 1901–Setúbal, 1957), who had converted to Catholicism in 1935 and was a vocal supporter of Francisco Franco and the Nationalists in the then ongoing Spanish civil war. See Guibert's translations of Campbell's *Adamastor* (Tunis: Mirages, 1936).

106. Le Baut, *Algérien universel*, 132. In his later translated anthology of Kabyle songs, Malek Ouary also points to suggestive similarities between Greek and Kabyle cultures; see *Poèmes et chants de Kabylie*, ed. Malek Ouary (Paris: Librairie Saint-Germain-des-Prés, 1974), 32.

107. Quoted in Le Baut, *Algérien universel*, 118.

108. Jean-Joseph Rabéarivelo, *Presque-songes: Poëmes hova: Traduits par l'auteur*, pref. Robert Boudry, ill. Urbain-Faurec (Antananarivo, 1934); *Traduit de la nuit* (Tunis: Mirages, 1935).

109. As in, for example, "Dis-moi, serait-il malade? / Aux mains des Chrétiens prisonnier?" [Tell me, might he be ill? / Prisoner in the hands of the Christians?] (Amrouche, *Chants berbères de Kabylie*, 85).

110. In his own estimation, this preface is one of his major poetic achievements, as he notes in a letter to Roy dated December 23, 1941: "Everyone has forgotten that I wrote *Étoile secrète*, that my introduction to *Les chants* is one of the most beautiful texts on poetry ever written in French" (*D'une amitié*, 23).

111. Jean Amrouche, "Témoignage d'un compagnon de service," in *Milosz: Textes et documents inédits*, ed. Armand Guibert (Paris: Poésie 42, 1942): 67–70 (67–68).

112. Patrice de La Tour du Pin, *Une somme de poésie* (Paris: Gallimard, 1946), 220.

113. Amrouche, *Chants berbères de Kabylie*, 11–12.

114. Amrouche, 8.

115. Amrouche, 42.

116. Amrouche, 60. In the 1947 republication of *Chants berbères de Kabylie*, this effect is further enhanced by the repetition of the publisher's name, Edmond Charlot (Algiers, 1915–Béziers, 2004).

117. Amrouche, 40.

118. Amrouche, 41.

119. Amrouche, 44.

120. Jean Amrouche, "Pour une poésie africaine: Préface à des chants imaginaires," *Fontaine: Revue mensuelle de la poésie et des lettres françaises* 30 (1943): 531–43 (531).

121. Amrouche, 542.

122. Amrouche, 542 . See Rom. 13:14 (King James Version), "But put ye on the Lord Jesus Christ, and make not provision for the flesh, to *fulfil* the lusts *thereof*"; and Gal. 3:27 (King James Version), "For as many of you as have been baptized into Christ have put on Christ."

123. Amrouche, *Chants berbères de Kabylie*, 24.

124. Amrouche, 40.

125. For a brief introduction to Si Mohand, see Thomas C. Connolly, "Editor's Preface: Prelude to North African Poetry in French," *Yale French Studies* 137–38 (2020): 1–10 (1–5).

126. Mouloud Mammeri, *Les Isefra: Poèmes de Si Mohand-ou-Mhand; Texte berbère et traduction* (Paris: François Maspero, 1969), 79.

127. Mouloud Feraoun, *Les poèmes de Si Mohand* (Paris: Minuit, 1960), 47.

128. Youssef Nacib, *Anthologie de la poésie kabyle: Édition bilingue* (Algiers: Éditions Andalouses, 1993), 118.

129. "De la musique avant toute chose, / Et pour cela préfère l'Impair / Plus vague et plus soluble dans l'air, / Sans rien en lui qui pèse ou qui pose" [Music before everything else. / And to that end think odd and not even, / Uncertain of beat, dissolving more quickly, / With no weight to speak of, no feigning at all] (Paul Verlaine, *Paul Verlaine: A Bilingual Selection of His Verse*, trans. Samuel N. Rosenberg, ed. Nicolas Valazza [University Park: Pennsylvania State University Press, 2019], 152–53).

130. Nacib, *Anthologie de la poésie kabyle*, 120; Amrouche, *Chants berbères de Kabylie*, 46.

131. Mouloud Mammeri, "Évolution de la poésie kabyle," *Revue africaine* 422–23 (1950): 125–48 (145).

132. Feraoun, *Les poèmes de Si Mohand*, 8. In his exceptional study of Djaout and Lounis Aït Menguellet (b. Iboudraren, 1950), Ali Chibani further problematizes "asefru" by setting it alongside the Kabyle term "anza," that is, the keening or cry that can be heard at the spot where someone has been killed, usually on the anniversary of the murder. Where "anza" inscribes violence in an obsessional return of the same, "asefru" aims to break free from the circularity of time and the repetition of violence: "But [asefru] also finds itself confronted with the reality of this closure and requires countless poetic stratagems to escape from it" (Ali Chibani, *Tahar Djaout et Lounis Aït Menguellet: Temps clos et ruptures spatiales*, pref. Beïda Chikhi [Paris: L'Harmattan, 2012], 9).

133. Amrouche, *Chants berbères de Kabylie*, 39–40.

134. Amrouche, 39.

135. Mammeri, *Les Isefra*, 73; Nacib, *Anthologie de la poésie kabyle*, 31, 120.

136. Jean-Marie Dallet, *Dictionnaire kabyle-français: Parler des At Mangellat, Algérie* (Paris: Société d'études linguistiques et anthropologiques de France, 1982–85), 216–17. See also Nacib, *Anthologie de la poésie kabyle*, 31, 120.

137. Dallet, *Dictionnaire kabyle-français*, 565; Nacib, *Anthologie de la poésie kabyle*, 120.

138. Dallet, 31.

139. Amrouche, *Chants berbères de Kabylie*, 40.

140. Amrouche, 20.

141. Amrouche, 21.

142. Amrouche, *Journal*, 87.

143. Amrouche, "Notes sur la grâce de ravissement en poésie," 162.

144. Habib Tengour, *Traverser*, ill. Abdallah Benanteur (La Rochelle: Rumeur des âges, 2002), 24; "oily sea-foam laps at the foot of the rusty / rocks recalling the barter of olives and wheat / and the fantasies of rhapsodists / who passed on to each other in secret the myth of / Aphrodite" (Habib Tengour, *Crossings*, trans. Marilyn Hacker [Sausalito: Post-Apollo Press, 2013], 39).

145. Jean Amrouche, *Sous le feu la cendre*, ed. Tassadit Yacine Titouh (Paris: Non Lieu, 2012).

146. Henri Kréa, *La révolution et la poésie sont une seule et même chose*, pref. Jean Amrouche, frontispice Ferró, illus. Kijno (Paris: Pierre Jean Oswald, 1960). This book title is later used as the title of a poem in Tahar Djaout's *Solstice barbelé: 1973–1975*, 20.

147. Jean Amrouche, "Rhapsodie sur le seuil," preface to, *La révolution et la poésie sont une seule et même chose*, by Kréa, 7–10 (8).

148. Amrouche, 7.

149. Amrouche, 10.

150. See Le Baut, *Algérien universel*, 308; Ali Chibani, "Jean Amrouche a été un homme qui n'a jamais manqué de courage quand il s'est agi de défendre sa 'famille humaine,'" *El Watan*, July 5, 2022, https://elwatan-dz.com/ali-chibani-poete-essayiste-jean-amrouche-a-ete-un-homme-qui-na-jamais-manque-de-courage-quand-il-sest-agi-de-defendre-sa-famille-humaine. Amrouche continued to appear regularly on Radio-Lausanne and Radio-Genève until June 1961.

151. Charles de Gaulle, "Discours sur l'autodétermination de l'Algérie, 16 septembre 1959," https://www.charles-de-gaulle.org/wp-content/uploads/2017/03/Discours-de-lautodetermination-de-lAlgerie.pdf.

152. Amrouche, "Rhapsodie sur le seuil," 7–10.

153. Amrouche and Césaire had both spoken at the meeting of the Action Committee of Intellectuals against the Continuation of the War in North Africa" in Paris at the Salle Wagram on January 27, 1956, alongside Alioune Diop, Michel Leiris, André Mandouze, Jean-Paul Sartre, Robert Barrat, and others (Le Baut, *Algérien universel*, 289–90).

154. Aimé Césaire et al., "Hommages à Jean Amrouche," *Présence africaine* 46, no. 2 (1963): 187–96 (188). The apparent typing error ("nation" instead of "notion") is not entirely inapposite, as will become evident.

155. "All effective remedies are denied him. The French route, as well as the Malagasy route, in both temporal senses, the upstream of the fabulous ancestors and the revolutionary downstream [vers l'amont des ancêtres fabuleux et vers l'aval révolutionnaire], neither is able to welcome and guarantee his human passage on firm ground" (Amrouche, preface to *Jean-Joseph Rabearivelo et la mort*, iii).

156. "Afloat in the current of enemy time, he incessantly ascends its flow toward the origin, which he sometimes touches, and at those moments, the seal of eternity is applied to mortal language and confers on it the attributes of divine speech" (Amrouche, "Témoignages: Jean Amrouche," 262).

157. Césaire et al., "Hommages à Jean Amrouche," 188. Césaire might also have evoked Baudelaire, as Amrouche quotes the line "Adieu donc, chants du cuivre et soupirs de la flûte!" [So, farewell, songs of brass and sighs of the flute!] from "Le goût du néant" [The Taste of Nothingness] (Charles Baudelaire, *Œuvres complètes*, ed. Claude Pichois, 2 vols. [Paris: Gallimard, 1976], 1:76 (1:76)), when he writes, "silences et soupirs des flûtes de roseau" [silences and sighs of reed flutes].

158. Césaire et al., "Hommages à Jean Amrouche," 188.

159. Rimbaud, *Œuvres complètes*, 303.

160. Césaire et al., "Hommages à Jean Amrouche," 188. As Cavallaro puts it, this line is "one of the banner formulas" of *Illuminations* (Adrien Cavallaro, "*Illuminations* [Herméneutique et poétique]" in *Dictionnaire Rimbaud*, ed. Adrien Cavallaro, Yann Frémy, and Alain Vaillant [Paris: Classiques Garnier, 2021]: 362–90 (379)).

161. Césaire et al., "Hommages à Jean Amrouche," 188–89.

162. Quoted in Césaire et al., "Hommages à Jean Amrouche," 189. Note that Césaire inserts punctuation and italics that are absent from Amrouche's original text.

163. Césaire et al., 189.

164. Kréa will say that Amrouche represented "for the writers of North Africa what Césaire represented for those of the Black world" (Césaire et al., "Hommages à Jean Amrouche," 190).

165. Abdellatif Laâbi, "À propos du 'Polygone étoilé' de Kateb Yacine," *Souffles* 4 (1966): 44–46 (45).

166. El-Mahdi Acherchour, *L'œil de l'égaré: poème*; Jamel Eddine Bencheikh, *Cantate pour le pays des îles: poème* (Paris: Marsa, 1997), 41.

167. Rimbaud, *Œuvres complètes*, 313.

168. The Kabyle for "threshold" is "amder, imedran" and signifies not only the threshold of a dwelling under a doorway or window, and a wooden beam, but also, in the geological sense, "the edge of a natural basin found in the bed of a dried river" (Dallet, *Dictionnaire kabyle-français*, 487).

169. Quoted in Le Baut, *Algérien universel*, 149.

170. André Gide—whom Amrouche first met in Tunis in 1942—encouraged Amrouche to establish *L'Arche* to challenge the primacy of the *Nouvelle revue française*, then under the direction of the collaborationist Pierre Drieu La Rochelle. Founded in Algiers in 1944 by Amrouche and Jacques Lassaigne, *L'Arche* was moved to Paris after the liberation of France and ceased publication in 1947. For Gide and Amrouche's complete epistolary exchange, annotations, and commentary, see *André Gide, Jean Amrouche: Correspondance, 1928–1950*, ed. Pierre Masson and Guy Dugas (Lyon: Presses universitaires de Lyon, 2010).

171. Kateb Yacine, "Amrouche, cet inconnu," *Jeune Afrique* 142 (July 8–14, 1963): 26 (26).

172. Kateb Yacine, "De grandes espérances," *L'Arc* 19 (1962): 73–75 (75).

173. Kateb Yacine, "Amrouche, cet inconnu," 26.

174. "*Nedjma* par Kateb Yacine," June 23, 1956, Chaîne nationale, Radiodiffusion-Télévision Française (RTF), Archive INA–Radio France, https://www.radiofrance.fr/franceculture/nedjma-nee-d-un-exorcisme-par-kateb-yacine-8561151.

175. Amrouche and Roy, *D'une amitié*, 104.

176. Quoted in Le Baut, *Algérien universel*, 235.

177. In his introduction to Fadhma Aït Mansour Amrouche's *Histoire de ma vie*, Kateb Yacine begins by saying that her son, Jean, would have been best placed to present his mother's book: "In a sense he was the preliminary torrent of this living source [le torrent précurseur de cette source vive] from which he drew, from his earliest childhood, along with his sister Taos, the gift of poetry that would never leave them" (Kateb Yacine, "Jeune fille de ma tribu," introduction to *Histoire de ma vie*, by Fadhma Aït Mansour Amrouche, pref. Vincent Monteil [Paris: François Maspéro, 1968]: 11–15 (11)).

178. Kateb Yacine, *Nedjma: roman* (Paris: Seuil, 1956), 138.

179. Kateb Yacine, 172.

180. "It only rarely rains on the eastern Algerian plain, but when it does it pours; the miraculously pregnant Seybouse then delivers herself, the untimely spewings of a dying river, vomited up by the ungrateful banks it has nourished . . . the downpour erupts, degenerates, an aborted sneeze; the constellations drown from one night to the next in the spray, vaporized like squadrons in a camouflage of mist" (Kateb Yacine, 66).

181. Kateb Yacine, 177–78.

182. Kateb Yacine, 179.

183. Kateb Yacine, 178. As Tamalet Talbayev writes, the Oued El Kebir restores "the prestigious lexeme Guadalquivir to its Arabic etymology" (Tamalet Talbayev, *The Transcontinental Maghreb*, 61).

184. Audisio designates the unpredictable torrent of the wadi as a figure for "North African genius," which is held in check by a deliberately developed discipline or "solar thought" (Gabriel Audisio, "Tête d'Africa ou le génie de l'Afrique du Nord," *Cahiers du sud* 310 [1951]: 437–51 (448)).

185. Quoted in Déjeux, "La littérature nord-africaine de langue française en quête d'un langage authentique," 6. See also Jean Déjeux, "Réception critique de *Nedjma* en 1956–57," in *Actualité de Kateb Yacine*, ed. Jacqueline Arnaud (Paris: L'Harmattan, 1993): 109–26 (118).

186. Jacqueline Arnaud, introduction to *L'œuvre en fragments*, by Kateb Yacine, ed. Jacqueline Arnaud (Paris: Sindbad, 1986): 9–29 (15).

187. Khatibi, *La blessure du nom propre*, 88.

188. Meddeb, *Instants soufis*, 86. See also Meddeb's description of the ninth-century Iranian Sufi Abū Yazīd Bisṭāmī: "Le transi de Bestam dont la bouche débordait d'extases, comme le fleuve pendant la crue" [The ecstatic of Basṭām, whose mouth overflowed with excess, like a river in spate] (Abdelwahab Meddeb, *Blanches traverses du passé* [Saint-Clément-de-Rivière: Fata Morgana, 1997], 17).

189. Quoted in Meddeb, *Instants soufis*, 86. From the Greek "θεοπάθεια" [theopatheia], meaning "the suffering of God," theopathy is the "sympathetic passive feeling excited by the contemplation of God; susceptibility to this feeling; sensitiveness or responsiveness to divine influence; pious sentiment" (*Oxford English Dictionary*, s.v. "theopathy (*n.*)," July 2023, https://doi.org/10.1093/OED/7504526572).

190. Charles Baudelaire, "Fusées," in *Œuvres complètes*, 1:649–67. See also Abdelwahab Meddeb, "La subversion de Hallâj ou le secret divulgué," in *Le voyage initiatique*, ed. Nadia Benjelloun (Paris: Albin Michel, 2011): 53–72 (56–57).

191. Guillaume Apollinaire, "Pressentiment d'Amérique," in *Œuvres poétiques*, pref. André Billy, ed. Marcel Adéma and Michel Décaudin (Paris: Gallimard, 2005): 497 (497).

192. Du Pin, *La Quête de joie*, 63–64.

193. Quoted in *Poèmes choisis*, by Patrice de La Tour du Pin, ed. Claude Arnaud, Emmanuel de Calan, and Jean-Matthieu de l'Epinois (Paris: Gallimard, 2010), 219.

194. Khaïr-Eddine, *Soleil arachnide*, 25.

195. Quoted from a diary entry dated November 1936; see Amrouche, *Journal*, 70.

196. Émile-Félix Gautier, *Le Sahara, avec 4 cartes dans le texte* (Paris: Payot, 1923), 48.

197. Henri Begouën, "Les vestiges des terrasses de l'oued Igharghas [*sic*] et le dessèchement du Sahara," *XV*e *Congrès international d'anthropologie et d'archéologie préhistorique (Suite) et V*e *Session de l'Institut international d'anthropologie, Paris, 20–27 septembre 1931* (Paris: Nourry, 1933): 250–59 (252).

198. Gautier, *Le Sahara*, 73–74.

199. Gautier, 74. By "chott," Gautier understands a "temporary lake," most often with salt deposits (79, 136).

200. Jacqueline Arnaud, "Les villes mythiques et le mythe de Nedjma dans le roman de Kateb Yacine," *Journée Kateb Yacine: Actes du colloque organisé par le Département de français (5 mai 1984)* (Manouba: Publications de la faculté des lettres, 1990): 9–17 (9). Kateb later extends the geographical scope of *Nedjma* to the Tunisian island of Djerba at the southern end of the Gulf of Gabès, thought to be the home of the lotus-eaters—or "λωτοφάγοι" [lōtophagoi]—in Greek mythology, in three prose texts entitled "Djerba, l'île de l'étrangère" (1958), "Le lotos" (1964), and "Les poissons sautent" (1965) (Kateb Yacine, *L'œuvre en fragments*, 146–57). See Tamalet Talbayev, *The Transcontinental Maghreb*, 69–78.

201. Compare to Audisio's *Héliotrope*, which begins, "There is only one sea: the Mediterranean. After that there are seas, oceans, water. But here, I am speaking of *the Sea*, the Only, mine. Or ours, let's say" (Gabriel Audisio, *Héliotrope* [Paris: Gallimard, 1928], 11).

202. Gautier, *Le Sahara*, 51.

203. Tamalet Talbayev, *The Transcontinental Maghreb*, 42–43.

204. Plato, *The Dialogues of Plato*, trans. R. E. Allen, vol. 3, *Ion, Hippias Minor, Laches, Protagoras* (New Haven: Yale University Press, 1996), 22.

205. Maurice Blanchot, *L'entretien infini* (Paris: Gallimard, 1969), 572.

206. Charles Baudelaire to Sainte-Beuve, January 15, 1866, in *Correspondance*, ed. Claude Pichois and Jean Ziegler, 2 vols. (Paris: Gallimard, 1993–99), 2:583.

207. R. E. Allen, "Comment," in *The Dialogues of Plato*, 3:3–7 (3:3).

208. Blanchot, *L'entretien infini*, 571–72.

209. Amrouche, "Notes sur la grâce de ravissement en poésie," 162.

210. Blanchot, *L'entretien infini*, 572.

211. Khatibi, *Figures de l'étranger*, 91.

212. Blanchot, *L'entretien infini*, 572.

213. Roland Barthes, *La préparation du roman I et II: Cours et séminaires au Collège de France (1978–1979 et 1979–1980)*, ed. Nathalie Léger (Paris: Seuil, 2003), 203.

214. Khatibi, *Maghreb pluriel*, 39.

215. Blanchot, *L'entretien infini*, 554.

216. Barthes, *La préparation du roman*, 203.

217. Édouard Glissant, *La cohée du Lamentin: Poétique V* (Gallimard, 2005), 124.

218. Khatibi, *Maghreb pluriel*, 54.

219. Abdelkébir Khatibi, "Repères," *Pro-Culture. Revue maghrébine: science / écriture / analyse* 12 (1978): 48–52 (49).

CHAPTER 2

1. Jean-Paul Sartre, "Orphée noir," preface to *Anthologie de la nouvelle poésie nègre et malgache de langue française*, ed. Senghor, ix–xliv.

2. Jean-Paul Sartre, *Qu'est-ce que la littérature?* (Paris: Gallimard, 1948).

3. Richard H. Watts, "Difference/Indifference: Sartre, Glissant, and the Race of Francophone Literature," in *Race after Sartre: Antiracism, Africana Existentialism, Postcolonialism*, ed. Jonathan Judaken (Albany: State University of New York Press, 2008): 193–209 (195).

4. Sénac hosted programs on Algerian radio, including "Le poète dans la cité" (1964–65) and "Poésie sur tous les fronts" (1967–71). For his work as a critic, see Hamid Nacer-Khodja, *Jean Sénac, critique algérien*, pref. Guy Dugas (Algiers: El Kalima, 2013).

5. Rachid Boudjedra, *Lettres algériennes* (Paris: Grasset et Fasquelle, 1995), 74.

6. Aimé Césaire, "Maintenir la poésie," *Tropiques* 8 (1943): 7–8 (8).

7. Ovid, *Ovid in Six Volumes*, trans. Frank Justus Miller, vol. 4, *Metamorphoses in Two Volumes*, 2 vols. (Cambridge: Harvard University Press, 1976), 10.1–85, 2:64–71.

8. Sartre, "Orphée noir," xix.

9. Sartre, xx.

10. Quoted in Sartre, xix–xx; Mallarmé, *Divagations*, 264.

11. Sartre, "Orphée noir," xvii.

12. These can be traced to Arthur de Gobineau's 1853 "Essai sur l'inégalité des races humaines" [Essay on the Inequality of the Human Races], via Guillaume Apollinaire's theories on "fetish-art" (Christopher L. Miller, *Blank Darkness: Africanist Discourse in French* [Chicago: University of Chicago Press, 1985], 88).

13. Sartre, "Orphée noir," xvii.

14. Sartre, xvi.

15. Sartre thereby amplifies Breton's claim that Césaire's *Cahier* is "the greatest lyrical monument of our time" (André Breton, "Un grand poète noir," in *Œuvres complètes*, by Aimé Césaire, 3 vols. [Fort-de-France: Éditions Désormeaux, 1976]: 1.31–39 (1.35)). Bwejeri is not alone in describing Sartre's assertion as suspect (Jean Bwejeri, "*Orphée noir* ou la lettre qui tue: Éléments pour une évaluation du concept sartrien de négritude," *Les lettres romanes* 43, nos. 1–2 (1989): 85–99 (88)).

16. Jean Sénac, *Avant-Corps, précédé de Poèmes iliaques et suivi de Diwân du Noûn* (Paris: Gallimard, 1968).

17. Rabah Belamri, *Jean Sénac: Entre désir et douleur* (Algiers: Office des publications universitaires, 1989), 54.

18. Jean Sénac, *Poèmes*, pref. René Char (Paris: Gallimard, 1954). Sénac and Camus were close friends until divergent opinions on the Algerian War drove them apart around 1957. Toward the end of his life, Sénac dedicated *Les désordres* [Disturbances] to his former mentor: "Camus loved these poems. They were dedicated to him. Gallimard refused them. They slept in a suitcase. After fifteen years (the war, the ruptures, *Jacques Orphée des Halles*, independence, 'tu es belle comme un comité de gestion' [you are beautiful like a management committee], the 'corpoème,' Char intact, Vietnam, Palestine, May 1968, Algiers faithful as a sore), between derision and Vertigo, a friendship momentarily dislocated resumes" (Jean Sénac, *Les désordres* [Paris: Librairie Saint-Germain-des-Prés, 1972], 7). For more on their turbulent relationship, see Bernard Mazo, *Jean Sénac, poète et martyr*, foreword by René de Ceccatty, pref. Hamid Nacer-Khodja (Paris: Seuil, 2013); Hamid Nacer-Khodja, *Albert Camus, Jean Sénac; ou, Le fils rebelle*, pref. Guy Dugas (Paris: Paris-Méditerranée / Birkhadem: EDIF 2000, 2004); Hamid Nacer-Khodja, *Albert Camus, Jean Senac, or the Rebel Son*, trans. Kai Krienke (East Lansing: Michigan State University Press, 2018).

19. Jean Sénac, *Matinale de mon peuple*, pref. Mostefa Lacheraf, ill. Abdallah Benanteur (Rodez: Subervie, 1961).

20. Jean Sénac, *Le soleil sous les armes: Eléments d'une poésie de la résistance algérienne* (Rodez: Subervie, 1957), 21.

21. Nacer-Khodja describes Sénac's relation to homosexuality as a "painful quest," incompatible with his Christian upbringing (Hamid Nacer-Khodja, "Érotique, poétique, politique," postface to *Œuvres poétiques*, by Jean Sénac, pref. René de Ceccatty [Arles: Actes Sud, 2019]: 785–802 (791)).

22. Sénac, *Avant-corps*, 54–55.

23. Frantz Fanon, *L'an V de la révolution algérienne* (Paris: François Maspero, 1959).

24. Assia Djebar, *Le blanc de l'Algérie: récit* (Paris: Albin Michel, 1995), 152.

25. Belamri notes that these transformations were accompanied by formal innovations, including an accrued use of parentheses, of dashes, of suspension points, and of the reverse question mark "⸮". Belamri identifies "⸮"—used to signal irony—as a mode of expression somewhere between the question mark and exclamation point (Belamri, *Entre désir et douleur*, 53). Sénac previously deployed "⸮" in *Le torrent de Baïn: poèmes* (Die: Relâche, 1962).

26. Sénac, *Avant-corps*, 12. Sénac further explores the notion in "Notes sur le corpoème (1972–1973)," *CELAAN* 7 (2009): 82–89. See also Claude Fintz, "Éro-

tisme, méditerranéité et identité dans le 'corpoème' de Jean Sénac: Les imaginaires congruents du corps, de l'écriture, de la nation," in *Penser le corps au Maghreb*, ed. Monia Lachheb (Tunis: IRMC / Paris: Karthala, 2012): 241–56 (246).

27. Quoting Peterson's description of Frantz Fanon's take on Albert Memmi (Peterson, *Dubois, Fanon, Cabril*, 100).

28. Louis Segond (Geneva, 1810–Geneva, 1885) was a Swiss theologian, whose French translation of the Bible was first published in 1871 and revised and republished in 1910. See Louis Segond, trans., *La sainte Bible qui comprend l'ancien et le nouveau testament traduits sur les textes originaux hébreu et grec* (Paris, 1923).

29. Jean Sénac, *Ébauche du père: Pour en finir avec l'enfance* (Paris: Gallimard, 1989). The novel was composed during Sénac's exile in France between 1959 and 1962. For an incisive analysis of the figure of the father in Sénac's life and writings, as well as of theater and theatricality in this novel, see Dominique Combe, "Jean Sénac, le roman impossible," *Awal* 10 (1993): 37–49; previously published in *Critique* 527 (1991): 246–59.

30. Charles Baudelaire, "Peintures murales d'Eugène Delacroix à Saint-Sulpice," in *Œuvres complètes*, 2:729–31.

31. Gen. 32:24–31 (King James Version), quoted in Sénac, *Ébauche du père*, 124–25.

32. See Khatibi's telling of this episode in *Par-dessus l'épaule*, 80.

33. The French for comma is "une virgule," but in the Spanish familiar to Sénac and his mother it is "una coma."

34. In a somewhat related context, Glissant notes, "In this litany, the comma (,) indicates a relation, the hyphen (-) an opposition, the colon (:) a sequence" (Édouard Glissant, *Poétique de la relation* [Paris: Gallimard, 1990], 236).

35. Sénac, *Avant-corps*, 11. For Sénac, the question of naming extends to being called Algerian, or what he calls in a letter to Camus, "ce tout petit mot algérien" [this little word, Algerian] (quoted in Nacer-Khodja, *Le fils rebelle*, 158). See also Katia Sainson, "Jacob's Wound: Jean Sénac, Albert Camus, and the Question of Algerian Nationalism," *French Review* 83, no. 6 (2010): 1202–15 (1210).

36. "The ruse is everywhere. And even in creolization, in the poetic that would find favor with us, the ruse is never absent. The key is to know where the ruse ends, where innocence begins" (Jacques Derrida, in dialogue with Édouard Glissant at the Parlement international des écrivains in Strasbourg, France, November 6, 1993. https://edouardglissant.world/lieux/jacques-derrida-edouard-glissant/).

37. Sartre, *Qu'est-ce que la littérature*, 17.

38. Sénac, *Avant-corps*, 12.

39. Sénac, 122.

40. Gen. 32:25 (King James Version).

41. Gen. 32:31 (King James Version).

42. Shams-i Tabrīzī features in a list of inspirational "voyous"—or "poet-thugs"—in "Poubelles précieuses" [Precious Trash] and as a possible lover in "Non pas Chams de Tabriz mais Jacques" [Not Shams-i Tabrīzī but Jacques] (Sénac, *Avant-corps*, 30, 65).

43. Djaout, *Solstice barbelé*, 60.

44. Isabelle Renaud-Chamska describes the rhythm of Patrice de La Tour du Pin's *Quête de joie*, discussed in the previous chapter, as also bearing "this tragic mark of a congenital dislocation of the hip, a wound similar to that which affects Jacob after

the nocturnal struggle with the angel at Yabboḳ" (Isabelle Renaud-Chamska, "La *Quête* au cœur: Un colloque sur *La Quête de joie* de Patrice de La Tour du Pin," in *Patrice de La Tour du Pin: "La Quête de joie" au cœur d'"Une Somme de poésie"*; *Actes du colloque au Collège de France, 25–26 septembre 2003*, ed. Isabelle Renaud-Chamska [Geneva: Droz, 2005], 7–11 (10–11)).

45. The word "étreinte" comes from the Latin verb "stringō, stringere," meaning both "to press, tighten, compress" (i.e., "to constrain") and "to unsheathe, to draw a sword from its scabbard" (Félix Gaffiot, *Dictionnaire illustré latin-français* [Paris: Hachette, 1934], 1484).

46. Sénac, *Avant-corps*, 122.

47. Mammeri, *Les Isefra*, 197.

48. Mammeri, 68. See also Nacib, *Anthologie de la poésie kabyle*, 105.

49. Sénac, *Avant-corps*, 38.

50. Anna Gréki, *Algérie, capitale Alger*, pref. Mostefa Lacheraf, frontis. Edgard Naccache, translated into Arabic by Tahar Cheriaa (Tunis: SNED, 1963), 58.

51. Kaouther Adimi, *Nos richesses: roman* (Paris: Seuil, 2017), 20.

52. Sénac, *Avant-corps*, 122. Note that Sénac sometimes signs with the Arabic pseudonym "Yahia El Ouahrani," that is, "Jean of Oran." See Jean-Pierre Péroncel-Hugoz, "Yahia El Ouahrani," *Le Monde*, September 30, 1983, 18.

53. Sartre, "Orphée noir," xxxix.

54. Aimé Césaire, *Discours sur la négritude* (Paris: Présence Africaine, 1955), 84.

55. Ovid, *Metamorphoses in Two Volumes*, 11.10–13, 2:120–21.

56. Pierre Bourdieu, *Les règles de l'art: Genèse et structure du champ littéraire* (Paris: Seuil, 1998), 344–45.

57. Bourdieu, 344.

58. Sartre, "Orphée noir," xxv.

59. Sartre, xxx–xxxi.

60. Ovid, *Metamorphoses in Two Volumes*, 10.78–85, 2:70–71.

61. Sartre, "Orphée noir," xxxiii.

62. Sartre, xxxiii.

63. Césaire, *Œuvres complètes*, 1:50.

64. Sartre, "Orphée noir," xxxii.

65. Quoted in Belamri, *Entre désir et douleur*, 23.

66. Sartre, "Orphée noir," xxxii; Léon Laleau, "Sacrifice," in *Anthologie de la nouvelle poésie nègre et malgache de langue française*, ed. Senghor, 108–9 (108).

67. Sartre, "Orphée noir," xxxiv.

68. Sartre, xxxiv.

69. Sartre, xx.

70. Mallarmé, *Œuvres complètes*, 2:211.

71. Mallarmé, 2:211.

72. Mallarmé, 2:211. For an extended discussion of the stakes of this critical poem, see Thomas C. Connolly and Liesl Yamaguchi, "*Incipit*: On Poetry and Crisis," *Nineteenth-Century French Studies* 50, nos. 1–2 (2021–22): 1–49.

73. Sartre, "Orphée noir," xx.

74. Sartre, xli.

75. Aimé Césaire to Maurice Thorez, Octobre 1956, in *Œuvres complètes*, 3:460–73 (3:466).

76. Frantz Fanon, *Peau noire, masques blancs*, in *Œuvres*, foreword by Fondation Franz Fanon, pref. Achille Mbembe, intro. Magali Bessone (Paris: La Découverte, 2011): 45–257 (171).

77. Sénac and Fanon met at the First International Congress of Black Artists and Writers at the Sorbonne, Paris, in September 1956. Upon Fanon's death on December 6, 1961, Sénac wrote a short eulogy entitled "Bonjour Fanon" in *Poésie au sud: Jean Sénac et la nouvelle poésie algérienne d'expression française* (Marseille: Archives de la ville de Marseille, 1983), 76. See also Hamid Nacer-Khodja, "Jean Sénac–Frantz Fanon, d'une filiation idéologique," *Algérie Littérature-Action* 153–56 (2011): 122–26; Laura Prosdocimi, "Retrouver Jean Sénac dans les paroles de Frantz Fanon," *Awal* 10 (1993): 89–92.

78. Quoted in Fanon, *Peau noire, masques blancs*, 239.

79. Fanon, 239.

80. Sénac, *Avant-corps*, 106.

81. Sénac, 107.

82. See "Alors / Il retirait son slip, dans l'effusion des cris / Plongeait" [Then / He removed his underpants, among the outpouring of shouts / Dove] (Sénac, 107); "Tu veux un autographe ؟ / L'enfant du Noûn entre-bâilla la serviette de couleurs qui lui ceignait les reins, / et brandissait son sexe: / Tu veux un autographe ؟" [You want an autograph ؟ / The child of the nūn half opened the colored towel that covered his loins, / and brandished his penis / You want an autograph ؟] (Sénac, 109).

83. Quoted in Belamri, *Entre désir et douleur*, 10. The original reads, "La réalité sans l'énergie disloquante de la poésie, qu'est-ce?" [Reality without the dislocating energy of poetry, what is it?] (René Char, *Œuvres complètes*, intro. Jean Roudaut [Paris: Gallimard, 1983], 399). Char provides the preface to Sénac's first major publication, *Poèmes* [Poems] in 1954: "Les poèmes qui m'accompagnent ici aujourd'hui sont ceux de Jean Sénac. Ils chantent à longue voix nourrie et pure le paysage de l'atelier immense du soleil, atelier qui a la nuit pour toiture et l'homme comme exploit décevant et merveilleux. Le vent ami tourne dans mes doigts les pages du cahier où une écriture de jeune homme *s'établit* en poésie. / FORTIFICATIONS POUR VIVRE" [The poems that accompany me here today are those of Jean Sénac. They sing in a long, rich, and clean voice the landscape of the sun's immense workshop, a workshop that has the night for its roof and man as a disenchanting and breathtaking exploit. The friendly wind turns the pages of the notebook between my fingers, where the writing of a young man *establishes itself* in poetry. / FORTIFICATIONS FOR LIVING] (René Char, "Avant-propos," in *Poèmes*, by Sénac, 7–8 (7–8)). In addition to his mother, Jeanne Comma, his "son," Jacques Miel, Patrick Mac Avoy, Jean Genet, and Antonin Artaud, Sénac dedicates *Ébauche du père* to Char and refers to him as "(ton Dieu)" [your God] in "Interrogation" (Sénac, *Avant-corps*, 113).

84. Sénac, 107–8.

85. Sénac, *Le soleil sous les armes*, 20.

86. Jean Sénac, "L'Algérie d'une libération à l'autre," *Le Monde diplomatique* (August 1973): 22 (22).

87. Sénac, *Avant-corps*, 97. In light of this poem, consider Rabah Belamri's *Corps seul: poèmes* (Paris: Gallimard, 1998), which includes the lines "l'ange rebelle se débat . . . la route mène au gué de l'inquiétude" [the rebel angel struggles . . . the road

leads to the ford of anxiety] (25) and the poem "Jabbok inversé" [Inverted Yabboḳ], dedicated to the memory of Jean Sénac, his friend and mentor (64–65).

88. Fanon, *Peau noire, masques blancs*, 108.

89. Frantz Fanon, *Les damnés de la terre* in *Œuvres*, 419–681 (496).

90. Simone de Beauvoir, *Force of Circumstance*, trans. Richard Howard (New York: G. P. Putnam's Sons, 1965), 591.

91. Jean-Paul Sartre, preface to *Les damnés de la terre*, by Frantz Fanon (Paris: François Maspero, 1961), 7–26 (26). In his own preface to this same work, then Algerian president Abdelaziz Bouteflika describes Sartre's preface as "superbe et écrasante" [stunning and crushing] (Algiers: ANEP, 2006), 3–6 (3)).

92. Sénac, "Au pas lent des caravanes" (*Matinale de mon peuple*) in *Œuvres poétiques*, 256 (256).

93. Peterson, *Dubois, Fanon, Cabril*, 97.

94. Sénac, *Avant-corps*, 122.

CHAPTER 3

Epigraph: "my flute implicates itself and ends" (Mohammed Khaïr-Eddine, *Soleil arachnide*, 100).

1. Khaïr-Eddine, *Moi l'aigre*, 26–28.

2. See, for example, Hédi Abdel-Jaouad, "Mohammed Khaïr-Eddine: The Poet as Iconoclast," *Research in African Literatures* 23, no. 2 (1992): 145–50 (147, 150); Rachida Saïgh Bousta, "Mohammed Khaïr-Eddine: Repères et portrait du poète errant," in *Mohammed Khaïr-Eddine, texte et prétexte: Actes du colloque international, 20–22 novembre 1996, Université Cadi Ayyad, Marrakech* (Rabat: Publications du ministère des affaires culturelles, 1999): 11–16 (12, 16); and Khalid Lyamlahy, "Le poète et sa 'vieille marotte calamiteuse': Figures et variations du grotesque dans la poésie de Mohammed Khaïr-Eddine," *Irish Journal of French Studies* 20 (2020): 14–47 (17).

3. "Poésie ininterrompue" was produced by Claude Royet-Journoud and broadcast on *France Culture* between April 7, 1975, and April 1, 1979. Royet-Journoud was the editor and publisher of Khaïr-Eddine's first chapbook, "Nausée noire" [Black Nausea] (London: Siècle à mains, 1964). Abigail Lang identifies "Poésie ininterrompue" as having provided a unique platform where poets could read from their own works in progress, enabling "the rise of public readings in France" ("Bien ou mal lire, telle n'est pas la question: *Poésie ininterrompue*, archives sonores de la poésie," in *Les poètes sur les ondes*, ed. Pierre-Marie Héron and Céline Pardo [Rennes: Presses universitaires de Rennes, 2018]: 1–12 (5). Michel Murat perceives the 1970s as a pivotal moment in the performance of poetry in French ("'Lire ce qui est écrit comme ce qui est imprimé'," *Fabula* [2019], http://www.fabula.org/colloques/document6366.php).

4. Mohammed Khaïr-Eddine, *Agadir* (Paris: Seuil, 1967), 83.

5. Khaïr-Eddine, *Ce Maroc!*, 76–77.

6. Khaïr-Eddine, 11.

7. "Poésie ininterrompue," *France Culture*, October 19, 1975, 6:18ff. Lucette Finas (b. Grenoble, 1921) was then professor of literature at Université Paris VIII–Vincennes.

8. Jean-Roger Bourrec, "'(. . .) Une science pour faire face, le cas échéant': (Mohammed Khaïr-Eddine à Casablanca, années 1960. Témoignage)," in *Hommage à Mohammed Khaïr-Eddine*, ed. Jean-Paul Michel et al. (Paris: Préau des collines, 2011): 113–17 (113).

9. Tahar Ben Jelloun, "Khaïr-Eddine ou la fureur de dire," *Le Monde,* December 1, 1995, ii (ii).

10. Ben Jelloun, ii.

11. Abdelmajid Benjelloun, "Mohammed Khaïr-Eddine, ou le non d'être né," in *Hommage à Mohammed Khaïr-Eddine*, ed. Michel et al., 126-27 (126).

12. Jean-Paul Michel, "'J'arrache les clous de mon corps trop haut pour être pleuré'," in *Hommage à Mohammed Khaïr-Eddine*, ed. Michel et al., 118–25 (123).

13. Marc Gontard, *La violence du texte: Études sur la littérature marocaine de langue française* (Paris: L'Harmattan / Rabat: Société marocaine des éditeurs réunis, 1981), 54.

14. In a diary entry from the final months of his life, Khaïr-Eddine speaks, with justification perhaps, in highly unflattering terms of university academics: "Les profs d'université vous font manger du sable à la place du couscous" [University professors give you sand when all you want is couscous] (Mohammed Khaïr-Eddine, *Journal d'un moribond* [Rabat: Dar Al Amane, 2012], 28).

15. See Abderrahman Tenkoul, *Littérature marocaine d'écriture française: Essai d'analyse sémiotique* (Casablanca: Afrique Orient, 1985), 145.

16. Abdel-Jaouad, "The Poet as Iconoclast," 146.

17. Habib Tengour, "Le surréalisme maghrébin," in *L'arc et la lyre: Dialogues (1988–2004),* by Habib Tengour, ed. Mourad Yelles (Algiers: Casbah Éditions, 2006): 99–105 (102).

18. Tengour, 101.

19. Tahar Djaout, *L'exproprié: roman* (Algiers: SNED, 1981), 90–91. See also "Ici, / à l'ombre de la / Kahéna, seule iconoclaste de notre histoire, / je dis mon anti-manifeste / et rends hommage à M. K. E. qui, le premier, / décida de jeter son sang aux latrines / et de faire peau neuve" [Here, / in the shadow of / Kahina, the only iconoclast in our history, / I pronounce my anti-manifesto / and pay homage to M. K. E., who was the first / to determine to throw his blood down the toilet / and to grow a new skin] (Djaout, 71).

20. In addition to his early short works *Nausée noire* in 1964 and *Faune détériorée* (Bram: Encres-vives, 1966), Khaïr-Eddine's collections of poems include *Soleil arachnide* (1969), *Ce Maroc!* (1975), *Résurrection des fleurs sauvages* (1981), and *Mémorial* (Paris: Le Cherche Midi, 1991).

21. Michiel de Vaan, *Etymological Dictionary of Latin and the Other Italic Languages* (Leiden / Boston: Brill, 2008), 473.

22. "Poésie ininterrompue," 2:58ff.

23. Mladen Dolar, *A Voice and Nothing More* (Cambridge: MIT Press, 2006), 71.

24. "Poésie ininterrompue," 6:28ff.

25. Khaïr-Eddine, *Ce Maroc!*, 77.

26. Mohammed Khaïr-Eddine, *Une odeur de mantèque* (Paris: Seuil, 1976), 159. See also the description of Azro Wado after the poet's return in 1979: "Située au creux d'un cirque rocheux sur lequel planent indéfiniment des escadrilles de corbeaux qui hantent les abattoirs et la cime des palmiers environnants, elle croupit au

soleil, loin de tout, mais fascinante" [Situated in the hollow of a circus of rock, over which ceaselessly glide squadrons of crows that haunt the slaughterhouses and the tops of the surrounding palm trees, it stagnates under the sun, far from everything, but still fascinating] (Mohammed Khaïr-Eddine, "Redécouverte du sud," *Lamalif* 112 [1980]: 38–43 (41)).

27. Khaïr-Eddine, "Un homme-poème," 45.

28. Deleuze and Guattari, *Capitalisme et schizophrénie 2*, 383–84.

29. "Poésie ininterrompue," 14:12ff.

30. "Poésie ininterrompue," 14:28ff.

31. Mallarmé," *Œuvres complètes*, 1:234.

32. David Sylvester, *Francis Bacon: The Human Body* (London: Hayward Gallery, 1998), 22.

33. Claude Imbert, "Empiricism Unhinged: From Logic of Sense to Logic of Sensation," in *Introduction to the Philosophy of Gilles Deleuze*, ed. Jean Khalfa (London: Continuum, 2003): 133–48 (144).

34. Michael Peppiatt, *Francis Bacon in the 1950s* (Norwich: Sainsbury Centre for Visual Arts, 2006), 24.

35. Louis Marin, *On Representation*, trans. Catherine Porter (Stanford: Stanford University Press, 2001), 346.

36. Deleuze, *Logique de la sensation*; *Francis Bacon: The Logic of Sensation*, trans. Daniel W. Smith (London: Continuum, 2006).

37. Dolar, *A Voice*, 69.

38. Deleuze, *The Logic of Sensation*, x.

39. Deleuze, *Logique de la sensation*, 1:17.

40. Dolar, *A Voice*, 69.

41. Deleuze, *Logique de la sensation*, 1:17.

42. Imbert, "Empiricism Unhinged," 144.

43. Deleuze, *The Logic of Sensation*, xii.

44. Abderrahman Tenkoul, "Writing in Movement: A Poetics of Undecidability?" in *The World in Movement: Performative Identities and Diasporas*, ed. Alfonso de Toro and Juliane Tauchnitz (Leiden / Boston: Brill, 2018): 229–37 (234).

45. Deleuze and Guattari, *Capitalisme et schizophrénie 2*, 383.

46. Khaïr-Eddine, *Soleil arachnide*, 54–56.

47. Mohammed Khaïr-Eddine, *Scorpionic Sun*, trans. Conor Bracken (Cleveland: Cleveland State University Poetry Center, 2019), 35–36; translation modified.

48. Other poems in *Soleil arachnide* that adopt the epistrophic stanza include "Mutinéries" (57–58) and "Flibuste" (59–60). See also Mohammed Khaïr-Eddine, "Maturités," *Encres vives* 55 (1965): 14.

49. Glissant, in dialogue with Derrida, Parlement international des écrivains, *op. cit.*

50. Deleuze and Guattari, *Capitalisme et schizophrénie 2*, 422.

51. Deleuze, *Logique de la sensation*, 1:27.

52. "Entretiens avec Francis Bacon," *France Culture*, April 2–4, 1975, 15:30ff., https://www.franceculture.fr/emissions/les-nuits-de-france-culture/francis-bacon-parler-de-peinture-c-est-impossible. Bacon returns to this notion—of making a Sahara of the mouth—on several occasions. See David Sylvester, *Interviews with Francis Bacon, 1962–1979* (New York: Thames and Hudson, 1980), 56. It may stem

from a similar formulation made by Alberto Giacometti in 1947: "But if, on the other hand, one began by analyzing a detail, the end of the nose, for example, one was lost. One could have spent a lifetime without achieving a result. The form dissolved, it was little more than granules moving over a deep black void, the distance between one wing of the nose and the other is like the Sahara, without end, nothing to fix one's gaze upon, everything escapes [la distance entre une aile du nez et l'autre est comme le Sahara, pas de limite, rien à fixer, tout échappe]" (Alberto Giacometti to Pierre Matisse, 1947, in *Alberto Giacometti*, ed. and intro. Peter Selz [New York: Museum of Modern Art, 1965]: 14–29 (18–19)).

53. Deleuze, *Logique de la sensation*, 1:65.

54. Deleuze, 1:65.

55. Deleuze, 1:65.

56. Compare this line to the passage in Tournier's 1967 novel *Vendredi ou les limbes du Pacifique*. Robinson climbs a tree and reflects on its function as a vast lung, when he sees Friday fly a kite made from the skin of a dead goat: "*The leaf lung of the tree, the tree lung itself, and therefore the breathing wind* [*La feuille poumon de l'arbre, l'arbre poumon lui-même, et donc le vent de respiration*], thought Robinson. He daydreamed of his own lungs, stretched out, a bush of purple flesh, a polyparium of living coral, with pink limbs, and mucous sponges. . . . Over by the shore, a large bird the color of old gold, in the shape of a lozenge, swung capriciously high in the air. Friday, fulfilling his mysterious promise, was making Andoar fly" (Michel Tournier, *Vendredi ou les limbes du Pacifique* [Paris: Seuil, 1967], 167).

57. Deleuze, *Logique de la sensation*, 1:67.

58. Deleuze, *The Logic of Sensation*, xv.

59. Pierre Fédida, *L'Absence* (Paris: Gallimard, 1978), 112.

60. Fethi Benslama, *La nuit brisée: Muhammad et l'énonciation islamique* (Paris: Ramsay, 1988), 81–82.

61. Deleuze, *Logique de la sensation*, 1:55.

62. Sylvester locates this painting at the end of the first of Bacon's two peaks, which runs from 1945 to 1953. The second peak, from 1970 to 1976, saw the creation of a dozen large triptychs, most of them studies of the male nude, "realized in a conscious wish to exorcise the pain of [lover George] Dyer's death" (Sylvester, *Francis Bacon*, 29).

63. Deleuze, *Logique de la sensation*, 1:56.

64. See also "lion giclant," where "gicler" [to spurt] is related to the Provençal "cisclar" [to cry out loud, to whistle, to wind and rain].

65. Compare to "ēminēre" [to stick out, protrude], "ēminulus" [projecting], and "minēre" [to lean forward, project] (De Vaan, *Etymological Dictionary of Latin and the Other Italic Languages*, 380).

66. M'hamed Issiakhem, *La mère et la main coupée*, ca. 1965, oil on canvas, Musée de l'institut du monde arabe, Paris.

67. "abandoning the end of their thirst / the best days resurface / to accompany the cicada disguised as a flute" (El-Mahdi Acherchour, *L'œil de l'égaré*, 32).

68. Khaïr-Eddine, "Bucolique" [Bucolics] in *Ce Maroc!*, 42 (42).

69. Khaïr-Eddine, "Peuple du ciel chu sur moi" [People of the Sky Fallen on Me] in: Khaïr-Eddine, 43–44 (43).

70. Khaïr-Eddine, "De Casa à Bogota" [From Casa to Bogota] in: *Résurrection des fleurs sauvages*, 9–11 (10).

71. The notion of the flute as a figure for revolutionary Algerian poetics appears in what has become a seminal text of francophone Maghrebi poetry, namely Sénac's "Salut aux écrivains et artistes noirs," read aloud at the first Congrès des écrivains et artistes noirs on September 22, 1956, and which concludes with the following lines: "Frères Noirs, les Écrivains Algériens, / s'ils osent élever la voix tandis que leurs frères tombent, / c'est pour vous transmettre le relais de leur Espérance, / cette flûte de nos montagnes / où la Liberté s'engouffre, / s'unit au souffle de l'homme / et chante!" [Black Brothers, if Algerian Writers / Dare to raise their voices while their brothers perish, / it is to transmit to you the relay of their Hope, / this flute of our mountains / where Liberty is ensconced, / unites with the breath of man / and sings!] (Sénac, *Œuvres poétiques*, 272).

72. Ovid, *Fasti*, trans. James G. Frazer, rev. G. P. Goold (Cambridge: Harvard University Press, 1931), 6.701, 372–73.

73. Apollodorus, *The Library*, trans. James G. Frazer, 2 vols. (Cambridge: Harvard University Press, 1921), 1.4.2, 1:31.

74. Diodorus Siculus, *Library of History*, 12 vols. (Cambridge: Harvard University Press, 1935), 3.59, 2:273.

75. In a draft of "L'Après-midi d'un faune," Mallarmé's faun says, "Ma jeunesse coula par les flûtes, j'offrais / À la fleur entrouverte un solo que le frais / Vent de la nuit jetait en transparente pluie" [My youth flowed through the flutes, I offered / To the partly opened flower a solo that the cool / Night breeze cast in transparent rain] (Mallarmé, *Œuvres complètes*, 1:831).

76. Ovid, *Metamorphoses in Two Volumes*, 6.385–86, 1:314–15.

77. Ovid, 6.387.

78. Ovid, 6.388.

79. Ovid, 6.388.

80. Ovid, 6.389.

81. Ovid, 6.389–90.

82. Ovid, 6.390–91.

83. Deleuze, *Logique de la sensation*, 1:22.

84. Especially if we hear in "virgula" [little stick] the flute that Marsyas can no longer play.

85. Saïgh Bousta, "Mohammed Khaïr-Eddine," 14.

86. Deleuze, *Logique de la sensation*, 1:37.

87. This poem preempts a more explicit description of torture, perpetrated by the police, in *Moi l'aigre*: "The sight before their eyes was so horrific that they were frozen to the spot: a man, whose body was cut into small bloody pieces, lay on an 'operating' table in the middle of a room where four police-butchers were walking up and down. The body of the man, completely naked, was vomiting puddles of blood. The police had 'worked' on him so well that it seemed difficult to identify him. His lips had been carefully excised and placed on the ashes of a brazier at the end of the table. An acerbic grin was spread across the man's so-called face" (Khaïr-Eddine, *Moi l'aigre*, 129).

88. Compare the sun's thread to the title of Celan's 1967 collection, *Fadensonnen* [Thread-Suns]. There appear to be several discreet references to Celan in Khaïr-

Eddine. "Le roi" ends with the line "*parmi le lait noir de ma palmeraie*" [among the black milk of my palmery] (Khaïr-Eddine, *Soleil arachnide*, 65-73 (73)), which echoes the opening line of Celan's best-known poem, "Todesfuge" [Death-Fugue]: "Schwarze Milch der Frühe wir trinken sie abends" [Black milk of dawn we drink it at evening] (Paul Celan, *Die Gedichte: Neue kommentierte Gesamtausgabe in einem Band*, ed. Barbara Wiedemann [Berlin: Suhrkamp, 2018]: 46–47 (46)).

89. Sartre, preface to *Les damnés de la terre*, 26.

90. Jacques Rancière, "The Cause of the Other," *Parallax* 4, no. 2 (1998): 25–33 (28). See also Lia Brozgal, *Absent the Archive: Cultural Traces of a Massacre in Paris, 17 October 1961* (Liverpool: Liverpool University Press, 2020); and Hannah Feldman, "The Eye of History: Photojournalism, Protest, and the *Manifestation* of 17 October 1961," in *From a Nation Torn: Decolonizing Art and Representation in France, 1945–1962* (Durham: Duke University Press, 2014), 159–99.

91. "Arrhythmia: initial asymmetry, loss of memory, wandering in solitude, desert without traces. Strange the end of every life" (Khatibi, *Aimance*, 108).

92. "Poésie ininterrompue," 7:42ff.

93. Philippe Monbrun, "La notion de retournement et l'*agôn* musical entre Apollon et Marsyas chez le ps.-Apollodore: Interprétation d'un mythe," *Kernos* 18 (2005): 269–89 (273). Compare to the poem "Errance" by Rouchedy Chafaï (Sour El-Ghozlane, 1933–Colombes, 2022), which seeks specifically to combine the functions of voice and flute: "Quand l'ânonnante flûte épelle le désert / Interminable syllabaire / Que peut nommer l'enfant bercé par ce coran / Aveugle à peine né sur le bât du chameau / / O complorante flûte jumelle de nos voix / Image d'un miroir dans un miroir déteint / Orant la litanie de nos espoirs sans fin / Quêtant toujours plus loin herbages pour leurs fêtes . . ." [When the faltering flute spells out the desert / Endless syllabary / What can a child cradled by this Qur'ān name / Blind barely born on the camel's pack / / O bewailing twin flute of our voices / Mirror image of a faded mirror / Reciting the ceaseless litany of our hopes / Always searching new grazing for their feasts] (*Exils et demeures*, intro. Georges Mailhos [Paris: L'Harmattan, 1998]: 39 (39)).

94. Plato, *Republic*, ed. and trans. Christopher Emlyn-Jones and William Preddy, 2 vols. (Cambridge: Harvard University Press, 2013), 3.271, 1:271.

95. Monbrun, "La notion de retournement," 274.

96. Deleuze, *Logique de la sensation*, 1:27.

97. Apollodorus, *The Library*, 1.4.2, 1:29.

98. Jean Sénac, "Le levain et la fronde," in *Anthologie de la nouvelle poésie algérienne*, ed. Jean Sénac (Paris: Librairie Saint-Germain-des-Prés, 1971): 5–38 (38).

99. Mohammed Khaïr-Eddine, "'L'écrivain et le citoyen' (1979)," in Mohammed Khaïr-Eddine, *Le temps des refus: Entretiens, 1966–1995*, ed. Abdellatif Abboubi (Paris: L'Harmattan, 1998): 65–71 (69).

CHAPTER 4

Epigraphs: "I know that in your hands / so many suns are woven" (Djaout, *Solstice barbelé*, 39); "Of course, I'm nothing more than a Barbarian" (Djaout, L'Exproprié, 51).

1. Tahar Djaout, *L'arche à vau-l'eau: Poèmes, 1971–1973* (Paris: Saint Germain-des-Prés, 1978).

2. Tahar Djaout, *Insulaire & cie.*, ill. Denis Martinez (Sigean: L'Orycte, 1980).

3. Tahar Djaout, *L'oiseau minéral*, ill. Mohammed Khadda (Sigean: L'Orycte, 1982).

4. Tahar Djaout, *L'étreinte du sablier: poèmes* (Oran: CRIDSSH, 1983). A number of the poems published in these collections first appeared in literary journals including *Alif, Action Poétique, Présence Africaine*, and *Souffles*. See also Djaout, *Les mots migrateurs*; and the posthumous *Pérennes*, ill. Hamid Tibouchi, pref. Jacques Gaucheron (Montreuil: Le temps des cerises, 1996).

5. Djaout, *L'exproprié*, 34–35.

6. Tahar Djaout, *Les chercheurs d'os: roman* (Paris: Seuil, 1984).

7. Tahar Djaout, *Les rets de l'oiseleur: nouvelles* (Algiers: ENAL, 1984).

8. Tahar Djaout, *L'invention du désert: roman* (Paris: Seuil, 1987).

9. Tahar Djaout, *L'exproprié: roman* (Paris: Majault, 1991).

10. Djaout, *Les vigiles*. Djaout was one of the first of many journalists, writers, artists, and intellectuals to be killed in Algeria in the 1990s. Lâadi Flici (b. Algiers, 1937) was assassinated in March 1993, the poet Youcef Sebti (b. El Milia, 1943) in December of the same year, and the playwright Abdelkader Alloula (Ghazaouet, 1939–Paris, 1994) the following March. Joaquim "Vincent" Grau was shot in his bookstore, La librairie des beaux-arts, on rue Didouche Mourad on February 21, 1994. See *Le blanc de l'Algérie* by Assia Djebar, who writes to remember these dead and others. The Parlement international des écrivains was founded in November 1993 as a response to Djaout's assassination. At launch, its executive members included Christian Salmon, Adonis, Breyten Breytenbach, Pierre Bourdieu, Jacques Derrida, Édouard Glissant, Toni Morrison, and Salman Rushdie. The group was dissolved in 2003.

11. Tahar Djaout, *Le dernier été de la raison: roman* (Paris: Seuil, 1999).

12. Dominique D. Fisher, *Écrire l'urgence: Assia Djebar et Tahar Djaout* (Paris: L'Harmattan, 2007), 22.

13. Eric Sellin, "Tahar Djaout (1954–1993)," *World Literature Today* 68, no. 1 (1994): 71–73 (71). See also Wadi Bouzar, "The French-Language Algerian Novel," *Research in African Literatures* 23, no. 2 (1992): 51–59 (55).

14. As Bekri explains, "Of course, the [title of *Ruptures*] is in the plural, because the writer's critical gaze is both demanding and alert, neither compromising nor complacent" (Tahar Bekri, *Littératures de Tunisie et du Maghreb (essais), suivi de Réflexions et propos sur la poésie et la littérature* [Paris: Harmattan, 1994], 135).

15. For an introduction to the revolutionary aims of this journal, see Robyn Creswell, *City of Beginnings: Poetic Modernism in Beirut* (Princeton: Princeton University Press, 2019), 181–82.

16. Boudjedra, *Lettres algériennes*, 60.

17. Kateb Yacine, "Le monde entier pour objet," in *Le poète comme un boxeur: Entretiens, 1958–1989*, ed. Gilles Carpentier (Paris: Seuil, 1994): 45–50 (45); first published in *France-Observateur*, December 31, 1958.

18. Hamid Abdelkader, "Tahar Djaout, tel que je l'ai connu," in *Présence de Tahar Djaout, poète*, ed. Amin Khan (Algiers: Barzakh, 2013): 23–29 (24).

19. Isaac-Célestin Tchého, "À livre ouvert avec Tahar Djaout," *Horizons maghrébins* 11 (1987): 27–33 (30). See also Tahar Djaout, "L'Histoire est une usurpation," where he writes, "I still consider poetry a privileged and uncompromising form of

expression that tolerates neither compromise nor imperfection" (*Notre Librairie* 95 [1988]: 26–27 (27)).

20. Quoted in Marc Gontard, "Tuez-le mes fils, il couve un verbe subversif . . . ," *Kaleïdoscope critique: Hommage à Tahar Djaout* (Algiers: Équipe de recherche ADISEM, Université d'Alger, 1995): 39–47 (43).

21. Youcef Merahi, *Tahar Djaout, ou, Les raisons du cri: Étude et choix de texte* (Tizi Ouzou: SARL, 1998), 15.

22. Tahar Djaout, *Les vigiles: roman* (Paris: Seuil, 1991).

23. For a brief consideration of bureaucracy in *Les vigiles*, see Imane Terhmina, "Tales of the Civil Service: Bureaucracy, Democracy, and Justice in Francophone African Literature" (PhD diss., Yale University, 2020), 152–78.

24. Phillip C. Naylor, *France and Algeria: A History of Decolonization and Transformation* (Gainesville: University Press of Florida, 2000), 170. For Naylor, Lemdjad's struggle to have his invention recognized by the state invites the reader to reflect on the state as "a manufactured product, not wanting to be reinvented" (171). This reading is enhanced by Deleuze and Guattari, when they remind us that "weaving reconstitutes a bottom by placing the knots on one side" and that it was "these characteristics that enabled Plato to use the model of weaving as the paradigm for 'royal science,' in other words, the art of governing people or operating the State apparatus" (Gilles Deleuze and Félix Guattari, *A Thousand Plateaus: Capitalism and Schizophrenia*, trans. Brian Massumi [Minneapolis: University of Minnesota Press, 1987], 475). On weaving as a metaphor for governing, see Plato, *Statesman*, ed. Julia Annas and Robin Waterfield, trans. Robin Waterfield (Cambridge: Cambridge University Press, 1995), 279c ff.

25. Raji Vallury, "Politicizing Art in Rancière and Deleuze: The Case of Postcolonial Literature," in *Jacques Rancière: History, Politics, Aesthetics*, ed. Gabriel Rockhill and Philip Watts (Durham: Duke University Press, 2009): 229–48 (240).

26. Vallury, 243.

27. For an earlier treatment of the loom, see the final novel in Mohammed Dib's *Algérie* trilogy, *Le métier à tisser* (Paris: Seuil, 1957). For a comparison of *Le métier à tisser* and *Les vigiles*, see Christiane Ndiaye, "Dib et Djaout: Le métier à tisser en deux temps," *Nouvelle Revue Synergies Canada* 6 (2013): n.p., https://doi.org/10.21083/nrsc.v0i6.2867.

28. Charles Baudelaire, "Réflexions sur quelques-uns de mes contemporains," in *Œuvres complètes*, 2:129–81 (2:145).

29. Djaout, *Les vigiles*, 33.

30. Franz Kafka, *Die Erzählungen* (Frankfurt am Main: S. Fischer Verlag, 1961), 94.

31. Djaout, *Les vigiles*, 38–39.

32. Djaout, 149.

33. Djaout, 149.

34. Olga Soffer, "Recovering Perishable Technologies through Use Wear on Tools: Preliminary Evidence for Upper Paleolithic Weaving and Net Making," *Current Anthropology* 45, no. 3 (2004): 407–13 (407).

35. Mallarmé, *Œuvres complètes*, 2:23; quoted in Assia Djebar, *Ces voix qui m'assiègent . . . en marge de ma francophonie* (Paris: Albin Michel, 1999), 86.

36. Djaout, *Les vigiles*, 34.

37. Djaout, 34.

38. As Lacoste-Dujardin reminds us, "Women have an exclusive role when it comes to weaving, this clothing industry" (Camille Lacoste-Dujardin, *Le conte kabyle: Étude ethnologique* [Algiers: Bouchene, 1970], 288).

39. Djaout, *Les vigiles*, 33.

40. Walter Benjamin, *Illuminations: Essays and Reflections*, trans. Harry Zohn, ed. and intro. Hannah Arendt (New York: Schocken, 2007), 91.

41. Benjamin, 91.

42. "Every poet dreams of a geometry of the mind" (Khatibi, *Quatuor poétique*, 57).

43. Paris: François Maspero, 1976.

44. Paris: Éditions Awal, 1986.

45. Paris: Plon, 1952.

46. Paris: Plon, 1955.

47. Paris: Plon, 1965.

48. Jean Déjeux, "Mammeri Mouloud (1917–1987): L'écrivain," *Encyclopédie berbère* 30 (2010): 4543–47.

49. For further reading, see Tassadit Yacine Titouh, *La face cachée de Mammeri* (Algiers: Koukou, 2021); and Amin Zaoui, *Éternel Mammeri, un intellectuel pas comme les autres* (Béjaïa: Tafat, 2017).

50. *Poèmes kabyles anciens*, ed. Mouloud Mammeri (Paris: François Maspero, 1980).

51. Mouloud Mammeri, introduction to *Poèmes kabyles anciens*, 7–57 (16).

52. Claude Hagège, *L'homme de paroles: Contribution linguistique aux sciences humaines* (Paris: Fayard, 1985), 110.

53. Susan Petrilli, Augusto Ponzio, *Semiotics Unbounded: Interpretive Routes through the Open Network of Signs* (Toronto: University of Toronto Press, 2005), 417.

54. Mammeri, introduction to *Poèmes kabyles anciens*, 11. In his transcription of Zuni songs, Dennis Tedlock has recourse "to typographical contrasts in the size, layout, and spacing of the characters, alone capable of rendering, more or less, this vocal gesture" (Paul Zumthor, "Le rythme dans la poésie orale," *Langue française* 56 [1982]: 114–27 (117)). No such attempt is made here by Mammeri.

55. Anthologies of Kabyle poetry in French translation include: Adolphe Hanoteau, *Poésies populaires de la Kabylie du Jurjura* (Paris: Imprimerie impériale, 1867); Si Ammar Ben Saïd Boulifa, *Recueil de poésies kabyles (Texte Zouaoua) traduites, annotées et précédées d'une étude sur la femme kabyle* (Algiers: A. Jourdan, 1904); Jean Amrouche, *Chants berbères de Kabylie* (Tunis: Monomotapa, 1939); Malek Ouary, *Poèmes et chants de Kabylie* (Paris: Librairie Saint-Germain-des-Prés, 1974), which presents poems recorded between 1945 and 1955; Mouloud Mammeri, *Poèmes kabyles anciens* (Paris: François Maspero, 1980). Amrouche's edition was later reissued, edited by Tassadit Yacine and with a preface by Mouloud Mammeri, with the Kabyle texts restored (Paris: L'Harmattan, 1989). For a critical genealogy of these translations, see Jane E. Goodman, *Berber Culture on the World Stage: From Village to Video* (Bloomington: Indiana University Press, 2005), 97–119.

56. In conversation with Bourdieu, Mammeri also points to the professional and peripatetic "ameddaḥ" (pl. "imeddaḥen"), a reciter of existing poems (from the triconsonantal root meaning "to proclaim, to publicize, to speak a lot"), and the "afṣiḥ"

(pl. "lefṣiḥ," "lfeṣḥa"), who both creates and recites poems, and who responds to events as and when they occur (Pierre Bourdieu, *Algerian Sketches*, ed. Tassadit Yacine, trans. David Fernbach (Cambridge, MA: Polity Press, 2013), 232). "Afṣiḥ" comes from the Arabic root "فصح" [faṣuḥa], meaning "to improvise, to be eloquent" (Marcelin Beaussier, *Dictionnaire pratique arabe-français contenant tous les mots employés dans l'arabe parlé en Algérie et en Tunisie, ainsi que dans le style épistolaire, les pièces usuelles et les actes judiciaires* [Algiers: Librairie Adolphe Jourdan, 1887], 507).

57. Bourdieu, *Algerian Sketches*, 228.

58. Bourdieu, 251.

59. Bourdieu, 251–52.

60. Alain Mahé, *Histoire de la Grande Kabylie: XIXe–XXe siècles: Anthropologie historique du lien social dans les communautés villageoises* (Saint-Denis: Bouchène, 2006), 118.

61. Kamel Chachoua, *L'islam kabyle: Religion, État et société en Algérie* (Paris: Maisonneuve et Larose, 2001), 27.

62. Chachoua, 26.

63. Mohamed-Amokrane Zoreli, "La thèse de M. Mammeri sur la *Tamusni* et l'*Amusnaw*: Fondements d'une épistémologie kabyle," *La revue du MAUSS* 59 (2022): 167–87.

64. Boaventura de Sousa Santos, *Epistemologies of the South: Justice against Epistemicide* (Boulder: Paradigm Publishers, 2014).

65. Mammeri, introduction to *Poèmes kabyles anciens*, 56.

66. See Mohamed Benrabah, *Language Conflict in Algeria: From Colonialism to Post-Independence* (Bristol / Buffalo / Toronto: Multilingual Matters, 2013), 140.

67. Kateb Yacine, "C'est africain qu'il faut se dire (1987): Entretien avec Tassadit Yacine," in *Le poète comme un boxeur*, 101–20 (119).

68. Tahar Djaout, "Lettre à Da Lmulud," in *Mouloud Mammeri Amusnaw: Bio-bibliographie (1917–2009)*, ed. Boussad Berrichi (Biarritz: Atlantica-Séguier, 2010): 19–22 (20).

69. Djaout, 20.

70. Djaout, *Les vigiles*, 35.

71. Malek Ouary, *Poèmes et chants de Kabylie*, 26.

72. Ouary, 160.

73. Tahar Djaout, *Les rets de l'oiseleur: nouvelles* (Algiers: ENAL, 1984).

74. Ouary, *Poèmes et chants de Kabylie*, 159. Djaout's avian imaginary is celebrated in Moncef Ghachem's poem of mourning, "Oiseau, *in memoriam Tahar Djaout*": "Ramier dans la coupole du temple / Loriot dans la ruine cendrée / Pélican des eaux imaginaires / Rossignol dans la nuit mauve et bleue" [Pigeon in the temple cupola / Oriole in the ashen ruins / Pelican of imaginary waters / Nightingale in the mauve and blue night] (*Nouba*, ill. Tahar Mgadmini [El Ghazala: L'or du temps, 1997]: 17–20 (19)).

75. Djaout, *Les vigiles*, 193–94.

76. In a lecture entitled "Weiblichkeit" [Femininity], Freud claims that women have never contributed to the discoveries of human civilization, except for the invention of "plaiting" [Flechten] and "weaving" [Weben]: "Nature herself would seem to have given the model which this achievement imitates by causing the growth at maturity of the pubic hair that conceals the genitals. The step that remained to be taken

lay in making the threads adhere to one another" (in *New Introductory Lectures on Psychoanalysis*, trans. James Strachey [New York: W. W. Norton, 1965]: 112–35 (132).

77. Freud, 132.

78. Ouary, *Poèmes et chants de Kabylie*, 25–26. Consider the poem "Solitude," which begins as follows: "Me voici seule en la maison, / avec les montants du métier" [Here I am alone in the house / with the uprights of the loom] (Ouary, 144).

79. Khatibi, *Aimance*, 102.

80. Djebar, *Ces voix qui m'assiègent*, 75.

81. The title poem gives to understand that "solstice" should be understood etymologically as the moment the sun stands still, a "sunstead" that precedes "le soleil couchant" [the setting sun], one meaning of the Arabic "مغرب" [maghrib] (Djaout, *Solstice barbelé*, 13). The title may therefore point to a time that precedes the Maghreb, perhaps to "Barbarie," hinted at in the echoes of "barbelé" [barbed, barbed wire], or to what is now sometimes called "Tamazgha."

82. The four other sections are entitled "Bitumer les rosaires," "Il y a dans mon crâne un soleil qui bat la chamade," "Aléatoires," and "Réminiscence d'un soleil." In her review of *Solstice barbelé*, Josette Bryson reserves criticism only for "Aléatoires," whose flippant, schoolboy style and mix of English and French she considers out of keeping with the rest of the book (review of *Solstice barbelé*, by Tahar Djaout, *French Review* 52, no. 1 (1978): 177–78 (178).

83. Ovid, *Metamorphoses V–VIII*, ed. and trans. D. E. Hill (Warminster: Aris and Phillips, 1992), 6.18, 38–39.

84. Homer, *The Iliad*, trans. A. T. Murray, 2 vols. (Cambridge: Harvard University Press, 1963), 5.733–37, 1:249.

85. Ovid, *Metamorphoses V–VIII*, 6.129–30, 43; translation modified. See the case of the flute player Marsyas, who competes unsuccessfully with Apollo and his lyre, which Ovid recounts later in book six. In Spenser's rewriting of the myth, Arachne realizes that she has been beaten when she sees the butterfly that Athena includes in the border of her tapestry and that "seem'd to live, so like it was in sight" (Edmund Spenser, *The Complete Poetical Works of Edmund Spenser* [Boston: Houghton Mifflin, 1908], 120). Neither Ovid nor Djaout makes any mention of butterflies.

86. William Shakespeare, *Troilus and Cressida*, ed. Kenneth Palmer (London / New York: Methuen, 1982), 5.2.151, 278.

87. Ovid, *Metamorphoses V–VIII*, 6.132–33, 42–43.

88. Ovid, 6.136, 42–43.

89. Ovid, 6.140–45, 42–43.

90. Roland Barthes, *Le plaisir du texte* (Paris: Seuil, 1973), 85.

91. Naomi Schor, *Breaking the Chain: Women, Theory, and French Realist Fiction* (New York: Columbia University Press, 1985), 3–4.

92. Glenn W. Most, "'What Is a Classic Text?,'" *Poetica* 52 (2021): 1–12 (3-4).

93. Nancy K. Miller, "Arachnologies: The Woman, the Text and the Critic," in *The Poetics of Gender*, ed. Nancy K. Miller (New York: Columbia University Press, 1986): 270–95 (271).

94. Miller, "Arachnologies," 272.

95. Miller, 288.

96. Miller, 288.

97. Djaout perceives himself as doing something similar with the French language: "The French that I write is different; it comes from another place where 'métissage' is very important, is much more possible than in France. French is not totally assumed by me in a perspective of purity. . . . There is a kind of fracture that I introduce into French, a particular way of claiming a 'métissage' that prohibits entry to the French language purists" (quoted in Tchého, "À livre ouvert avec Tahar Djaout," 31).

98. Miller, "Arachnologies," 288.

99. Khatibi, *Figures de l'étranger*, 106–9.

100. Khatibi, 172.

101. Djaout, *Solstice barbelé*, 24. See also Rimbaud's "Les premières communions": "Elle avait rêvé rouge. Elle saigna du nez" [She had dreamed red. She was bleeding from the nose] (Rimbaud, *Œuvres complètes*, 139–43 (141)).

102. Émile Littré, *Dictionnaire de la langue française*, 4 vols. (Paris: Librairie Hachette, 1863–69), 2:2074.

103. Spenser, *Complete Poetical Works*, 119.

104. Note that the Kabyle for "poem" or "poetry" [asefru] can also mean "riddle, enigma" or "the explication of a dream" (Dallet, *Dictionnaire kabyle-français*, 217).

105. Djaout, *Solstice barbelé*, 25.

106. Qur'ān 29:40 (Kazimirski's translation, p. 322).

107. Matt. 7:24–27 (King James Version).

108. Edward Westermarck, *Ritual and Belief in Morocco*, 2 vols. (New Hyde Park: University Books, 1968), 2:356. In Berber tradition, the spider is a feminine symbol representing hard work, patience, and harmony. It often features in Berber carpet and other textile patterns.

109. Djaout, *Solstice barbelé*, 26.

110. Djaout, 27.

111. The section "Réminiscence d'un soleil" includes "Terrasse. *Sénac toujours présent*" [Terrasse. *Sénac always present*], "Cet espoir possible. *A mes amis d'Alger, en souvenir de l'époque où nous rêvions de châteaux en Espagne (et en Poésie)*" [This possible hope. *To my friends in Algiers, in memory of the time when we used to dream of castles in the air (and in Poetry)*], and "Soleil bafoué" [Scorned sun] (Djaout, *Solstice barbelé*, 55–60).

112. Annunciata Crugnola, ed., *Scholia in Nicandri Theriaka, cum glossis* (Milan / Varese: Istituto Editoriale Cisalpino, 1971), 39.

113. Bourdieu, *Algerian Sketches*, 260.

114. Djaout, *Solstice barbelé*, 28.

115. In Djaout's short story "Le reporter" [The Reporter], a journalist suffering from writer's block describes his metamorphosis into a town beginning with the letter "T": "I was roasting so much that at the end, arms stretched out and body open to the passage of wasps and sea anemones, I became a small town with porous arteries and peeling walls. A T-shaped city impaled by the sun and dragged across the rocks of a hamada. Tipasa? Tigzirt? Timimoun? Tiznit? Tafilalet? Tabarka? But the city that *superimposes itself* is different. Not Maghrebi. However, in its rainbow tattoos it spells out a man, weaver of light. Cherkaoui. Martinez[.] Khadda" (Djaout, *Les rets de l'oiseleur*, 16). The narrator suggests that a painter such as Ahmed Cherkaoui (1934–67), Denis Martinez (b. 1941), or Mohammed Khadda (1930–91) might

be a "tisseur de lumière" [weaver of light]. Djoher Amhis-Ouksel, however, claims that epithet to describe Djaout in a study entitled *Ce tisseur de lumière: Lecture de l'œuvre de Tahar Djaout* (Algiers: Casbah, 2014).

116. Denis Martinez and Djaout first met through the auspices of poet and painter Hamid Tibouchi (b. Tibane, 1951) (Rachid Hammoudi, *Tahar Djaout: Un talent cisaillé* [Tizi Ouzou: L'Odyssée, 2012], 38). Martinez was one of the founding members of Aouchem (from "وشام" [wishām], meaning "tattoos"), a group of artists that promoted the incorporation of indigenous styles, motifs, and materials into modern Algerian art. He taught at the École des beaux-arts in Algiers between 1963 and 1993 and subsequently at the École supérieure d'art in Aix-en-Provence. For Djaout's writings on Martinez, see Tahar Djaout, *Une mémoire mise en signes: Écrits sur l'art*, ed. Michel-Georges Bernard, pref. Hamid Nacer-Khodja (Algiers: Kalima, 2014), 61–75. For more illustrations accompanying Djaout's poems, see Denis Martinez, *Bouches d'incendie: Œuvre graphique*, with contributions by Messaour Boulanouar, Abdelhamid Laghouati, Tahar Djaout, Hamid Tibouchi, Omar Azradj, and Ahmed Hamdi (Algiers: ENAP / Paris: Publisud, 1983).

117. There appear to be deliberate echoes here of Sénac's poem "Alger, ville ouverte!": "Notre corps vibre, multiplié, comme s'il était déjà quelque âme gigantesque" [Our body vibrates, multiplied, as if it were already some gigantic soul] (Sénac, *Avant-corps*, 57).

118. There is no male version of "tteryel," a feature that "ogress," as a gendered derivative of "ogre," cannot express. In Kabyle, the male ogre is "awarzeniu" (Nabile Farès, *L'ogresse dans la littérature orale berbère: Littérature orale et anthropologie* [Paris: Karthala, 1994], 8).

119. Farès, 14.

120. See "L'Ancêtre ravalé par le vagin infanticide de la terre souricière et n'arrivant jamais à se défaire de la hargne accumulée sous sa chéchia—occiput battant le rythme arachnéen des sagaies" [The Ancestor swallowed by the infanticidal vagina of the mousetrap earth and never managing to rid himself of the aggression accumulated under his shashiya—back of the skull beating the arachnidian rhythm of the assegais] (Tahar Djaout, *L'exproprié* [Algiers: SNED, 1981], 141); and "il est poète / débauché / il tire le couteau à chaque propos / il prostitue la syntaxe / pour en faire un vagin enfanteur de cauchemars" [he is a poet / debauched / he draws his knife at every comment / he prostitutes syntax / to make of it a vagina that gives birth to nightmares] (Djaout, "Le breviaire du roi" in *L'arche à vau-l'eau*, 69–70 (69)). Khatibi ascribes fear of the vagina to a dissymmetry between male and female sexual organs: "The penis cannot be considered the equivalent of the vagina, which is a cosmic space where elemental interplay (of air, water) takes place: kissing, sucking, ejaculating, these are all ways of inscribing a divine tattoo on the woman's body . . . the penis/breast tries hard to cover up its fear of absorption, from which was born the ever-present myth of the devouring vagina: Astarte, 'Ayshah Qandīshah" (Khatibi, *La blessure du nom propre*, 167–68).

121. Camille Lacoste-Dujardin, "Maghreb: Éléments de mythologie kabyle," in *Dictionnaire des mythologies et des religions des sociétés traditionnelles et du monde antique*, ed. Yves Bonnefoy, 2 vols. (Paris: Flammarion, 1981): 2:45-48 (2:45-46).

122. Lacoste-Dujardin, 2:46. Dallet gives her proper name as "yemma jiđa" (Dallet, *Dictionnaire kabyle-français*, 829).

123. Lacoste-Dujardin, "Maghreb," 2:46.

124. Djaout, *Le dernier été de la raison,* 63.

125. Djaout, *L'invention du désert,* 115.

126. "I am abandoning my arachnean poetry in search of an equatorial life" (Sophie Elgoulli, *Vertige solaire,* pref. Jean Éthier-Blais [Tunis: 1981], n.p).

127. Compare to Mouloud Feraoun's *Le fils du pauvre,* in which the protagonist and (part-time) narrator is a teacher called Fouroulou Menrad, "a scrambling of Mouloud Feraoun" (Nicholas Harrison, *Our Civilizing Mission: The Lessons of Colonial Education* [Liverpool: Liverpool University Press, 2019], 91).

128. Djaout, *Les vigiles,* 168.

129. Ovid, *Metamorphoses V–VIII,* 6.144–45, 42.

130. Djaout, *Les vigiles,* 170.

131. Djaout, 173.

132. Djaout, 176.

133. Djaout, *Solstice barbelé,* 25.

134. Khatibi, *Quatuor poétique,* 35; Johann Wolfgang von Goethe, "Vorschmack," in *Gedichte aus dem Nachlass: West-östlicher Divan* (Zurich: Artemis Verlag, 1962): 684 (684).

135. In the Qur'ān, "زيادة" [ziyādah] means "increase" and refers to seeing the face of God in the Hereafter, a reward given to God's select servants.

136. Djaout, *Les vigiles,* 215.

137. Djaout, 216.

138. Djaout, 172.

139. Djaout, 217.

140. Kafka, *Die Erzählungen,* 121.

141. Djaout, *Les vigiles,* 204–5.

142. Mohamed Walid Bouchakour, "*Les vigiles* de Tahar Djaout: Cartographie d'un roman urbain," (master's thesis, Université d'Alger 2, 2012–13), 143.

143. Tighilt's article is no longer accessible on the newspaper's website (https://www.liberte-algerie.com/culture/le-chant-ancien-ahiha-ressuscite-290776). For a detailed case study of the "aḥiḥa" see: Mehenna Mahfoufi, "Chant d'évocation amoureuse de type *aḥiḥa* des Aït Issaad de Grande Kabylie," in *Littérature orale arabo-berbère* 19-20 (1988–89): 109–43. See also Djaout's poem "Ahal et ahiha": "je te regarde rêver / pendant qu'halètent tes seins / et qu'éclate l'*ahiha* / sur tes lèvres / fleurs de grenadier" [I watch you dream / while your breasts breathe heavily / and the *ahiha* bursts / on your / pomegranate flower lips] (Djaout, *L'arche à vau-l'eau,* 46).

144. Djaout, *Les vigiles,* 205.

145. Jean Amrouche, "Je ne peux pleurer qu'en Kabyle," in *Un Algérien s'adresse aux Français,* 299–301 (299).

146. Federico García Lorca, "Arquitectura del cante jondo," in *Obras completas, I: Prosa y poesía,* ed. Andrés Soria Olmedo (Madrid: Biblioteca Castro, 2019): 125–44 (127); "Deep Song" in *Deep Song and Other Prose,* ed. and trans. Christopher Maurer (New York: New Directions, 1980): 23–41 (25).

147. Lorca, "Arquitectura del cante jondo," 127; *Deep Song and Other Prose,* 25.

148. Jean Amrouche, introduction to *Chants berbères de Kabylie,* 19.

149. Kateb Yacine, "Toujours la ruée vers l'or (1988): Entretien avec Médiène Benamar," in *Le poète comme un boxeur,* 121–33 (132).

150. Bernadette Rey Mimoso-Ruiz, "Tahar Djaout entre rire et conte," *Horizons maghrébins* 52 (2005): 48–55 (53).

151. Tahar Djaout, "Un film sur Kateb," *Revue Celfan* 5, no. 3 (1986): 17–19 (18).

152. Paul Zumthor, foreword to *Flatus vocis: Metafisica e antropologia della voce*, by Corrado Bologna (Bologna: Il Mulino, 1992): 9–12 (9).

153. Zumthor, "Le rythme dans la poésie orale," 125.

154. Paul Zumthor, *Oral Poetry: An Introduction*, trans. Kathryn Murphy-Judy (Minneapolis: University of Minnesota Press, 1990), 228.

CHAPTER 5

1. This is the opening word of the ninety-sixth sura, "The Blood Clot." The first fives verses of this sura are considered to have been the first revealed to the Prophet, in Mecca in 610, twelve years before the migration to Medina in 622, which marks the start of the Islamic calendar.

2. Fethi Benslama, "La répudiation originaire," in *Idiomes, nationalités, déconstructions: Rencontre de Rabat avec Jacques Derrida* (Casablanca: Toubkal, 1998): 113–53 (143). See also Fethi Benslama, *La nuit brisée: Muhammad et l'énonciation islamique* (Paris: Ramsay, 1988), 34.

3. Khatibi, *Quatuor poétique*, 40.

4. Abdelkébir Khatibi, "Civilisation du signe," in *L'art calligraphique de l'Islam*, by Abdelkébir Khatibi and Mohamed Sijelmassi (Paris: Gallimard, 1994): 6–7 (6).

5. Khatibi, 6. See also "The extreme desire of every writer is, after all, the invention of the reader and the revelation of their inhibited power" (Khatibi, *Quatuor poétique*, 38).

6. Qur'ān 26:225–26 (Nasr et al.'s edition, pp. 925–26); see Seyyed Hossein Nasr, Caner K. Dagli, Maria Massi Dakake, Joseph E. B. Lumbard, and Mohammed Rustom, eds., *The Study Quran: A New Translation and Commentary* (New York: HarperOne, 2015).

7. Khatibi, *Quatuor poétique*, 40.

8. Khatibi, *Dédicace à l'année qui vient*, illus. Mechtilt (Saint-Clément-de-Rivière: Fata Morgana, 1986).

9. Khatibi, *Par-dessus l'épaule*, 11–46, 157–84.

10. Abdelkébir Khatibi, *Le livre de l'aimance: Proses artistiques*, ill. Mohamed Krich (Rabat: Marsam, 1995).

11. Abdelkébir Khatibi, *Aimance*, frontis. and vignettes Gérard Titus-Carmel (Neuilly-sur-Seine: Al Manar, 2003).

12. Isa. 29:11 (King James Version). According to Ibn Isḥāq, Muḥammad first explained to Gabriel that he could not read: "While I was sleeping, the angel Gabriel arrived with a roll of cloth on which something was written. He said *'iqra.'* I said *mâ' aqra'u* (negation of *qara'*), and so he suffocated me with the cloth until I thought that I was dead" (Muhammad Ibn Isḥāq, *Sirat Ibn Ishāq* [Konya, 1981], 48; quoted in Benslama, *La nuit brisée*, 91).

13. Khatibi, *La blessure du nom propre*, 116.

14. Khatibi, 116.

15. Réda Bensmaïa, "Writing Metafiction: Khatibi's 'Le Livre du sang,'" *SubStance* 21, no. 3 (1992): 103–14; Yasser Elhariry, "Khatibi Misses the Mark," *Yale French Studies* 137–38 (2020): 125–46.

16. Khatibi, *Quatuor poétique*, 21.

17. Khatibi, 21.

18. Khatibi, 34. Such poetic mysticism is often accompanied by what Khatibi calls a "courtly mode" that translates this desire for eternity into the present moment. Much like Goethe, Khatibi also seeks to "renew . . . the tradition of courtly love" (Khatibi, 38). The first section of *Aimance* is entitled "Nouveau mode courtois" [New Courtly Mode] (Khatibi, *Aimance*, 9).

19. Khatibi, *Quatuor poétique*, 21.

20. Khatibi, 59.

21. Khatibi, 28.

22. Lafcadio Hearn, *Kwaidan: Stories and Studies of Strange Things* (Boston / New York: Houghton, Mifflin and Company, 1904), 1–20.

23. Khatibi, *Par-dessus l'épaule*, 29; *Le livre de l'aimance*, 26.

24. For a range of recent critical perspectives on "aimance," see Françoise Bétourné, "L'amour est toujours réciproque dans la sphère d'aimance," *Cliniques méditerranéennes* 69 (2004): 87–115; Laurent Dubreuil, "Poétiques de l'énallage," *Expressions maghrébines* 12, no. 1 (2013): 57–72; Valentina Valle Baroz, "L'aimance dans l'œuvre d'Abdelkébir Khatibi" (unpublished manuscript), https://www.academia.edu/6376346/LAimance_dans_loeuvre_dAbdelkébir_Khatibi; Teresa Villa-Ignacio, "Aimancipation," *PMLA* 137, no. 2 (2022): 362–69; Hassan Wahbi, *Abdelkébir Khatibi: La fable de l'aimance* (Paris: L'Harmattan, 2009) and *Petit éloge de l'aimance* (Neuilly-sur-Seine: Al Manar, 2019). Note that George Collins translates "aimance" as "lovence" (Jacques Derrida, *The Politics of Friendship*, trans. George Collins [London: Verso, 1997], 7, 24–25).

25. Khatibi, *Par-dessus l'épaule*, 7. Balibar suggests that Sharon Marcus's term "amity"—used to describe forms of friendship and affection between women—might also be considered a "fair approximation" of "aimance" (Étienne Balibar, "*Aimance* / 'lovence,'" *Dictionary of Untranslatables: A Philosophical Lexicon*, ed. Barbara Cassin, Emily Apter, Jacques Lezra, and Michael Wood, trans. Steven Rendall, Christian Hubert, Jeffrey Mehlman, Nathaniel Stein, and Michael Syrotinski [Princeton: Princeton University Press, 2014], 605). Marcus writes, "Female amity gave married and unmarried women the opportunity to play the social field with impunity, since a woman could show devoted love, lighthearted affection, fleeting attraction, and ardent physical appreciation for multiple female friends without incurring rebuke" (Sharon Marcus, *Between Women: Friendship, Desire, and Marriage in Victorian England* [Princeton: Princeton University Press, 2007], 58).

26. Khatibi, *Par-dessus, l'épaule*, 167; *Le livre de l'aimance*, 48, *Aimance*, 123.

27. Khatibi, *Par-dessus l'épaule*, 167; *Le livre de l'aimance*, 48; *Aimance*, 123.

28. Khatibi, *Par-dessus l'épaule*, 33; *Le livre de l'aimance*, 30.

29. Khatibi, *Par-dessus l'épaule*, 28; *Le livre de l'aimance*, 25; *Aimance*, 102.

30. Khatibi, *Par-dessus l'épaule*, 33; *Le livre de l'aimance*, 30.

31. Khatibi, *Par-dessus l'épaule*, 33; *Le livre de l'aimance*, 30.

32. Khatibi, *Dédicace à l'année qui vient*, 95.

33. Khatibi, *Aimance*, 25.

34. Mallarmé, *Œuvres complètes*, 1:37–38; letter to Eugène Lefébure, May 3, 1868, in *Correspondance: 1854–1898*, ed. Bertrand Marchal (Paris: Gallimard, 2019): 207–9 (208).

35. "Ptyx" appears in Victor Hugo's poem "Le satyre" (*Œuvres complètes: Poésie V–VI; La légende des siècles*, 45 vols. [Paris: Imprimerie nationale / Ollendorff / Albin Michel, 1904–52]: 6:3–25 (6:3)).

36. Khatibi, *La langue de l'autre*, 80.

37. Plato, *The Dialogues of Plato*, 3:13.

38. Plato, 3:14.

39. Édouard Pichon, *Le développement psychique de l'enfant et de l'adolescent: Évolution normale—Pathologie—Traitement; Manuel d'étude* (Paris: Masson, 1936), 73, 115. For Pichon, the first sign of "aimance oblative" occurs when the child develops sphincteral discipline.

40. Emmanuel Mounier, *Traité du caractère* (Paris: Seuil, 1946), 150.

41. Balibar, "*Aimance* / 'lovence'," 605. Note that this entry is not included in the French original; see *Vocabulaire européen des philosophies: Dictionnaire des intraduisibles*, ed. Barbara Cassin (Paris: Seuil / Le Robert, 2004).

42. Abdelkébir Khatibi, "L'aimance et l'invention d'un idiome," in *Œuvres de Abdelkébir Khatibi II: Poésie de l'aimance*, pref. Marc Gontard (Paris: Éditions de la Différence, 2008): 124–45 (126).

43. Jacques Derrida, *Politiques de l'amitié; suivi de L'oreille de Heidegger* (Paris: Galilée, 1994), 23.

44. Khatibi, "L'aimance et l'invention d'un idiome," 128. See also Abdelkébir Khatibi, "Protocole," in *Le livre de l'aimance*, 5–6 (5).

45. Khatibi, *Par-dessus l'épaule*, 160; *Le livre de l'aimance*, 41; *Aimance*, 116.

46. Jane Hiddleston, "The Artist's Journey, or, the Journey as Art: Aesthetics and Ethics in *Pèlerinage d'un artiste amoureux* and Beyond," in *Abdelkébir Khatibi: Postcolonialism, Transnationalism, and Culture in the Maghreb and Beyond*, ed. Jane Hiddleston and Khalid Lyamlahy (Liverpool: Liverpool University Press, 2020): 305–25 (312).

47. Khalid Lyamlahy, "The Carpet as a Text, the Writer as a Weaver: Reading the Moroccan Carpet with Abdelkébir Khatibi," in *Abdelkébir Khatibi: Postcolonialism, Transnationalism, and Culture in the Maghreb and Beyond*, 279–303 (297).

48. Dubreuil, "Poétiques de l'énallage," 57–58, 65.

49. "Over the shoulder of a woman, what do you see? —another woman, she replies" (Khatibi, *Aimance*, 105).

50. Khatibi, *La langue de l'autre*, 81.

51. Khatibi, 81.

52. Khatibi, *Dédicace à l'année qui vient*, 16; *Aimance*, 36. Note that in *Aimance*, "La vierge de nulle part" does not appear on a separate page but is set apart from the text that follows by a large gap. Compare also to "la vierge - de - nulle - part" (Khatibi, 100; *Par-dessus l'épaule*, 25) and to "la vierge-de-nulle-part" (*Le livre de l'aimance*, 22).

53. Khatibi, *Dédicace à l'année qui vient*, 17. "La Vierge dicible à la cheville tressée" can be traced to "l'Androgyne à la cheville tressée" [the Androgyne with the braided ankle], namely the prostitute Muthna, in Khatibi's *Le livre du sang* (Paris: Gallimard, 1979): "Ta cheville si tressée et si svelte a-t-elle reçu le baiser d'un dieu?" [Has your braided and slender ankle received the kiss of a god?] (79, 153).

54. Giulia Sissa, *Greek Virginity*, trans. Arthur Goldhammer (Cambridge: Harvard University Press, 1990) 2.

55. Claude Calame, *Les chœurs de jeunes filles en Grèce archaïque I: Morphologie, fonction religieuse et sociale* (Rome: Edizioni dell'Ateneo e Bizzarri, 1977), 65.

56. Isa. 7:14 (King James Version).

57. See also "بكارة" [bakārah], meaning "virginity"—from the triconsonantal root for "to rise early"—which, as Khatibi writes, "contains the idea of spring, of a spring cloud which will cause rain, symbol of fecundity and fertility." He continues, "The radical of this word insists on the beginning, on the primacy of one thing over everything else, and the fact that it is not initiated by anything. Intact, pure, such is the entity of the body in question, whether it is that of a woman or of a female . . . or of a vine stock that produces grapes and their pleasures" (Abdelkébir Khatibi, *Le corps oriental* [Paris: Hazan, 2002], 69).

58. Khatibi, *La langue de l'autre*, 82. For Nabile Farès, the placelessness of "nulle part" is above all a dangerous and disenfranchising fiction: "Ils / racontaient / ou fabulaient / sur nous: que nous / n'étions nés / Nu L ll / e part / sans-vie / sans-corps / sans-yeux / sans-mains / sans-os / sans-cris / et / sans-histoires" [They / told / or fantasized / about us: that we / were born / No W he / ere / life-less / body-less / without eyes / without hands / without bones / without cries / and / without histories] (Farès, *L'état perdu*, 39).

59. Khatibi, *Par-dessus l'épaule*, 25; *Le livre de l'aimance*, 22. When this fragment is reproduced in *Aimance*, the neologism "l'offrance" is replaced by "l'offrande" [offering, sacrifice, gift, donation] (100).

60. Khatibi, *Figures de l'étranger*, 110.

61. "Have you considered al-Lāt and al-ʿUzza and Manāt, the third, the other?" (Qur'ān 53:19–20 [Nasr et al.'s edition, pp. 1292–93]). According to some traditions, at the end of the twentieth verse of the fifty-third sura—called "al-Najm" or "The Star"—Satan whispered to the Prophet an additional two verses, commonly known as the Satanic Verses or the Story of the Cranes ("qiṣṣat al-gharānīq"), which appear to accept the idols as legitimate deities: "Verily, they are high flying cranes! And their intercession is indeed anticipated/hoped for" (Qur'ān, 1292). However, the following verse—"Unto you males and unto Him females?" (53:21, Qur'ān, 1293)—appears to refute this notion, by asking why God would choose female offspring that even men would not want for themselves, in keeping with pre-Islamic Arab cultural norms.

62. Khatibi, *Figures de l'étranger*, 107–8.

63. Khatibi, 110.

64. Gunnar Ekelöf, *Dīwān över Fursten av Emgión* (Stockholm: Albert Bonniers Boktryckeri, 1965); *Sagan om Fatumeh* [The Tale of Fatumeh] (Stockholm: Albert Bonniers Boktryckeri, 1966); *Vägvisare till underjorden* [Guide to the Underworld] (Stockholm: Albert Bonniers Boktryckeri, 1967).

65. Gunnar Ekelöf, *Dīwān sur le prince d'Emgion*, trans. Carl Gustaf Bjurström and André Mathieu, pref. Georges Perros (Paris: Gallimard, 1973); *La légende de Fatumeh (Dīwān II)*, trans. Carl Gustaf Bjurström and André Mathieu (Paris: Gallimard, 1979); *Guide pour les enfers: poèmes*, trans. Carl Gustaf Bjurström and André Mathieu, pref. Pierre Emmanuel (Paris: Gallimard, 1979). See also Gunnar Ekelöf, "Dīwān sur le prince d'Emgion," trans. Carl Gustaf Bjurström and André Mathieu, *Le nouveau commerce* 18–19 (1971): 87–102. Ekelöf also edited and translated an anthology of modern French poetry, *Hundra år modern fransk dikt från Baudelaire till surrealismen* (Stockholm: Albert Bonniers Boktryckeri, 1934).

66. Ekelöf, *Dīwān över Fursten av Emgión*, 9.

67. Ekelöf, 43.

68. Baudelaire, *Œuvres complètes*, 1:116.

69. Baudelaire, 1:692. Compare to Jacqueline Arnaud's reading of Kateb's Nedjma as "virgin . . . and polyandrous woman" ("Les villes mythiques et le mythe de Nedjma dans le roman de Kateb Yacine," *Journée Kateb Yacine: Actes du colloque organisé par le Département de français [5 mai 1984]* [Manouba: Publications de la faculté des lettres, 1990]: 9–17 (16)).

70. Ekelöf, *Vägvisare till underjorden*, 78. The Latin text rewrites a phrase from *The Satyricon*, where Quartilla responds to a suggestion from Psyche: "'Ita, ita' inquit Quartilla 'bene admonuisti. Cur non, quia bellissima occasio est, devirginatur Pannychis nostra?'" ["Quite right," said Quartilla. "You did well to remind me. This is a most auspicious moment, so why shouldn't our Pannychis lose her maidenhead?"] (Petronius, *The Satyricon*, trans. and intro. P. G. Walsh [Oxford: Clarendon Press, 1996], 18).

71. Ekelöf, *Dīwān över Fursten av Emgión*, 72.

72. Ekelöf, 44.

73. Gunnar Ekelöf, *Selected Poems*, trans. W. H. Auden and Leif Sjöberg, intro. Göran Printz-Påhlson (New York: Pantheon, 1971), 44. Pierre Emmanuel says, "I immediately appropriated these prayers to the 'Mother of No-One' [Mère de Personne], and its amorous invocation of a femininity without figure, the invitation to fall in love with Nothingness" (Pierre Emmanuel, "Gunnar Ekelöf, le voyant et la vierge," preface to *Guide pour les enfers*, 7–24 (7)). Emmanuel—elected to the Académie française in 1968—was much admired by Jean Amrouche, who devoted an article to him entitled "Présence d'un grand poète: P. Emmanuel" in *La Tunisie française littéraire* on May 16, 1941.

74. Khatibi, *Quatuor poétique*, 67. As Nasrin Qader demonstrates, Khatibi undertakes his own preliminary explorations of the space between virgin and prostitute, law and transgression, desire and consummation in *Le livre du sang* ("5. Figuring the Wine-Bearer," in *Narratives of Catastrophe: Boris Diop, Ben Jelloun, Khatibi* [New York: Fordham University Press, 2009], 153–87).

75. See Conradin Perner, *Gunnar Ekelöfs Nacht am Horizont und seine Begegnung mit Stéphane Mallarmé: Mit zahlreichen Übers. aus dem Schwed. und einer vollst. Übertr. ins Deutsche von Gunnar Ekelöfs "En natt vid horisonten" (Eine Nacht am Horizont)* (Basel / Stuttgart: Helbing Lichtenhahn, 1974).

76. Mallarmé, *Œuvres complètes*, 1:19.

77. Ekelöf, *Vägvisare till underjorden*, 58–59.

78. See also "Éloge de la jeune fille" [In Praise of the Young Girl] by Victor Segalen, on whom Khatibi writes in *Figures de l'étranger*. The poem includes the following lines: "Ceci est réservé à la seule Jeune Fille. . . . À celle qui a des seins et qui n'allaite pas / un cœur et n'aime pas / un ventre pour les fécondités, mais décemment demeure stérile. / À celle riche de tout ce qui viendra / qui va tout choisir, tout recevoir, tout enfanter peut-être" [This is reserved for the Young Girl. . . . One who has breasts and who does not give suck / a heart and does not love / a belly for fecundities, remaining decently sterile. / One rich with all that is to come / who will choose everything, receive everything, give birth to everything, perhaps] (Victor Segalen, *Stèles* [Paris: G. Crès, 1922], 77–78).

79. Ekelöf, *Dīwān över Fursten av Emgión*, 104. As Ekelöf explains, "In contrast to Theotokos, the Mother of God, [Atokos], a goddess of Asia Minor, gave birth to neither god nor child but is the mother of all" (Ekelöf, *Vägvisare till underjorden*, 109).

80. Ekelöf, 29.

81. Emmanuel, "Gunnar Ekelöf, le voyant et la vierge," 13.

82. Ekelöf, *Dīwān sur le prince d'Emgion*, 92.

83. As Georges Didi-Huberman explains, "Tertullian dubs a virgin that gives birth *monstruosa*; he calls her a 'sign of contradiction' (*signum contradicibile*)" ("La couleur de chair ou Le paradoxe de Tertullien," *Nouvelle revue de psychanalyse* 35 [1987]: 9–49 (27)).

84. "(or the angel Gabriel / flying to make / a child in your / back" (Derrida, *Glas*, 218).

85. Khatibi, *Dédicace à l'année qui vient*, 66.

86. Khatibi, 17.

87. Khatibi, 18.

88. Khatibi, *Aimance*, 80.

89. Khatibi, *Par-dessus l'épaule*, 27; *Le livre de l'aimance*, 24; *Aimance*, 101.

90. Khatibi, *Par-dessus l'épaule*, 167; *Le livre de l'aimance*, 48; *Aimance*, 123 (not italicized).

91. Khatibi, *Par-dessus l'épaule*, 26; *Le livre de l'aimance*, 23; *Aimance*, 100–101.

92. We should acknowledge how unusual the appeal to Velázquez is. José Ortega y Gasset notes that "Velasquez was not attracted by [poets], nor were they stirred by his art" (introduction to *Velasquez: Six Color Reproductions of Paintings from the Prado Museum* [New York: Oxford University Press, 1946]: 5–21 (19)). At court, Velázquez received few tributes from the poets he rubbed shoulders with, even from those he painted, such as Luis de Góngora (Córdoba, 1561–Córdoba, 1627). See the portrait *El poeta don Luis de Góngora y Argote* (1622), which hangs in the Museum of Fine Arts, Boston, and which Ortega y Gasset calls "the splendid head of an intellectual, burdened with resentment and wrath, like that of many another famous poet" (Ortega y Gasset, 6).

93. Gilles Deleuze, *Le pli: Leibniz et le baroque* (Paris: Minuit, 1988), 164.

94. Other pupils of Francisco Pacheco (Sanlúcar de Barrameda, 1564–Seville, 1644) include Francisco de Zurbarán (Fuente de Cantos, 1598–Madrid, 1664) and Alonso Cano (Granada, 1601–Granada, 1667).

95. This seems likely given that the model strongly resembles the Virgin in Velázquez's 1619 *Adoración de los Magos* (Museo Nacional del Prado), often considered a portrait of the painter's own family, including himself and his father-in-law. David Davies and Enriqueta Harris suggest that the model was his sister Juana, born in 1609, although this would make her too young to be "at the age of puberty" in 1618 (David Davies, ed., *Velázquez in Seville* [Edinburgh: National Galleries of Scotland, 1996], 156).

96. See Montañés's statue *Virgin of the Immaculate Conception*, which features in the altarpiece of the Chapel of St. Catherine in the church at El Pedroso: "The Virgin stands looking downwards to her right, her hands clasped together, and her right leg bent. She is placed on a crescent moon, with a cherub's head at the center. Her cloak and robe are decorated by *estofado* designs in blue, gold and pink" (Davies, *Velázquez in Seville*, 154). "Estofado" describes a method used in polychromy

to produce patterns imitating embroidered materials, in which a layer of gold leaf is applied to the surface of the wood, overpainted with colored pigments, and then revealed by scratching away the paint. Velázquez painted Montañés's portrait, now in the Museo del Prado, Madrid, in 1635.

97. As Sara T. Nalle explains, Seville was "a city passionately committed to the cult of the Virgin" such that, in the early seventeenth century, "the all-consuming religious question was not the spread of Protestantism across Europe, nor the continued presence of Islam in the Iberian Peninsula, but the doctrine of the Immaculate Conception" ("Spanish Religious Life in the Age of Velázquez," in *The Cambridge Companion to Velázquez*, ed. Suzanne L. Stratton-Pruitt [Cambridge: Cambridge University Press, 2002]: 109–29, 214–17 (114)).

98. Alexander Walker, trans., *The Protoevangelium of James: Greek and English Texts* (Philadelphia: Dalcassian, 2019). For a brief contextualization, see Luigi Gambero, *Mary and the Fathers of the Church: The Blessed Virgin Mary in Patristic Thought*, trans. Thomas Buffer (San Francisco: Ignatius Press, 1999), 35–42.

99. "Och Joachim tog emot henne / grönt fladdrade hans mantel / Han stödde med vänstra handen hennes armbåge / och tryckte lätt med sin högra fot / på hennes vänstra toffel av rött saffian" (Ekelöf, "Joachim och Anna" in *Sagan om Fatumeh*, 37–38 (38)); "And Joachim received her / His mantle fluttering green behind him / With his left hand he supported her right elbow / And lightly pressed with his right foot / On her left slipper of red morocco" (Ekelöf, "Joachim and Anna" in *Selected Poems*, 102 (102)).

100. Origen, *Homilies on Luke; Fragments on Luke*, trans. Joseph T. Lienhard (Washington, D.C.: Catholic University of America Press, 1996), Homily 7.2, 28.

101. Boniface Ramsey, *Ambrose* (London / New York: Routledge, 1997), 51.

102. Luigi Gambero, *Mary in the Middle Ages: The Blessed Virgin Mary in the Thought of Medieval Latin Theologians*, trans. Thomas Buffer (San Francisco: Ignatius Press, 2005), 237–38.

103. Gambero, 243–52.

104. Manfred Hauke, *Introduction to Mariology*, trans. Richard Chonak (Washington, DC: Catholic University of America Press, 2021), 237.

105. Kristeva notes that the establishment of the dogma of the Immaculate Conception showed the Catholic Church "to be more dialectical and more subtle than the Protestants, who were already engendering the first suffragettes." She continues, "It is frequently suggested that the flourishing of feminism in the Protestant countries is due, among other things, to the fact that women there are allowed greater initiative in social life and ritual. But one wonders if it is not also due to Protestantism's *lacking* some necessary element of the Maternal which in Catholicism has been elaborated with the utmost sophistication by the Jesuits (and which again makes Catholicism very difficult to analyze)" (Julia Kristeva, "Stabat Mater," trans. Arthur Goldhammer, in *The Female Body in Western Culture: Contemporary Perspectives*, ed. Susan Rubin Suleiman [Cambridge: Harvard University Press, 1986]: 99–118 (105); originally published as "L'héréthique de l'amour," *Tel Quel* 74 [1977]: 30–49, and later as "Stabat Mater," in *Histoires d'amour* [Paris: Denoël, 1983], 225–47).

106. 1 Kings 18:44 (King James Version).

107. Ronald Cueto, "The Wilder Shores of Carmelite Spirituality: Ravens, Deserts, Clouds and Prophecies in the Discalced Reform," in *Leeds Papers on St. John of the Cross: Contributions to a Quatercentenary Celebration*, ed. Margaret A. Rees (Leeds: Trinity and All Saints College, 1991): 63–104 (103).

108. Ortega y Gasset is even more forthright, stating that no sooner had Velázquez left Seville "than he determined to paint no more religious pictures" (introduction to *Velasquez*, 16). Later paintings nevertheless include *Christ after the Flagellation Contemplated by the Christian Soul* (National Gallery, London, probably 1628–29); *The Crucifixion* (Museo del Prado, 1632); *The Temptation of St. Thomas* (Museo Diocesano de Arte Sacro, Orihuela, 1632); and *The Coronation of the Virgin* (Museo del Prado, 1641–44), in which there are echoes of *Immaculate Conception.*

109. Khatibi, *Quatuor poétique*, 23.

110. Mallarmé, *Œuvres complètes*, 2:170.

111. Abdelkébir Khatibi, "Intersignes," in *Imaginaires de l'autre: Khatibi et la mémoire littéraire*, ed. Christine Buci-Glucksmann et al. (Paris: L'Harmattan, 1987): 123–31 (124).

112. Khatibi, *Aimance*, 103. Compare to the almost identical rendition of this phrase in *Le livre de l'aimance* (27), where in place of "désiré" [desired] we read "aimé" [loved].

113. Kateb Yacine, *Nedjma*, 178.

114. Kateb Yacine, 178.

115. Nabile Farès, *Le miroir de Cordoue* (Paris: L'Harmattan, 1994), 140.

116. Khatibi, *Par-dessus l'épaule*, 8.

117. Khatibi, 8.

118. Ibn Kathīr, *The Islamic View of Jesus (Peace Be upon Him)*, trans. Tamir Abu As-Su'ood Muhammad, ed. Noha Kamal Ed-Din (Mansoura: Dar al-Manarah, 2002), 10.

119. Kathīr, 10.

120. Qur'ān 3:35 (Nasr et al.'s edition, p. 141).

121. Khatibi, *Dédicace à l'année qui vient*, 27.

122. The sura "Maryam" contains nearly a third of all instances in the Qur'ān of the Divine Name "الرحمن" [al-raḥman], meaning "the merciful," but related to the Arabic "رحم" [raḥim], or "womb."

123. Qur'ān 19:16–17 (Nasr et al.'s edition, pp. 768–69); translation modified.

124. Helmut Gätje, *The Qur'ān and Its Exegesis: Selected Texts with Classical and Modern Muslim Interpretations* (London: Oneworld Publications, 2000), 121. Although Khatibi allows angelic mystery to infiltrate his poetic universe, he also questions the celestial order: "Est-ce désormais une fête folle / De croire aux anges mystérieux?" [Is it now madness / To believe in mysterious angels?] (Khatibi, *Dédicace à l'année qui vient*, 70); "Les anges ne sont que noms d'oiseaux exotiques / Et le paradis une pure mosaïque de lauriers" [Angels are nothing more than names of exotic birds / And paradise a pure mosaic of laurels] (Khatibi, 105).

125. Qur'ān 21:91 (Nasr et al.'s edition, p. 825).

126. This precise formulation is repeated in Qur'ān 66:12: "And Mary, the daughter of 'Imrān, who preserved her chastity" (Nasr et al.'s edition, p. 1392).

127. Nasr et al., *The Study Quran*, 769.

128. Ibn Kathīr, *The Islamic View of Jesus*, 27.

129. For example, al-ʿĀmilī, *Tafsīr al-bayān* (Cairo, n.d.), 114; Maḥmūd Muḥammad Ḥamza, *Tafsīr al-qur'ān al-karīm* (Cairo, 1960), 35; ʿAbd al-Karīm al-Khaṭīb, *Al-Tafsīr al-qur'ānī li'l-qur'ān* (Cairo, n.d.) 2:730.

130. Muḥammad Jamāl al-Dīn al-Qāsimī, *Tafsīr al-Qāsimī* (Cairo, 1914), 4:133.

131. Such circumspect credence should be contrasted with the skepticism attributed to the midwife Salome in James the Less's *Protoevangelium*, who, in an echo of Thomas doubting Christ's resurrection, insists, "'Unless I insert my finger and test her condition, I will not believe that a virgin has given birth.' . . . And Salomé inserted her finger to test her condition. And she cried out, saying, 'Woe for my wickedness and unbelief; for I have tempted the living God, and behold, my hand falls away from me, consumed by fire.'" (J. K. Elliott, ed., *The Apocryphal New Testament: A Collection of Apocryphal Christian Literature in an English Translation* [Oxford: Clarendon, 1993], 19.3–20.1, 64–65).

132. Khatibi, *Le corps oriental*, 8.

133. Khatibi, 34.

134. Abdelwahab Bouhdiba, *La sexualité en Islam* (Paris: Presses universitaires de France, 1975), 47.

135. Khatibi, *Le livre du sang*, 14.

136. Khatibi, *Dédicace à l'année qui vient*, 102.

137. Khatibi, *Par-dessus l'épaule*, 26; *Le livre de l'aimance*, 23; *Aimance*, 100–101.

138. Khatibi, *Dédicace à l'année qui vient*, 74; *Aimance*, 65.

139. Dubreuil, "Poétiques de l'énallage," 65.

140. Wehr, *A Dictionary of Modern Written Arabic*, 110.

141. Maulānā Jalāluddīn, active in Anatolia—or "Rūm," the land of the Romans, whence the nickname Rūmī—often calls upon Mary as a model of virtue: "In her room Mary had seen something / that won her heart, something intensely alive. / That trusted spirit rose from the face of the earth / like a sun or moon rising in the East / like beauty unveiled. / / Mary, who was undressed, began to tremble, / afraid of the evil that might be in it. / This kind of thing could cause / Joseph to cut his own wrist. / It flowered in front of her like a rose, / like a fantasy that lifts its head in the / heart" (Jalaluddin Rumi, *The Rumi Collection*, ed. Kabir Helminski [Boston: Shambhala Publications, 1998], 231; this passage trans. Nevit Ergin, with Camille Helminski).

142. Deleuze, *Le pli*, 165.

143. Khatibi, *Figures de l'étranger*, 111.

144. "Ciphered tattoo: / khamsah /vulva /rhythm" (Khatibi, *La blessure du nom propre*, 93).

145. Khatibi, 100.

146. Khatibi, 99.

147. Fernand Braudel, "Conflits et refus de civilisation: Espagnols et morisques au XVIe siècle," *Annales. Histoire, Sciences Sociales* 2, no. 4 (1947): 397–410 (397).

148. Louis Aragon identifies with the last Muslim king of Spain at the opening of *Le fou d'Elsa: poème* (*Œuvres poétiques complètes II*, ed. Olivier Barbarant, Jamel Eddine Bencheikh, François Eychart, Marie-Thérèse Eychart, Philippe Forest, Bernard Leuilliot [Paris: Gallimard, 2007], 489–938 (494ff.)). Sénac does something similar in the poem "Ordalie de novembre" [November Ordeal]: "Et le chant d'une

flûte en mes veines surprend / Le mal de Boabdil sous les murs de Grenade" [And the song of a flute in my veins surprises / The suffering of Boabdil under the walls of Granada] (Sénac, *Avant-corps*, 53–56 (55)).

149. Nalle, "Spanish Religious Life in the Age of Velázquez," 126.

150. Antonio Feros, "'Sacred and Terrifying Gazes': Languages and Images of Power in Early Modern Spain," in *The Cambridge Companion to Velázquez*, 68–86 (82). For a brief history of the Moriscos and their expulsion from Spain, see Braudel, "Conflits et refus de civilisation"; and Antonio Feros, *Kingship and Favoritism in the Spain of Philip III, 1598–1621* (Cambridge: Cambridge University Press, 2000), 198–205.

151. *Expulsion of the Moriscos by Philip III* (1627) was destroyed in a fire at the Real Alcázar in Madrid on Christmas Eve 1734. It is said to have depicted Philip III standing next to an allegory of Spain, in the form of a woman, pointing toward the Moriscos as they boarded boats to cross the Mediterranean Sea. For Palomino's description of the painting, see Francisco Pacheco and Antonio Palomino, *Lives of Velázquez*, trans. Nina Ayala Mallory, intro. Michael Jacobs (London: Pallas Athene, 2006), 71–72. Velázquez's competitors included Vincenzo Carducci (Vicencio Carducho), who created a drawing in pencil and pen entitled *La expulsión de los moriscos* (Museo del Prado, Madrid).

152. Ortega y Gasset, introduction to *Velasquez*, 6.

153. Pacheco and Palomino, *Lives of Velázquez*, 141.

154. See *The Virgin of the Immaculate Conception with Miguel Cid* (Cathedral of Seville, 1619); *Inmaculada Concepción con Mateo Vázquez de Leca* (Private collection, Seville, 1621); *Inmaculada Concepción* (Iglesia de San Lorenzo, Seville, 1623–24). See also Zurbarán's painting of the same title—dated 1628–30—in the Prado Museum, Madrid.

155. Qur'ān 19:23–25 (Nasr et al.'s edition, pp. 770–71). Herber identifies the palm tree as the plant most often found tattooed on the skin of sex workers in Morocco in the early twentieth century (Joseph Herber, "Les tatouages des prostituées marocaines," *Revue d'ethnographie et de sociologie* [1919]: 264–73 (265)).

156. Khatibi, *La blessure du nom propre*, 96.

157. Khatibi, 96–97.

158. Kristeva says that Mary's biography is made to parallel that of Jesus, being not only immaculately conceived, and thereby free from original sin, but also free from death, and so subject to dormition (koimēsis) and assumption (Kristeva, "Stabat Mater," 102).

159. Khatibi, *La blessure du nom propre*, 31.

160. Khatibi, 93.

161. Khatibi, 76, 86.

162. Only one painting of a nude has ever been attributed to Velázquez, namely the *Toilet of Venus*, also known as *The Rokeby Venus* (National Gallery, London, 1647–51), in which the viewer looks over the shoulder ("par-dessus l'épaule") of the naked girl.

163. Habib Tengour and Mourad Yelles, "Dialogue des 'Andalouses,'" in *L'arc et la lyre: Dialogues (1988–2004)*, by Habib Tengour, ed. Mourad Yelles (Algiers: Casbah Éditions, 2006), 11–62 (19). The poem "Salut" begins with the lines: "*Une ivresse belle m'engage / Sans craindre même son tangage / De porter debout ce salut*" (Mallarmé, *Œuvres complètes*, 1:4).

164. Khatibi and Sijelmassi, *L'art calligraphique de l'Islam*, 214.

165. Mallarmé, *Œuvres complètes*, 1:387.

166. Qur'ān 4:171 (Nasr et al.'s edition, p. 268).

167. Mallarmé, *Œuvres complètes*, 2:174.

168. Khatibi, *Par-dessus l'épaule*, 14; *Le livre de l'aimance*, 10; *Aimance*, 90.

169. Jacques Derrida, *La dissémination* (Paris: Seuil, 1972), 206.

170. "Oh brothers! If our syntax itself / is not a cog of freedom . . ." (Jean Sénac, "Salut aux écrivains et artistes noirs" in *Œuvres poétiques*, 271–72 (271)).

171. Barbara Johnson, *The Critical Difference: Essays in the Contemporary Rhetoric of Reading* (Baltimore: Johns Hopkins University Press, 1980), 67.

172. Roland Barthes, *Mythologies* (Paris: Seuil, 1957), 178.

173. Abdelkébir Khatibi, "Un étranger professionnel," *Textuel* 32 (1997): 139–41 (140–41).

174. Khatibi, *La langue de l'autre*, 37.

175. Khatibi, "Un étranger professionnel," 140.

176. Khatibi, *La langue de l'autre*, 80.

177. Abdelkébir Khatibi, *Pèlerinage d'un artiste amoureux: roman* (Monaco: Éditions du Rocher, 2003), 193.

178. Derrida, *La dissémination*, 240.

179. Abdelkébir Khatibi, *Vœu de silence*, ill. Abdelkébir Rabi (Neuilly-sur-Seine: Al Manar, 2000), 16; Khatibi, *Quatuor poétique*, 17.

180. Mallarmé, *Œuvres complètes*, 2:715. Derrida mistakenly refers to this text by Mallarmé as a letter, where in fact Guillemot visits Mallarmé at Valvins (Derrida, *La dissémination*, 205).

181. Mallarmé, *Œuvres complètes*, 2:234.

182. Khatibi and Sijelmassi, *L'art calligraphique de l'Islam*, 46.

183. Khatibi, *Le corps oriental*, 15.

184. Wehr, *A Dictionary of Modern Written Arabic*, 879.

185. Arthur Rimbaud to Paul Demeny, May 15, 1871, in *Œuvres complètes*, 342–49 (346).

186. Wehr, *A Dictionary of Modern Written Arabic*, 906.

187. Qur'ān 3:47 (Nasr et al.'s edition, p. 144; translation modified). See also Qur'ān 19:20, "How shall I have a boy when no man has touched me, nor have I been unchaste?" (Nasr et al.'s edition, p. 769), where the same verb is used.

188. Wehr, *A Dictionary of Modern Written Arabic*, 906–7.

189. Khatibi, "L'aimance et l'invention d'un idiome," 125.

190. Khatibi, *Dédicace à l'année qui vient*, 59. For a modified version, see Khatibi, *Aimance*, 57.

191. Khatibi, *Par-dessus l'épaule*, 45. See also Sénac's poem "Ni le baiser" [Neither the Kiss]: "Dans la maison lustrale / Il y a tant de graffiti / Que les murs en sont vierges / Et de nouveau la parole possible" [In the house of purification / There is so much graffiti / That the walls have turned virgin / And inscription is again possible] (*Avant-corps*, 23 (23)).

192. Khatibi, *Par-dessus l'épaule*, 28; Khatibi, *Le livre de l'aimance*, 25. When reprised in *Aimance*, "la vierge" becomes "le vierge" (102).

193. Khatibi, *Maghreb pluriel*, 18.

194. Khatibi, *La blessure du nom propre*, 93.

195. Khatibi, 63–64.

CHAPTER 6

Epigraph: "The moon last night already was at full." This quotation from Dante Alighieri's *Divine Comedy* (*Inferno*, 20.127) concludes Abdelwahab Meddeb's novel *Phantasia* (Paris: Seuil, 2003 [Paris: Éditions Sindbad, 1986]), 172). It is likely a temporal reference to Good Friday, the day of Christ's crucifixion and death, which probably took place the day following the first night of the Jewish feast of Pessach, or Passover, that is, a day after the full moon that marks the fifteenth night of the month of Nissan.

1. Abdelwahab Meddeb and Tahar Djaout, "Surprise de l'hybridation," *Parcours maghrébins* 3 (1986): 8–9 (8).

2. H. B. Tristram, *The Land of Moab: Travels and Discoveries on the East Side of the Dead Sea and the Jordan* (London: John Murray, 1873), 28.

3. David Fieni, *Decadent Orientalisms: The Decay of Colonial Modernity* (New York: Fordham University Press, 2020), 155. Just such a hippodrama briefly enters the narrative at the end of the sixth chapter: "In my head, a TV screen broadcasts a fantasia [une fantasia] on the arid steppe, light horse race, galloping on soft ground" (Meddeb, *Phantasia*, 109).

4. Jocelyne Dakhlia, "*No man's langue*: Une rétraction coloniale," in *Trames de langues: Usages et métissages linguistiques dans l'histoire du Maghreb*, ed. Jocelyne Dakhlia (Paris: Maisonneuve et Larose, 2004): 259–71 (268).

5. Dakhlia, 267–68; Hugo Schuchardt, "Die Lingua franca," *Zeitschrift für Romanische Philologie* 33 (1909): 441–61 (447). Other instances of such titles in modern Maghrebi literature might include Meddeb's *Talismano* (Paris: Bourgois, 1979), Assia Djebar's *L'amour, la fantasia* (Paris: J. C. Lattès, 1985), Abdelkébir Khatibi's *Vomito blanco* (Paris: Union générale d'éditions, 1974), and Mohammed Khaïr-Eddine's *Une odeur de mantèque* (Paris: Seuil, 1976).

6. Abdelkébir Khatibi, "Bilinguisme et littérature," in *Maghreb pluriel*, 177–207 (180ff.). See Alison Rice, *Time Signatures: Contextualizing Contemporary Francophone Autobiographical Writing from the Maghreb* (Lanham: Lexington Books, 2006), 278–79; Yasser Elhariry, *Pacifist Invasions: Arabic, Translation, and the Postfrancophone Lyric* (Liverpool: Liverpool University Press, 2017), 10–11.

7. For a broad and detailed introduction to "fantaisie" in the long Romantic tradition—and especially the influence of the German "Phantasie"—see Bernard Vouilloux, "Éléments pour l'archéologie d'une notion," in *La fantaisie post-romantique*, ed. Jean-Louis Cabanès and Jean-Pierre Saïdah (Toulouse: Presses universitaires du Mirail, 2003), 19–58.

8. Begun in Milan in 387 and completed at Hippo (now Annaba) in 391.

9. Augustine, *On Music (De musica)*, trans. Robert Catesby Taliaferro, in *The Immortality of the Soul, The Magnitude of the Soul, On Music, The Advantage of Believing, On Faith in Things Unseen* (Washington, DC: Catholic University of America Press, 2002): 151–379 (356–57).

10. Augustine, 357.

11. Augustine, *Confessions*, trans. Carolyn J.-B. Hammond, vol. 1, bks. 1–8 (Cambridge: Harvard University Press, 2014), 106.

12. Augustine, 106. Meddeb describes Augustine's *Confessions* as "branded by the same obdurate sun of childhood that had tanned his skin and his mind" (Meddeb, *Phantasia*, 71).

13. Augustine, *On Music (De musica)*, 357.

14. Meddeb, *Phantasia*, 14.
15. Meddeb, 14.
16. Meddeb, 14.
17. Meddeb, 18–19, 28–30, 43–44, 46, 50, 55, 121, 136, 146, 149, 150, 159.
18. Meddeb, 19, 29, 44, 46.
19. Meddeb, 20.
20. Meddeb, 24, 30, 55.
21. Meddeb, 117.
22. Meddeb, 159.
23. Meddeb, 44.
24. Jambet, preface to *Instants soufis*, 19.
25. James A. W. Heffernan, *Museum of Words: The Poetics of Ekphrasis from Homer to Ashbery* (Chicago: University of Chicago Press, 1993), 3.
26. Veronica Amadessi, "Pour une nouvelle poétique de l'extase: Abdelwahab Meddeb et l'héritage des poètes arabes et persans de l'Antiquité et du Moyen Âge. Comparaisons et pistes de lecture intertextuelles" (PhD diss., Università di Bologna, 2009); Maya Boutaghou, "Le testament soufi de Abdelwahab Meddeb," *Expressions maghrébines* 16, no. 2 (2017): 135–53.
27. Meddeb, *Phantasia*, 18.
28. Qur'ān 96:1–5 (Nasr et al.'s edition, p. 1537).
29. Meddeb, *Phantasia*, 18.
30. Savary, *Le Coran*, 33. Claude-Étienne Savary's *Le Coran* (1783) is the second translation of the Qur'ān into French, following Du Ryer's 1647 version. Savary draws extensively on Marracci's 1698 Latin translation.
31. Djaout, *Une mémoire mise en signes*, 75.
32. Khatibi, *Dédicace à l'année qui vient*, 38.
33. Meddeb, *Phantasia*, 19.
34. Meddeb, 19.
35. John 1:14 (King James Version).
36. Meddeb, *Instants soufis*, 145.
37. Meddeb, *Phantasia*, 73.
38. Meddeb, 73. Similar formulations can be found in *De trinitate*, although the notion is repeated widely in Augustine's writings (Augustine, *The Trinity*, trans. Stephen McKenna [Washington, DC: Catholic University of America Press, 2002], 4.20, 164 and 7.5, 235).
39. Pierre Courcelle, "Saint Augustin 'Photinien' à Milan (*Confessions* VII, 19, 25)," *Ricerche di storia religiosa* 1 (1954): 63–71 (65). See also William Mallard, "The Incarnation in Augustine's Conversion," *RechAug* 15 (1980): 80–98.
40. Meddeb, "L'icône mentale," 63.
41. Meddeb, "L'islamisme est la maladie de l'islam," n.p. See also *Contre-prêches: Chroniques* (Paris: Seuil, 2006), 9–17; and *Sortir de la malédiction: L'islam entre civilisation et barbarie* (Paris: Seuil, 2008), 19.
42. Meddeb, *Phantasia*, 29.
43. Meddeb, 29. See Exod. 20:4 (King James Version).
44. Benslama, *La nuit brisée*, 31.
45. Meddeb, *Phantasia*, 29.
46. Meddeb, 29.

47. Meddeb, 146–47.
48. Meddeb, 27.
49. Meddeb, 27.
50. Meddeb, 65.
51. Meddeb, 67.
52. Meddeb, 67–68.
53. Meddeb, 68.
54. Meddeb, 68.
55. Meddeb and Djaout, "Surprise de l'hybridation," 8. The historic prevalence of aniconism is also the starting point for Abdelfattah Kilito: "I have often wondered how the Arabs of old were able to do without images. Apparently, they did not care much for them; or at least they made no effort to perpetuate their own. What Hārūn al-Rashīd, al-Mutanabbī, or Averroes looked like, we will never know" (Abdelfattah Kilito, *La querelle des images* [Casablanca: EDDIF, 1995], 9).
56. Meddeb and Djaout, "Surprise de l'hybridation," 9.
57. Meddeb, *Phantasia*, 18.
58. Meddeb, 25–26.
59. A ceiling painting by Pontormo no longer exists (Louis Alexander Waldman, "New Light on the Capponi Chapel in S. Felicita," *Art Bulletin* 84, no. 2 [2002]: 293–314 (293)).
60. "Abdelwahab Meddeb: Hommage," interview with Christine Goémé, part 2 of 5 in "À voix nue," *France Culture*, first broadcast on December 23, 2014, 14:38ff., https://www.franceculture.fr/emissions/voix-nue/abdelwahab-meddeb-25-hommage.
61. Amy Knight Powell, *Depositions: Scenes from the Late Medieval Church and the Modern Museum* (New York: Zone Books, 2012), 10.
62. Col. 1:15 (King James Version).
63. Powell, *Depositions*, 39.
64. Meddeb, *Phantasia*, 69.
65. Meddeb, 159.
66. Meddeb, 70–71.
67. Abdelwahab Meddeb, "Hallâj revisité," *Parcours maghrébins* 1 (1986): 42–44 (44).
68. Meddeb, 44.
69. Giorgio Vasari, *The Lives of the Artists*, trans. Julia Conaway Bondanella and Peter Bondanella (Oxford: Oxford University Press, 2008), 406.
70. Pontormo, *Study for the Capponi Chapel Pietà* (Christ Church Picture Gallery, Oxford, probably before September 1526). For its reproduction, see Waldman, "New Light," 301.
71. Note that on the skyline of the scene depicted in the window, the deposition of Christ from the cross is also portrayed.
72. Doris Wild, "Ein Selbstbildnis Pontormos," in *Josef Strzygowski-Festschrift* (Klagenfurt: Artur Kollitsch, 1932): 182–85 (184–85).
73. The Capponi Chapel is dedicated to the pietà.
74. Meddeb, *Phantasia*, 27.
75. Meddeb, 28.
76. Rabat: Stouky, 1981. Meddeb implicitly proposes Khaïr-Eddine as the Maghreb's response to Aimé Césaire in his poetic hommage to the great Martinican

poet: "... je retiens aussi le voyage / vers le Souss et l'arrière-pays qui relie Agadir / à Mogador où survivent les Berbères Haha / ou encore sur les sentiers du Tafraout / le domaine de Mohammed Khaïr Eddine / « ... *j'habite un troupeau de chèvres tirant sur la tétine / de l'arganier le plus désolé* ... » pour rendre la vision / des caprins grimpant les vastes frondaisons / suçant les glands les dépouillant de leur chair ..." [... I also recall the journey / toward Sous and the hinterland that links Agadir / to Mogador where the Berbers survive Haha / or even on the pathways of Tafraout / the domain of Mohammed Khaïr Eddine / '... *I live among a herd of goats that tug on the teats / of the most desolate argan tree* ...' to render the vision / of goats climbing the vast foliage / sucking the nuts stripping the flesh away ...] (Abdelwahab Meddeb, "Portrait de l'artiste en soufi: Dix fragments," *Po&sie* 144 [2013]: 97–114 (99)).

77. Paul de Man, *The Rhetoric of Romanticism* (New York: Columbia University Press, 1984), 6.

78. "For Meddeb, the problem is neither to secularize [Islam] nor to update it, but to make it circulate and, by this very gesture, to return each culture—sickened and strangled by the repressions it imposes on itself and on other cultures—to a more liberated circulation. Neither transpositions, nor hybrids, but connections where each language knows and whispers something of the secrecy imposed as enigma and silence on the other, where each culture repairs something of the prohibition that amputates and disfigures the other" (Antoine Raybaud, *Le besoin littéraire* [Monaco: Éditions du Rocher, 2000], 252).

79. Leo Steinberg, "Pontormo's Capponi Chapel," *Art Bulletin* 56, no. 3 (1974): 385–99 (387).

80. Meddeb, *Phantasia*, 26.

81. Meddeb, "Portrait de l'artiste en soufi," 106.

82. Scored for soprano and alto soloists, two violins, viola, cello, and organ. Note that Aya sings "de sa voix coranique" [with her Qur'ānic voice] from the "Lamento d'Ariane" by Monteverdi (Meddeb, *Phantasia*, 165).

83. Meddeb, "L'icône mentale," 54–55.

84. Wehr, *A Dictionary of Modern Written Arabic*, 420.

85. Meddeb, *Phantasia*, 36.

86. Saint Paul claims that the crucifixion is a "scandal" for the Jews and "foolishness" for the Greeks (1 Cor. 1:23 [King James Version]).

87. Khaïr-Eddine, "Nausée noire," n.p.

88. Khaïr-Eddine, "Au pays des Multifaces" in *Résurrection des fleurs sauvages*, 91–92 (91).

89. Meddeb, *Phantasia*, 167. Compare to Salah Stétié, for whom Christ is "a character of great humanity" and "the most perfect figuration possible of compassion" but who also insists on "leaving the crucifixion to one side" on the grounds that it "is just a way of emphasizing the appropriation of humanity's pain by means of a real or symbolic projection" (Stétié, *Fils de la parole*, 220–21).

90. Khatibi, *La blessure du nom propre*, 100–101. See also Herber—from whom Khatibi draws—who stresses that although the cross is a common motif in Moroccan tattooing, "it is simply the result of the crossing of two lines" and not in any way a Christian symbol (Joseph Herber, "Tatouages curatifs au Maroc," *Revue d'Ethnographie et des traditions populaires* 9 [1928]: 179–87 (184)).

91. Qur'ān 4:157 (Nasr et al.'s edition, pp. 262–63). See Ibn Kathīr, the fourteenth-century theologian and historian, who says that on the Day of Judgment, Jesus himself will explain that "Allah saved him by rendering one of his disciples a lookalike of Jesus on whom they took their revenge" (Ibn Kathīr, *The Islamic View of Jesus*, 59).

92. Meddeb, "L'icône mentale," 48; Wehr, *A Dictionary of Modern Written Arabic*, 453–54.

93. "Quomodo enim eas solveret in cruce phantasmatis, quod de illo credideram? quam ergo falsa mihi videbatur mors carnis eius, tam vera erat animae meae, et quam vera erat mors carnis eius, tam falsa vita animae meae, quae id non credebat" [After all, how could he undo those hostilities by the cross of (as I then believed about him) an imaginary being? The more the death of his flesh seemed to me to be false, the more true was the death of my soul; while the more the death of his flesh was in fact true, the more false was the life of my soul, because it did not believe in it] (Augustine, *Confessions*, 212–15).

94. Meddeb, *Instants soufis*, 85.

95. See Meddeb, 86–87. See also Bāyazīd Bisṭāmī, *Les dits de Bistami: Shatahât*, trans. and ed. Abdelwahab Meddeb (Paris: Arthème Fayard, 1989).

96. Quoted in Meddeb, *Phantasia*, 28.

97. Meddeb, *Instants soufis*, 87. See also Abdelwahab Meddeb, "La subversion de Hallâj ou le secret divulgué," in *Le voyage initiatique*, ed. Nadia Benjelloun (Paris: Albin Michel, 2011): 53–72.

98. Quoted in Meddeb, *Phantasia*, 28.

99. Quoted in Meddeb, "La subversion de Hallâj," 56; Meddeb, *Instants soufis*, 86.

100. Quoted in Pierre Rocalve, *Louis Massignon et l'islam* (Damascus: Institut français de Damas, 1993), 53. See also Louis Massignon, "Perspective transhistorique sur la vie de Hallâj," in *Dîwân*, by Husayn Mansûr Hallâj, pref. and trans. Louis Massignon (Paris: Seuil, 1981): 12–38 (18).

101. Meddeb, *Instants soufis*, 88. See also Meddeb, *Talismano*, 33.

102. Meddeb, *Instants soufis*, 88.

103. This also means "stopping, putting up, staying; descending, coming on, befalling, overtaking; setting in, advent, arrival, beginning, dawn; substitution," from the verb "حل" [ḥalla] [to untie, unbind, unfasten, unravel, undo, solve, dissolve, resolve, etc.] (Wehr, *A Dictionary of Modern Written Arabic*, 198–99).

104. Meddeb, *Instants soufis*, 88.

105. It is generally thought that al-Ḥallāj's ashes were scattered in the Tigris, which runs through the city of Baghdad.

106. Meddeb, *Phantasia*, 29.

107. Meddeb, "L'icône mentale," 63.

108. Meddeb, *Phantasia*, 150.

109. A model for the book may be Mohamed Aziza's *La calligraphie arabe* (Tunis: Société tunisienne de diffusion, 1961), which includes a section called "Écritures de fantaisie" [Fantasy Inscriptions] (85–87). The calligraphy that appears on the cover of the 2003 Seuil edition of *Phantasia* is also reproduced here, where it is described as "Calligraphic composition in the shape of a labyrinth" (Aziza, *La calligraphie arabe*, 123, 139). Aziza (b. Tunis, 1940)—who also writes under the pseudonym

Chems Nadir—is a poet and the author of *L'image et l'Islam: L'image dans la société arabe contemporaine* (Paris: Albin Michel, 1973).

110. Meddeb, *Phantasia*, 155. Compare to the reproduction *Composition in the Form of a Floral Tughra* (Aziza, *La calligraphie arabe*, 90, 138). Note that "rutilement" [glistening, shining], from the verb "rutiler" [glisten, shine], is coined by Rimbaud in his 1871 poem "Le bateau ivre" [The Drunken Ship] (Rimbaud, *Œuvres complètes*, 162–64 (163)).

111. Meddeb, *Phantasia*, 26.

112. Meddeb, 26.

113. Meddeb, 26.

114. Meddeb, 155.

115. Meddeb, 26.

116. Meddeb, 26, 155.

117. Meddeb, 155–56.

118. Meddeb, 26.

119. Khatibi, *La blessure du nom propre*, 75.

120. Meddeb, *Phantasia*, 18.

121. Meddeb, 19.

122. Meddeb, 155.

123. Meddeb, 155.

124. Meddeb, 74.

125. Meddeb, 156.

126. Meddeb, 156.

127. Meddeb, 156.

128. Meddeb, 29.

129. Hédi Abdel-Jaouad, *Fugues de Barbarie: Les écrivains maghrébins et le surréalisme* (New York: Les mains secrètes, 1998), 91.

130. Abdelwahab Meddeb, *Tombeau d'Ibn Arabi* (Paris: Noël Blandin, 1990).

131. Yasser Elhariry, "Abdelwahab Meddeb, Sufi Poets, and the New Francophone Lyric," *PMLA* 131, no. 2 (2016): 255–67 (266).

132. Elhariry, 256.

133. Hoda El Shakry, "Abdelwahab Meddeb and the Po/Ethics of Sufism," *Expressions maghrébines* 16, no. 2 (2017): 95–115 (103).

134. Habib Tengour, "Maghrebian Surrealism [Essay and Manifesto]," trans. Pierre Joris, *Jacket2*, January 13, 2017, https://jacket2.org/commentary/habib-tengour-maghrebian-surrealism-essay-manifesto.

135. Lucy McNeece, "La présence de l'absent," *Expressions maghrébines* 15, no. 1 (2016): 77–98 (81).

136. Fieni, *Decadent Orientalisms*, 138.

CHAPTER 7

Epigraph: "The flowers that bedizen the paths of life are a test" (Qur'ān 20:131 [Savary's translation]).

1. Michel Houellebecq, *Soumission* (Paris: Flammarion, 2015).

2. Michel Houellebecq, *Submission*, trans. Lorin Stein (New York: Farrar, Straus and Giroux, 2015), 17.

3. Houellebecq, *Soumission*, 180.

4. Rimbaud's first experience of a Muslim country had been the time he spent in Java in July and August 1876. For an account of this period, see Jean-Jacques Lefrère, *Arthur Rimbaud* (Paris: Fayard, 2001), 747–57.

5. Jean-Jacques Lefrère, ed., *Sur Arthur Rimbaud, Correspondance (1891–1900)* (Paris: Fayard, 2010), 908; Arthur Rimbaud, *Correspondance*, ed. Jean-Jacques Lefrère (Paris: Fayard, 2007), 265.

6. Lefrère, *Sur Arthur Rimbaud*, 912; Rimbaud, *Correspondance*, 277.

7. Alfred Bardey, *Barr-Adjam: Souvenirs d'Afrique Orientale, 1880–1887* (Paris: CNRS, 1981), 220.

8. Rimbaud, *Correspondance*, 355. To mark the one hundredth anniversary of Rimbaud's birth, the Bibliothèque nationale exhibited a Qur'ān similar to the one that used to belong to Rimbaud. This volume, published in 1865, is now preserved in the library of the Institut du monde arabe in Paris. Also displayed was a "nineteenth-century manuscript Qur'ān from Harar" (*Arthur Rimbaud: Exposition organisée pour le centième anniversaire de sa naissance* [Paris: Bibliothèque nationale, 1954], 59).

9. Pierre Brunel, *Rimbaud: Biographie; Étude de l'œuvre* (Paris: Albin Michel, 1995), 61.

10. Steve Murphy, *Stratégies de Rimbaud* (Paris: Honoré Champion, 2004), 249.

11. Miller, *Blank Darkness*, 139. Miller limits his study to, on the one hand, the references to Africa and Africans in the poet's work—that is, all traces of "le mythe du nègre chez Rimbaud"—and, on the other, critical, historical, and anecdotal discourse on Rimbaud's time in Africa, or what he calls "le mythe de Rimbaud chez les nègres."

12. Hédi Abdel-Jaouad, *Rimbaud et l'Algérie* (New York: Les mains secrètes, 2002), 82.

13. A Sunni order founded by 'Abd al-Qādir al-Jīlānī (Gilan, 1077–Baghdad, 1166); Graham Robb, *Rimbaud* (London: Picador, 2000), 408.

14. Quoted in Henri d'Acremont, "En Abyssinie: Sur les traces de Rimbaud," *Revue hebdomadaire* 41, no. 35 (1932): 410–21 (419).

15. d'Acremont, 420. See also the letter from Ottorino Rosa to his employer in Aden, the Triestine trader Vittorio Bienenfeld, dated February 1, 1890: "The charm of this truly unbearable trip is compounded by the aggravations of the Abyssinians. The other day, the soldiers beat Rimbaud with sticks" (quoted in F. Reyna, "Rimbaud au Harrar à travers une correspondance inédite," *Panorama* [1944]: 1, 6 (6)).

16. Léonce Lagarde to Paul Claudel, September 7, 1919, in *Sur Arthur Rimbaud*, 1039 (1039). This letter was first published in Marguerite-Yerta Méléra, "Nouveaux documents autour de Rimbaud," *Mercure de France* (1930): 44–76 (74).

17. Giovanni Dotoli, *Rimbaud, l'Italie, les italiens: Le géographe visionnaire* (Paris: Presses de l'Université de Paris–Sorbonne, 2004), 96.

18. Ugo Ferrandi to Ezio Maria Gray, October 1913, in *Rimbaud, l'Italie, les italiens*, 230–31 (231). For the original publication of the letter, see Carlo Zaghi, *Rimbaud in Africa: Con documenti inediti* (Naples: Guida, 1993), 841–42.

19. "The first line of Arabic characters is illegible. The second line, which is incomplete, could be read as 'incense carrier.' The third might be interpreted as follows: Abdoh Rinb(o)—the title Abdallah is often given to foreigners who convert to Islam. Rimbaud's mother would continue to use her son's seal after his death, un-

aware of its significance" (*Arthur Rimbaud: Exposition organisée pour le centième anniversaire de sa naissance,* 59). For an alternative reading of the seal, see Salah Stétié, *Rimbaud, le huitième dormant,* ill. Jean Messagier (Saint-Clément-de-Rivière: Fata Morgana, 1993), 24, 116n10.

20. Quoted in Jean Bourguignon and Charles Houin, *Vie d'Arthur Rimbaud,* ed. Michel Drouin (Paris: Payot, 1991), 111. Guerdon maintains that this account is likely accurate, given that it contradicts Isabelle's "deep intentions" (David Guerdon, "L'itinéraire alchimique d'Arthur Rimbaud," in *Rimbaud multiple,* ed. Alain Borer, Jean-Paul Corsetti, and Steve Murphy, pref. Alain Borer [Gourdon: D. Bedou / Paris: J. Touzot, 1989]: 100–112 (111)).

21. Partially published, first in *La Vogue* (May–June 1886), and again in October as *Les illuminations,* pref. Paul Verlaine (Paris: Publications de La Vogue, 1886).

22. For a similar critical perspective, see Samia Kassab-Charfi, who identifies the deep imbrication of Rimbaud's poetic works in prose and the philosophical preoccupations of Abdelkébir Khatibi ("Le songe rimbaldien de Khatibi," in *Rimbaud "littéralement et dans tous les sens": Hommage à Gérard Martin et Alain Tourneux* (Paris: Classiques Garnier, 2012): 189–207). See also Elhariry, who—in his reading of *Les déserts de l'amour*—asks, "What does the Muslim ear hear in the Rimbaldian text? What does the Arabic eye see?" (Yasser Elhariry, "8e Dormant: Vers une poétique franco-arabe; Salah Stétié lecteur de Rimbaud," *Parade sauvage* 27 [2016]: 169–82 (170)).

23. Rimbaud, *Œuvres complètes,* 167.

24. Kees Versteegh, *The Arabic Language* (New York: Columbia University Press, 1997), 56.

25. Rimbaud, *Œuvres complètes,* 167.

26. Rimbaud, 313–14.

27. Khatibi, *La blessure du nom propre,* 180.

28. Savary, *Le Coran,* 2:1.

29. Rimbaud, *Œuvres complètes,* 294.

30. Rimbaud, 344.

31. Qur'ān 18:27 (Kazimirski's translation, p. 233). An earlier edition of this translation (1841, p. 231) reads "excès" [excess] instead of "déréglement" [disordering].

32. Kazimirski, *Le Koran* (1869), 233n2.

33. A. de Biberstein Kazimirski [*sic*], *Dictionnaire arabe-français contenant toutes les racines de la langue arabe, leurs dérivés, tant dans l'idiome vulgaire que dans l'idiome litéral* [*sic*], *ainsi que les dialectes d'Alger et de Maroc,* 2 vols. (Paris: Maisonneuve, 1860), 2:577.

34. Elhariry, *Pacifist Invasions,* 197. See also Yasser Elhariry, "Arabic and the Postfrancophone Poetics of Maghrebi Literature," *Oxford Research Encyclopedia of Literature* (April 19, 2023), https://doi.org/10.1093/acrefore/9780190201098.013.1302.

35. Rimbaud, *Œuvres complètes,* 272.

36. Valeria Zotti, "Rimbaud 'Sage bâtard' et le Coran," in *Les Afriques de Rimbaud,* ed. David Ellison, Ralph Heyndels, and Paulette Hacker (Fasano: Schena / Paris: Presses de l'Université de Paris-Sorbonne, 2006): 47–59 (56).

37. Claude Jeancolas, *Le dictionnaire Rimbaud* (Paris: Balland, 1991), 84.

38. "Hortic. *Plante bâtarde,* Wild or ungrafted plant. . . . Plant that bears the name of a genus to which it does not belong" (Pierre Larousse, *Grand dictionnaire univer-*

sel du XIXe siècle, 17 vols. [Paris: Administration du Grand dictionnaire universel, 1866–90], 2:349).

39. "Calligr. Writing with full downstrokes and rounded liaisons, based on both the 'ronde' and the 'coulée,' hence its name" (Larousse, 2:350). See also "'Écriture bâtarde,' or simply 'bâtarde,' writing ordinarily leaning, with full downstrokes, rounded liaisons from above, and heads without loops" (Émile Littré, *Dictionnaire de la langue française*, 4 vols. [Paris: Librairie Hachette, 1863–69], 1:309).

40. "Bâtard, arde, adj. et subst," *Trésor de la langue française informatisé*, atilf.atilf.fr.

41. Yves Bonnefoy, *L'arrière-pays* (Paris: Gallimard, 1998), 52.

42. Kazimirski, *Dictionnaire arabe-français*, 2:1248.

43. Hassan Massoudy, *Calligraphie arabe vivante*, with Isabelle Nitzer, pref. Guy Jacquet (Paris: Flammarion, 1981), 70.

44. Djaout, *L'invention du désert*, 103.

45. Mohamed Kacimi, "Frédéric Rimbaud, chef de bureau arabe," *Europe: Revue littéraire mensuelle* 69 (1991): 82–87 (83). See also Charles Henry L. Bodenham, *Rimbaud et son père: Les clés d'une énigme* (Paris: Les belles lettres, 1992), 29–57.

46. Frédéric Rimbaud and O. Mac Carthy, "Les sauterelles à Sebdou en 1849," *La revue de l'Orient, de l'Algérie et des colonies: Bulletin et actes de la société orientale, algérienne et coloniale de France* 12 (1852): 373–81. For an interpretation of this article, see Abdel-Jaouad, *Rimbaud et l'Algérie*, 90–94.

47. Rimbaud and Mac Carthy, "Les sauterelles à Sebdou en 1849," 379; quoting Kazimirski, *Le Koran* (1844), 438. Rimbaud and Mac Carthy change the future tense of the verb "sortiront" [they will emerge] to the simple past tense "sortirent" [they emerged].

48. Kacimi, "Frédéric Rimbaud, chef de bureau arabe," 86.

49. Bourguignon and Houin, *Vie d'Arthur Rimbaud*, 53; initially published as Jean Bourguignon and Charles Houin, "Arthur Rimbaud," *Revue d'Ardenne et d'Argonne* 4, no. 1 (November–December 1896): 1–10 (3).

50. Simon Godchot, *Rimbaud ne varietur*, 2 vols. (Nice: Chez l'auteur, 1936), 1:5–6.

51. Rimbaud, *Œuvres complètes*, 10–14, 813–15. Rimbaud's poem is based on texts by the historian Sallust and Virgil. For an extended close reading of this poem, see Abdel-Jaouad, *Rimbaud et l'Algérie*, 14–80.

52. Rimbaud, *Œuvres complètes*, 265.

53. Sénac, *Avant-corps*, 29.

54. Meddeb, "Hallâj revisité," 44.

55. Kacimi, "Frédéric Rimbaud, chef de bureau arabe," 82.

56. "The fresh complexion that had made him look like an English child for so long had given way, in this interval of two years, to the darker shade of a Kabyle" (Ernest Delahaye, *Rimbaud* (Reims / Paris: Revue littéraire de Paris et de Champagne, 1905), 185).

57. Abdelwahab Meddeb, *Pari de civilisation*, pref. Christian Jambet (Paris: Seuil, 2009), 17.

58. Rimbaud, *Œuvres complètes*, 306.

59. Edward J. Ahearn, *Rimbaud: Visions and Habitations* (Berkeley: University of California Press, 1983), 246.

60. Martin Heidegger, *Zur Sache des Denkens* (Frankfurt am Main: Vittorio Klostermann, 2007), 83–84.

61. Suzanne Bernard, "Notes," in *Œuvres*, by Arthur Rimbaud, ed. Suzanne Bernard (Paris: Frères Garnier, 1960): 355–555 (510).

62. Bruno Claisse, *Rimbaud ou le dégagement rêvé: Essai sur l'idéologie des "Illuminations"* (Charleville-Mézières: Musée-Bibliothèque Arthur Rimbaud, 1990), 52.

63. Antoine Adam, "Notes," in *Œuvres complètes*, by Arthur Rimbaud, ed. Antoine Adam (Paris: Gallimard, 1972): 807–1055 (999–1000).

64. Ross Chambers, "Rimbaud et le regard créateur," *Saggi e ricerche di letteratura francese* 10 (1969): 197–228 (222).

65. Ernest Delahaye, *Les illuminations et Une saison en enfer de Rimbaud* (Paris: Albert Messein, 1927), 65–66.

66. Anne-Emmanuelle Berger, *Le banquet de Rimbaud: Recherches sur l'oralité* (Seyssel: Champ Vallon, 1992), 140.

67. Jean-Pierre Richard, *Poésie et profondeur* (Paris: Seuil, 1955), 205.

68. Gleize, *Poésie et figuration*, 84–85.

69. Richard, *Poésie et profondeur*, 205.

70. Quoted in Louis Massignon, *Les allusions instigatrices* (Saint-Clément-de-Rivière: Fata Morgana, 2000), 35.

71. Émile Dermenghem, "Baya et l'Afrique," *Derrière le miroir: Exposition Baya, Galerie Maeght*, (Paris: Pierre à feu, 1947): 3, 6 (3). See also Alice Kaplan, "Seeing Baya Anew," *New York Review of Books*, May 11, 2023, https://www.nybooks.com/articles/2023/05/11/seeing-baya-anew-women-in-their-garden/.

72. Richard, *Poésie et profondeur*, 202.

73. Richard, 202.

74. Richard, 204.

75. Rimbaud, *Œuvres complètes*, 153.

76. Richard, 289.

77. Massignon, *Les allusions instigatrices*, 49.

78. De Man, *The Rhetoric of Romanticism*, 6.

79. Jean-Paul Sartre, *Saint Genet: Comédien et martyr* (Paris: Gallimard, 1952), 470.

80. Quoted in Sartre, 469.

81. Berger, *Le banquet de Rimbaud*, 136.

82. Berger, 136.

83. Derrida, *Glas*, 21.

84. ". . . the tribe of Rimbaud and of Mohand ou M'hand, of Hannibal, of Ibn Khaldūn and of Saint Augustine . . ." (Kateb Yacine, "Jeune fille de ma tribu," 14).

85. Rimbaud, *Œuvres complètes*, 191–93.

86. Qur'ān 18:30 (Kazimirski's translation [1869], p. 233).

87. Qur'ān 56:15–16 (Kazimirski's translation, p. 443).

88. Qur'ān 56:17 (Kazimirski's translation, p. 443).

89. Rimbaud, *Œuvres complètes*, 247.

90. Rimbaud, 125.

91. Rimbaud, 126.

92. Brunel, *Rimbaud: Biographie; Étude de l'œuvre*, 12.

93. Léon Valade to Émile Blémont, October 5, 1871, in *Correspondance*, by Rimbaud, 90.

94. Paul Verlaine, *Les poètes maudits: Tristan Corbière, Arthur Rimbaud, Stéphane Mallarmé* (Paris: Léon Vanier, 1884), 17.

95. Paul Verlaine, *Œuvres complètes*, 5 vols (Paris: Léon Vanier, 1907–8) 5:366.

96. Delahaye, *Rimbaud*, 185.

97. Qur'ān 20:102 (Kazimirski's translation [1869], p. 254).

98. Kazimirski proposes the following meanings for "zaraqun": "1. Blue, bluish, *or* livid color. 2. Blindness [Cécité]. 3. Crying, teary-eyed" (Kazimirski, *Dictionnaire arabe-français*, 1:986).

99. Kazimirski, 1:986.

100. Rainer Maria Rilke, *Werke in drei Bänden*, intro. Beda Allemann, 3 vols. (Frankfurt am Main: Insel Verlag, 1966): 1:439–82 (1:454).

101. Kazimirski, *Le Koran* (1869), 254n1. According to a Kabyle saying, a man with blue eyes descends from an ogress: "azemṛaq bbwallen yuɣ aẓaṛ si tteryel" (Dallet, *Dictionnaire kabyle-français*, 829).

102. Qur'ān 2:10 (Savary's translation [1826]).

103. Qur'ān 2:10 (Marracci's translation [1698], vol. 2, p. 445).

104. Qur'ān 2:10 (Sale's translation [1856], p. 262).

105. Sale, *The Koran* (1856), 262.

106. Qur'ān 26:225–26 (Kazimirski's translation, pp. 301–2). Kazimirski explicates these verses as follows: "That is to say, they abandon themselves to their imagination, and take up all sorts of subjects" (Kazimirski, 301).

107. "As for the flowers, short and strikingly colored, they are, are they not? imitations, artificial, and created to mimic the mosaic" (Mallarmé, *Œuvres complètes*, 2:383).

108. Khatibi, "II. Vertige," 227–54.

109. Khatibi, 232.

110. Khatibi, 229.

111. Khatibi, 229.

112. Khatibi, 234.

113. Khatibi, 235.

114. Khatibi, 239.

115. Abdelkébir Khatibi, *L'art contemporain arabe: Prolégomènes* (Neuilly-sur-Seine: Al Manar, 2001), 111.

116. Abdelkébir Khatibi, *Il faut bien savoir gré à Melehi . . .* , leaflet from the archives of Pauline de Mazière, April 1981, presented in the exhibition *L'Atelier, 1971–1991* at the Musée d'art contemporain in Rabat, Spring 2023; reproduced in *Legends: Ventes aux enchères; Samedi 10 avril 2021 à 17h, Hôtel des ventes CMOOA, Casablanca*, 97.

117. Khatibi, *Pèlerinage d'un artiste amoureux*, 211.

118. Khatibi, *Le livre du sang*, 134.

119. Khatibi, *Figures de l'étranger*, 83.

120. Gleize, *Poésie et figuration*, 102–3.

121. Massignon, *Les allusions instigatrices*, 39.

122. Pierre Lauxerois, *"L'opéra fabuleux," suivi de "Sous la lumière qu'on a créée": Deux essais sur Arthur Rimbaud* (Lausanne: L'Âge d'Homme, 2001), 219.

123. Bernard, "Notes," 511.

124. Christian Pagès, "À propos de la 'rose d'eau' de Rimbaud," *Parade sauvage* 4 (1986): 112 (112).

125. Arthur Rimbaud, *Œuvres complètes: Poésie, prose et correspondance*, ed. Pierre Brunel (Paris: Librairie Générale Française, 1999), 483.

126. Arthur Rimbaud, *Œuvres complètes*, ed. André Guyaux and Aurélia Cervoni (Paris: Gallimard, 2009), 167.

127. Khatibi notes that the believer folds and unfolds the prayer rug, or "سجادة" [sajjādah], with a certain pleasure because it "evokes—for those who are initiated into the imaginary of Islamic monotheism—the correspondence between the garden, the carpet, and Paradise: an inexhaustible metaphor in decorative effects" (Khatibi, *Le corps oriental*, 44).

128. Khatibi, "II. Vertige," 235.

129. Chambers, "Rimbaud et le regard créateur," 224.

130. Chambers, 224.

131. Richard, *Poésie et profondeur*, 205.

132. Richard, 207.

133. Derrida, *Glas*, 21.

134. Khatibi, "II. Vertige," 233.

135. Michel de Certeau, "extase blanche," *Traverses* 29 (1983): 16–18 (16).

CONCLUSION

1. Sigmund Freud, *Jenseits des Lustprinzips* (Vienna: Internationaler Psychoanalytischer Verlag, 1921), 58.

2. Lyotard, *Rudiments païens*, 22–23.

3. Freud, *Jenseits des Lustprinzips*, 64.

4. Friedrich Rückert, *Die Verwandlung des Abu Seid von Serug, oder die Makamen des Hariri in freier Nachbildung*, 2 vols. (Stuttgart / Tübingen: Cotta, 1837), 1:24.

5. Wehr, *A Dictionary of Modern Written Arabic*, 398. Rückert was the author of *Oestliche Rosen* (1822), inspired by Goethe's *West-östlicher Divan* (1819).

6. Elhariry, *Pacifist Invasions*, 204.

7. Charles Baudelaire, *Le spleen de Paris (Petits poèmes en prose)*, in *Œuvres complètes*, 1:273–363.

8. Qur'ān 48:17 (Nasr et al.'s edition, p. 1252). As Rückert points out in a footnote, this is intended to apply specifically to those who would otherwise be expected to participate in jihad, or holy war (*Die Verwandlung des Abu Seid von Serug*, 1:24).

9. Lyotard, *Rudiments païens*, 24.

10. Lyotard, 24.

11. Foucault, "Two Lectures," 83.

12. Lyotard, *Rudiments païens*, 24.

13. Lyotard, 28.

14. Lyotard, 29.

15. Lyotard, 29.

16. A similar concern motivates the title of a seminal anthology of North African poetry in English translation, referred to by its editors as "Diwan Ifrikiya," but published as *Poems for the Millennium, Volume Four: The University of California Book of North African Literature*, ed. Pierre Joris and Habib Tengour (Berkeley: University of California Press, 2012), 2.

17. Pascal Quignard, *Lycophron et Zétès* (Paris: Gallimard, 2010), 138.

18. Dallet, *Dictionnaire kabyle-français*, 218.

19. Kateb Yacine, "Nazim Hikmet ou le chant des exilés," in *Minuit passé de douze heures: Écrits journalistiques, 1947–1989*, by Kateb Yacine, ed. Amazigh Kateb (Paris: Seuil, 1999): 235–40 (236); first published in *Jeune Afrique* 213 (January 1965): 29.

20. Wehr, *A Dictionary of Modern Written Arabic*, 668.

21. Khaïr-Eddine, *Moi l'aigre*, 79.

22. Wehr, *A Dictionary of Modern Written Arabic*, 668.

23. Kazimirski, *Dictionnaire arabe-français*, 2:450; Wehr, *A Dictionary of Modern Written Arabic*, 668.

24. Kazimirski, *Dictionnaire arabe-français*, 2:449.

25. Kazimirski, 2:449.

26. Kazimirski, 2:449.

27. Kazimirski, 2:449.

28. Kazimirski, 2:449.

29. Farès, *Le miroir de Cordoue*, 21. In a similar vein, Moroccan poet Mohamed Hmoudane writes: "J'entre à Cordoue / Architecturée par le Coran" [I enter Córdoba / Engineered by the Qur'ān] (*État d'urgence: poème*, ill. Bouchaïb Maoual [Tangier: Virgule éditions, 2016], 41).

30. Compare to Raymond Queneau's autobiographical "roman en vers" [novel in verse], *Chêne et chien* (Paris: Gallimard, 1952), and to Georges Perros's "poème roman" [novel-poem] *Une vie ordinaire* (Paris: Gallimard, 1967).

31. Mohammed Dib, *L. A. Trip: Roman en vers* (Paris: Éditions de la Différence, 2003), 28, 30.

32. Fernand Braudel, "Les espagnols et l'Afrique du Nord de 1492 à 1577," *Revue africaine* 69 (1928): 184–233, 351–462 (193).

33. Tamalet Talbayev, *The Transcontinental Maghreb*, 3.

34. Talbayev, 166.

35. Talbayev, 8.

36. Talbayev, 3.

37. Talbayev, 4.

38. Talbayev, 4.

39. Elhariry, *Pacifist Invasions*, 204.

40. Bensmaïa, *Experimental Nations*, 2.

41. Albert Memmi, "Portrait du colonisé," *Esprit* 250, no. 5 (1957): 790–810 (806); *Anthologie des écrivains maghrébins d'expression française*, 17.

42. Malek Haddad, *Écoute et je t'appelle: Poèmes précédés de Les zéros tournent en rond* (Paris: François Maspero, 1961), 21, 9.

43. Sénac, *Le soleil sous les armes*, 20; "L'Algérie d'une libération à l'autre," 22.

44. Mohammed Dib, *L'arbre à dires* (Paris: Albin Michel, 1998), 193.

45. Amrouche, "Je ne peux pleurer qu'en Kabyle," 301.

46. Mohammed Khaïr-Eddine, *Légende et vie d'Agoun'chich* (Paris: Seuil, 1984).

47. Abdelwahab Meddeb, Jabbar Yassin Husin, and Xavier Person, "Entretien," in *Abdelwahab Meddeb* (Poitiers: Office du livre en Poitou-Charentes, 1993): 15–30 (15).

48. Mourad Bourboune, "Je ne puis garder le silence," *Le nouvel observateur* 16 (March 4, 1965): 12–13 (12).

49. Mouloud Mammeri and Abdallah Mazouni, "Entretien sur la littérature algérienne," in *Culture et enseignement en Algérie et au Maghreb*, by Abdallah Mazouni (Paris: Maspero, 1969): 215–27 (221).

50. Jacques Derrida, *Le monolinguisme de l'autre; ou, La prothèse d'origine* (Paris: Galilée, 1996), 46.

51. Abdelkébir Khatibi, *Amour bilingue*, ill. Abdeslam Guenouni (Saint-Clément-de-Rivière: Fata Morgana, 1983).

52. Khatibi, *La langue de l'autre*, 41. For a brief treatment of this debate set in the broader historical context of a Maghrebi lingua franca, see Jocelyne Dakhlia, "*No man's langue*: Une rétraction coloniale," 261–62. For an extended discussion, including reflections on the proximity of deconstruction and decolonization, see Rice, *Time Signatures*, 290–99.

53. Quoted in Jean Scemla, "Entretien avec Khatibi," *Bulletin de l'Association Victor Segalen* 2 (1989): 9–10 (9).

54. Elhariry, *Pacifist Invasions*, 4.

55. Khatibi, *Maghreb pluriel*, 188.

56. Albert Thibaudet, *La poésie de Stéphane Mallarmé: Étude littéraire* (Paris: Gallimard, 1926), 20.

57. Khatibi, *La langue de l'autre*, 43.

58. Franz Rosenzweig to Gershom Scholem, March 10, 1921, in *Briefe und Tagebücher*, by Franz Rosenzweig, ed. Rachel Rosenzweig, Edith Rosenzweig-Scheinmann, and Bernhard Casper, 2 vols. (The Hague: Martinus Nijhoff, 1979): 2:698–700 (2:699).

59. Quoted in Tchého, "À livre ouvert avec Tahar Djaout," 30–31.

Index

FLASHPOINTS

1. *On Pain of Speech: Fantasies of the First Order and the Literary Rant*, Dina Al-Kassim
2. *Moses and Multiculturalism*, Barbara Johnson, with a foreword by Barbara Rietveld
3. *The Cosmic Time of Empire: Modern Britain and World Literature*, Adam Barrows
4. *Poetry in Pieces: César Vallejo and Lyric Modernity*, Michelle Clayton
5. *Disarming Words: Empire and the Seductions of Translation in Egypt*, Shaden M. Tageldin
6. *Wings for Our Courage: Gender, Erudition, and Republican Thought*, Stephanie H. Jed
7. *The Cultural Return*, Susan Hegeman
8. *English Heart, Hindi Heartland: The Political Life of Literature in India*, Rashmi Sadana
9. *The Cylinder: Kinematics of the Nineteenth Century*, Helmut Müller-Sievers
10. *Polymorphous Domesticities: Pets, Bodies, and Desire in Four Modern Writers*, Juliana Schiesari
11. *Flesh and Fish Blood: Postcolonialism, Translation, and the Vernacular*, S. Shankar
12. *The Fear of French Negroes: Transcolonial Collaboration in the Revolutionary Americas*, Sara E. Johnson
13. *Figurative Inquisitions: Conversion, Torture, and Truth in the Luso-Hispanic Atlantic*, Erin Graff Zivin
14. *Cosmopolitan Desires: Global Modernity and World Literature in Latin America*, Mariano Siskind
15. *Fiction beyond Secularism*, Justin Neuman
16. *Periodizing Jameson: Dialectics, the University, and the Desire for Narrative*, Phillip E. Wegner
17. *The Practical Past*, Hayden White
18. *The Powers of the False: Reading, Writing, Thinking beyond Truth and Fiction*, Doro Wiese
19. *The Object of the Atlantic: Concrete Aesthetics in Cuba, Brazil, and Spain, 1868–1968*, Rachel Price
20. *Epic and Exile: Novels of the German Popular Front 1933–1945*, Hunter Bivens
21. *An Innocent Abroad: Lectures in China*, J. Hillis Miller
22. *Form and Instability: East Europe, Literature, Postimperial Difference*, Anita Starosta
23. *Bombay Modern: Arun Kolatkar and Bilingual Literary Culture*, Anjali Nerlekar
24. *Intimate Relations: Social Reform and the Late Nineteenth-Century South Asian Novel*, Krupa Shandilya
25. *Media Laboratories: Late Modernist Authorship in South America*, Sarah Ann Wells
26. *Acoustic Properties: Radio, Narrative, and the New Neighborhood of the Americas*, Tom McEnaney

27. *The New Woman: Literary Modernism, Queer Theory, and the Trans Feminine Allegory*, Emma Heaney
28. *Civilizing War: Imperial Politics and the Poetics of National Rupture*, Nasser Mufti
29. *Late Colonial Sublime: Neo-Epics and the End of Romanticism*, G. S. Sahota
30. *Globalizing Race: Anti-Semitism, Empire, and the Politics of Scale in Modern French and European Culture*, Dorian Bell
31. *Domestications: American Empire, Literary Culture, and the Postcolonial Lens*, Hosam Mohamed Aboul-Ela
32. *Behold an Animal: Four Exorbitant Readings*, Thangam Ravindranathan
33. *Capital Letters: Hugo, Baudelaire, Camus, and the Death Penalty*, Ève Morisi
34. *Immaterial Archives: An African Diaspora Poetics of Loss*, Jenny Sharpe
35. *Figures of the World: The Naturalist Novel and Transnational Form*, Christopher Laing Hill
36. *Imperfect Solidarities: Tagore, Gandhi, Du Bois, and the Forging of the Global Anglophone*, Madhumita Lahiri
37. *Fictional Environments: Mimesis, Deforestation, and Development in Latin America*, Victoria Saramago
38. *How to Read a Moment: The American Novel and the Crisis of the Present*, Mathias Nilges
39. *Secondhand China: Spain, the East, and the Politics of Translation*, Carles Prado-Fonts
40. *New World Maker: Radical Poetics, Black Internationalism, and the Translations of Langston Hughes*, Ryan James Kernan
41. *The Idea of Indian Literature: Gender, Genre, and Comparative Method*, Preetha Mani
42. *Concepts of the World*, Effie Rentzou
43. *Traces of the Unseen*, Carolina Sá Carvalho
44. *Cannibal Translation: Literary Reciprocity in Contemporary Latin America*, Isabel C. Gómez
45. *Entranced Earth: Art, Extractivism, and the End of Landscape*, Jens Andermann
46. *Dwelling in Fiction: Poetics of Place and the Experimental Novel in Latin America*, Ashley R. Brock
47. *Disoriented Disciplines: China, Latin America, and the Shape of World Literature*, Rosario Hubert
48. *Forms of Mobility: Genre, Language, and Media in African Literary Cultures*, Stephanie Bosch Santana